SYSTEMIC SEX THERAPY

Edited by
Katherine M. Hertlein
Gerald R. Weeks
Nancy Gambescia

 Routledge
Taylor & Francis Group
New York   London

Routledge
Taylor & Francis Group
711 Third Avenue,
New York, NY 10017

Routledge
Taylor & Francis Group
2 Park Square
Milton Park, Abingdon
Oxon OX14 4RN

International Standard Book Number-13: 978-0-7890-3669-8 (Softcover)

Library of Congress Cataloging-in-Publication Data

Systemic sex therapy / edited by Katherine M. Hertlein, Gerald R. Weeks & Nancy Gambescia.
    p. ; cm.
Includes bibliographical references and index.
ISBN 978-0-7890-3668-1 (hardbound : alk. paper) -- ISBN 978-0-7890-3669-8 (pbk. : alk. paper)
    1. Sex therapy. 2. System theory. I. Hertlein, Katherine M. II. Weeks, Gerald R., 1948- III. Gambescia, Nancy.
    [DNLM: 1. Couples Therapy--methods. 2. Marital Therapy--methods. 3. Sexual Dysfunction, Physiological--therapy. 4. Sexual Dysfunctions, Psychological--therapy. WM 430.5.M3 S995 2008]

RC557.S928 2008
616.89'1562--dc22   2008024926

Visit the Taylor & Francis Web site at
http://www.taylorandfrancis.com

and the Routledge Web site at
http://www.routledge.com

SYSTEMIC
SEX
THERAPY

Dedication

To Adam Joseph with love—may you experience as much joy and wonder in your life as you have brought to ours

KH

To Nancy Love—For the love you bring to my life

GW

To Michael, Matt, and Lauren—With love

NG

Contents

Acknowledgments

Many people have helped us in the creation of this book. First, we would like to thank the numerous contributors who have made this book a success. We consider ourselves very lucky to work with such an esteemed class of authors. Their insights, writing, and dedication to this project will surely shape the field of sex therapy, and we are appreciative of their significant efforts. We would also acknowledge the support from our family and friends throughout this endeavor. Thank you to Eric Hertlein, Nancy Love, and Michael Chenet for providing us support during the completion of this project. There are also a number of people who served as writing mentors to the first editor, including (but not limited to) Dr. Fred Piercy, Dr. Joseph Wetchler, Dr. Lorna Hecker, and Dr. Terry Trepper. Each spent a significant amount of time helping to shape ideas into publications. Dr. Piercy also took it upon himself to be a formal writing mentor, and I am extremely grateful for his energy, time, and exceptional knowledge. We thank the staff at both Haworth Press and Taylor & Francis for their support of this project, specifically the work of Rob Owen. He continually provided valuable guidance and direction in the preparation of this manuscript and guided us through the pragmatic issues related to publication. Finally, we would also like to acknowledge the hard work of our graduate assistants in preparation of this manual, including Lisa Crammer-Schapiro, Shelley Sendak, Armeda Stevenson, and Blendine Hawkins.

Preface

Authors frequently write texts because they cannot find a book that they feel is appropriate for a course they are teaching. We were motivated by this reason and many others in our desire to publish *Systemic Sex Therapy*. As marriage and family therapists, we were searching for a book that would serve as an introduction to the field of sex therapy from a systems perspective. The target audiences for this book are graduate students in marriage and family therapy programs or students and professionals who want a truly fresh perspective on sex therapy. We also wanted to write a book that is comprehensive, concise, highly focused on treatment, and user friendly. Current books on the market impress us as being outdated, too advanced, simplistic, unfocused, or too diffuse in content.

This book's main purpose is to accomplish what we believe no other book in the field of sex therapy has ever fully done. It is based on systems theory. In the introduction to their book, Masters and Johnson (1970) state that there is no such thing as an "uninvolved partner." They discuss the importance of the conjoint marital unit in therapy. This theoretical position leads the reader to assume they view problems from this framework. However, as the book unfolds it becomes clear that their work is informed by a behavioral perspective. From this perspective, the only real use for couple therapy is to see the partner as an essential informant regarding the problem and a surrogate therapist for the homework assignments. We can skip forward to the latest edition of *Principles and Practices of Sex Therapy* (Leiblum, 2007). In her introductory chapter Leiblum states, "... sex therapy is fundamentally couple therapy—without including the partner, crucial information is lost and the therapeutic outcome is compromised" (p. 8). Former editions of this book (1980; 1989; 2000) have taken the same position although not as explicitly. Unfortunately, Leiblum's books are also primarily behaviorally grounded and view couple therapy from the same limited perspective as Masters and Johnson. This view is not surprising since the field of sex therapy has been clearly dominated by

behavioral principles and most of the writing has been done by behaviorists and physicians.

We do not intend to discard the invaluable work of behaviorally
informed therapists. Our framework is broad enough to embrace this perspective and many more within the much larger context of systems theory.
We believe that the couple is the essential unit of therapy, but not in the
limited view of the behavioral tradition. Our assumption is that many sexual dysfunctions reflect difficulties in the couple relationship. This basic
assumption has many implications for sex therapy that are highlighted in
this volume. Our assertion is that (1) sexual problems may reflect problems at many different levels in the couple ranging from lack of communication to underlying intimacy problems, (2) the resolution of the couple's
problems are necessary to remedy many sexual problems, (3) unconscious
factors in the couple's relationship may impede or sabotage the couple
being able to develop a more satisfying sexual relationship, (4) a sexual
problem in one partner may "mask" a sexual and/or relational problem in
the other, (5) the sexual problem may be unconsciously maintained by the
couple, and (6) the homework should be designed so that each partner is
given respect and receives something from the exercise that enhances his
or her relationship on multiple levels.

The systems framework used in this text was developed by Weeks (1977)
in a formative paper and elaborated through many texts on couple therapy
(Weeks, 1989; Weeks, Gambescia, & Jenkins, 2003; Weeks & Hof, 1987;
1994; 1995; Weeks, Odell, & Methyen, 2005; Weeks & Treat, 1992; 2001),
and subsequently applied to two common sexual dysfunctions (Weeks &
Gambescia, 2000; 2002). The theory that informs this book is called the
intersystems theory (Weeks, 1989). It is an advance over traditional systems
theory described in books like Gurman and Kniskern's (1991) *Handbook
of Family Therapy* that in the early years disregarded the importance of the
individual within the system. Our theory encompasses the simultaneous
consideration of individual, interactional, and family-of-origin factors in
both the etiology and treatment of a problem. Not every couple or problem
may have these three factors, but they are all considered.

In addition to this theoretical framework, our book is integrative as well
but not in the limited way as used in the Leiblum (2007) text. In Leiblum's
text, integration is essentially viewed as the incorporation of medical and
psychological aspects with what we believe is an overemphasis on the former and underemphasis on the latter. Our view of integration is that of
the individual, including individual psychopathology and biological or
medical concerns, couple issues from multiple levels, and the influence

of the family of origin on couple development, functioning, and dysfunction in all aspects of the relationship. Weeks and Gambescia (2000; 2002) successfully utilize this approach in understanding and treating erectile dysfunction and hypoactive sexual desire and treating these problems by incorporating both medical and psychological factors. For reasons beyond our comprehension, behaviorally oriented writers have not incorporated the concept of a theoretically based approach to integration into their writings. Perhaps part of the reason is discussed in our last chapter on the lack of theory in the field of sex therapy in general.

In summary, we believe this book has several unique features not found in any other texts on sex therapy.

- **Grounding in Systems Theory.** This volume is the first that truly takes a systems perspective. The couple is viewed as the unit of treatment based on the assumptions described above. This view transcends the tradition view of the partner as an informant and using the partner as a homework surrogate.
- **Systemic/Behavioral Focus.** Specifically, it will use the framework of the intersystem approach that we have successfully used in two prior books on sex therapy. This approach will move the book beyond traditional behavioral sex therapy approaches to a much broader systemic framework where individual, couple, and intergenerational factors are considered in both the etiology and treatment (if all are present).
- **Clinical Innovation.** Advances in the field of sex therapy have been primarily medical for the past decades. This text not only renders a new theoretical framework, but encourages clinical innovation in the understanding and treatment of sexual problems.
- **Greater Focus on Implementation than Competing Works.** Many books give the reader the technique and expect the clinician to automatically know how to implement it. Techniques are relatively easy to learn. We will describe the technique, discuss its implementation, and provide some case material to illuminate the use of the technique system.

The contributors to this text were asked to follow a standard outline for the core treatment chapters. These are the chapters that describe the traditionally defined sexual problems. Of course, some variation will exist depending on how much literature and insight we currently have into the role each factor plays in the etiology and treatment of the disorders.

- **Definition and Description of Disorder.** The definition should reflect the *DSM IV-TR*'s (2004) material regarding definition and clinical criteria. Authors were asked to include reviews of other descriptions in the literature and any other information on the development of the classification.

- **Etiology.** What are the known or suspected causes of this disorder from the multiple perspectives mentioned in the intersystem approach (e.g., individual/medical, interactional/couple, and intergenerational)?
- **Assessment.** How is this disorder assessed using the present theoretical framework?
- **Treatment.** Treatment should be discussed from the perspective of the intersystem approach (e.g., individual/medical, interactional/couple, intergenerational). It is important to take the clinician from the beginning to the end of treatment focusing on stages of treatment, techniques, implementation of techniques, examples of how to implement techniques, homework exercises, how to deal with noncompliance or homework failure, etc.
- **Research and Future Directions.** A brief review of research supporting the treatment, and if possible, directions for future development (e.g., new medical treatments for ED, PE, and inhibited orgasm, new therapeutic techniques, etc.) should be provided.

The book is organized into several sections. The first section provides an overview of some of the basics of sex therapy, and serves as a way to orient the new professional to the field. It is composed of three chapters: "What Every Sex Therapist Needs to Know" by Jane Ridley, "The Profession of Sex Therapy" by Peggy Kleinplatz, and "Toward a New Paradigm in Sex Therapy" by Katherine Hertlein and Gerald Weeks. Ridley's chapter outlines both the personal attributes and the knowledge base required by aspiring sex therapists. It focuses on the interconnected and interdependent nature of sexuality through the discussion of social norms, introduction to sexual difficulties, and the anatomy and physiology of sex and the sexual response cycle. It further identifies contemporary "hot" issues in the field, including the medicalization of sex therapy. Finally, the chapter by Hertlein and Weeks shifts the current paradigm of sex therapy by providing an integrative approach based on Sternberg's triangle and the intersystem approach. In a departure from eclectic approaches, this framework synthesizes information from the fields of healthcare, couples therapy, psychology, sexuality, and communication to inform treatment of sexual problems. Following this is Hertlein's chapter on integrating technology in sex therapy practice. This chapter details how couples become vulnerable to having problems with technology and their relationships from an intersystemic perspective, and then uses the intersystemic perspective as a guide to treating the couple's vulnerable areas.

The second section is comprised of chapters describing how the inter-system approach can be utilized for the treatment of specific sexual dys-functions. Gerald Weeks, Katherine Hertlein, and Nancy Gambescia focus on using the approach to treat hypoactive sexual desire disorder; Nancy Gambescia, Shelley Sendak, and Gerald Weeks outline how this approach is used for the treatment of erectile dysfunction. Stephen Betchen has included a chapter on using the intersystems approach with couples strug-gling with premature ejaculation. This chapter depicts how premature ejaculation and relational dynamics are intertwined, and presents a sys-temic and integrative model designed to treat the disorder, attending to medical issues, and combining aspects of psychoanalytic conflict theory and psychodynamic family-of-origin work with basic sex therapy prin-ciples and exercises. The chapter on delayed ejaculation, written by Sallie Foley, outlines the multitude of biopsychosocial factors that contribute to the emergence of delayed ejaculation and describes how the intersystem approach is applied to the treatment of this presenting problem. Kevan Wylie and Ruth Hallam-Jones discuss the systemic approach in its applica-tion to inhibited arousal in women. In this chapter, they discuss their use of a garden metaphor and encourage the use of this metaphor through-out treatment. They also provide a wealth of resources for the assessment and treatment of this problem. Marita McCabe contributed the chapter on anorgasmia in women, which maps out the complex factors contributing to the development of this condition, focusing on intersystemic etiology and outlining specific treatment for each of these factors. In the chapter on painful intercourse, Marta Meana proposes a multidisciplinary intersys-tems approach to etiology, assessment, and treatment of dyspareunia and vaginismus. Meana also proposes an integrative approach as the optimal standard of care, with the collaboration of sex therapy, gynecology, and physical therapy. The last chapter, rounding out the dysfunction chapters, is Martha Turner's chapter on sexual addiction. Here, Turner reviews the complex etiology of the development of a sexual addiction and outlines treatment from an integrative model.

The third section of this book is devoted to special topics. Katherine Hertlein, Gerald Weeks, and Nancy Gambescia have contributed a chap-ter on infidelity treatment, using the intersystems approach as well as providing an outline for intervention from a theoretical base. Gambescia and Weeks outline how to implement sensate focus from a systemic per-spective. Johan Verhulst and Jon Reynolds contributed a chapter on sexual pharmacology. This chapter discusses the medicalization of sex and the impact certain drugs have on relationship and sexual functioning, and explores sexual pharmacology from a systemic perspective. Finally, Terry Trepper, Sophia Treyger, Jenifer Yalowitz, and Jeff Ford contribute a chapter on solution-focused sex therapy. Such an approach is consistent with the needs of managed care to work quickly. Additionally, this approach is consistent with many aspects of the intersystems approach and could be subsumed as a part of the larger model.

The last section of the book outlines future directions. In "Sex Therapy: A Panoramic View" by Weeks, Gambescia, and Hertlein, the authors review where the field of sex therapy has been, where it is now, and where it is going. Topics include the predominantly behavioral focus, the need for integration, the medicalization of sex therapy, working with special populations, and gaps in theory.

We sincerely hope that students, clinicians, and academics will benefit greatly from this book. It is our firm belief that this book will become the standard text in our field as well as move the field to the next stage of its development theoretically while giving students practical information.

Katherine M. Hertlein

Gerald R. Weeks

Nancy Gambescia

Editors

Katherine M. Hertlein, Ph.D. is an assistant professor in the Department of Marriage and Family Therapy at the University of Nevada, Las Vegas. She earned her master's degree in marriage and family therapy from Purdue University Calumet and her Ph.D. in marriage and family therapy from Virginia Tech. She has published in several journals including the *Journal of Marital and Family Therapy, The Family Journal, Journal of Couple and Relationship Therapy, American Journal of Family Therapy, Contemporary Family Therapy, Journal of Feminist Family Therapy,* and *Journal of Clinical Activities, Assignments, and Handouts in Psychotherapy Practice.* She serves as reviewer for several journals, as a co-editor of a book on therapy interventions for couples and families, and as a co-editor of a book for the clinical treatment of infidelity. Her areas of interest include infidelity treatment, research methodology and measurement, and training in marriage and family therapy.

Gerald R. Weeks, Ph.D. is professor and chair of the Department of Marriage and Family Therapy at the University of Nevada, Las Vegas. He is a licensed psychologist, fellow, approved supervisor, and clinical member of the American Association of Marriage and Family Therapy, and is board certified by the American Board of Professional Psychology and the American Board of Sexology. He has published 18 books, including major contemporary texts in the fields of sex, marital, and family therapy. Dr. Weeks is the past president of the American Board of Family Psychology and has lectured extensively throughout North America and Europe on sex, couple, and psychotherapy. Dr. Weeks has close to 30 years of experience in practicing and supervising sex, couple, and family therapy.

Nancy Gambescia, Ph.D. maintains an active private practice specializing in relationship and sex therapy. She teaches and supervises psychotherapists in the assessment and treatment of sexual dysfunctions and couples therapy. She has 30 years of clinical and teaching experience in working with couples. Dr. Gambescia is an approved supervisor and clinical member of the American Association of Marriage and Family Therapy, Society for Sex Therapy and Research, and a certified sexologist and diplomate of the American Board of Sexology. She has coauthored three books: *Erectile Dysfunction, Hypoactive Sexual Desire, and Treating Infidelity* (Norton) and several chapters in textbooks that focus on relationship and sexual issues. She completed her clinical training at the Council for Relationships (formerly Marriage Council of Philadelphia) and her doctorate at the University of Pennsylvania (1983).

Contributors

Stephen J. Betchen, D.S.W. is an AAMFT-approved supervisor and AASECT-certified supervisor with a full time private practice in New Jersey specializing in couples and sex therapy. He has published two books and several scholarly articles on relationships.

Sallie Foley, LMSW is the director of the Center for Sexual Health at the University of Michigan Health Systems and teaches at the University of Michigan. She has a private practice in psychotherapy and consultation in Ann Arbor. She is on the medical advisory board for the Intersex Society of North America and is an AASECT-certified sex therapist. She writes and lectures frequently on the subject of human sexuality.

Jeffrey J. Ford, M.S., MFT received his B.S. at the University of Utah in psychology. He earned his M.A. in marriage and family therapy at Purdue University Calumet. He has practiced therapy in Indiana, Illinois, and Utah and is a member of the American Association of Marriage and Family Therapy. He has published articles about the practice of marriage and family therapy. In addition to his clinical practice, he has been an instructor of psychology and adolescent development.

Ruth Hallam-Jones is an independent clinician providing sexual and relationship assessment, psychotherapy, and sexual medicine resources. She uses retreats based on systemic residential sex therapy. She also provides individual and group training for professionals. She has worked as a nurse and a sexual and relationship therapist for over 30 years. An experienced and creative clinician, Ruth has gained her understanding of systemic work with patients with sexual and relationship problems not just from her training but also from working in community and residential psychiatry and psychotherapy settings in Sheffield, Rotherham, and the Maudsley, London, and from the residential sex therapy used by Restoration Therapy.

She has also worked for ten years in outpatient sexual medicine services. Until recently she coordinated training and was the senior psychotherapist at Porterbrook Clinic, Sheffield, UK.

Peggy J. Kleinplatz, Ph.D. is Associate Professor of Medicine at the University of Ottawa. She is a clinical psychologist, board certified in sex therapy, sex education and as a diplomate in sex therapy. Since 1983, she has been teaching human sexuality at the School of Psychology, University of Ottawa, where she received the Prix d'Excellence in 2000. She is Chair of Certifications for the American Association of Sex Educators, Counselors and Therapists. Dr. Kleinplatz has edited two books, most notably *New Directions in Sex Therapy: Innovations and Alternatives* (Brunner-Routledge, Philadelphia, 2001), a book intended to challenge, expand, and diversify the field of sex therapy. Her current research focuses on optimal sexuality, particularly in the elderly and other marginalized populations.

Marita P. McCabe, Ph.D. is a professor of psychology and foundation director of the Health and Well Being Research Priority Area at Deakin University in Melbourne, Australia. She is Australian editor of *Sexual and Marital Therapy*, and is on the editorial board of the *Journal of Sex Research*. She has over 300 publications in refereed journals, most of which are concerned with human sexuality. Professor McCabe has obtained research grants and supervised postgraduate students conducting studies on sexual dysfunction, sex and disability, sexual harassment, sexual abuse, rape, extramarital affairs, and adolescent sexuality. She has conducted a series of studies that have investigated the etiology and most effective method of treatment for sexual dysfunction. She has recently devised and evaluated two Internet-based treatment programs for the treatment of erectile dysfunction and the treatment of female sexual dysfunction.

Marta Meana, Ph.D. is an associate professor in the Department of Psychology at the University of Nevada, Las Vegas. She earned her Ph.D. in clinical psychology from McGill University in Montreal and was a postdoctoral fellow in women's health at the Toronto Hospital. The author of numerous peer-reviewed articles, chapters, and conference papers on women's sexual health, Dr. Meana has focused mostly on the sexual pain disorders and, more recently, on the characteristics of female sexual desire. She has won various research and teaching awards and is currently president-elect nominee for the Society for Sex Therapy and Research.

Jonathan K. Reynolds, PharD, FASCP is a clinical assistant professor at the College of Pharmacy at Washington State University. His teaching assignments include pharmacotherapy and communications courses. He maintains a clinical site at the Snake River Community Clinic where he works in the pharmacy and has a collaborative practice with the physicians. He also maintains a clinical site at the Idaho Veterans' Home in Lewiston.

Jane Ridley, B.A., PQSW trained as a social worker at the London School or Economics and at the University of Newcastle, and as a mature student at the Institute of Psychiatry. She ran the Richmond Fellowship training in residential care of the recovering mentally ill for seven years and joined Dr. M. Crowe in 1983 at the Marital and Sexual Therapy Clinics. She was instrumental in developing the course in relationship and sexual therapy, which offered both M.Sc. and diploma at the Institute of Psychiatry at Maudsley. She further developed her work in supervision, running courses for experienced therapists. She has also been chair of the Family, Marital and Sexual Section of United Kingdom Council for Psychotherapy and a member its governing board. She is currently in private practice. Her writing includes joint authorship of *Therapy with Couples: A Behavioural-Systems Approach To Relationship and Sexual Problems,* 2nd edition (Crowe M. and Ridley J., Eds., Blackwell Science, 2000), and authorship of *Intimacy in Crisis* (Whurr, 1999). In 2007 she contributed to *The Handbook of Clinical Adult Psychology,* 3rd edition (Stan Lindsay and Graham Powell, Eds., Routledge, Philadelphia).

Shelley K. Sendak, Ph.D. holds a Ph.D. in sociology. Her areas of interest include visual sociology, gender studies, and women's sexuality. She has published a women's studies textbook and several works on homoerotica. Her visual essays have appeared in social work, gerontology, family studies, and inequality textbooks. Her interest in women's sexuality has led her to further her studies in clinical sexology from the American Academy of Clinical Sexology and Marriage and Family Therapy at the University of Nevada, Las Vegas.

Terry S. Trepper, Ph.D. is Professor of Psychology at Purdue University Calumet. He is an APA Fellow, an AAMFT clinical member and approved supervisor, an AASECT-certified sex therapist, and a diplomate in the American Board of Sexology. He is editor of the *Journal of Family Psychotherapy* and editor-in-chief of *Psychotherapy, Clinical Interventions*

& Behavioral Health (Haworth/Taylor & Francis). Dr. Trepper is the co-author of *More than Miracles: The State of the Art in Solution Focused Therapy* (with Steve de Shazer, Yvonne Dolan, Harry Korman, Eric McCollum, and Insoo Berg); co-author (with Mary Jo Barrett) of *Systemic Treatment of Incest: A Therapeutic Handbook* (Brunner/Routledge); *Treating Incest: A Multiple Systems Perspective* (Haworth Press); *101 Interventions in Family Therapy* (with Thorana Nelson) (Haworth Press, 1993); *101 More Interventions in Family Therapy* (1995); and *Family Solutions for Substance Abuse* (with Eric McCollum) (Haworth Press, 2001). He was the recipient of the American Association for Marriage and Family Therapy 1998 Significant Contribution to the Field of Marriage and Family Therapy Award and the 2004 American Psychological Association Florence W. Kaslow International Family Psychology Award. He maintains a private practice in family psychology in northwest Indiana.

Sophia Treyger, M.S. earned her degree in marriage and family therapy from Purdue University, Calumet. She has written extensively for www.RelationShip911.com and www.BreakUp911.com. The websites are clearinghouses for information on how to enhance relationships and cope with breakup-related issues. They also provide an interface for therapists and clients to interact. Ms. Treyger has written articles that complement therapy and are assigned as homework by therapists to their clients. She has conducted research on factors that promote a positive female lesbian identity. Her clinical interests include working with disadvantaged and marginalized women, couples, adolescents, and specifically in the fields of sex therapy and education. She has written articles featured in the *American Journal of Family Therapy* and *The Therapist's Notebook II* (Haworth, New York, 1998).

Martha Turner, M.D. graduated from Temple Medical School, completed an internship in pediatrics at Pittsburgh Children's Hospital, and then returned to Philadelphia for a residency in adult psychiatry at The Institute of Pennsylvania Hospital. During her residency she treated people with drug and alcohol addictions. She stayed on at the institute as an assistant director on the substance abuse unit for four years and then moved fully into private practice. She moved her practice to Bryn Mawr, Pennsylvania in 1993. In 1983, one of her alcoholic patients revealed a sexual addiction. Learning about the challenging disorder gave new direction and a subspecialty to Dr. Turner's practice. She developed an outpatient program of therapy groups for recovering sex addicts and partners called Sexual Trauma and Recovery (STAR). STAR includes educational groups, structured groups for early recovering people, and advanced groups for trauma resolution and the development of social and relationship skills. Treating sex addicts and their partners encompasses attachment disorders, childhood sexual abuse, and posttraumatic stress disorder. Dr. Turner is board certified in psychiatry and addiction medicine. She is also certified in Eye Movement Desensitization and Reprocessing (EMDR) and Emotional Transformation Therapy (ETT). These treatments use colors and lights to safely and quickly help people through their suffering. In 2007 she received the Carnes Achievement Award for her contributions to the field of sexual addiction treatment.

Johan Verhulst, M.D. earned his degree from the University of Leuven in Belgium and completed his residency training in psychiatry at the University of Utrecht in Holland. After his return to Belgium he established a program for marital and sex therapy at the University of Leuven. In 1978 he joined the Department of Psychiatry and Behavioral Sciences of the University of Washington Medical School in Seattle, where he is currently an emeritus associate professor. Dr. Verhulst also has a faculty appointment at the Kinsey Institute for Research in Sex, Gender and Reproduction at Indiana University in Bloomington.

Kevan R. Wylie, M.D., MB, DSM, FRCP, FRCPsyc earned his medical degree at Liverpool Medical School in 1985 and went on to postgraduate training in London, earning a diploma in therapy with couples (1993) and a diploma in sexual medicine (1994). He obtained his doctorate M.D. in couples sex therapy in 1999. He is an associate member of both British Association of Urological Surgeons and the Royal College of Obstetrics and Gynaecologists and a fellow of the RCP London and the RCPsych. Obtaining his first consultancy in Sheffield in 1995, he went on to a full time post in sexual medicine in June 1999. Dr. Wylie now works across two trusts as clinical lead for Porterbrook Clinic and consultant lead for andrology (urology) at the Royal Hallamshire Hospital. He is supported by five full-time nurses and therapists across both institutes as well as numerous accredited part-time clinicians from various clinical backgrounds, including psychotherapists, counselors, doctors and nurses, and researchers. Over his career, Dr. Wylie has published over 100 articles and book chapters, including 65 peer-reviewed publications.

Jennifer Yalowitz, M.A. is a marriage and family therapist in private practice in Munster, Indiana. She specializes in solution-focused therapy to help her clients bring about the change that betters their lives and relationships. She earned a master's degree in marriage and family therapy at the Marriage and Family Therapy program at Purdue University Calumet. She also teaches as adjunct faculty at Purdue University Calumet and is a member of the American Association of Marriage and Family Therapists.

1

What Every Sex Therapist Needs to Know

Jane Ridley

Contents

Introduction

If you are considering training as a sex therapist today it is essential that you are a resilient and flexible person yet able to be firm about your own and others' boundaries. You will constantly learn new aspects of yourself, your motivation, your sexual orientation, your moral and social code, your prejudices and excitements. This means you will simultaneously be developing and changing.

You may often explore with clients an unfamiliar world that provokes in you ideas, feelings, and fantasies that have been strangers to you; guilt or shame may become more familiar, as will sexual and other powerful feelings. Being open to monitoring your reactions must become part of you and your daily work. Allowing yourself to learn and to respond to the clients' world with empathy and without judgment will be enriching. A central aspect of becoming a sex therapist is your own curiosity, openness, and preparedness to learn, without prejudice.

Your openness must also encompass the clients' reactions, attitudes, feelings, or fantasies toward you. Your age, dress, ethnicity, voice tone, choice of language, social or religious attitudes, likes and dislikes, and prejudices will be observed, noted, and judged by your clients. Since you rapidly become part of your clients' system, how you are perceived by clients will influence the outcome of your work together.

In the process of becoming a sex therapist, there is much to learn and understand. Definitions of normal sexual behavior or characterizations and understanding of sexual difficulties or dysfunctions are central. A clear knowledge of the anatomy and physiology of male and female sexuality, the sexual response cycle, and the impact of life events and aging on sexuality must be understood within a historical context and within the individual, couple, family, or social network as well as taking into account people's ethnic or religious affiliations. Physical and mental health, drug or alcohol abuse, domestic violence, previous sexual or emotional abuse, and other traumatic experiences all have an impact on individuals' sexual life. Specialist knowledge and skills may need to be learned to work with these client groups. Evidence from research and evaluative studies is constantly emerging that may affect how one understands or approaches aspects of human behavior and that must be constantly monitored and responded to.

Disentangling the interaction among organic, physical, individual, interrelational, social, and environmental factors can make you feel part of an elaborate web without boundaries. However, developing these skills depends on an awareness of the complex interaction between the physical and organic aspects of sexuality and the individual's internal and external psychological world as well as the social network surrounding the individual or couple. Thinking and working systemically greatly facilitates this process. It is essential to use supervision to explore not only what is happening to clients but also what issues are being raised for you. Regular supervision will become an essential routine (Giami, 2001; Mann, 1997; Ridley, 2006).

Historically, therapy has developed along separate theoretical routes (Ridley, 2006). More recently there has been a movement toward an integrative approach enabling therapists to select, from the rich range of theoretical options, the approach most suited to each particular client. Crowe and Ridley (2002) describe a hierarchy of alternative interventions (ALIs), which offers the therapist guidelines on why and when to choose which approach and when it may be useful to move up or down the hierarchy during therapy to an alternative intervention. Weeks and Hof (1994, 1995) develop the intersystem approach for this purpose. Clarity about the therapist's use of theory and the ability to move between theories is an essential skill: "A good postulate here is; fire your theory before you fire your client, or your client fires you" (Weeks and Hof, 2005). Throughout this book the intersystems approach is used when assessing the impact on individuals' sexual function, the interplay between their psychological makeup and the interpersonal and social environment they inhabit. This parallels Crowe and Ridley's model for assessment.

As sex therapists learn more about clients, difficult moral or legal issues can arise. Conflict between loyalty to the client and or client confidentiality, may seem at odds with society's requirements. Knowing the limits of therapy and working within the professional codes of practice and the legal framework are essential and challenging (AAMFT, 2001; BASRT, n.d.). Sex therapists do not work outside the legal and social framework of their country (even though occasionally it may feel that way). Working together with other professionals and knowing the limits of sexual therapy, when to seek help from other coprofessionals, and when to refer clients are basic requirements. Working together with psychiatrists, doctors, social workers, probation, prison, or other welfare agencies then becomes a support for both therapist and client.

These personal attributes and rich knowledge base are essential requirements for the sex therapist who wishes to learn the intervention skills described throughout this book and developed during clinical practice under professional supervision.

Sexuality and Sexual Behavior

Social Norms

Human survival depends on the physiological fact that, for the next generation to be conceived, men and women must have sexual intercourse, however brief—although in-vitro fertilization (IVF) is now available to a select few. Societies have developed different ways of coping with this powerful and necessary creative force. In a multicultural society at the beginning of the 21st century, one is faced with a multitude of social, religious, or ethnic practices affecting the individual, couple, or family. Any attempt to understand what is seen as "normal" sexual behavior must take into account this rich context.

Gender and gender issues such as whether lesbians, gays, bisexuals, or transsexuals have similar sexual experiences as heterosexual men and women and whether men's and women's approach to sex is different will affect the way sexuality is understood (Basson, 2002; Komisaruk, Beyer-Flores, & Whipple, 2006; Ridley, 1999).

In 1973 the American Psychiatric Association ceased to consider homosexuality as pathological: "It is hard to overestimate the impact of this decision. First declaring homosexuals as 'normal', or at least as normal as heterosexuals, undermined laws, civil commitment procedures and the practice of therapy itself" (Nichols & Shernoff, 2007, p. 393). The legal acceptance of gay and lesbian long-term relationships through the Civil Partnerships Act 2004, which was implemented December 5, 2005, questions previous approaches to sexuality and sexual behavior in the United Kingdom.

Kinsey and coworkers (Kinsey, Pomeroy, & Martin, 1948; Kinsey, Pomeroy, Martin, & Gebhard, 1953) were among the first to study and publish material regarding the sexual behavior of Americans between 1938 and 1952 and opened up sexual behavior as an appropriate area for study. Newport (1997), examining the concept of *norms*, writes, "The concept of a norm is mysterious because it refers to a concept which exists 'out there' as part of culture, but is something which generally, unlike laws, for example, is never written down or codified formally" (p. 1). He continues,

> Survey research provides an excellent mechanism for social scientists to use to analyse a society's norms. If 80% of the members of a society agree that certain behaviour is appropriate in a given situation, then it can be hypothesised that

this represents a fairly widely shared norm. If only 20% agree, the behaviour is more appropriately characterised as deviant, rather than normative. (ibid.)

Newport writes of the tension that exists between the basic sex drive and culture's attempts to control or channel "this amazingly powerful instinct" (Gallup Poll, 1997, p. 1).

The tensions described by Newport (1997) are seen clearly between generations. Regarding premarital sex, 71% of those over 65 said premarital sex was wrong, while 75% of those 18 to 29 years of age said it was not wrong. In the group over 65, 6% had lived together before marriage compared with 50% of the 18- to 29-year-olds. Seidman and Rieder (1994) examined sexual behavior in more detail by reviewing American surveys and analyzed the 1988–1990 General Social Survey, which indicated that most American males at that time had experienced intercourse by 16 to 17 years of age and females by 17 to 18 years of age. The majority of 18- to 24-year-olds surveyed had had multiple serial partners, whereas the 25- to 59-year-olds had been relatively monogamous. Regarding extramarital relationships, surprisingly perhaps, both older and younger Americans had a similar view: 79% said it is always wrong for a married person to have sexual relationships outside marriage, and only 3% said it is not wrong at all. However, when examining what people actually do, rather than what they say, 80% of the public believe that half or more married people have committed adultery.

In relation to extramarital relationships in the United Kingdom, Wellings, Field, Johnson, and Wadsworth (1994, p. 249) write, "Disapproval of extramarital sexual relationships extends to all age groups.... There is no clear age related trend in these data." They urge that "care needs to be taken here in distinguishing attitudes from behavior. Disapproval of behavior does not mean that people refrain from it. Adultery is still one of the most widely cited grounds for divorce in Britain. But, practice aside, the principle of monogamy is held in very high regard" (ibid, p. 249). Physical sexual exclusivity may be more important to women than to men, although paradoxically men may expect their partners to be faithful to them (Ridley, 1999; Wellings et al., 1994). Hence, a paradoxical difference occurs between what may be seen as social norms and individual behavior.

In contrast, Nichols and Shernoff (2007) believe that little should be taken for granted "including the two-gender system, the assumption of heteronormality, and romantic views like the belief that monogamy and high sex drive are compatible" (p. 381).

Heterosexual/Homosexual Issues

The Gallup Poll review (Newman, 1997) states, "Americans have a complex set of attitudes about homosexual relations.... 52% say that homosexuality should not be considered an acceptable alternative lifestyle" (p. 3), with 59% indicating that homosexual behavior is morally wrong. As we have seen in the United Kingdom, although since December 2005 there has been legal acceptance of civil partnerships, there is little consensus among religious or political leaders. However, according to the poll, 25% of adults have had heterosexual anal intercourse, and up to 20% of adult men reported having had a homosexual experience, with 1% to 6% reporting such an experience during the previous year.

Views about sodomy—usually defined as anal or oral copulation with a member of the same or opposite sex—continue to vary from country to country. Much of the resistance to the acceptance of anal or oral sexual contacts between consenting adults in private tend to come from church organizations or affiliations. Both American and British data indicate that around 25% of heterosexual couples have had anal intercourse and suggest that "oro-genital contact may be experienced by increasing proportions of those who have not yet had vaginal intercourse ... as a risk reduction strategy in the face of AIDS" (Wellings et al., 1994, p. 157). It is noteworthy that "stimulating the rectum could add to the quality of orgasm" for women and may account for the "experience of orgasm in men receiving mechanical stimulation of the prostate during anal intercourse" (Komisaruk et al., 2006, p. 78). This is one of many aspects of sexual behavior raising problems of acceptance within the framework of norms. If these behaviors are not "normal," then how are they to be understood—as problems, variations, or dysfunctions? The boundaries are often blurred (Popovic, 2006).

Professional organizations can also be at odds with what society accepts. Paraphilias, for example, as defined by the American Psychiatric Association (APA) are "recurrent intense urges and sexually arousing fantasies involving either non-humans, or the suffering or humiliation of oneself or one's partner, and even children or consenting adults" (APA, 2000, p. 566). This behavior "must cause clinically significant distress or impairment in social, occupational, or other important areas of functioning" (p. 566). Are we therefore to assume that unless there is clinically significant distress, paraphilias can be placed within the normal spectrum of human behavior?

The Aging Population

By the year 2030, nearly 20% of people in the United States will be 65 years or older (Bradford & Meston, 2007). This trend is not restricted to America; worldwide, adults 60 and over are the most rapidly growing population (World Health Organization, 2002). Many myths and misconceptions inhibit the understanding of the norms of sexual needs and desires of this population (Hodson & Skeen, 1994). Contrary to some myths the sexual life of the older couple may slow down but continues into late age; this is understandably dependent on factors such as the availability of a partner, illness, and the impact of some medications. Changes that do occur affect men and women slightly differently.

Although erectile functioning tends to decline from midlife into old age, erectile failure is not inevitable. Typical changes include a delay in gaining a full erection, less rigidity of the erect penis, lessening sensitivity of the penis, and fewer erections during sleep (Wespes, 2002). The orgasmic responses may change, taking longer to achieve orgasm with a less forceful ejaculation and less volume of semen (Schiavi, 1999).

In aging women, a difference may be seen between desire and arousal, as there seems to be a steep decline in sexual desire (DeLamater & Sill, 2005) but sexual satisfaction may remain higher in older women than in men (AARP, 2005). The lining of the vagina thins, and vaginal lubrication and engorgement of the clitoral and vaginal tissues is slower and less robust; these features usually follow menopause and consequent loss of estrogen. As a result, there may be an increased risk of vaginal pain, urethral irritation, and urogenital infections (Society of Obstetricians and Gynaecologists of Canada, 2004). Myths about sexuality and aging and a lack of awareness of the needs of the older person can detrimentally hinder development of a therapeutic alliance.

Sexual Abuse, Rape, Domestic Violence

Until the 1960s sexual abuse of girls by males or females and its impact on sexuality was rarely discussed (Jehu, 1979; 1989). Greater awareness, often through clinical experience, recently identified the issue of male sexual abuse. Within the context of a discussion about norms, what does this mean? Was sexual abuse seen as an acceptable aspect of family life until the 20th century? Do rape and domestic violence fall into this same category? Genital mutilation is illegal in the United Kingdom but is still performed within some British cultural groups and is often understood as a necessary religious or "circumcision ritual." Such dilemmas are part of what must be dealt with when becoming a sex therapist.

Tiefer (2002) questions robustly the way sexuality has been understood and corralled by "experts who know a lot about the body mechanics rather than those who understand learning, culture and imagination" (p. 134). She prefers to understand sex as an aspect of human potential but its interpretation within each society as a social construct. She also wonders whether sex is a talent such as music or mathematics and writes that "to insist that everyone is equally talented at sex is fraudulently democratic" (ibid., p. 156). Her view of normality is challenging and well worth thinking through. Sex therapists working with clients whose norms are not their own should be sensitive and respectful of the client.

Diagnosis and Prevalence of Sexual Difficulties

The *Diagnostic and Statistical Manual of Mental Disorders*, 4th ed., text revision (*DSM-IV-TR*; APA, 2000) is used worldwide for diagnosis and treatment of both male and female sexual difficulties. Its validity is currently questioned. There is increasing disagreement about the prevalence of sexual problems, and an intelligent debate is developing regarding what constitutes a sexual problem or "dysfunction." Komisaruk et al. (2006), drawing from the National Health and Social Life Survey (NHSLS; Laumann, Paik, & Rosen, 1999), indicate that 43% of women and 31% of men in the United States are affected by sexual problems. However, the researchers did not ask about the level of distress, now seen as a defining characteristic.

Kaplan (1995) focuses specifically on desire disorders within a clinic population: "38% of the 5,580 patients with diagnosed sexual disorders whom we say between 1972 and 1992 met the criteria for sexual desire disorders" (p. 10). This upward trend is fueled possibly by the aging population and the impact of AIDS. Orgasmic problems are again dependent on individuals' level of distress. A nonrandom sample of couples found that 63% of women reported arousal and orgasmic problems although they were happily married, and 85% said they were happily married (Frank, Anderson, & Rubinstein, 1978).

DSM-IV-TR (APA, 2000) includes within it *dyspareunia* and *vaginismus*. Binik, Meana, Berkeley, and Khalife (1999) argue cogently that these are not sexual problems but problems of pain and fear of pain and should be treated as such. Low or absent desire in men is also being debated, as is the issue of rapid ejaculation, previously called premature ejaculation (Althof, 2007). There is little information regarding delayed ejaculation; the prevalence rates range widely from 1% to 10% (Spector & Carey, 1990) with a possible increase with age. Erectile dysfunction is considered to be a common and distressing aspect of male sexuality, with possibly 50% of men over 60 expressing concerns (Rosen, 2005).

Assessment in the Absence of Greater Clarity

A thorough assessment and proper diagnosis of the client, or client system, is essential. It is the basis of the treatment plan and therapeutic approach chosen. The present discussions are invigorating, if occasionally confusing. For the new recruit into sex therapy a wonderful opportunity is now available to be aware of the diagnostic criteria and the discussions encircling them and, more importantly, to recognize the individuality of the clients and to be less focused on medicalizing sexuality and to develop a therapeutic alliance that respects the uniqueness of each individual seeking help.

The Anatomy and Physiology of Sexuality

An appreciation of the anatomy and physiology of sexuality is necessary. Undue emphasis has led to a mechanistic view of sexuality, largely resulting from Masters and Johnson's (1966) approach to their material and subsequent interpretations. An emphasis on the context and complexity of sexuality helps to avoid this. Sexuality cannot be separated from the total context individuals or couples inhabit. Their social, religious, ethical, community, and familial systems and individual makeup will all have an important influence on their understanding of and response to sexuality. The meaning given to dancing, music, eating, clothing, scents, setting, and ambiance or the meaning of a glance, the movement of a hand, or the wiggle of a bottom will all have a personal and social context within which individuals or couples respond. The anatomy and physiology of individuals must be set and understood within these interconnecting systems.

Exploring the Internet provides a clear picture that young people are searching for factual information. See, for example, the Teen Sex Guide

(2006) at Student.com that describes the male genitalia in detail, and the website http://www.bygirlsforgirls.org, which is dedicated to providing helpful information of the female sex organs to girls who are interested in knowing the makeup of their bodies.

This is good factual information, but the focus is on the genitalia. What is missing is any attempt to describe the total person; see Kaplan (1975), where there are no anatomical drawings of genitalia. Focus on the genitalia ignores the importance of the skin as the largest erogenous zone and also overlooks other areas of sensitivity such as the potential tenderness of the breasts, around the mouth, under the nails, or the inner thigh. Clients can be encouraged to learn about their uniqueness by mapping their own or their partner's body and experiencing their own "erogenous zones."

Individuals are highly affected by life experiences; inappropriate sexual touching of the breast in childhood, for example, may make the breast area "off limits" because of the association, however repressed. The position of the light, odors, sounds, and music may all have powerful positive or negative associations that may affect the responsiveness of individuals to touch or sensuality. Unless these are seen as powerful aspects of the sensual or sexual experience, much will be missed by the therapist.

Paradoxically, sex therapists must have a good understanding of anatomy and physiology and the sexual response cycle, since many clients are poorly informed and can often be helped by a simple explanation of how the body works. It is important to have sufficient knowledge to identify when a physical examination or referral to a specialist may be necessary. Understanding the impact of aging or illness on the sexual relationship is part of the sex therapist's daily tasks. Bancroft (1990, currently being updated) is still one of the better resource books for a more complete picture.

The Sexual Response Cycle

Masters and Johnson's (1966) study of human sexual response is a landmark in the understanding of male and female sexual responses, built upon by succeeding clinicians and researchers. They set the direction that sex therapy would travel for many years. How they presented their material and succeeding professionals interpreted the research may be responsible for overemphasizing the physical aspect of sexuality. Nevertheless, their research formed the basis for ongoing investigations.

The Four Phases and Two Physiological Changes

Masters and Johnson (1966) divide up the sexual cycle into four specific phases through which individuals progress: from excitement to plateau to orgasm and finally to resolution. Significantly they described this as a "purely arbitrary design" (p. 7), which "is inadequate for evaluation of finite psychogenic aspects of elevated sexual tensions" (ibid.). Women are described as "having the response potential of returning to another orgasmic experience from any point in the resolution phase," which they describe as the "multiple orgasmic expression" (ibid., p. 65). Although the authors are aware of male–female differences, these tend to get lost in their excitement at discovering "similarities, not the differences" (ibid., p. 8) between the male and female sexual response cycle. These differences are now being addressed (Basson, 2007; Ridley, 1999).

Masters and Johnson (1966) describe the sexual responses as the result of two principal physiological changes: (1) increase in blood flow to various parts of the body (vasocongestion); and (2) an increase in muscle tension (myotonia). Detailed physiological changes in the female or male were noted as they moved through the phases of the cycle.

Male–Female Similarities and Differences

Masters and Johnson (1966) are at pains to emphasize that the clitoris and the penis are anatomically similar but that the clitoris does not respond as quickly as the penis to stimulation, whether direct or indirect, and that this is an error in thinking about female sexual responses. Additionally, they challenge the notion of the clitoris having an erection paralleling the male erection. The clitoris is described "as a unique organ, since no such organ exists within the anatomic structure of the human male" (ibid., p. 45). The different rates of excitement and engorgement between male and female responses are emphasized as well as the need for the clitoris to be stimulated to enable female orgasm. The vagina was studied with similar intensity.

In describing the female orgasm, Masters and Johnson (1966) emphasize three key areas that impact the female orgasm: the physiological, psychological, and sociological. Sociologically, the authors do recognize that female orgasmic attainment never has achieved the undeniable status afforded the male ejaculation. They predict that the human female now has an undeniable opportunity to realistically develop her own sexual response levels.

The male sexual arousal cycle, as described by Masters and Johnson (1966), is simpler than the female's. Again, the four phases—excitement, plateau, orgasm, and resolution—are noted. The whole body, similar to the female, shows physical evidence of sexual tension following two basic patterns—(1) vasocongestion and (2) myotonia (both widespread and specific). The male orgasm and ejaculation is described using the same three areas as the female: physiologic, psychologic, and sociologic. Masters and Johnson comment that sociological pressures have played a trick on the two genders; fears of performance in the female have been directed toward gaining an orgasm and in the male toward erection.

An important contribution of Masters and Johnson (1966) is their detailed study of the impact of aging on sexuality. They were able to crucially challenge the myths of the death of sexual activity with age but to describe a slowing down of the sexual arousal system and accompanying minor changes. Their work focuses exclusively on the functions and dysfunctions of the genitalia. They identify erectile and ejaculatory problems for men and women with problems relating to penetration and orgasm. These became categories established in the *Diagnostic and Statistical Manual of Mental Disorders,* 3rd ed. (*DSM-III;* APA, 1980). This had the twofold impact of having sexual problems taken seriously while also emphasizing the medical and physical aspects as dominant.

The Significance of Desire

Kaplan (1975; 1995) challenges Masters and Johnson's (1966) focus on the genitalia and added a crucial dimension: sexual desire. She believes, as a result of her clinical experience, that Masters and Johnson miss this essential element and thus ignore sexual problems relating to desire. As a result, hypoactive sexual desire (HSD) disorders were included in *DSM-III* (APA, 1980). Kaplan (1995) believes that "the pathological decrease of these patients' libido is essentially an expression of normal regulation of sexual motivation gone awry" (p. 3).

Kaplan's (1975; 1995) treatment approach includes *erotic techniques* and their accompanying emotional impact on clients and couples. She is concerned about the unconscious conflicts, fears, and desires that she feels may cause or exacerbate sexual difficulties and are evident within the therapeutic process between clinicians and their clients or patients. Kaplan (1995) draws attention to the "wider psychic matrix of which sexuality is an integral and beautiful part" (p. 7). Her contribution adds greatly to the understanding of the emotional and social aspects of sexuality. Paradoxically, the inclusion of hypoactive sexual desire as a disorder in *DSM-III* added significantly to the medicalization of female sexuality.

The Analytic Contribution

The psychoanalytic field has tended to take a very separate perspective on female and male sexuality, within which a fascinating and often fierce dialogue continues (Bassin, 1999). Students should be aware of these debates and their impact on theories regarding female and male development. Karen Horney (in Bassin, 1999) aptly describes the skeleton around which such dialogues rage.

Seen from the analytic perspective, Horney (in Bassin, 1999) lists the following characterizations of *growing boys*:

- They have naïve assumptions that girls as well as boys possess a penis.
- They have a realization of the absence of the (female's) penis.
- They have a belief that girls have suffered punishment that also threatens them.
- The girl is regarded as inferior.
- They are unable to imagine how girls can ever get over this loss or envy.
- They dread girls' envy.

Horney then lists ideas about *girls' development* as follows:

- For both sexes, only the male genital plays any part.
- They discover with sadness the absence of a penis.
- They believe that they once possessed a penis and lost it by castration.
- Castration is conceived of as the infliction of punishment.
- They regard themselves as inferior (i.e., penis envy).
- They never get over the sense of deficiency and inferiority and have to constantly master afresh their desire to be a man.
- They desire throughout life to take revenge on men for possessing something they lack.
- Concepts such as penis envy—or the castrating woman from the psychoanalytic field—have become popularly accepted wisdom.

The Complex Female

An intense and fascinating debate is occurring, largely in America, regarding the complexity of female sexuality. Beverly Whipple has carried out detailed research into the nature of the female orgasm, which is best summarized in Komisaruk et al. (2006). Emphasis is placed on women being asked about the level of distress they experience, as this is now believed to be a key component in the diagnosis of sexual disorder. Komisaruk et al. also challenge the linear sequence derived from Masters and Johnson's (1966) four phases (i.e., excitement, plateau, orgasm, resolution) and believe it to be "unhelpful in assessing and managing women's sexual problems and disorders" (Komisaruk et al., 2006, p. 64). Basson (2002) and Basson et al. (2003) seek to redefine the nature of female sexuality: "Now nearly four decades later, we know that sexual interest, motivation, arousal and pleasure are triggered and experienced quite differently by men and women" (Leiblum, 2007, p. 6).

In 2003 a second consensus conference reviewing *DSM-IV-TR* (APA, 2000) recommended that instead of a single diagnosis of female sexual arousal disorder there should be four: (1) primarily physical; (2) primarily subjective; (3) combined physical and subjective arousal disorder; and (4) a newly defined arousal disorder, persistent genital arousal (Basson, 2007). While these emphasize the complex nature of female sexuality, the determination that these difficulties should be included in *DSM-IV-TR* (APA, 2000) inevitably adds further impetus to the medicalization of female sexuality. The diagnosis of male sexual disorders has not been formally reassessed but is likely to occur particularly in the areas of what constitutes rapid or premature ejaculation.

The Dual Control Model for Men

Bancroft and colleagues (2005) sought to clarify the nature of male sexuality. A concept of an inhibitory factor that operates against an excitatory factor, the *dual control model* provides a useful theoretical model with which to examine male sexuality, in particular erectile difficulties. It is worth remembering what Masters and Johnson noted in 1966: "Penile erection may be impaired easily by the introduction of asexual stimuli" (p. 183). Within this model the Sexual Inhibition/Sexual Excitation Scales (SIS/SES) are used (Janssen, Vorst, Finn, & Bancroft, 2002a, 2002b). The propensity for sexual inhibition, due to the threat of performance failure (SIS I), or the propensity for sexual inhibition, due to the threat of performance consequences (SIS II), is measured. The propensity for sexual excitation (SES) is also measured.

According to this theoretical model, sexual arousal, including genital response, depends on both an active excitation response plus reduction of inhibitory tone together with the relative absence of inhibitory response to the sexual situation. Further research is obviously necessary, but the concepts of an inhibitory system that may work against the excitatory system certainly resonate with clinical experience.

Gender differences are now recognized regarding intimacy needs; fear of or need for intimacy as well as differences in a partnership such as between closeness and distance and between emotional and practical are now understood to affect individuals' or couples' experience of their sexual life (Popovic, 2005; Ridley, 1999). Sexual preferences like being lesbian, gay, or bisexual are increasingly encompassed as part of the rich spectrum of personal and interpersonal sexuality (Davies & Neal, 2002), although much work is still necessary.

Overemphasizing the Medical Aspects of Sexuality?

An overemphasis on the physical and medical aspects of sexuality can develop in both the client and practitioner (Hart & Wellings, 2002; Tiefer, 2002). When sexual difficulties are viewed as an illness or physical, it is easiest to seek a medical solution rather that to examine possible contributing aspects of personal or interpersonal life. The arrival of Viagra (Pfizer, New York) and similar drugs has provided such an opportunity (Ashton, 2007; Finger, 2007); additionally, many men's sex lives have also been improved. Paradoxically, when using a drug, personal or interpersonal difficulties may be highlighted and then addressed. A search for a similar drug for women is under way while at the same time attempting to resist the medicalization of women's sexuality (Tiefer, 2002).

An important area, however, is that of the impact of illnesses both mental and physical, which are real and do need to be treated medically. Illnesses such as depression, diabetes, or heart problems can have a serious impact on quality of life, including the sexual life. Equally, essential medication can treat the illness but may impact negatively on sexual abilities. Working with clients to find an appropriate balance between these conflicting elements requires an ability to take seriously the physical and medical circumstances faced by each client (Gill & Hough, 2007).

Conclusion

Before embarking on a career as a sex therapist, you may want to ask yourself if you can accept the personal and professional challenges you will face. Wanting to help is not good enough. A sound, wide-spectrum knowledge base must be learned during which your value system and prejudices will be challenged. You will need to be open to new experiences while retaining the ability to be both flexible and boundaried. Examining your own emotional and sexual responses under supervision will become part of your regular routine. Understanding the multilayered interaction between the inner and outer world of the client, the client system, and the wider social context will involve setting aside previously held perspectives. Knowing the limits of your knowledge and skill will mean that seeking advice or referring clients to other specialists may be necessary. Being prepared to question attitudes about what is normal, to value others whose way of life is different from your own, to learn from good research and evidence-based practice, to practice within the law, however complex, to cowork with medical and psychiatric specialists while continuing to value the whole person can test us all, but these are essential requirements of a sex therapist.

References

AAMFT (2001). *American Association for Marriage and Family Therapy Code of Ethics.* Retrieved July 13, 2007 from: http://www.aamft.org/resources/LRMPlan/Ethics/ethicscode2001.asp

AARP (2005). *Sexuality at mid-life and beyond: 2004 Update of attitudes and behaviour.* Retrieved July 13, 2007 from: http://www.aarp.org/research/family/lifestyles/2004_sexuality.html

Althof, S. E. (2007). Treatment of rapid ejaculation. Psychotherapy, pharmacotherapy, and combined therapy. In S. Leiblum (Ed.), *Principles and practice of sex therapy* (4th ed., pp. 212–240). New York: Guilford.

American Psychiatric Association (APA) (1980). *Diagnostic and Statistical Manual of Mental Disorders* (3rd ed.). Washington, DC: APA.

American Psychiatric Association (APA) (2000). *Diagnostic and Statistical Manual of Mental Disorders* (4th ed., text revision). Washington, DC: APA.

Anatomy and Physiology (2006). Anatomy and physiology. Retrieved July 26, 2007 from: http://www.bygirlsforgirls.org/anatomy.html

Ashton, A. K. (2007). The new sexual pharmacology. In S. Leiblum (Ed.), *Principles and practice of sex therapy* (4th ed., pp. 509–541). New York: Guilford.

Bancroft, J. (1990). *Human sexuality and its problems.* New York: Churchill Livingstone.

Bancroft, J., Herbenick, D., Barnes, T., Hallam-Jones, R., Wylie, K., Janssen, E., & BASRT members (2005). The relevance of the dual control model to male sexual dysfunction: Kinsey Institute/BASRT collaborative project. *Sexual and Relationship Therapy, 20,* 13–30.

Bassin, D. (1999). *Female sexuality, contemporary engagements.* Northvale, NJ: Jason Aronson.

BASRT (British Association of Sexual and Relationship Therapy) *Code of Practice.* Retrieved July 24, 2007 from: http://www.basrt.org.uk/downloads/EP_GP_Members.pdf

Basson, R. (2002). Are our definitions of women's desire, arousal and sexual pain disorders too broad and our definition of orgasmic disorder too narrow? *Journal of Sex and Marital Therapy, 28*(4), 289–300.

Basson, R. (2007). Sexual desire/arousal disorders in women. In S. Leiblum (Ed.), *Principles and practice of sex therapy* (4th ed., pp. 25–53). New York: Guilford.

Basson, R., Leiblum, S., Brotto, L., Derogatis, L., Fourcroy, J., Fulg-Meyer, K., et al. (2003). Definitions of women's sexual dysfunction reconsidered: Advocating expansion and revision. *Journal of Psychosomatic Obstetrics and Gynecology, 24,* 221–229.

Binik, Y. M., Meana, M., Berkeley, K., & Khalife, S. (1999). Dyspareunia: Is the pain sexual or the sex painful. *Annual Review of Sex Research, 36,* 210–235.

Bradford, A. & Meston, C. M. (2007). Senior sexual health: The effects of aging on sexuality. In L. VandeCreek, F. L. Peterson, & J. W. Bley (Eds.), *Innovations in clinical practice: Focus on sexual health* (pp. 35–46). Sarasota, FL: Professional Resource Press.

Civil Partnership Act (2004). Civil Partnership Act. Retrieved July 24, 2007 from: http://www.opsi.gov.uk/ACTS/acts2004/20040033.htm

Crowe, M. & Ridley, J. (2000). *Therapy with couples, a behavioural systems approach to relationship and sexual problems* (2nd ed.). Oxford: Blackwell Science.

Davies, D. & Neal, C. (2002). *Therapeutic perspectives on working with lesbian, gay, and bisexual clients.* London: Open University Press.

DeLamater, J. D. & Sill, M. (2005). Sexual desire in later life. *Journal of Sex Research, 42,* 138–149.

DeMaria, R., Weeks, G., & Hof, L. (1999). *Focused Genograms: Intergenerational assessment of individuals, couples and families.* Philadelphia: Brunner/Mazel.

Finger, W. W. (2007). Medication and sexual health. In L. VandeCreek, F. L. Peterson, & J. W. Bley (Eds.), *Innovations in clinical practice: Focus on sexual health* (pp. 47–62). Sarasota, FL: Professional Resource Press.

Frank, E., Anderson, A., & Rubenstein, D. (1978). Frequency of sexual dysfunction in "normal" couples. *New England Journal of Medicine, 299,* 111–115.

Gallup Poll Review from the Poll Editors. *Sexual norms: Where does America stand today?* Retrieved August 26, 2008, from http://www.hi-ho.ne.jp/taku77/refer/sexnorm.htm

Giami, A. (2001). Counter-transference in social research: George Devereux and beyond. *Papers in Social Research Methods, Qualitative Series, no 7.* Methodology Institute, London School of Economics and Political Science.

Gill, K. M. & Hough, S. (2007). Sexual health of people with chronic illness and disability. In L. VandeCreek, F. L. Peterson, & J. W. Bley (Eds.), *Innovations in clinical practice: Focus on sexual health* (pp. 223–245). Sarasota, FL: Professional Resource Press.

Hart, G. & Wellings, K. (2002). Sexual behaviour and its medicalisation: In sickness and in health. *British Medical Journal, 45,* 896–900.

Hodson, D. S. & Skeen, P. (1994). Sexuality and ageing: The Hammerlock of myths. *Journal of Applied Gerontology, 13,* 219–235.

Janssen, E., Vorst, H., Finn, P., & Bancroft, J. (2002a). The Sexual Inhibition (SIS) and Sexual Excitation (SES) scales I: Measuring sexual inhibition and excitation proneness in men. *Journal of Sex Research, 39,* 114–126.

Janssen, E., Vorst, H., Finn, P., & Bancroft, J. (2002b). The Sexual Inhibition (SIS) and Sexual Excitation (SES) scales II: Predicting psychophysiological response patterns. *Journal of Sex Research, 39,* 127–132.

Jehu, D. (1979). *Sexual dysfunction. A behavioural approach to causation, assessment and treatment.* New York: John Wiley and Sons.

Jehu, D. (1989). *Beyond sexual abuse.* Chichester, England: Wiley.

Kaplan, H. S. (1975). *The illustrated manual of sex therapy.* Herts, England: Granada.

Kaplan, H. S. (1987). *The illustrated manual of sex therapy,* 2nd ed., New York: Brunner/Mazel.

Kaplan, H. S. (1995). *The sexual desire disorders: Dysfunctional regulation of sexual motivation.* New York: Brunner-Mazel.

Kinsey, A. C., Pomeroy, W. B., & Martin, C. E. (1948). *Sexual behaviour in the human male.* Philadelphia, PA: W. B. Saunders.

Kinsey, A. C., Pomeroy, W. B., Martin, C. E., & Gebhard, P. H. (1953). *Sexual behaviour in the human female.* Philadelphia, PA: W. B. Saunders.

Komisaruk, B. R., Beyer-Flores, C., & Whipple, B. (2006). *The science of orgasm.* Baltimore, MD: Johns Hopkins University Press.

Laumann, E. O., Paik, A., & Rosen, R. C. (1999). *National Health and Social Life Survey.* Chicago: University of Chicago Press.

Leiblum, S. R. (2007). Sex therapy today: Current issues and future perspectives. In S. Leiblum (Ed.), *Principles and practice of sex therapy* (4th ed., pp. 3–25). New York: Guilford.

Mann, D. (1997). *Psychotherapy, an erotic relationship. Transference and counter-transference passions.* New York: Brunner-Routledge.

Masters, W. H. & Johnson, V. E. (1966). *Human sexual response.* Boston: Little, Brown.

Maurice, W. L. (2007). Sexual desire disorders of men. In S. Leiblum (Ed.), *Principles and practice of sex therapy* (4th ed., pp. 181–211). New York: Guilford.

Morin, J. (1995). *The erotic mind: Unlocking the inner sources of sexual passion and fulfillment.* New York: HarperCollins.

Newport, F. (1997). *Gallup Poll Review from the Poll Editors, Sexual Norms: Where does America stand today?* New York: Gallup Organisation.

Nichols, M. & Shernoff, M. (2007). Therapy with sexual minorities: Queering Practice. In S. Leiblum (Ed.), *Principles and practice of sex therapy* (4th ed., pp. 379–416). New York: Guilford.

Popovic, M. (2005). Intimacy and its relevance in human functioning. *Sexual and Relationship Therapy, 20,* 31–49.

Popovic, M. (2006). Psychosexual diversity as the best representation of human normality across cultures. *Journal of Sexual and Relationship Therapy, 21,* 171–187.

Ridley, J. (1999). *Intimacy in crisis.* London: Whurr.

Ridley, J. (2006). The subjectivity of the clinician in psychosexual therapy and training. *Sexual and Relationship Therapy, 21*(3), 319–331.

Rosen, R. C. (2005.) Reproductive health problems in ageing men. *Lancet, 366,* 183–185.

Schiavi, R. C. (1999). *Ageing and male sexuality.* Cambridge, England: Cambridge University Press.

Seidman, S. N. & Rieder, R. O. (1994). A review of sexual behaviour in the United States. *American Journal of Psychiatry, 151,* 330–341.

Society of Obstetricians and Gynaecologists of Canada (2004). The detection and management of vaginal atrophy. *International Journal of Gynaecology and Obstetrics, 88,* 222–228.

Spector, I. P. & Carey, M. P. (1990). Incidence and prevalence of the sexual dysfunctions: A critical review of the empirical literature. *Archives of Sexual Behaviour, 19,* 389–408.

Teen Sex Guide (2006). *Teen sex guide.* Retrieved July 26, 2007 from: http://www.student.com/sexguide.php

The Sexuality Guide (2007). *Male genitals.* Retrieved July 24, 2007 from: http://www.student.com/sexguide_a.php?id=92

Tiefer, L. (2002). Sexual behaviour and its medicalisation. *British Medical Journal, 325*(7354), 45.

Weeks, G. & Hof, L. (1994). *The marital relationship therapy casebook: Theory and application of the intersystem model.* New York: Brunner/Mazel.

Weeks, G. & Hof, L. (1995) *Integrative solutions: Treating common problems in couples therapy.* New York: Brunner/Mazel.

Wellings, K., Field, J., Johnson, A. M., & Wadsworth, J. (1994). *Sexual behaviour in Britain: The national survey of sexual attitudes and lifestyles.* London: Penguin Books Ltd.

Wespes, E. (2002). The ageing penis. *World Urology Journal, 20,* 36–39.

World Health Organisation (2002). *Active ageing: A policy framework.* Retrieved July 13, 2007 from: http://whqlibdoc.who.int/hq/2002/WHO_NMH_NPH_02.8.pdf

2

The Profession of Sex Therapy

Peggy J. Kleinplatz

Contents

Introduction

This chapter reviews the history of sex therapy and recent trends in the field including the medicalization of sexual dysfunction and responses to medicalization. The professional life of the sex therapist is described, highlighting the various sex therapy organizations, the personal and professional process of becoming a sex therapist, and the ethical principles of sex therapy. Finally, the controversy over the distinctiveness of sex therapy—or lack thereof—and therefore whether certification of sex therapists is warranted are considered.

The History of Sex Therapy

Throughout the 20th century until the development of sex therapy, sexual problems were either unspoken or were the province of religion, philosophy, and, to a minor extent, medicine. They were often discussed in "marriage manuals," which had some nifty little ideas about how much sex was desirable, which kinds of sexual activity were appropriate, and, for that matter, what constituted sex (Van de Velde, 1926). Whatever ideas they put forth were based on the values and beliefs of the era, with no basis in sexology, that is, the scientific study of sexuality. In addition, sexuality was a major focus of the work of psychoanalysis, which dealt with the whole person and his or her development rather than targeting sexual problems for treatment. Although psychoanalysis had the advantage of aiming for substantive personality change (Freud, 1917/1963), it was time intensive, was hardly cost-effective, and dealt with the individual alone rather than the couple or society, that is, the context in which sexual difficulties tend to arise and be manifest.

In the late 1940s and early 1950s, the work of Alfred Kinsey and his colleagues helped to revolutionize what could be studied by sexologists by seeking to describe and categorize the spectrum of normal sexual behaviors. The popularity of Kinsey's work, even though it was highly controversial, helped to pave the way for the study of the physiology of sexual response in the laboratory by William Masters and Virginia Johnson (1966). Their findings mapped out the sequence of the four stages of what they termed the *human sexual response cycle,* consisting of excitement, plateau, orgasm, and resolution. This laboratory research in turn laid the foundations—and provided the credibility—for Masters and Johnson's (1970) text, *Human Sexual Inadequacy,* which described the sexual disorders and their treatment. This seminal book essentially created the field of sex therapy. Sexual problems came to be defined largely in terms of deviations from the physiological norms found among subjects engaging in sexual acts in the lab. Deviations from Masters and Johnson's (1966) model of the human sexual response cycle later came to be reified as the criteria for defining sexual disorders in the American Psychiatric

Association's various editions of the *Diagnostic and Statistical Manual of Mental Disorders* (*DSM*).

The evolution of sex therapy and the current status of sexual problems and their treatment cannot be understood without further attention to the basic precepts and concepts Masters and Johnson elucidated. A gynecologist, Masters became interested in the scientific study of sexuality and, specifically, the treatment of sexual disorders. He was joined in his investigations and in the development of a treatment paradigm by social scientist Johnson. The foundation of their work was consistent with Masters' training as a physician. One of their major precepts was that sex is a biological function, not unlike urination, defecation, or respiration (Masters and Johnson, 1986). Much of their clinical work was aimed at eliminating psychosocially imposed obstacles (e.g., ignorance, fear, guilt, shame) to sexual function so that "natural" functioning could reassert itself. They stated that 90% of sexual problems were likely to be psychogenic and the remaining 10% of organic origin. (Although the discourse popular in the current Zeitgeist is reversed and would suggest that 90% of sexual problems are of organic etiology and only 10% are psychogenic, the mind–body dualism prevails.)

A second major precept proposed by Masters and Johnson was that the relationship should be the focus of treatment rather than targeting only the symptomatic patient. Regardless of which individual presented the problem, the couple would be required in therapy to achieve a solution. Ironically, they have been criticized for giving only lip service to the importance of the relationship in maintaining the problem (Weeks, 2005); the use of surrogates as part of their treatment paradigm betrays their belief that although two people may be necessary to effect symptom amelioration, the interchangeability of the partners suggests a neglect in this model of the role of the *intimate* relationship and the couple *system* in sexual problems. In short, the early pioneers talked about working with the couple but did not conceptualize or intervene systemically.

The treatment approach of Masters and Johnson consisted of brief, behaviorally oriented couples therapy with a strong educational component intended to target the symptoms of sexual dysfunction. The success of Masters and Johnson's approach as first reported in 1970 led to great interest in sex therapy and laid the groundwork for the entire field over the next decades. Unfortunately, the paradoxical effect of this "success" led to widespread acceptance of their methods without due consideration of underlying theoretical foundations—or lack thereof—allowing the prevailing assumptions to remain unexplored (Kleinplatz, 2001, 2003; Wiederman, 1998).

During the 1970s and 1980s, Masters and Johnson's work began to be critiqued for ignoring subjective aspects of sexual response such as desire, psychological arousal during sex, and satisfaction thereafter (Kaplan, 1977, 1979; Lief, 1977; Zilbergeld & Ellison, 1980) as well as for unorthodox reporting of outcome data, making it difficult either to interpret their findings or to replicate them. Helen Singer Kaplan (1974), trained in psychoanalysis, emphasized the need to assess not only for "immediate" factors blocking sexual response but also for "remote," developmental factors that might affect personality and relationships. Ironically, despite her insight as to the role of historical factors, she emphasized that "fortunately" it was easy enough to remediate symptoms without needing to deal with underlying dynamics except in recalcitrant cases (Kaplan, 1974). In 1977, both Kaplan and Harold Lief described the desire disorders as particularly common and vexing. The desire disorders were more complex than could be accounted for by studying the physiology of sexual response alone. Inhibited sexual desire, now known as hypoactive sexual desire disorder (HSDD), entered the *DSM* in 1980.

In the ensuing years, sex therapy has consisted primarily of brief, directive couples and, often, individual therapy blended with psychoeducational counseling and use of "homework" assignments. Sex therapy has historically been rather effective in treating the symptoms of sexual dysfunctions, at least compared with the track record of mainstream psychotherapy in treating its most prevalent presenting problems (e.g., depression, anxiety). As such, sex therapy assumed brand-name proportions, becoming the "Kleenex of psychotherapy," without much attention to the ill-defined, poorly explored, assumptions implicit in our treatment methods (Kleinplatz, 1996). A variety of sex therapists have attempted to articulate, broaden, and integrate treatment paradigms to focus more extensively on a wider and deeper array of issues, particularly relationship and systemic factors, including Weeks and the Intersystem model (1977, 1994; Weeks & Hof, 1987), LoPiccolo and the Post-Modern approach (1987), Schnarch and the Crucible model (1991, 1997) and Kleinplatz and the Experiential model (1996, 1998, 2004) developed by Mahrer (1996, Mahrer & Boulet, 2001).

Recent Trends in the Field

The burgeoning attention beginning to be given to integrate sexual and couples therapy was suddenly deflected by the introduction of sildenafil citrate, or Viagra (Goldstein et al., 1998) in March 1998. The introduction of a pharmacological intervention for treatment of a sexual dysfunction was not new in and of itself; however, a variety of factors made Viagra a popular option and an instant media star. The ease of administration combined with a curiously sex-negative, sociocultural environment and the relative theoretical void combined to shift public attention to a quick-fix solution for sexual problems.

Some history is useful to situate "the Viagra moment" in context. In a society that has long been ambivalent, at best, about sex education, let alone comprehensive sexuality education, the pull toward dealing with sexual problems as if they are somehow separate from the rest of our lives is irresistible. It is as if the people with sexual difficulties, the surrounding society, the pharmaceutical industry, and clinicians collectively entered into a silent pact: Let's just conspire to keep our sexual difficulties sealed off from the rest of the context in which they come into existence, are perceived as problematic, and require "fixing." Let us collude to treat the symptoms of sexual dysfunctions, as if the symptoms are the (possibly underlying) problems themselves. Let us prop up the sagging penis as if that alone will take care of his (and his partner's) deflated spirits, as if hard penises are all we need for sex, as if sex equals intercourse. Let's talk about our genitals—if we must talk about them at all—as if they are mechanical objects in need of repair rather than parts of whole persons silently asserting their discontent at unfulfilling intimate relations.

Such a pact was not so easy for as long as the treatment itself was unduly painful or cumbersome, as was the case with the biomedical treatment of erectile dysfunction prior to Viagra. Throughout the 1990s, my practice (and that of many colleagues) was replete with men who reported being diagnosed with "leaky blood vessels" (Kleinplatz, 2004). The major medical treatment for erectile dysfunction at that time was the use of intracavernosal injections of papaverine, phentolamine, and prostaglandin E_1 to produce rapid, firm, and long-lasting erections. (It remains the treatment of choice for many men who cannot use sildenafil citrate because of, for example, potentially dangerous interactions with nitrates.) The popularity of this treatment, however, was limited by the queasiness engendered by having to inject oneself in the penis (Althof & Turner, 1992; Althof et al., 1989; Irwin & Kata, 1994). It was hardly pleasant and difficult to administer inconspicuously. Even more so, it violated the belief system proclaiming that sex, defined as intercourse, was supposed to be "natural and spontaneous." I was struck by how quickly this epidemic of "leaky blood vessels" disappeared at precisely the same time the little blue pills appeared on the market (Kleinplatz, 2004). The latter were much easier to swallow.

The field of sex therapy was forced to react to the easy availability of a new, relatively safe and effective, nonintrusive method for treating erectile dysfunction without the theoretical foundations with which to conceptualize this innovation. It was as though the field was thrust into a collective (albeit silent) identity crisis (Giami, 2000), attempting to ascertain how to deal with this new option (e.g., as merely another intervention, adjunct, rival, ally, diagnostic tool) while unsure of our own clinical and professional objectives. How were we to deal with the new kid on the block while still unclear on who we want to be when we grow up?

In 1994, Schover and Leiblum warned of the encroaching medicalization of sex therapy. Long before the field had begun to grapple with its theoretical lacunae, "the Viagra moment" had arrived. In the interim, we had neglected to identify the basic questions a science of psychotherapy practice must encounter, while continuing to act as if we had all the answers (Kleinplatz, 2001, 2003). Here are just a few fundamental questions:

- How are we to understand sexual experience?
- What is the basis or origin of sexual desire?
- Are all people capable of some kind of sexual feeling?
- What is "normal" sexuality?
- What is the relationship between "normal" and "abnormal/dysfunctional" sexuality, and what can we learn about one from the other?
- What is optimal sexuality?
- What kinds of sex do we want to promote?
- How are we to conceptualize sexual problems?
- What are the meanings of those difficulties for the individual, the couple, and the system?
- What should our goals be in dealing with sexual problems?

Whereas it had been simple enough to ignore our own assumptions when we were the only game in town, with the introduction of Viagra the time was well overdue for us to reconsider the provisional principles underlying sex therapy praxis.

The Medicalization of Sexual Problems

Over the next five years, the increasing medicalization of sex therapy emerged in the forms of new pharmacological treatments, new organizations and conferences designed to teach non–sex-therapist physicians the rudiments of prescribing these drugs, and the marketing not only of the drugs but also a new discourse on sexual difficulties. Advertisements blanketed American television, magazines, and other media announcing first Viagra and later two other phosphodiesterase type 5 (PDE5) inhibitors: tadalafil, or Cialis (Eli Lilly and Company, Indianapolis, Indiana); and vardenafil, or Levitra (Bayer Pharmaceuticals Corporation, Pittsburgh, Pennsylvania). Each ad exhorted the audience or reader to "Ask your doctor." Unfortunately, the increasingly sex-negative atmosphere during those years led to funding cutbacks for teaching sex therapy and even basic training in medical schools about human sexuality and its problems (Kleinplatz, 2003). Thus, prospective patients were being instructed to contact physicians who were increasingly ill-equipped to handle the newly created demand for their services. The pharmaceutical industry funded conferences that taught physicians about urological aspects of erectile dysfunction with little attention to the sexological or relational dimensions. This fit quite well with the marketing of the discourse touting that 90% of erectile dysfunction was of organic etiology whereas only 10% was psychogenic or relational in origin. That notion, in turn, was especially appealing to individuals and couples who preferred to blame the malfunctioning penis rather than be forced to delve too deeply into the possibility of personal or interpersonal problems. Thus, a situation was created where the penis would "work" while the individual attached (or detached) was ignored.

In addition, the off-label prescription of other drugs for sexual difficulties was promoted increasingly in the 1990s and thereafter. Selective serotonin reuptake inhibitors (SSRIs) were recommended increasingly as a treatment for rapid ejaculation. Drugs such as Paxil (GlaxoSmithKline, Philadelphia, Pennsylvania), intended originally as antidepressants, demonstrated an adverse impact on sexual desire and response, diminishing or even preventing orgasm in many patients. SSRIs succeeded in slowing down men's ejaculations and were therefore used as an adjunct to (Assalian, 1994) or instead of conventional sex therapy for treatment of rapid ejaculation (Waldinger, 2003). SSRIs were also used in combination with antiandrogens to control paraphilic behavior. Various preparations of testosterone (oral, injectable, and transdermal) or dehydroepiandrosterone (DHEA) were promoted for treatment of the nebulous "female sexual dysfunction." Ubiquitous "experts" spoke in the media as if it were a given that desire or lack thereof was a direct result of levels of testosterone. It came as quite a surprise to the public in December 2004, when the U.S. Food and Drug Administration (FDA) rejected unanimously

Procter & Gamble's bid to seek approval for Intrinsa (Procter & Gamble Pharmaceuticals, Cincinnati, Ohio), their proposed testosterone patch for HSDD in women. Two studies released shortly thereafter affirmed the *lack* of correlation between androgen levels and female sexual desire (Davis, Davison, Donath, & Bell, 2005; Wierman et al., 2006).

The emphasis on biomedical interventions for sexual problems was also apparent in the new mechanical treatment of female sexual arousal disorder with the EROS-CTD (clitoral therapy device; Billups et al., 2001) and the use of physiotherapy to reduce genital and pelvic pain (Bergeron et al., 2002; Binik, 2005).

New professional organizations, often sponsored by the pharmaceutical industry, were formed and began to provide continuing education for physicians, especially gynecologists and urologists in treating sexual dysfunctions (see section below). Although there is a serious need for physicians to be trained in the comprehensive care of patients' sexual difficulties (Maurice, 1999; Moser, 1999), the instruction in many of these instances was largely about the high prevalence of sexual dysfunction and the need to be on the lookout for them, about checklists to evaluate for their symptoms, and about pharmacological information. The psychosocial and interpersonal context in which problems are generated was largely overlooked.

The phenomenal amount of attention garnered by Viagra led to great interest in the development of a female equivalent (Hartley, 2006) and the introduction into the clinical lexicon of the new phrase "Female Sexual Dysfunction." A new organization was established in 1998 with Irwin Goldstein (the urologist who first introduced sildenafil citrate [1998]) at the helm. It was known initially as the Female Sexual Function Forum (FSFF) and made up primarily of physicians, rather than clinicians trained/identifying as sex therapists. It is now known as the International Society for the Study of Women's Sexual Health (ISSWSH). It had followed the establishment in 1982 of the International Society for Impotence Research, which changed its name in 2000 to the International Society for Sexual and Impotence Research and subsequently to the International Society for Sexual Medicine [ISSM]. The vast majority of its members are urologists.) New journals, notably the *Journal of Sexual Medicine* (published by ISSM), were established and special issues of existing journals devoted to medical aspects of sexual problems were published. Winton (2000, 2001) documented the growing dominance of the medical model in the major sexology journals. The unfortunate demise in 2000 of the *Journal of Sex Education and Therapy* further illustrated the shift toward fragmentation of the field.

Responses to Medicalization

As the medicalization of sex therapy grew, so too did the developing resistance to and backlash against it. During the early 1990s, sociologists (e.g., Irvine, 1990; Jeffries, 1990; Reiss, 1990) had begun to criticize the field of sex therapy. They stated that the treatment of clients' problems one on one without attempting to change the social environment in which these problems are generated, maintained, and treated allows clinicians to make a profit by helping individuals adjust to a troubled norm while sustaining the dysfunctional status quo. In the successive years, sex therapists, too, began to question openly the tenuous, tacit assumptions built into our beginnings (Kleinplatz, 1996, 1998, 2003; Schnarch, 1991, 1997; Tiefer, 1991, 1996; Ussher, 1993). These shaky foundations made it easier for the field to be co-opted by reductionistic, biomedical models; correspondingly, they made it easy for the pharmaceutical industry to market treatments for sexual dysfunctions to clinicians and the public and to achieve buy-in.

In 2000, in response to the growing medicalization of sexuality and sexual problems, a group of sexologists coalesced under the leadership of Leonore Tiefer and proffered an alternate diagnostic framework for conceptualizing sexual difficulties. The Working Group for a New View of Women's Sexual Problems (Alperstein et al., 2002) recommended that all women's (and later, men's) sexual problems be assessed in terms of sociocultural, political, or economic factors; problems relating to partner and relationships; and psychological and medical factors. The call for multidimensional approaches to assessing and dealing with human sexuality (e.g., Ogden, 2001) has been welcomed in some quarters and been dismissed as regressive, outmoded, "feminist" complaints by others.

If in 1994 Schover and Leiblum decried the stagnation of sex therapy, a decade later the field had moved increasingly to splintering of the profession(s) (Kleinplatz, 2003). Although the demand for help with sexual problems continues unabated, the nature of the services provided often depends on which type of clinician with what type of training the client or patient happens to see. Perhaps more often, particularly in the United States, it is less a matter of happenstance and is related instead to health insurance coverage or lack thereof. With the rise of managed care in the 1990s, access to psychotherapy was curtailed severely, with most insurance plans refusing reimbursement for couples therapy. Although the increasing emphasis on *empirically supported treatments* and *best practices* seems logical enough, the most expedient treatment with the most clear-cut effectiveness in reducing symptoms of sexual dysfunctions may not be in the patient's best interests in an area as complex as sexuality. Studies of pharmaceutical interventions may show impressive results when criteria for effective outcome are "more restricted and unidimensional" (Heiman, 2002, p. 74) than in studies of individual or couples therapy. However, most couples are seeking more than "erections firm enough for penetration" or to be free of "vaginal spasms preventing intercourse;" they are hoping for sex that is desired and worth wanting, a feeling of connection with their partners during sex, and feelings of shared contentment thereafter.

At this time, the treatment of sexual problems and concerns often occurs in a fragmented fashion, with a need for richer paradigms and more integrated clinical care. Although there have been calls for interdisciplinary training for decades (cf. Moser, 1983), numerous institutional obstacles, real or perceived turf wars, and the lack of a coherent, cohesive, and multidimensional theoretical framework have impeded comprehensive care. The increased attention to symptoms of sexual problems in recent years presents clinicians with a remarkable opportunity to broaden the discourse around sexuality itself—to consider anew what men and women truly aspire toward as sexual beings and as partners and how we can help them attain their goals.

Professional Sex Therapy Associations

The oldest of the major North American sexology organizations, founded in 1957, is the Society for the Scientific Study of Sexuality (http://www.sexscience.org/), which focuses primarily on research into sexuality broadly rather than being limited to sex therapy alone. Its interdisciplinary membership of 1,000 or so sexologists consists largely of academics. The Society for Sex Therapy and Research (http://www.sstarnet.org/) was founded in 1975 and has maintained a relatively constant membership of approximately 250 sex therapist/researchers whose primary focus is on sexual difficulties and treatment of them. The primary, international, credentialing body for sex therapists is the U.S.-based American Association of Sexuality Educators, Counselors and Therapists (AASECT; http://www.aasect.org). AASECT was founded in 1967 and currently has approximately 2,000 members with an applied focus, of whom roughly 500 are certified as sex therapists or diplomates (i.e., experts) in sex therapy. In addition, sex therapists in Ontario, the most populous Canadian province, can be certified by the Board of Examiners in Sex Therapy and Counselling of Ontario

(BESTCO at http://www.BESTCO.info), which was founded in 1975. There are approximately 30 to 35 BESTCO-certified sex therapists at any given time. Although their model of training and evaluation and certification is not renowned outside Ontario, it probably deserves to set the standard for the profession (see the following section). As stated already, both ISSWSH and ISSM are composed largely of physicians who may treat sexual disorders in male or female patients, respectively, but who are not trained as nor identify as sex therapists.

The Personal and Professional Process of Becoming a Sex Therapist

Many students are curious about the process of becoming a sex therapist. Some assume that it must be a very glamorous field, with regular appearances on the *Oprah Winfrey Show* or in *Cosmopolitan* magazine. Others assume that becoming a sex therapist mostly requires a hearty appreciation for the joys of sex. The reality is neither so gilt-edged nor so simple. Becoming a sex therapist requires first and foremost that one become skilled at individual and couples therapy. That is, the process of becoming a sex therapist presupposes prior training and expertise in psychotherapy per se. Only those adept at psychotherapy (and licensed accordingly within their jurisdictions as discussed herein, at least if they are seeking to be certified by AASECT or BESTCO) will qualify for training in sex therapy. This requires graduate- or doctoral-level training in one of the fields that licenses psychotherapists: typically clinical psychology, social work, marital and family therapy, or medicine. (Others are possible, too, such as graduate degrees in counseling, depending on the jurisdiction and possibility of licensure.)

Above and beyond one's qualifications and license to practice psychotherapy, prospective sex therapists require fundamental knowledge of sexology and advanced training in sex therapy. AASECT (see http://aasect. org/certification.asp) requires that candidates for certification as sexuality educators, counselors, and therapists acquire at least 90 hours of course work covering such basics as the history of sexology; knowledge of sex research and literature; the anatomy and physiology of sexual response; developmental, sociocultural, and medical factors affecting sexual values and expression; gender roles; relationship issues; sexually transmitted infections and prevention issues; sexual abuse and its consequences; sexual orientation; and sexual minorities. In addition, prospective sex therapists require a minimum of 60 graduate course hours on sexual difficulties and how to deal with them in therapy. Among other things, this includes knowledge of the *DSM* sexual dysfunctions, gender disorders, and paraphilias as well as the more common problems (e.g., sexual desire discrepancy, disappointment with sex, lack of "connection") that bring individuals and couples into the offices of sex therapists; the major intrapsychic, interpersonal, psychosocial, and organic causes of sexual problems; theory and methods of assessment, diagnosis and clinical intervention (i.e., psychotherapeutic and medical) with sexual problems; models and methods of couples/systemic sex therapy; knowledge of the role of the sex therapist in working with other health professionals, whether generalists or specialists; and techniques for assessment of outcome. In addition, the sex therapist requires specialized knowledge of how other clinicians' interventions (e.g., treatment of depression, diabetes, cardiovascular disease, cancer) affect, engender, or exacerbate sexual problems. The role of the sex therapist today increasingly requires skill at advocating for one's clientele with other health-care practitioners who often have little time to investigate sexual problems or concerns. Sex therapists are also situated to advocate for sexual minorities within other systems.

Above and beyond didactic information, sex therapists are expected to complete several years of supervised (via direct observation or audio/ video recording) clinical training (generally at the postgraduate level) in the practice of sex therapy with a wide array of clients. This education should include therapy with individuals, couples, and sometimes groups, men and women, and sexual minorities and should involve learning to deal with a broad range of *DSM* disorders and other sexual concerns.

Both AASECT and BESTCO require that all certified members engage in a process of personal reflection and sexual values clarification. Sexual Attitude Reassessment (SAR) workshops, generally lasting a weekend or so, challenge participants to examine their own feelings, attitudes, and previously untested beliefs about sexuality in all its diversity and complexity. SARs involve experiential learning processes in small groups led by trained leaders who encourage participants to become aware of their own philosophies of sexuality and sexology. Therapists become aware of their own personal and professional limits and of the kinds of situations or clients they may not be ideally suited to serving well.

In addition to the previously mentioned requirements, BESTCO requires a three-year period of clinical training, supervision, and attendance at all twice-yearly, two-day meetings to become certified as a sex therapist. Thereafter, attendance at all meetings is a requirement for maintaining one's certification. Much of the sex therapy literature refers to a "biopsychosocial approach" or, conversely, to a "psychobiosocial approach" (Metz & McCarthy, 2003). Unfortunately, this is often merely lip service. By contrast, BESTCO meetings are truly interdisciplinary and are characterized by a remarkable atmosphere of mutual respect, collegiality, and desire to learn from one another's experience and expertise. Approximately half of BESTCO members are physicians, whereas the other half hold graduate or doctoral degrees in the social sciences. All BESTCO members must be full clinical members of the American Association of Marital and Family Therapists or must otherwise document and demonstrate competence in couples therapy before being allowed to enter the three-year apprenticeship period. The primacy of skill in couples therapy and the heavily interdisciplinary component make BESTCO unique within sex therapy associations. Although the primary theoretical orientation is systemic, there are psychodynamic, experiential, and cognitive behavioral approaches, too. BESTCO also has the distinction of requiring a series of examinations, at least one of which entails a case presentation in front of the entire BESTCO membership, with written synopsis and bibliography, before one can be certified as a sex therapist.

Some practitioners are trained and certified as sex counselors rather than as sex therapists. The major distinction is that sex counseling tends to be rather brief and focused on problem solving around time-limited concerns (e.g., choice of contraceptives, safer sex practices, dealing with sexual assault) rather than more intensive psychotherapy. Sex counselors tend to be employed by such agencies as Planned Parenthood or work in the community as nurses or guidance counselors rather than in psychotherapy practice as such.

Ethical Principles of Sex Therapy

Sex therapists are expected to study and follow the codes of ethics of their respective disciplines. AASECT members are also required to adhere to the organizations' code of ethics for sex therapists (see http://aasect.org/codeofethics.asp).

Issues such as integrity, confidentiality, and avoiding dual relationships are particularly salient in sex therapy, given the vulnerability that clients generally feel in revealing highly taboo and often hidden material. Similarly, ethical principles such as respect for diversity in values, sexual orientations, gender, and sensitivity to human rights issues—each impor-

tant in all psychotherapy—take on added dimension and importance in
sex therapy.

Some laypeople wonder if sex therapy entails talk therapy only or
whether treatment will involve sexual contact with the therapist or even
between the partners while in the therapist's office. In fact, no sexual
contact between therapist and clients is permissible. Although clients are
often given "homework" assignments (e.g., sensate focus exercises) for the
couple to share at home and then to discuss during the following session,
it would be unethical to have clients engage in sexual activity with the
therapist present.

Some confusion may be a remnant of the sensationalistic publicity
surrounding the early days of Masters and Johnson's work (1970) with
surrogate partners. Masters and Johnson believed strongly that effective
therapy required a couple present and refused to offer individual therapy. When men presented for therapy alone, a surrogate partner was provided for these clients to engage in the accompanying homework. (Single
women were presumed able to find their own sex therapy partners.)
Masters and Johnson eventually gave up their work with surrogates out
of fear of legal threats and possible repercussions. The use of surrogate
partners has continued as an adjunctive component of some sex therapy
although it is not widespread. Surrogate partners are now trained and
regulated by the International Professional Surrogates Association (IPSA;
http://www.SurrogateTherapy.org). These individuals are trained to work
with sex therapists and their clients and have their own code of ethics.
In all instances, they are to use touch appropriate to the client's needs as
assessed by the sex therapist; it is incumbent whenever physical contact is
used as any component of treatment for the therapist to justify the use of
whatever touch is prescribed in terms of the standards of care and of clinical goals appropriate to the case.

Is Sex Therapy a Distinct Modality?
The Case for Certifying Professionals

Recently, there has been controversy over whether sex therapy is a distinct
modality and, therefore, whether certification of sex therapists should
continue. In a 2007 Society for Sex Therapy and Research (SSTAR) presentation (ironically, on the occasion of receiving the Masters and Johnson
lifetime achievement award), Yitzhak Binik called for the abolition of sex
therapy certification. He argued that the theoretical basis of sex therapy

was negligible and therefore that the study of it, presumably the foundation for professional development in any field, was nonsensical. On this point there can be little dispute (Kleinplatz, 2001, 2003; Wiederman, 1998). Binik then argued that the psychotherapy techniques used in the treatment of sexual dysfunctions are hardly unique to sex therapy: The major interventions, including psychoeducational counseling, cognitive-behavioral homework assignments, communication skills education, and bibliotherapy are used rather extensively for a wide array of purposes by other varieties of psychotherapists. There is no technique used by sex therapists that is unique to sex therapy alone. This reasoning, too, is solid. Then what, if anything, makes sex therapy special? Binik would say that the time is well overdue to strip away the illusion of distinctiveness.

What makes sex therapy unique is the knowledge about human sexuality and sexology that practitioners must acquire during the training process. Unfortunately, this knowledge is increasingly difficult to obtain, whereas misleading and flat-out erroneous information about sexuality is ubiquitous. In North America, public and graphic discussion (and sometimes display) of sex is omnipresent, and, paradoxically, individuals feel increasingly alone with their sexual difficulties. The misinformation found on television, on the Internet, and in magazines we see at check-out stands and in physicians' waiting rooms continue to scare people and to leave them feeling sexually defective (Kim & Ward, 2004). In the media, misleading stories abound regarding, for example, the role of technique in sexual fulfillment, gender differences and similarities in arousal, sexuality and aging, "normal" levels of desire, hormones, and sexual orientation (Ménard & Kleinplatz, 2008). Ignorance and myths combined with the resulting fear, shame, and sense of inadequacy are precisely why so many of us continue to have extensive waiting lists. Unfortunately, the same lack of knowledge found in the public pervades the ranks of clinicians; none of us is immune to the consequences of being raised in a sex-negative culture. It is precisely to counter these effects that it is compulsory for certified sex therapists to undertake the aforementioned course work in the study of human sexuality and to attend an SAR.

In an ideal world, such course training would be unnecessary. Our childhood and adolescent years would prepare us for adult sexual relations, thus somewhat curtailing the need for help with sexual problems. Or failing that, given the crucial role of sexuality in personal well-being, all mental and medical health-care providers would naturally receive considerable training in sexology in the course of their undergraduate and graduate schooling; they would then be prepared to help clients/patients deal with their sexual difficulties. Not only is that not the case at present, but the cutbacks to training in human sexuality in recent years have also made the required knowledge increasingly and abysmally inaccessible within the bulk of American medical school (Kleinplatz, 2003) or clinical psychology programs.

As such, the major purpose of sex therapy certification remains consumer protection. Most certified sex therapists can rattle off a series of horror stories, where we have been brought in to take care of the casualties produced by other, duly licensed health-care providers: the woman who is told she will need long-term therapy because she is unable to reach orgasm during intercourse; the "impotent" man who is treated for the childhood origins of his fear of women when he has not been assessed until too late for diabetes mellitus; the woman who is given some lubricant for her lack of arousal when in fact, her relationship is so filled with vitriol she should be advised to listen to the wisdom of her dry vagina; two people in a relationship who are distressed about their sexual desire discrepancy are told to "just compromise," when sex is merely the battleground for far more complex power dynamics; the infertile couple who is told to "just relax" when both find themselves paralyzed by the rigors of infertility treatment, and the list continues.

More frighteningly, because *sex therapist* is not generally a registered title, anyone can advertise himself or herself as having an interest or expertise in treating sexual problems or even claim to be a sex therapist. In such instances, clients/patients assume they are in competent hands when there is no assurance of any skill, knowledge base, or clinical training to correspond with the clinician's claims. (And, of course, sometimes those advertising their willingness to deal with sexuality are not clinicians at all and are offering an entirely different service.) Thus, whereas we should hope with Binik (2007) that certification in sex therapy will ultimately become unnecessary, at the present time certification serves to protect the public from ignorant, incompetent, and unscrupulous "health-care" providers.

Conclusions

Sex therapy provides a wonderful and deeply meaningful professional life. Sex therapists serve clients/patients who are searching for more sexual pleasure, fulfillment, and intimacy. Given that sexual wishes, hopes, and fantasies touch the core of human existence, sex therapy can prove profoundly rewarding. We serve the public uniquely, in that few mainstream, individual, and couples therapists have the knowledge base, skill, training, and especially comfort level to deal in depth with complex sexual problems. More importantly, sex therapists are privileged with the opportunity to help people attain their most cherished and unspoken dreams, working not only to alleviate sexual disorders and dysfunctions but also to allow couples to experience their own erotic potentials (Kleinplatz, 1998, 2004, 2006; Kleinplatz & Ménard, 2007).

Resources

To Locate a Certified Sex Therapist

The Board of Examiners in Sex Therapy and Counselling of Ontario
www.BESTCO.info
American Association of Sexuality Educators Counselors and Therapists
www.AASECT.org

Major Sexology Associations and Opportunities for Continuing Education

The Society for the Scientific Study of Sexuality
www.sexscience.org
Society for Sex Therapy and Research
www.sstarnet.org
American Association of Sexuality Educators Counselors and Therapists
www.AASECT.org
Canadian Sex Research Forum
www.csrf.ca
The British Association for Sexual and Marital Therapy
www.basrt.org.uk

Distributors of Sex Toys and Educational/Sexually Explicit Videos

Come as You Are (an especially useful resource for sex toys and aids for the
disabled as well as the able-bodied)
www.comeasyouare.com
Good Vibrations
www.goodvibes.com
Sex Smart Films
www.sexsmartfilms.com

References

Alperstein, L., Ellison, C. R., Fishman, J. R., Hall, M., Handwerker, L., Hartley, H., et al. (2002). A new view of women's sexual problems. *Women and Therapy*, *24*(1–2), 1–8.

Althof, S. E. & Turner L. A. (1992). Pharmacological and vacuum pump techniques: Treatment methods and outcome. In R. Rosen & S. Leiblum (Ed.), *Erectile disorder: Assessment and treatment* (pp. 283–312). New York: Guilford Press.

Althof, S. E., Turner, L. A., Levine, S. B., Risen, C., Kursh, E., & Bodner, D. (1989). Why do so many people drop out from auto-injection therapy for impotence? *Journal of Sex and Marital Therapy*, *15*, 121–129.

American Psychiatric Association (2000). *Diagnostic and statistical manual of mental disorders* (4th ed., text revised). Washington, DC: Author.

Assalian, P. (1994). Premature ejaculation: Is it really psychogenic? *Journal of Sex Education & Therapy*, *20*(1), 1–4.

Bergeron, S., Brown, C., Lord, M.-J., Oala, M., Binik, Y. M., & Khalifé, S. (2002). Physical therapy for vulvar vestibulitis syndrome: A retrospective study. *Journal of Sex & Marital Therapy*, *28*(3), 183–192.

Billups, K. L., Berman, L., Berman, J., Metz, M. E., Glennon, M. E., & Goldstein, I. (2001). A new non-pharmacological vacuum therapy for female sexual dysfunction. *Journal of Sex & Marital Therapy*, *27*(5), 435–441.

Binik, Y. M. (2005). Should dyspareunia be retained as a sexual dysfunction in *DSM-V*? A painful classification decision. *Archives of Sexual Behavior*, *34*(1), 11–22.

Binik, Y. M. (2007, March 10). *Does sex therapy have a future?* Paper presented at the Annual Meeting of the Society for Sex Therapy and Research, Atlanta, GA.

Binik, Y. M., Meana, M., Berkley, K., & Khalifé, S. (1999). The sexual pain disorders: Is the pain sexual or is the sex painful? *Annual Review of Sex Research*, *10*, 210–235.

Davis, S. R., Davison, S. L., Donath, S., & Bell, R. J. (2005). Circulating androgen levels and self-reported sexual function in women. *Journal of the American Medical Association*, *294*(1), 91–96.

Ellison, C. R. (2001). Intimacy-based sex therapy: Sexual choreography. In P. J. Kleinplatz (Ed.), *New directions in sex therapy: Innovations and alternatives* (pp. 163–184). Philadelphia: Brunner-Routledge.

Freud, S. (1917/1963). Introductory lectures on psychoanalysis. In *The standard edition of the complete psychological works of Sigmund Freud* (Vol. 15 and Vol. 16, trans. James Strachey). London: Hogarth Press.

Giami, A. (2000). Changing relations between medicine, psychology and sexuality: The case of male impotence. *Journal of Social Medicine*, *37*, 263–272.

Goldstein, I., Lue, T., Padma-Nathan, H., Rosen, R., Steers, W., & Wicker, P. (1998). Oral sildenafil in the treatment of erectile dysfunction. *New England Journal of Medicine, 338,* 1397–1404.

Hartley, H. (2006). The 'pinking' of Viagra culture: Drug industry efforts to create and repackage sex drugs for women. *Sexualities, 9,* 363–378.

Heiman, J. (2002). Sexual dysfunction: Overview of prevalence, etiological factors, and treatment. *Journal of Sex Research, 39*(1), 73–78.

Irvine, J. M. (1990). *Disorders of desire: Sex and gender in modern American sexology.* Philadelphia: Temple University Press.

Irwin, M. B. & Kata, E. J. (1994). High attrition rate with intra-cavernous injection of prostaglandin E1 for impotency. *Urology, 43,* 84–87.

Jeffries, S. (1990). *Anticlimax: A feminist perspective on the sexual revolution.* London: Women's Press.

Kaplan, H. S. (1974). *The new sex therapy.* New York: Brunner/Mazel.

Kaplan, H. S. (1977). Hypoactive sexual desire. *Journal of Sex & Marital Therapy, 3*(1), 3–9.

Kaplan, H. S. (1979). *Disorders of sexual desire and other new concepts and techniques in sex therapy.* New York: Brunner/Mazel.

Kim, J. L. & Ward, L. M. (2004). Pleasure reading: Associations between young women's sexual attitudes and their reading of contemporary women's magazines. *Psychology of Women Quarterly, 28,* 48–58.

Kinsey, A. C., Pomeroy, W. B., & Martin, C. E. (1948). *Sexual behavior in the human male.* Philadelphia: Saunders.

Kinsey, A. C., Pomeroy, W. B., Martin, C. E. & Gebhard, P. H. (1951). *Sexual behavior in the human female.* Philadelphia: Saunders.

Kleinplatz, P. J. (1996). Transforming sex therapy: Integrating erotic potential. *Humanistic Psychologist, 24*(2), 190–202.

Kleinplatz, P. J. (1998). Sex therapy for vaginismus: A review, critique and humanistic alternative. *Journal of Humanistic Psychology, 38*(2), 51–81.

Kleinplatz, P. J. (2001). A critical evaluation of sex therapy: Room for improvement. In P. J. Kleinplatz (Ed.), *New directions in sex therapy: Innovations and alternatives* (pp. xi–xxxiii). Philadelphia: Brunner-Routledge.

Kleinplatz, P. J. (2003). What's new in sex therapy: From stagnation to fragmentation. *Sex and Relationship Therapy, 18*(1), 95–106.

Kleinplatz, P. J. (2004). Beyond sexual mechanics and hydraulics: Humanizing the discourse surrounding erectile dysfunction. *Journal of Humanistic Psychology, 44*(2), 215–242.

Kleinplatz, P. J. (2006). Learning from extraordinary lovers: Lessons from the edge. *Journal of Homosexuality, 50*(3/4), 325–348.

Kleinplatz, P. J. & Ménard, A. D. (2007). Building blocks towards optimal sexuality: Constructing a conceptual model. *Family Journal: Counseling and Therapy for Couples and Families, 15*(1), 72–78.

Lief, H. I. (1977). Inhibited sexual desire. *Medical Aspects of Human Sexuality, 7,* 94–95.

Loe, M. (2004). *The rise of Viagra: How the little blue pill changed sex in America.* New York: New York University Press.

LoPiccolo, J. (1992). Postmodern sex therapy for erectile failure. In R. C. Rosen & S. R. Leiblum (Eds.), *Erectile disorders: Assessment and treatment* (pp. 171– 197). New York: Guilford.

Mahrer, A. R. (1996). *The complete guide to experiential psychotherapy.* New York: Wiley.

Mahrer, A. R. & Boulet, D. B. (2001). How can Experiential Psychotherapy help transform the field of sex therapy? In P. J. Kleinplatz (Ed.), *New Directions in sex therapy: Innovations and alternatives* (pp. 234–257). Philadelphia: Brunner-Routledge.

Masters, W. H. & Johnson, V. E. (1966). *Human sexual response.* Boston: Little, Brown.

Masters, W. H. & Johnson, V. E. (1970). *Human sexual inadequacy.* New York: Bantam Books.

Masters, W. H. & Johnson, V. E. (1986). *Sex therapy on its twenty-fifth anniversary: Why it survives.* St. Louis: Masters and Johnson Institute.

Maurice, W. L. (1999). *Sexual medicine in primary care.* St. Louis: Mosby.

Ménard, A. D. & Kleinplatz, P. J. (2008). Twenty-one moves guaranteed to make his thighs go up in flames: Depictions of "great sex" in popular magazines. *Sexuality and Culture, 12*(1), 1–20.

Metz, E. M. & McCarthy, B. W. (2003). *Coping with premature ejaculation: How to overcome P.E., please your partner & have great sex.* Oakland, CA: New Harbinger.

Moser, C. (1983). A response to Reiss' "Trouble in Paradise." *Journal of Sex Research, 19*(2), 192–195.

Moser, C. (1999). *Health care without shame: A handbook for the sexually diverse and their caregivers.* San Francisco: Greenery Press.

Nicolson, P. (1993). Public values and private beliefs: Why do women refer themselves for sex therapy? In J. M. Ussher & C. D. Baker (Eds.), *Psychological perspectives on sexual problems: New directions in theory and practice* (pp. 56–76). New York: Routledge.

Ogden, G. (1994). *Women who love sex.* New York: Pocket Books.

Ogden, G. (2001). Integrating sexuality and spirituality: A group therapy approach to women's sexual dilemmas. In P. J. Kleinplatz (Ed.), *New directions in sex therapy: Innovations and alternatives* (pp. 322–346). Philadelphia: Brunner-Routledge.

Reiss, I. L. (1990). *An end to shame: Shaping our next sexual revolution.* New York: Prometheus Books.

Schnarch, D. (1991). *Constructing the sexual crucible: An integration of sexual and marital therapy.* New York: Norton.

Schnarch, D. (1997). *Passionate marriage.* New York: Norton.

Schover, L. R. & Leiblum, S. R. (1994). Commentary: The stagnation of sex therapy. *Journal of Psychology and Human Sexuality, 6*(3), 5–30.

Tiefer, L. (1991). Historical, scientific, clinical & feminist criticisms of "The Human Sexual Response Cycle" model. *Annual Review of Sex Research, II*, 1–24.

Tiefer, L. (1996). The medicalization of sexuality: Conceptual, normative, and professional issues. *Annual Review of Sex Research, 7,* 252–282.

Tiefer, L. (2001). The selling of "female sexual dysfunction." *Journal of Sex & Marital Therapy, 27*(5), 625–628.

Ussher, J. M. (1993). The construction of female sexual problems: Regulating sex, regulating woman. In J. M. Ussher & C. D. Baker (Eds.), *Psychological perspectives on sexual problems: New directions in theory and practice* (pp. 10–40). New York: Routledge.

Van de Velde, Th. H. (1926). *Ideal marriage: Its physiology and technique.* New York: Random House.

Waldinger, M. D. (2003). Rapid ejaculation. In S. B. Levine, C. B. Risen, & S. Althof (Eds.), *Handbook of clinical sexuality for mental health professionals* (pp. 257–274). New York: Brunner-Routledge.

Weeks, G. (1977). Toward a dialectical approach to intervention. *Human Development, 20,* 277–292.

Weeks, G. (1994). The intersystem model: An integrative approach to treatment. In G. Weeks & L. Hof (Eds.), *The marital-relationship therapy casebook: Theory and application of the intersystem model* (pp. 3–34). New York: Brunner/Mazel.

Weeks, G. & Hof, L. (Eds.). (1987). *Integrating sex and marital therapy: A clinical guide.* New York: W. W. Norton.

Weeks, J. (1985). *Sexuality and its discontents.* New York: Routledge.

Wiederman, M. (1998). The state of theory in sex therapy. *Journal of Sex Research, 35*(1), 88–99.

Wierman, M. E., Basson, R., Davis, S. R., Khosla, S., Miller, K. K., Rosner, W., et al. (2006). Androgen therapy in women: An Endocrine Society Clinical Practice guideline. *Journal of Clinical Endocrinology & Metabolism, 91*(10), 3697–3710.

Winton, M. A. (2000). The medicalization of male sexual dysfunctions: An analysis of sex therapy journals. *Journal of Sex Education and Therapy, 25*(4), 231–239.

Winton, M. A. (2001). Gender, sexual dysfunctions and the *Journal of Sex & Marital Therapy. Journal of Sex & Marital Therapy, 27*(4), 333–337.

Zilbergeld, B. & Ellison, C. R. (1980). Desire discrepancies and arousal problems in sex therapy. In S. R. Leiblum & L. A. Pervin (Eds.), *Principles and practice of sex therapy* (pp. 65–101). New York: Guilford Press.

3

Toward a New Paradigm in Sex Therapy

Katherine M. Hertlein
Gerald R. Weeks

Contents

Introduction

Integration in psychotherapy refers to taking into account various schools and models of therapy. Though many therapists purport to be practicing integrative models of sex therapy, they are in fact practicing technical eclecticism, only one element of the three in the process of integration. In technical eclecticism, various techniques of several models or systems of therapy are applied to a case "systematically and sequentially" (Stricker & Gold, 1996, p. 49). Though this approach is often used, it cannot truly be considered integration because it lacks guidance from a theoretical perspective. This is problematic because it is not connected with any framework that serves as a guide to predict and change human behavior.

Sex Therapy's Traditional Nonintegrative Stance

There are several areas where the field of sex therapy appears fragmented: (1) within professional organizations; (2) in theory; and (3) in research and practice. Fragmentation within the professional organizations is evident in the training emphases of the professional organizations devoted to couple and sex therapies. For example, organizations such as the American Association for Marriage and Family Therapy (AAMFT) and the American Counseling Association (ACA), which dictate standards of practice for couple therapists, only require that minimal fragments of human sexuality or sex therapy be taught. For example, although AAMFT's Commission on Accreditation for Marriage and Family Therapy Education (COAMFTE)-accredited programs delineate some training in sexuality in their programs requirements, the requirements only state that COAMFTE-accredited programs should include in their clinical knowledge component "content on issues of gender and sexual functioning, sexual orientation, and sex therapy as they relate to couple, marriage and family therapy theory and practice" (COAMFTE, 2002). The Council for Accreditation of Counseling and Related Educational Programs (CACREP), the accrediting body for counseling programs, states that there should be some focus on "human sexuality issues and their impact on family and couple functioning" and have some knowledge of sexual issues for college students and older adults (CACREP, 2001). In short, both these bodies set standards for couples therapy but fail to address sexuality and sexual problems. Likewise, the two most prominent sex therapy organizations, the American Association of Sex Educators, Counselors, and Therapists (AASECT) and the Society for the Scientific Study of Sexuality (SSSS), have emphasized the training of sex therapy but do not emphasize couples therapy in their process to becoming a certified sex therapist.

The minimal overlap between the professional organizations is reflected somewhat in the lack of overlap between the each field's theoretical developments and historical developments. For example, Masters and Johnson (1970) emphasized the importance of incorporating one's partner in sex therapy treatment with an identified patient; however, this partner was often used as a cotherapist in the treatment whose role was to work with the identified patient in completion of homework assignments. Kaplan (1974) mentioned couples issues in her text but stopped short of addressing how one might treat the relational problems faced by the couple. Further, Kaplan used a behavioral/psychodynamic approach in her treatment model, suggesting that the therapist should circumvent concurrent couples' problems and that sex therapy can proceed without attention to those issues. Rather than integrating central ideas from many already existing theories, most theorists have attempted to circulate their own ideas or to identify gaps in current treatment and theory where they can "make their mark" in the field.

Finally, research and practice are also affected by the fragmentation of current paradigms of sex therapy, as evidenced in analyses of three well-respected journals in the field of sex therapy. Ruppel (1994) examined the *Archives of Sexual Behavior* via content analysis and discovered that just over half of the articles published within a nearly 20-year span (1971–1990) did not contain a theoretical foundation. Likewise, Dubois and Weiderman (1997) found no articles in the *Journal of Sex and Marital Therapy* that were theory based. Additionally, the *Journal of Sex Research* published a special issue in 1998 that noted the lack of theory in both clinically oriented and research articles. Disconnect between theory and practice is not limited to journal articles but also occurs in the therapy room. Standard treatment is typically (1) not research informed and (2) tends toward eclecticism, with little to no understanding of basic principles of couples or behavioral therapies. In this way, sex therapy resembles a "cookbook" approach, with limited comprehension of underlying principles, behavior theory, couples therapy, and all the other elements that would constitute an integrative paradigm.

Integrative Paradigm

Our integrated sex therapy paradigm is informed by Sternberg's (1986) triangular theory of love, the intersystem approach (Weeks, 1994), and the theory of interaction (Strong & Claiborn, 1982). We believe these frameworks should be included in an integrated paradigm because they consistently attend to the emotions, cognitions, and behaviors of couples, address both sexuality and couples' issues, and operate effectively together to create a cohesive paradigm rather than a series of isolated interventions. Our model, though not the definitive integrative approach to sex therapy, reflects the result of a natural progressive process. This theoretical foundation for the approach was first presented by Weeks (1977) and was followed by Weeks and Hof (1987), who detailed one model of integration of sex and marital therapy. The intersystem approach can be used with a variety of clinical concerns and has specifically been applied to the treatment of sexual problems including erectile dysfunction (Weeks & Gambescia, 2000), hypoactive sexual desire disorder (Weeks & Gambescia, 2002), and infidelity (Weeks, Gambescia, & Jenkins, 2003). Rather than combining techniques in a technically eclectic approach, this framework (as it applies to such problems as erectile dysfunction and hypoactive sexual desire disorder) synthesizes our knowledge about couples therapy, sex therapy, medical therapy, psychology, and knowledge about larger systemic contexts.

Sternberg's Triangle of Love

Sternberg (1986), in conducting research in social psychology, developed a triangular theory of love. Sternberg believed that there are three components of love (commitment, intimacy, and passion) and that each of these components interact with one another in our relationships. The first component of the triangle, commitment, refers to the cognitive element of love—that is, the determination of whether couples stay together. Intimacy, the second component, describes the amount of closeness partners feel toward one another. This includes the extent of trust in the relationship, feelings of mutual respect, and the bond each would describe he or she has to the other partner. Finally, the affection, feelings of longing, and sexual attraction a couple demonstrates is known as the passion in a relationship.

Although Sternberg (1986) advanced the idea of the triangle to be used as a whole rather than utilizing the parts individually (all three components are necessary for adult loving relationships), this model has often been used in isolated components. Sex therapists might traditionally focus on the passion element, whereas traditional couple therapists might focus on intimacy and commitment. This divided focus can have significant treatment implications. For example, underlying fears of intimacy or varying levels of commitment might impact one's level of passion toward his or her partner. Therapies that do not address all aspects of the triangle may be vulnerable to treating one of the three elements of etiology and to truly not addressing the entire problem, making the problem vulnerable to resurgence.

The Intersystem Approach

This approach was generated from various theories of marriage and family therapy and synthesized using constructs to be described herein. The intersystem approach proposed by Weeks (1977) and refined later by Weeks and Cross (2004) represents an attempt to offer an integrative framework by focusing on individuals, couples dynamics, family-of-origin, and other important elements affecting a relationship. In the history of family therapy, the early approaches discarded the idea of individual diagnoses and anything having to do with individual dynamics and therapy (Sexton, Weeks, & Robbins, 2003). The intersystem approach balances its efforts in attention to the individual in the couple and family system as well as the systems themselves. This framework has five components:

1. Individual/biological/medical
2. Individual/psychological
3. Dyadic relationship
4. Family of origin
5. Society/culture/history/religion

Following is a description of this approach as it applies to couples in sex therapy. This approach is grounded in the therapist developing an appropriate case formulation, and treatment is organized around individual, interactional, and intergenerational components of the system.

Individual/Biological

A couple is made up of two individuals, each with distinct biologies and medical backgrounds. Because biological aspects differ for each partner, it is critical for the therapist to consider the influences of each individual's biology and medical concerns on the relationship and its affiliation to a couple's sexual problems. For example, in the treatment of erectile dysfunction, therapists are well advised to consider any medical problems potentially contributing to the dysfunction as well as hormonal issues that may be affecting the condition. Certain psychological disorders with biological components such as bipolar disorder may also contribute to problems experienced by a couple. In addition, certain medications can also impact one's sexual function. Selective serotonin reuptake inhibitors (SSRIs), particularly Paxil (GlaxoSmithKline, Philadelphia, Pennsylvania) and Remeron (Organon, West Orange, New Jersey), have significant sexual side effects including diminished libido and delayed or absent orgasm. It is imperative for therapists to acquire a list of all medications being taken by the clients and to be aware of the current information on these medications on sexual functioning. Once the therapist identifies that sexual functioning might in some way be impacted by medications, the therapist should contact the prescribing physicians and inquire as to other available alternatives, if available.

Individual/Psychological

The therapist then assesses the individual psychological composition of each partner. Psychological makeup is composed of, for example, personality (including personality disorders), psychopathology, intelligence, temperament, developmental stages and deficits, attitudes, values, defense mechanisms. It is through our psychological composition that we learn to understand sexuality and develop personal ways to exhibit it. For example, a person experiencing depression may not feel desire to engage in sexual activity, particularly if the depression is related to the relationship in some way. One's sexual intelligence may also have been acquired in such a way that elicits guilt about particular sexual activities, thus inhibiting desire. Therapists can gather information about an individual client's psychological composition through adequate history taking, utilizing both a sexual history and familial history. There may be a history of depression or other psychological issues as well as covert messages about sexuality impacting the current relationship.

Dyadic/Couple Relationship

Previously, behaviorally oriented sex therapies were conducted in such a way that included both partners, but not from a systemic perspective; rather, each partner in a couple was viewed as having an individual contribution to the problem (Masters & Johnson, 1970). The sex therapist should always maintain a systemic perspective (Weeks & Treat, 2001). Though it is important to assess the individual patterns of each partner, this approach goes one step further and addresses how these individual patterns manifest within the couple in terms of how they manage conflict, of communication, and of their level of intimacy and fears of intimacy. This is a unique contribution in that it treats the relationship as the client in addition to recognizing the contributions of each individual. For example, in cases of hypoactive sexual desire disorder, one partner may not feel desire while the other does not consider this problematic. A therapist working from a systemic perspective may identify the partner who does not consider the lack of desire problematic as having some fears toward intimacy, thus contributing to the fears of intimacy of the other partner, thereby decreasing desire even further. In other words, there can be unconscious collusion that is expressed by only one partner. It is in understanding these dynamics that the therapist addresses the individual and interactional components sustaining a sexual problem.

Family of Origin

One place where people learn about relationships and sexuality is in their families. Messages about sexuality can be covert or overt, internalized, and expressed in one's relationship. For example, some families do not discuss sexuality openly; as a result, children in these families may interpret this behavior as meaning that sexuality is inherently "bad" and that expression of such should be minimized. This can be problematic as these children become adults and begin to struggle with their emerging sexual feelings. They may in turn tell themselves that they are "bad" for having such feelings, thus impacting their self-esteem and inevitably their relationships. Some parents are overt in their condemnation of sexual behavior, again resulting in internal struggles for their children as they grow into adulthood and develop intimate relationships. Evidence of this impact is documented in research demonstrating that children from dysfunctional families with or without sexual abuse can lead to sexual dysfunctions such as hypoactive sexual desire disorder (Kinzl, Mangwerth, Traweger, & Biebl, 1996; Kinzl, Traweger, & Biebl, 1995). Therapists can assess for information about family history via a relationship/sexual genogram, published by Berman (1999) and Berman and Hof (1987). For more detailed information about this approach, consult DeMaria, Weeks, and Hof (1999).

Society/Culture/History/Religion

Finally, the therapist assesses the couple's environment and its effect on their relationship. Couples go to understand their background from the culture and history in which they were raised and are embedded. These influences shape one's beliefs, customs, and values around sexuality and sexual expression. Whereas some cultures may prohibit masturbation, other cultures dictate greater sexual permissiveness values. As norms change, a couple should work to understand the extent to which culture and contemporary society has played into their decision making, values, and behaviors as a couple. It is imperative that the therapist assess for the impact of culture, religion, and society on how a couple behaves and perceives themselves.

In sum, the intersystem approach works to integrate the individual, interactional, and transgenerational components that may be affecting sexual functioning. Integration begins before the treatment or assessment phase; in other words, it begins in the case conceptualization of the therapist. Therapists using this approach should be knowledgeable in the areas of couples and family therapy, sex therapy, and individual therapy; this should be reflected in the way they think about and intervene in a particular case. Because of the attention needed in so many areas, this is a difficult framework to master.

Theory of Interaction

Grounded in a social-psychological model, the theory of interaction posits that there are intrapsychic and interactional components active in relationships (Strong & Claiborn, 1982). This approach was incorporated specifically into couples work by Weeks (1994). We believe that this theory can

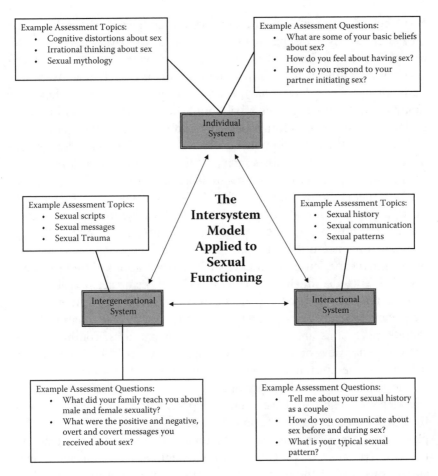

Example Assessment Topics:
- Cognitive distortions about sex
- Irrational thinking about sex
- Sexual mythology

Example Assessment Questions:
- What are some of your basic beliefs about sex?
- How do you feel about having sex?
- How do you respond to your partner initiating sex?

Individual System

The Intersystem Model Applied to Sexual Functioning

Example Assessment Topics:
- Sexual scripts
- Sexual messages
- Sexual Trauma

Example Assessment Topics:
- Sexual history
- Sexual communication
- Sexual patterns

Intergenerational System

Interactional System

Example Assessment Questions:
- What did your family teach you about male and female sexuality?
- What were the positive and negative, overt and covert messages you received about sex?

Example Assessment Questions:
- Tell me about your sexual history as a couple
- How do you communicate about sex before and during sex?
- What is your typical sexual pattern?

Figure 3.1 The Intersystem Approach showing the three systems and examples for sex therapy. (Adapted from Weeks, G., In G. Weeks & L. Hof (Eds.), *The marital-relationship therapy casebook: Theory and application of the intersystem mode* (pp. 3–34). New York: Brunner/Mazel, 1994. With permission.)

also be applied to working with couples within the context of sex therapy. This section reviews the components and discusses its implications in sex therapy treatment.

Intrapsychic Components

There are three intrapsychic components: interpretation, definition, and prediction. Interpretation refers to the meaning that is ascribed to an event, behavior, or problem. This is relevant to couples in that each partner may interpret his or her partner's behavior inaccurately. One's interpretation of another's behavior is often grounded in his or her previous experiences and learning histories. A partner who suffers from hypoactive sexual desire disorder may have a partner who interprets his or her behavior as unloving and uncaring. This attribution, though incorrect, will be what underlines the partner's future behavior and views about the relationship.

Definition, the next component, describes the reciprocal arrangement of how the relationship defines each partner and how each partner defines the relationship. Sager (1976) indicated that definitions and expectations can be either conscious and articulated, conscious and not articulated, or unconscious (and therefore not articulated). These definitions and expectations can infiltrate our view of our relationship without our knowledge and can influence our cognitions, affect, and behavior. A partner with more sexual experience might have variant expectations of frequency and behaviors included during sexual contact than his or her partner. If this expectation is articulated, partners can come to some agreement on the frequency and behaviors that will constitute part of their relationship. If these expectations are not articulated or unconscious, communication problems may develop between the couple, and it then becomes incumbent on the therapist to help the couple address the unspoken.

The third intrapsychic component, prediction, addresses the notion that to some degree we have a tendency to try to predict one's behavior, thoughts, or a particular outcome. Couples in sex therapy may not complete homework assignments, for example, because they anticipate failure. Unfortunately, this negative reinforcement received from avoiding an activity because of the fear of adverse effects may continue to reinforce avoidance behavior on a number of issues. It is quite common to prescribe a sensate focus exercise only to find that the couple avoided doing it. Conflict resolution programs for couples also often neglect the inclusion of strategies for dealing with avoidance (Weeks & Treat, 2001).

Interactional Components

The interactional components, which address the systemic aspects of relationships, include congruence, interdependence, and attributional strategy. Congruence refers to the degree to which couples share or agree on the how events are defined. A husband may consider his wife's online chatting with other men as a form of infidelity whereas the wife does not.

The perceptions of the event may be incongruent, but the couple can also agree that they define infidelity differently, thus being congruent. Another example is where one partner believes that he or she has sex often with his or her partner and the partner disagrees. This could be considered incongruency in the partner's perceptions. Incongruence, however, should only be addressed if the focus of the sessions is in coming to an agreement about frequency for the couple. Treatment goals should include acquiring information so that the couple can come to an agreement about the issue on which to be focused.

Interdependence pertains to the extent to which partners depend on one another. It includes how each partner trusts that the other will meet his or her needs. This can include how one meets another's emotional as well as sexual needs. For example, a husband may believe that he is meeting his wife's sexual desire, but according to the wife, he can or will not meet her needs. Couples who have relatively high levels of interdependence typically proceed through treatment quicker than couples with lower levels because they have a tendency to more freely accept change in their lives. In couples with lower levels of interdependence, discussion of commitment level may accompany a conversation about how each fulfills the other partner's needs. Low-level interdependence couples may also be more vulnerable to infidelity as one or both partners may believe that their needs are best met outside of the primary relationships (Weeks et al., 2003). Sex therapists should be attuned to the couple's interdependence level and should assess whether a conversation about commitment is warranted. Further, therapists should also address whether the need fulfillment partners have identified for each other is realistic and should develop realistic expectations.

Attributional strategy is the third interactional component. This refers to the manner in which partners ascribe meaning to an event. It is similar to the interpretation concept discussed earlier and specifically means whether a couple relates in a linear or circular fashion to one another. In a linear attribution strategy, couples attribute their partner's behavior (effect) to a stimulus (cause). A husband, for instance, might report that his wife "makes" him angry when she nags him about household chores; a wife might state that she cannot achieve orgasm because her husband's so-called premature ejaculation does not permit her to do so. Circular attribution strategies are those where partners examine the impact of their behavior on the other. In this case, the wife might state overtly that sex with him is not something she enjoys, thus sustaining the premature ejaculation. Reframing is one technique sex therapists can use to help the couple move from linear and blaming statements to a circular, positive view. Weeks and Treat (2001) discussed reframing in its application to sexual problems at length. The therapist might reframe the wife's displeasure in the previous example and the manifestation of premature ejaculation in the relationship as each partner trying desperately to please one another so hard that they both end up failing, reflecting how much they care about each other. This shifts the focus of the problem from a linear, individually focused problem to a relationship problem.

Bringing It Together: An Integrative Paradigm

The field of sex therapy has forked into many different roads. Though traditional sex therapy models typically emphasized behavioral components (i.e., Kaplan, 1974; Leiblum & Rosen, 1988, 2000; Masters & Johnson, 1970), our proposed framework provides a balanced effort toward understanding and addressing the cognitive and emotional components of sexual problems in addition. This is critical because cognition in sex therapy cases is typically significantly overlooked. Conducting an assessment of the negative thoughts accompanying sexual behavior and uncovering the positive thoughts should be a focus of diagnosis and treatment because it helps both couple and therapist understand the pattern of thoughts and its impact on the relationship (Weeks & Gambescia, 2000). Weeks and Gambescia (2000, 2002) present ideas for addressing cognitive and affective elements in the treatment of hypoactive sexual desire disorder and sexual dysfunction. We encourage therapists to be purposeful in providing assignments to the couple and in assessing couples' feelings and thoughts related to the homework. This information would communicate the therapist's warmth, genuineness, and caring attitude toward the clients. The joining relationship is enhanced and leads to greater compliance on the part of the clients.

Case Example*

Randy and Martha, a couple in their 40s, have been married for 15 years and have two children. Randy works as an executive for a software company, and Martha is a manager of a retail store. Martha is attending treatment at her husband's insistence due to her lack of interest and desire in sex. The following concepts from the case are illustrated as follows.

---

* This case represents a typical composite of hypoactive sexual desire disorder clients.

Sternberg's Triangular Theory of Love

Commitment

Martha indicates that, despite the lack of desire she has been feeling over the last few years, she is still very committed to her marriage and her family. Randy, too, reports that he is committed to Martha. Further, both believed that there were negative spiritual implications for divorced couples.

Intimacy

Both Martha and Randy worked long hours at their respective jobs. Further, Martha felt that she was primarily in charge of the household tasks and custodian to the children. She stated that she felt as if she were taking on increasing responsibilities in the household while Randy's responsibilities remained the same. As a result, Randy and Martha had difficulty setting aside time for togetherness. Martha had been socialized from a young age to be more nurturing than sexual whereas Randy was socialized to suppress vulnerabilities because to do so might threaten his self-worth and competence, leaving it difficult for Martha to connect with Randy on an intimate level as that side of him is more guarded. Martha stated that she learned to be more selective about the vulnerabilities she shares with Randy because she has been hurt in the past by his limited expression of feelings.

Passion

The couple agreed that, while both love one another, their sexual relationship, which manifested the most significant amount of passion in their relationship, was largely absent as a result of the lack of desire experienced by Martha. Martha did not view sexuality as that important of an aspect in the relationship, and with the problems already mentioned, nothing was happening to foster sexual desire.

Intersystem Components

- *Individual:* Martha reported that although she had been experiencing lack of desire for several years, it was really only within the last few years that she noticed it had worsened. In addition to the lack of desire, she noted that she felt more angry and depressed over the past few years. Prescribed Effexor (Wyeth, Madison, New Jersey) three months ago by her physician, she noted that her lack of desire further deteriorated along with her ability to orgasm. She cited her relationship with

Randy as a main source of her anxiety and depression and expressed significant anxiety about wanting to feel desire but not being able to do so. Randy noted that he has been feeling hopeless over the last few months, especially since Martha indicated things became worse after being prescribed Effexor. Randy viewed Martha's lack of desire as intentional withholding and had initially been angry with her. He was now filled with resignation and resentment. Finally, Martha defined herself as depressed and so did Randy, but he saw no part that he played in her depression.

- *Interactional:* Randy and Martha had little time together based on job schedules and household responsibilities. Martha reported that Randy often agreed to "help" with things around the house, but rarely if ever followed though with such promises. Further, Martha reported that she was angry and resentful toward Randy when he would offer to "help," as she saw this as still placing her in the role of household manager. Randy, who had narcissistic personality traits, overtly defined Martha to be a certain way, and Martha tried desperately to comply, as she had a dependent personality. Martha unconsciously used sexuality as one way to gain an upper hand in the relationship. Because the conflict between the couple was, for the most part, expressed covertly, there was tension between the couple.

- *Family of origin:* Randy and Martha indicated that they remained connected to one another over the years because of their common familial background. Randy stated that Martha could understand where he was coming from on many issues because both of them had been raised in alcoholic homes. Randy stated that his mother elevated him up to her level, describing himself as a parentified child, and Martha stated that her role in the family was similar, as a caretaker to her family. As an attempt to seek love and acceptance, both had experienced sex at an early age in their lives and still had yet to resolve the guilt over this issue. Further, Martha's family was highly religious, and she expressed guilt about having sex at all in addition to experiencing it early in life.

- *External factors:* Despite the degree of dysfunction in Martha and Randy's families of origin, divorce was a rare phenomenon in their family histories. Only one uncle on Randy's side was divorced, and the circumstances were that he had married young and was divorced within a short time. As previously mentioned, Randy and Martha are active in their local religious organization and believe in intact families. Martha and Randy also indicated that there were few people within their social network who were divorced.

Interactional Components

- *Interpretation:* Martha believed that her lack of desire toward Randy was a reflection of how she felt she was treated by him (i.e., resents his controlling behavior, so she controls their sex life). Randy interpreted her lack of desire as something that she is doing to punish him and does not believe that his attitude toward her has any influence on her actions.
- *Definition:* Both Randy and Martha define the problem as significantly impairing their relationship but are not willing to call it "quits." They are unable to define the lack of desire in terms of their own behavior and differ on how they define the level of desire each has: Randy says Martha has too little, whereas Martha says Randy has too much.
- *Prediction:* Randy indicates that he feels hopeless and likely predicts that nothing will change in the future until Martha gets some help. Martha does not predict that Randy's behavior or attitude toward her will change in the future, thus resulting in more of the same. Though both are hopeful that therapy may improve the desire issue, they are unable to see how it might have a larger impact on their relationship.
- *Congruence:* Because Randy believes the problem is that Martha has too little desire and Martha sees Randy as having too much desire, the couple's definitions of the problem are incongruent. As a result, the couple have difficulty agreeing on goals for treatment.
- *Interdependence:* Although both Randy and Martha have discussed divorce in the past, they do not recognize how their personalities complement one another. On some unconscious level, Martha sees Randy's narcissism and control as a part she lacks and is therefore drawn toward; Randy sees Martha's dependence as a good match to his controlling personality.
- *Attribution:* As discussed earlier, Martha blames her lack of desire on Randy (linear), just as Randy blames Martha's lack of desire on her unwillingness (linear). Neither party entertains the notion that each might have some influence on the other's behavior, affect, and cognitions.

Once this assessment across multiple areas is made, the therapist can develop a comprehensive case conceptualization. The therapist has multiple areas of intervention and can develop a treatment plan that details the issues germane to this couple.

Suggestions for Moving Toward Greater Integration

As sex therapy moves from a fragmented to more integrated framework, changes at multiple levels can help us achieve this goal. Though these cannot all be implemented immediately, the spirit of these suggestions is to continue to push the field of sex therapy into developing a comprehensive theoretical framework.

1. Envision sexual problems from an expansive, multivariate framework. This includes conceptualizing the etiology of a sexual problem, the treatment, client type, and other elements from a more comprehensive framework. For example, sex therapists should consider the impact of medications or organic conditions on sexual functioning. This condition can have significant implications for the couple's relationship because it can increase performance anxiety and overall psychology of not one but both partners. Conversely, individual issues such as personality problems and major illnesses like depression can affect one's sexual functioning. In addition to the problems an individual contributes to the relationship, a conflicted couple can also experience sexual problems.

2. Neutralize the present emphasis on treating some sexual problems solely with medications. This conceptualization can be problematic because a portion of the etiology may not be organically based. The agenda of the pharmaceutical answer is one primarily driven by pharmaceutical companies and does not address the variety of other etiologies that may be present. Likewise, therapists need to recognize that there may be an organic component to a sexual dysfunction that is primarily psychogenic and may refer the client for a medical evaluation to address any organic issues that might be best served through medical intervention. We advocate, first, collaboration between a physician prescribing the medications and the sex therapist working with the couple and, second, education regarding the potential multiple etiologies of sexual problems to physicians, therapists, and clients. Even when problems have a primarily organic basis there is a psychological overlay for each individual and systemic concern to address.

3. Therapists and researchers should become more familiar with a comprehensive conceptual framework and with theoretical and metatheoretical issues. Scholars and clinicians can engage in more theory-building activities. Journal editors and reviewers should be more aware of the inclusion and integration of theory in scholarly articles and should encourage theory-based submissions.

4. Sex therapy should be placed within the larger context of health care. It presently is viewed as a separate discipline and profession. Part of this is due to the fragmentation discussed earlier. Graduate training programs in marriage and family therapy, psychology, counseling, psychiatry, medicine, and other health-care programs should integrate sex therapy overtly in their training. Once included, sex therapy should be

integrated with the knowledge in that particular area rather than be discussed as a separate and distinct topic.

5. Bridging the gap between the fields with a stake in sex therapy should be initiated by the professional organizations. Organizations such as AAMFT, ACA, and AASECT should consistently work to integrate their fields as a way to provide the most comprehensive education about sex therapy treatment. Training in each program is currently limited to the elements relevant to each discipline, with minimal focus on the others' discipline. The focus on sexuality could be strengthened in many disciplines.

6. Facilitate movement away from theoretical purism. Previous theorists have been interested in developing a theory that departs from other theories and one in which they can take ownership. We encourage a movement toward integrative theorists who consider multiple views in their approach.

7. Begin to bridge research and practice in sex therapy, exploring the ways sex therapy is informed by research and generating research questions based on treatment. This bridging will inspire therapists to employ best practices and limits the risk of considering only one theoretical approach.

The Future of Sex Therapy

The field of sex therapy has made slow advances in the past 20 years, and some of these advances have been spurred by developments in the medical community. We believe that the partnership that exists between therapists and physicians has been very advantageous for many clients. However, it has also led to some problems being viewed in a strictly medical framework, and the psychological frame has been ignored. The field of sex therapy lacks an overarching model demonstrating to therapists how to attend to issues of couples therapy, family therapy, sex therapy, health care, and individual treatment. This paradigm shift encourages sex therapists to consider each of these issues in treatment and how they can result in a more comprehensive case conceptualization and ultimately better treatment for sexual problems.

As the field of sex therapy moves from the "sacred" models toward truly integrative models, we will gain a more comprehensive perspective on sex therapy. Although we advocate a paradigm shift that encourages therapists and researchers to consider etiology and interventions from multiple perspectives, we also anticipate this goal to be an ongoing process and are cautious of approaches who advocate a "complete" theoretical model, as this limits possibilities to incorporate new and different information.

Advances will be made in theory and from empirical studies that will inform any existing approach. It is through this shift in paradigms that we can develop a more descriptive picture of etiology and treatment for sexual problems.

References

Berman, E. (1999). Gender, sexuality, and romantic love genograms. In R. DeMaria, G. Weeks, & L. Hof (Eds.), *Focused genograms: Intergenerational assessment of individuals, couples, and families* (pp. 145–176). New York: Brunner/Mazel.

Berman, E. & Hof, L. (1987). The sexual genogram—Assessing family-of-origin factors in the treatment of sexual dysfunction. In G. Weeks & L. Hof (Eds.), *Integrating sex and marital therapy: A clinical guide* (pp. 37–56). New York: W. W. Norton.

Commission on Accreditation for Marriage and Family Therapy Education (COAMFTE) (2002). Standards of Accreditation Version 10.3. *American Association for Marriage and Family Therapy.* Retrieved February 16, 2006 from: http://www.aamft.org/about/COAMFTE/standards_of_accreditation.asp

Council for Accreditation of Counseling and Related Educational Programs (CACREP) (2001). 2001 Standards. *Council for Accreditation of Counseling and Related Educational Programs.* Retrieved March 17, 2006 from: http://www.cacrep.org/2001Standards.html#3

DeMaria, R., Weeks, G., & Hof, L. (1999). *Focused genograms: Intergenerational assessment of individuals, couples, and families.* New York: Brunner/Mazel.

Dubois, S. L. & Weiderman, M. W. (1997, June). *The journal of sex and marital therapy: A content analysis of articles from 1974–1995.* Paper presented at the annual meeting of the Mid-continent Region, Society for the Scientific Study of Sexuality, Chicago.

Kaplan, H. S. (1974). *The new sex therapy.* New York: Brunner/Mazel.

Kinzl, J., Mangweth, B., Traweger, C., & Biebl, W. (1996). Sexual dysfunction in males: Significance of adverse childhood experiences. *Child Abuse and Neglect, 20,* 759–766.

Kinzl, J., Traweger, C., & Biebl, W. (1995). Sexual dysfunctions: Relationship to childhood sexual abuse and early family experiences in a nonclinical sample. *Child Abuse and Neglect, 19,* 785–792.

Leiblum, S. R. & Rosen, R. C. (1988). *Sexual desire disorders.* New York: Guilford Press.

Leiblum, S. R. & Rosen, R. C. (Eds.). (2000). *Principles and practice of sex therapy* (3rd ed.). New York: Guilford Press.

Masters, W. H. & Johnson, V. (1970). *Human sexual inadequacy.* Boston: Little, Brown.

Ruppel, H. J., Jr. (1994). *Publications trends in the sexological literature: A comparison of two contemporary journals.* Unpublished doctoral dissertation, Institute for the Advanced Study of Human Sexuality.

Sager, C. (1976). *Marriage contracts and couples therapy.* New York: Brunner/Mazel.

Sexton, T., Weeks, G., & Robbins, M. (2003). *Handbook of family therapy.* New York: Brunner/Routledge.

Sternberg, R. (1986). A triangular theory of love. *Psychological Review, 93,* 119–135.

Stricker, G. & Gold, J. R. (1996). Psychotherapy integration: An assimilative, psychodynamic approach. *Clinical Psychology: Science and Practice, 3,* 47–58.

Strong, S. & Claiborn, C. (1982). *Change through interaction: Social psychological processes of counseling and psychotherapy.* New York: Wiley.

Weeks, G. (1977). Toward a dialectical approach to intervention. *Human Development, 20,* 277–292.

Weeks, G. (1994). The intersystem model: An integrative approach to treatment. In G. Weeks & L. Hof (Eds.), *The marital-relationship therapy casebook: Theory and application of the intersystem mode* (pp. 3–34). New York: Brunner/Mazel.

Weeks, G. & Cross, C. (2004). The intersystem model of psychotherapy: An integrated systems approach. *Guidance and Counselling, 19,* 57–64.

Weeks, G. & Gambescia, N. (2000). *Erectile dysfunction: Integrating couple therapy, sex therapy, and medical treatment.* New York: W. W. Norton.

Weeks, G. & Gambescia, N. (2002). *Hypoactive sexual desire: Integrating couple and sex therapy.* New York: W. W. Norton.

Weeks, G., Gambescia, N., & Jenkins, R. (2003). *Treating infidelity.* New York: W. W. Norton.

Weeks, G. & Hof, L. (Eds.) (1987). *Integrating sex and marital therapy: A clinical guide.* New York: W. W. Norton.

Weeks, G. & Treat, S. (2001). *Couples in treatment* (Rev. ed.). New York: Brunner/Routledge.

4

The Integration of Technology into Sex Therapy

Katherine M. Hertlein

Contents

Introduction

Richard Feynman (1988), noted physicist, once said, "For a successful technology, reality must take precedence over public relations, for Nature cannot be fooled" (p. 237). Indeed, this appears to be true in the ways that couples are affected by technology: The use of technology must be leveled with a dose of reality to preserve the positive elements and to enhance the successful integration of such technology in our lives and relationships.

The purpose of this chapter is to integrate the use of technology positively within the intersystems approach for the treatment of sexual dysfunction. First, a presentation is given of the problems facilitated by technology in couples relationships, particularly related to sex and sexual dysfunction and technology's role in contributing to problems within each level of the intersystems approach. Second, the pros of using technology in couples relationships is presented. Finally, treatment strategies are outlined that incorporate technology consistent with the intersystems approach.

The Use and Impact of Technology in Our Daily Lives

The use of technology has increased dramatically over the past decade. For example, 10 years ago the number of people using computers who accessed the Web daily was 9 million, and those who accessed the Web at least one time per week was 20 million; in 2006, a study documented more than 1 billion computer users worldwide, 197 million of which were Americans (Computer Almanac Industry, 2006). Similarly, there were a reported 207 million cell phone subscribers in the United States in 2005, up from just 33 million subscribers in 1995 (Infoplease, 2005).

The frequency of computer use and technology changes not only our lives but also the manner in which people relate to one another. Cooper and Sportolari (1997) reported that people who use computers engage in less inhibited behavior while online than they do in face-to-face communications. Over half of compulsive Internet users indicate that they flirt online (Greenfield, 1999), and more than one third report that they masturbate online, with 42% admitting to engaging in an online affair. In a study exploring how people use their cell phones, approximately 41% report that they use it to make calls to fill in time while they are waiting or traveling. Also, 57% of cell phone users report they always leave their cell phone on (AOL, 2006).

There are also several studies examining the impact of technology (specifically Internet use) on couples relationships. Schneider (2000, 2003), for example, conducted a study with female participants exploring the impact of cybersex addiction on their relationship and family, discovering that cybersex was a main factor in the decision to separate or divorce. In another study, Cooper, Galbreath, and Becker (2004) found that the reasons men engaged in online sexual behavior were primarily the same as what affected the men's offline relationships. In cases of Internet infidelity, Whitty (2005) discovered that Internet infidelity might have different effects on the primary relationship than face-to-face infidelity because of the greater emphasis on an emotional connection with another partner. Secrecy, another component of technology, can also significantly affect couples relationships. For example, each member of a couple might have his or her own email accounts, cellular telephones, or pagers. Secrecy around the exchange of information via emails, voicemails, or text messaging can also be problematic for a couple (Cooper, Delmonico, & Burg, 2000a, 2000b; Cooper, Scherer, Boies, & Gordon, 1999). Approximately one quarter of all cell phone users (but 39% of users aged 18–29) reported that they are not always truthful about where they are on their cell phone when asked (AOL, 2006).

Other problems that a couple may experience as a result of technology include financial problems related to greater Internet use, putting themselves at an increased risk for STDs (Elford, Bolding, & Sherr, 2001; McFarlane, Bull, & Reitmeijer, 2000; Toomey & Rothenberg, 2000), relational problems such as a reduction in intimacy with their primary partner (Schneider, 2000), lack of completing everyday tasks, and Internet problems related to their employment (Cooper, Månsson, Daneback, Tikkanen, & Ross, 2003; Cooper, Morahan-Martin, Mathy, & Maheu, 2002; Morahan-Martin & Schumacher, 2000; Underwood & Findlay, 2004). Almost one quarter of cell phone users reported that they frequently feel compelled to answer their phone, even if it rings during mealtimes (AOL, 2006).

This increased usage of technology in our lives results in a series of interruptions in everyday life. Cell phones, laptops, and handheld computers with wireless access allow individuals to be contacted almost anywhere at any time. Such contact can infringe on a couple's time together. Employers, for example, have the ability to contact their employees via cell phone after working hours and request that they attend to important business. Such contact can put a couple's date or time together "on hold" while the partner attends to the issues outlined by the employer. Cell phone interruptions are attributed not only to employers but also to anyone who can contact individuals and pull their time away from their partner while couples are out together. Friends, family, and others also have the potential to interrupt a couple's time together at any time and place, particularly if the partners in the relationship already have difficulty with maintaining boundaries and carving out time to protect the relationship. Further, individuals frequently have the ability (and often execute this ability) to check their work email while at home. Such opportunities blur the boundaries between work and home, thus potentially creating more problems for a couple or family. Finally, the relationships between the couple and the larger systems can also be disrupted by the exclusive use of cell phones. For example, family members of the couple can only talk to one person at a time as opposed to a home line with multiple phones in a house, where both partners can speak to someone on the other end of the line simultaneously.

Henline and Harris (2006) conducted an investigation on the pros and cons of technology within relationships. They explored how individuals use a variety of pieces of technology and the negative impacts it creates in one's life. Specifically, the forms of technology investigated included cell phones (i.e., text messaging and telephone capabilities), the Internet (i.e., online chatting, email and instant messaging, websites, blogs and other social networks, online meetings, and pornography), computers (i.e., video games and virtual relationships), and television and movies. The researchers found that, in many cases, communication through technology creates difficulty in understanding the true intentions of the message. For example, sarcasm across messages may be missed because the reader is relying heavily on the actual text. In some cases, this miscommunication can be problematic and disruptive to a couple's communication pattern.

Another finding was that in some cases, with the increased accessibility afforded by the Internet and cell phones, there is a greater likelihood in couples of feeling "smothered" by their partners. In other cases, the accessibility allowed individuals to work from home and therefore to compromise time with the primary partner. Further, respondents reported that there was an opportunity for individuals to get wrapped up with online activities and to neglect relationship or household responsibilities. The accessibility and availability of technology can monopolize individuals' time and, in some cases, can provide an opportunity for them to avoid their partner or the problems within the relationship. In terms of clinical implications, Henline and Harris (2006) reported that technology may affect the time and effort that individuals put into their primary relationship.

Additionally, individuals can use it as a tool to avoid their partner, and they may be distracted from investing in their primary relationships due to the increased consumerism available online.

Pros of Using Technology in Relationships

Although there are certainly negative impacts of technology in couples relationships, advanced technology also can have a positive impact on couples and families. Therapists can use the Internet for sexual or marital enrichment of their couples in therapy (Schnarch, 1997). For example, couples have another opportunity to communicate with one another via email or instant messenger during a busy workday. This can enrich a relationship because, as couples frequently report, they spend little physical time together with the other time constraints of work, child care, and other responsibilities (Hertlein, 2004). Further, the coupling of the personal computer and access to the Internet allow couples to send pictures and other digital images such as short movies to each other as well as to friends and family across the globe. In terms of a sexual relationship, couples can send digital images to each other throughout the day and even upload these images onto their desktop at work or at home. Couples can enjoy sending e-cards to one another or love letters through an instant medium. Frequently, online e-cards can be sent at no cost and are therefore an affordable way to do something special and unexpected for one's partner. Also, the sender can decide whether the card should be sent immediately or select a day in the future for the card to be sent. With such technology, it becomes more difficult to forget to send a wish on an anniversary or another special milestone in the couple's relationship.

Long-distance relationships become easier to maintain in an age of instant communication. First, individuals can socialize with a wide variety of people online without geographic restrictions in who they are meeting. This enables them to be more selective in their dating and establishment of a relationship. Once a relationship is established for those who are geographically separated, the day-to-day communication over the Internet can facilitate the growth of the relationship on an emotional level. Most research finds that couples who communicate online report increased levels of emotional intimacy and connection than do those in relationships whose primary setting is offline (i.e., Cooper & Sportolari, 1997). Further, the advances in technology allow these couples to communicate at an affordable level. Cell phone packages and monthly Internet access packages allow these partners to communicate with one another for a great deal of time at a low cost (Cooper, 2002).

Couples can even enjoy free time together interacting via online games or a massively multiplayer online game (MMORPG). This gives couples the opportunity not only to "talk" online but also to interact and be entertained at, again, a relatively low cost. Such games can be used by couples who are separated by distance in addition to couples who already live close together. In short, couples have the opportunity to stay connected in a way they never have had before.

Henline and Harris (2006) also reviewed the benefits of technology use in couples relationships. They discovered that individuals feel that the advances in technology affords them more opportunities to contact their partner and to develop emotional relationships with others without relying on physical attraction in the early stages of a relationship. Further, advances in technology provide a chance to develop common interests (i.e., online game playing or interactive components), to keep conversations private, and to develop new ways of resolving conflict. As a result of these findings, Henline and Harris suggested that technology can facilitate time together, conflict resolution, and technology-related relational investment or building a connection between themselves and someone else as a base for a deep relationship.

Application of the Intersystems Approach: Factors Related to Problem Formation

The intersystems approach, as identified by Weeks and Hertlein (2008) (see Chapter 3 in this volume) is an integrative framework that assesses and treats several aspects of the couple's relationship in sex therapy treatment. Five areas covered in the framework:

1. Individual biological factors
2. Individual psychological factors
3. Couple/dyadic factors
4. Family-of-origin factors
5. Sociocultural factors

In the application to technology, certain vulnerabilities need to be considered that can affect a couple's sexual relationship. Each of these factors as applied to technology is described in the following sections.

Individual/Biological and Psychological Factors

Certain individual characteristics can contribute to the problems a couple might have with a relationship. For individuals who want to maintain a certain degree of secrecy in their lives separate from their partners, technology such as the Internet and cell phones can provide an easy method for maintaining the desired level of secrecy. Further, individuals who are vulnerable to being sexually compulsive may encounter increased opportunities provided by technology to become sexually compulsive. Individuals with disorders such as personality disorders may use technology as a way to demonstrate their superiority or to manipulate their partner. Age might also be a factor. Daneback, Cooper, and Månsson (2005) found that women between 35 and 49 years of age tended to have more experience with cybersex than men in the same group. Individuals who were in the 50–65 age range tended to have less experience with cybersex. Additionally, as compared with heterosexual men, men oriented toward same-sex relationships were four times more likely to engage in cybersex (ibid.).

One's individual experience with technology may also be a factor that can contribute to technology-related problems for couples. If one partner has greater familiarity with the Internet than the other, he or she may be aware of more strategies to maintain privacy while online or using cell phones. Those more familiar with the Internet may also have greater opportunities for developing intimate relationships with others or may feel a greater degree of comfort in using technology to escape his or her relationship problems. The development of a more intimate relationship online can potentially result in the disruption of the primary couple's sex life. In addition, some people can become addicted to the Internet. Young, Griffin-Shelley, Cooper, O'Mara, and Buchanan (2000) described the factors leading to cybersex addiction (i.e., anonymity, convenience, and escape). Schneider (2000, 2003) identified sexually addictive behaviors facilitated by the Internet as including the following:

- Viewing/downloading pornography and masturbating
- Reading/writing sexually explicit letters and stories
- Using email to set up meetings
- Placing ads to meet sexual partners
- Visiting sexually oriented chat rooms
- Interactive affairs (including real-time viewing of others' bodies)

Individuals may have a predisposition to becoming addicted to the Internet. Such an addiction can be detrimental to daily functioning and couples relationships. For example, the amount of time addicts spend online can interfere with their job performance, household responsibilities, and the time spent with their partner. Carnes (2001) reported on several factors related to cybersex addiction and suggested that cybersex addiction is often associated with a quick escalation in the amount and type of sexual behavior: "Cybersex appears to speed up the process of addiction even in people who appear not to be predisposed to any addictive disorder" (p. 71). Denial is also a component in cybersex addiction. Further, cybersex escalates to other nonvirtual behavior patterns, such as moving toward engaging in prostitution. The computer and the Internet can also become sexualized for the individual. Individuals learn to associate a keyboard, monitor, or other neutral items with sexual response. For further discussion on the treatment of sexual addiction, see Chapter 12 in this volume.

Other individual traits have also been found to be associated with technology usage. Using a sample of 323 individuals in committed relationships, Henline and Harris (2006) found that greater differentiation of self is associated with higher levels of intimacy and lower levels of alone or conjoint technology usage. In other words, individuals who demonstrated a better ability to balance their emotional processes in decision making reported higher levels of intimacy with their partner and were less likely to use technology as a way to establish intimacy. Anolli, Villani, and Riva (2005) found that although people who chatted online were from a variety of personality groups, they were also more likely to be those who needed constant support and approval.

Couple/Dyadic Factors

Certain couple factors also contribute to the negative impact of technology with a couple. Fear of intimacy may be one factor that makes a couple more vulnerable to sexual/relationship problems related to technology. Couples who fear intimacy may find it more comfortable to communicate online or over the phone versus communicating face to face (for some, representative of a more vulnerable situation). Consistently communicating in this way may impair a couple's ability to manage conflict. For example, individuals may find it easy to elude their partners by merely turning off a cell phone or simply avoiding or blocking emails. Certainly, if communication between a couple is disrupted, sexual dysfunction or infidelity can also develop (Weeks, Gambescia, & Jenkins, 2003). One couple with sexual problems also reported various marital problems that interfered with experiencing desire for each other. They were a conflict-avoidant couple who never argued directly but would literally email each other from different rooms rather than confront conflict directly.

Another couple factor may be the context of their relationship. In some cases, couples who have maintained a long-distance relationship primarily with the assistance of technology (via email, cell phones, and pagers) may experience greater difficulty in communicating in real time once they shift their relationship from long distance to local. The impact on sex for these couples is that they may have to learn to develop a deeper emotional relationship with one another to fully enjoy a sexual relationship. In some circumstances, the couple may believe that the shifting from long distance to a local relationship will have no significant changes on their relationship and will encounter difficulties without consideration as to the impact of the transition on the couple. One such difficulty is the mismatch between expectations and reality, thus impacting both the emotional and physical relationship that the couple shares.

Family-of-Origin Factors

Family-of-origin factors may also contribute to a couple's problems related to technology. For example, a variety of MMPORGs allow families, friends, and couples to connect with one another while living several states and countries away. In such cases, family dynamics may play out over these games and affect the primary couple's relationship. If, for example, a husband spends one day a week playing with his family online and possibly neglects his wife or household tasks, feelings such as anger, resentment, or jealousy may develop in his wife. To confront the behavior, however, his wife may suggest to him that she does not value the time spent with his family, which may result in conflict around to whom the husband is more loyal.

Another family-of-origin factor relates to how comfortable each person's family has been with implementing technology in their lives. For example, families with greater implementation of technology may have an easier time adapting to advances in technology in the family. When one partner has been accustomed to technological advances and is paired with an individual who comes from a family unaccustomed to such techniques, the couple can be divided among daily decisions related to household management.

For example, one individual comfortable with technology may suggest that the couple only use cell phones in their home, whereas the other partner who is less comfortable with technology may argue that they should have a landline phone. Couples may also argue about the time each can spend online as it compares to interference with maintaining the household.

Sociocultural Factors

An increased use of technology is part of the social fabric of our society. In many ways, we are expected to keep up with the changes in technology usage to stay current with our contemporaries. In some cases, however, the increase in demands of using technology can negatively impact our sexual and emotional relationship with our partners.

Some sociocultural factors related to technology can also contribute to a couple's problems related to sexuality. Many individuals hold jobs that are greatly facilitated by increased usage of technology, including being able to check email from home, receiving phone calls from employers and coworkers while at home, and having increased opportunities to work from home. This can blur the lines between home and work life and can result in reduced intimacy between partners. In many cases, the blending of work and home can create difficulties for couples in trying to separate home and work. Increased stress in the home as a result of increasing work demands can certainly impact a couple's sexual relationship, potentially resulting in reduced arousal and decreased desire. Further, some individuals may find themselves so involved online that they do not even think about having sex or about their relationship.

Application of the Intersystems Approach: Technology-Based Solutions in Sex Therapy

Individual/Biological Factors

Technology can be useful in several ways for addressing the individual/ biological issues related to sexual dysfunction. First, there are many places online for clients to seek help for medical issues. For example, sites such as WebMD, Medline Plus, and Medicine.net are all places where anyone can read about various symptoms associated with a variety of illnesses and conditions. Although these sites are not intended for people to use as a self-diagnostic tool, they can point individuals in the right direction and can give them direction in terms of seeking appropriate medical assistance.

Individual/Psychological Factors

The Internet has become a place of sexual information and education (Cooper & McLoughlin, 2001). Technology can be useful to clients with psychological vulnerabilities by providing resources, support, and networking opportunities. Depressed clients, for example, can find support within the many online communities that exist for the management of depressive disorders. Such online resources as chat rooms, community blackboards, or psychoeducational websites offer support and information about the disorder and point users to resources such as books, research, or other sites. For example, the National Institute of Mental Health provides information outlining the symptoms of depression, causes, effective treatments, and information on where to get help. In the words of one Internet user:

> I have a mental illness and the Internet has literally been my lifeline to the world for some four and a half years now. If I'm not comparing notes with any number of advocates/self-advocates throughout the day, I am on some level at least maybe once a day, many times in the company of others, holding someone's virtual hand for a moment until that same flood of emotion I know myself too well washes over the person whose face I most likely will never, ever see. So often, all it takes is for people out there to know someone else acknowledges them, validates them and the existence of their battles. (CNN, 2005)

Such disorders can impact sex because depression, anxiety, or other mental health issues can create a lack of sexual desire. Further, medications prescribed to address the psychiatric problems can also result in decreased desire or orgasm and can affect one's performance (Seagraves & Balon, 2003). In this way, the Internet provides both educational and communicative functions—it educates the user on the effects of medications or of their symptoms, provides a forum for connecting with others, and, in so doing, also normalizes symptomology, side effects, frustrations, and experiences.

Couple/Dyad Factors

Incorporating technology into sex therapy along the lines of the dyadic factors can include a variety of options. Couples who have a history of difficulty communicating, for example, can increase the number of opportunities they have to connect with each other during a busy day via cell phones, email, pagers, and instant messaging. For couples who are experiencing a significant amount of discord, technology provides a way for them to write out their thoughts in an email format and to send the message immediately as a way to resolve an issue rather than waiting until they see each other, thus providing a greater potential for things to escalate.

Family-of-Origin Factors

Technology also can help mitigate the effects of family-of-origin factors. Computer users may discover that they are not alone in the way their family of origin communicated about sex. Through chat rooms and other community networking sites, users can identify how other individuals managed the messages heard by their families of origin and can work to develop their own strategies for sifting through messages.

Sociocultural Factors

Using technology to address the sociocultural factors contributing to sexual dysfunction include time management skills and developing boundaries. Though in many circumstances the pressures to respond to immediate requests via email, cell phones, and pagers can interrupt a couple's sexual life, technology has also made it fairly easy to establish boundaries. For example, away messages can be placed on email accounts and can allow email users a break from the perceived need to check their email, thereby allowing time for the couple to spend with one another without the interruption of other communication. Further, cell phone users can relatively easily turn off their phone to prevent interruptions while still maintaining the ability to collect messages and retrieve them at a later time. Advances in technology have made it possible for users to set boundaries around family time easier than in the past.

Case Example

Ruth and Gary, a biracial couple, came to therapy to address Gary's relationship with a woman with whom Ruth believed he had had an affair. This woman was someone whom Gary reported was a close friend of his, but he denied any romantic nature to the relationship. Gary stated that this woman was also married with children and believed that Ruth was making a "bigger deal" of the relationship than she should.

Ruth stated that though she recently discovered the relationship, she had evidence that it had been ongoing for five years. She had discovered the relationship while looking through phone records when trying to get reimbursed for work. She found a number that she did not recognize and asked Gary about it. Gary reported that it was just a friend of his, but Ruth reported that she was suspicious because there were several calls a day. When she reviewed previous phone bills and went back as far as she could, she discovered that the contact between Gary and the third party had been consistent over the last five years. Ruth had no access to phone records beyond that time and suspected that the relationship had been taking place for some time before then. When she confronted Gary about it, she stated that he denied everything. He asserted his position that he and the woman were good friends. As a result of the tension between the couple, Ruth reported that it was difficult for her to feel aroused toward Gary and that this lack of arousal was complicating their relationship even further.

Technology was creating problems for this couple in that Gary's relationship was primarily maintained through his cellular communications with the third party. First, communication maintained through cell phones contributed to the accessibility of the relationship. The fact that the relationship was accessible to Gary at work, at home, and in the car became especially problematic for Ruth. Further, the accessibility of the relationship created an environment of secrecy. Ruth became increasingly concerned that Gary was able to carry on his relationship with the third party at his convenience while maintaining the routine of his relationship with Ruth. Another aspect of technology that created conflict between the couple was the phone calls by the other woman received by Ruth. She reported that she, too, was becoming harassed by the other woman and had instructed Gary to tell the woman to stop calling. Gary stated that he was unable to stop her and that she made her own choices.

From an individual factor perspective, Gary's reliance on his cell phone and pager provided an easy method of communicating with the third party without being detected. In terms of the couple's relationship, both Ruth and Gary reported that their relationship began under stressful circumstances. Ruth reported that her father did not support the relationship and told her that she would be cut out of his life if she married Gary. Within this context, the couple became cut off from other family members and began to depend solely on one another. This was particularly pronounced when Ruth and Gary began to experience problems—as Gary began to become frustrated with Ruth's accusations, he stopped responding to her phone calls and emails, and Ruth noted that there was a great deal "riding" the outcome of this relationship, given that she had cut off from her father and risked that relationship for her marriage. From a sociocultural perspective, both Ruth and Gary were professional individuals living in a mid-sized city. Such responsibilities provided both with cell phones and pagers and with legitimate reasons by which they would be able to use the pager on weekends or times when they were off work.

In treatment, the therapist worked with each individual to rely less on the technology that initially separated them and to rely more on experiencing technology together as a way to solve the problem the couple was facing. Specifically, the therapist provided the couple with several websites where they could learn communication skills. As a result, Ruth began to trust that Gary was behaving appropriately online and was open with what he was sharing online rather than maintaining another relationship in secret. In addition to the work on the emotional infidelity component, the therapist helped the couple to develop new rules and to establish a new contract for their relationship that addressed technology. Ruth and Gary both agreed that part of the problem in the relationship was that when they were married 25 years ago, the unspoken marital contract did not include the technological advances that had become part of everyday life. With the sociocultural factors, Gary agreed to speak to his office about rotating the pager responsibilities to help Ruth feel more secure about his pager use. Additionally, the therapist worked with the couple to integrate the use of technology in each partner's personal life. Ruth began to text message and email Gary as a way to use the communication devices to strengthen their relationship. Gary reported that he enjoyed hearing from Ruth in this way during the workday and believed that once he returned home, he felt more connected to Ruth since they had already been talking via electronic devices during the day. Ruth reported that she felt more connected to Gary and that she was developing more trust with him.

The therapist also gave the couple the assignment of seeking out chat rooms or other online forums where couples were reporting similar experiences. In so doing, Ruth found that her experience of reduced arousal was not uncommon among other partners in her position. This normalization was powerful for her; she stated that she felt less pressured to "fix" the problem and recognized that a whole community of people was in a similar place. Gary, too, was able to connect with others who had been through the experience and were able to give Gary perspective as to what it is like to be in his position but could give him confidence that his situation would improve.

Future Directions

As technological advances continue to develop, couple and family therapists will be faced with more challenges related to technology and their lives. Therapists need to continue to develop strategies to address the influence of technology in people's lives as well as to identify ways to use the technology to improve interpersonal relationships. Technology in our lives gives therapists the opportunity to develop creative strategies tailored to the needs of each individual and couple. Though most of the research related to technology and sexuality has focused on the frequency and nature of electronic communications, future research should focus on developing more ways to use advances in technology to improve sexual functioning in relationships, specifically exploring the manner in which technology's interactive components can enhance relational functioning.

References

Anolli, L., Villani, D., & Riva, G. (2005). Personality of people using chat: An online research. *Cyberpsychology and Behavior, 8*(1), 89–95.

AOL (2006). *AP-AOL-PEW Research center mobile lifetime survey.* Retrieved December 19, 2006 from: http://mobile1.aol.com/survey

Carnes, P. J. (2001). Cybersex, courtship, and escalating arousal: Factors in addictive sexual desire. *Sexual Addiction and Compulsivity, 8,* 45–78.

Computer Almanac Industry (2006). *Worldwide Internet users top 1 billion in 2005.* Retrieved December 19, 2006 from: http://www.c-i-a.com/pr0106.htm

Cooper, A., Delmonico, D. L., & Burg, R. (2000). Cybersex, users, abusers, and compulsives: New findings and implications. *Sexual Addiction & Compulsivity, 7*(1–2), 5–29.

Cooper, A., Galbreath, N., & Becker, M. A. (2004). Sex on the internet: Furthering our understanding of men with online sexual problems. *Psychology of Addictive Behaviors, 18*(3), 223–230.

Cooper, A., Månsson, S., Daneback, K., Tikkanen, R., & Ross, M. W. (2003). Predicting the future of internet sex: Online sexual activities in Sweden. *Sexual & Relationship Therapy, 18*(3), 277–291.

Cooper, A. & McLoughlin, I. (2001). What clinicians need to know about Internet sexuality. *Sexual and Relationship Therapy, 16*(4), 321–327.

Cooper, A., Morahan-Martin, J., Mathy, R. M., & Maheu, M. (2002). Toward an increased understanding of user demographics in online sexual activities. *Journal of Sex & Marital Therapy, 28*(2), 105–129.

Cooper, A., Scherer, C. R., Boies, S. C., & Gordon, B. L. (1999). Sexuality on the Internet: From sexual exploration to pathological expression. *Professional Psychology: Research and Practice, 30*(2), 154–164.

Cooper, A. & Sportolari L. (1997). Romance in cyberspace: Understanding online attraction. *Journal of Sex Education & Therapy, 22*(1), 7–14.

Daneback, K., Cooper, A., & Månsson, S. (2005). An Internet study of cybersex participants. *Archives of Sexual Behavior, 34*(3), 321–328.

Elford, J., Bolding, G., & Sherr, L. (2001). Seeking sex on the Internet and sexual risk behaviour among gay men using London gyms. *AIDS, 15*(11), 1409–1415.

Feynman, R. P. (1988). *What do you care what other people think? Further adventures of a curious character.* New York: W. W. Norton.

Greenfield, D. N. (1999). *Virtual addiction: Sometimes new technology can create problems.* Retrieved September 28, 2005 from: http://www.virtual-addiction.com/pdf/nature_internet_addiction.pdf

Henline, B. H. & Harris, S. M. (2006, October 19–22). *Pros and cons of technology use within close relationships.* Poster presented at the annual conference of the American Association for Marriage and family Therapy, Austin, TX.

Hertlein, K. M. (2004). *Internet infidelity: An examination of family therapist treatment decisions and gender biases.* Unpublished doctoral dissertation. Virginia Polytechnic Institute and State University, Blacksburg.

Hertlein, K. M. & Weeks, G. R. (2008). Toward a new paradigm in sex therapy. In K. M. Hertlein, G. R. Weeks, & N. Gambescia, Eds., *Systemic Sex Therapy.* Boca Raton: Taylor & Francis.

Infoplease (2005). *Cell phone subscribers in the US.* Retrieved December 19, 2006, from: http://www.infoplease.com/ipa/A0933563.html

McFarlane, M., Bull, S. S., & Reitmeijer, C. A. (2000). The internet as a newly emerging risk environment for sexually transmitted diseases. *Journal of the American Medical Association, 284*(4), 443–446.

Morahan-Martin, J. & Schumacher, P. (2000) Incidence and correlates of pathological Internet use among college students. *Computers in Human Behavior, 16*(1), 13–29.

Schnarch, D. (1997). Sex, intimacy, and the Internet. *Journal of Sex Education and Therapy, 22*(1), 15–20.

Schneider, J. P. (2000). Effects of cybersex addiction on the family: Results of a survey. *Sexual Addiction & Compulsivity, 7*, 31–58.

Schneider, J. P. (2003). The impact of compulsive cybersex behaviours on the family. *Sexual & Relationship Therapy, 18*(3), 329–354.

Seagraves, R. & Balon, R. (2003). *Sexual pharmacology: Fast facts.* New York: W. W. Norton.

Toomey, K. E. & Rothenberg, R. B. (2000). Sex and cyberspace—virtual networks leading to high-risk sex. *Journal of the American Medical Association, 284*(4), 485–487.

Underwood, H. & Findlay, B. (2004). Internet relationships and their impact on primary relationships. *Behavior Change, 21*(2), 127–140.

Weeks, G. R., Gambescia, N., & Jenkins, R. E. (2003). Treating infidelity: Therapeutic dilemmas and effective strategies. New York: W. W. Norton & Co.

Whitty, M. T. (2005). The realness of cybercheating: Men's and women's representations of unfaithful Internet relationships. *Social Science Computer Review, 23*(1), 57–67.

Young, K. S., Griffin-Shelley, E., Cooper, O'Mara, J., & Buchanan, J. (2000). Online infidelity: A new dimension in couple relationships with implications for evaluation and treatment. *Sexual Addiction & Compulsivity, 7*(1–2), 59–74.

5

The Treatment of Hypoactive Sexual Desire Disorder

Gerald R. Weeks
Katherine M. Hertlein
Nancy Gambescia

Contents

Introduction

Hypoactive sexual desire disorder (HSDD) is one of the most common pre-senting problems in the practice of sex and couple therapy; approximately 20% of men and 33% of women are affected by low or absent sexual desire (Laumann, Palik, & Rosen, 1999). The incidence is higher in the clinical population: More than 50% of couples in treatment complain of insuffi-cient sexual desire within their relationship (Segraves & Segraves, 1991).

Although HSDD is prevalent, it is also among the most complex and difficult sexual problems to treat because it can be caused by any number of biopsychosocial factors. For instance, the source of HSDD is often a combination of factors such as the individual's feelings and beliefs about sexual intimacy, relationship issues, and, in some cases, family-of-origin difficulties and traumas. Hormone imbalances and other physical fac-tors might also be contributory. Further, HSDD can occur in conjunction with other sexual dysfunctions in either partner (Weeks & Gambescia, 2002). For example, a woman who experiences pain with intercourse may gradually lose her desire for sex, or a man may become disinterested in his partner with orgasm problems. Treatment, therefore, cannot follow a short protocol-based model but must be comprehensive, flexible, and tailored to each couple.

Definition

To appropriately diagnose HSDD, three criteria must be met according to the *Diagnostic and Statistical Manual of Mental Disorders,* 4th ed., text revision (*DSM-IV-TR;* APA, 2000). First, there is a lack of sexual fantasy and desire to engage in sexual activity. This absence of fantasy and desire must produce marked personal or interpersonal distress. Sometimes the distress is more pronounced in the individual who would like to feel desire but cannot experience it. In other cases, the distress affects both partners, particularly if there is a distinct discrepancy in sexual appetite resulting in, for example, frustration or disappointment. Finally, HSDD cannot be met by another Axis I disorder or another sexual dysfunction and cannot be a byproduct of a general medical condition or the result of substance abuse.

HSDD can be a *lifelong* condition in which absence of sexual desire is a typical state for the person. Alternately, when an individual has experienced a change in his or her sexual appetite, the term *acquired* is used; desire has been present, normally for a period of several years, but there has been a noticeable decline over time. The change can be gradual or precipitous (APA, 2000).

An individual with *generalized* lack of desire does not have a sexual appetite under any circumstance regardless of the partner or situation. Typically, this individual does not engage in sexual fantasy or any type of self-pleasuring. The *situational* type, on the other hand, is marked by selective desire, in certain situations or with specific partners (APA, 2000). For example, the person might feel desire when alone but not with a spouse or might feel desire toward an affair partner but not with one's established partner.

A Systemic Approach

The purpose of this chapter is to present a comprehensive method of treating HSDD. We have called our model *intersystemic* because it deals with the interfacing of three general areas:

1. Each partner's biological and psychosocial dynamics
2. The couple's relationship
3. Factors learned within the families of origin and expressed in the present

Since HSDD symptoms are usually embedded within the couple's relationship dynamics, the sexual symptom is not treated in isolation (Weeks, 1994, 2004; Weeks & Gambescia, 2002). Instead, all components of the system are considered in assessment and treatment.

The Individual

The individual partners contribute unique ingredients to the couple's overall sexual functioning, including biological factors such as hormonal status, age, and physical health. For instance, normative changes of aging can affect the homeostasis of the hormonal system and adversely impact sexual desire. In one case, a happily married woman feared she had fallen out of love for her husband of 25 years because she experienced a marked decline in sexual desire after menopause. The partners were concerned and worried about her lack of desire and the meaning she ascribed to this change in their relationship.

Psychological strengths, limitations, values, attitudes, psychopathology, and so forth are also included in this category. For example, an individual with low self-esteem can seem indifferent about enjoying the pleasures of sexual intimacy. Often, the partner in this situation worries that the lack of interest is a reflection of diminished sexual attraction or interest in the relationship. Another emotion that can inhibit sexual desire is anxiety; apprehension and worry can impede sexual pleasure (Katz & Jardine, 1999).

Interactional

Numerous relational factors have an effect on the sexual climate of a relationship. Some of these factors include discrepancies in sexual appetites or attraction, levels of resentment, discord, disagreements about power and control, and the lack of communication. We have often seen a partner express resentment indirectly through avoidance and disinterest in sex. Sometimes, lack of desire is the only form of establishing power in a relationship that is unbalanced. In other instances of partner-specific

HSDD, the individual can ostensibly seem disinterested in relational sex but enjoys frequent solo sexual activity.

Intergenerational

Each partner is strongly influenced by familial religious beliefs, culture, attitudes, values, and expectations toward sex. For example, early exposure to a highly repressive familial environment can distort adult perceptions of normal sexual feelings and behaviors. Often, sexual ignorance, secrecy, mythology, and trauma are learned within the family of origin and through early social experiences. As adults, individuals will often reexamine acquired beliefs about sex. Also, as times change, the couple will reinterpret their sexual behavior through other lenses (Weeks, 2004). This lens may include the partner's own developmental changes as well as environmental/societal influences that can dampen or enhance early education about sexual intimacy.

Problems with Nonsystemic Approaches

A major problem in the treatment of HSDD has been the fragmentation of therapy into distinct categories dealing with marital, sexual, and family issues separately. This difficulty stems from the fact that sex, marital, and family therapy are often seen as distinct and separate entities (Weeks, 2004). Additionally, some treatment models focus on the symptom bearer and overlook the contribution of each partner in the development, maintenance, and treatment of the sexual difficulty. Therapies grounded by an individualistic/behavioral perspective are inadequate because they are not systemic. Sexual problems affect the couple, the partners contribute to the problem in a number of ways, and the couple is the focal point of treatment.

Another obstacle in the treatment of sexual dysfunctions is the bifurcation of medical versus psychological therapies. Currently, pharmacological treatment of sexual problems has become so popular that, regardless of etiology, some individuals seek medicines over psychotherapy for sexual problems. Frequently, the individual hypothesizes that the cause of HSDD is physical and therefore obtains treatment from a medical practitioner without including the partner in the decision-making process. Various hormonal, psychotropic, and off-label (not approved for the intended use) treatments may be attempted to increase sexual desire. The individual may become pessimistic about correcting the problem if the remedies do not work as expected. Often, the relational components of the problem were never assessed in the first place, so treatment might not be successful. Conversely, many psychotherapists are not comfortable seeking medical consultations when necessary; thus, important biological information is missed. Since HSDD is often a result of combined etiologies, the systemic therapist must consider several etiologies and be flexible in selecting treatment modalities. The reader is referred to an interesting chapter by Ashton (2007) for a comprehensive discussion of the new sexual pharmacology.

Some of the current approaches to HSDD propose new diagnostic criteria and differentiate indices of desire between genders (Basson, 2007; Maurice, 2007). We agree that men and women often experience desire differently and that the woman's sexual appetite is strongly influenced by her relationships and contextual factors. One of the most controversial ideas to come out of this newer body of literature is the presupposition that women in long-term relationships do not experience spontaneous sexual desire (Basson, 2000, 2001a, 2001b). This assumption has been challenged in an excellent and highly sophisticated conceptual critique (Both & Everaerd, 2002). Further, Basson (2000, 2001a, 2001b, 2007) proposed that women engage in sex for many nonerotic reasons, such as the wish for emotional closeness, and that desire and arousal often emerge from the nonerotic motivations. Our clinical experience suggests that many women in long-term relationships remain quite interested in sex and become frustrated to the point of considering divorce when their partners lose desire.

The systemic approach addresses the totality of factors that engender and maintain sexual symptoms. This approach was fully described in our text *Hypoactive Sexual Desire* (Weeks & Gambescia, 2002). Reviews of other psychological and physiological treatment modalities and their effectiveness can be found in Ullery, Millner, and Willingham (2002) and Heiman (2002).

Clinical Assessment

Preliminary Assessment

Treating HSDD involves a comprehensive assessment that begins with the first telephone contact. The therapist notes which partner ostensibly has the problem, the duration, and what the couple hopes to gain from treatment. Is the symptomatic partner taking the initiative for treatment or placating the significant other? In the next few sessions, the therapist begins to generate hypotheses regarding the causes of the problem. Initial impressions and reactions are gathered about the individual partners and their relationship, including recent significant changes in each partner's life. Early in treatment, the therapist begins to establish treatment goals by exploring and identifying the couple's expectations of treatment.

Focused Appraisal

Next, the therapist directs the assessment to the sexual relationship by asking focused questions in the session and also suggesting that the couple think about them at home as part of a deeper exploration:

1. How often do you have sex?
2. How often do you feel like having sex?
3. Do you believe your desire level is too low?
4. When did you first notice losing desire for sex? What was happening at that time?
5. Did you lose desire rapidly or slowly?
6. What was your level of sexual desire earlier in your relationship?
7. Any changes in your health? What medications are you taking now?
8. On a scale of 1 to 10 how much desire do you feel in general? Prior to sex? During sex?
9. How often do you think about sex or fantasize about romantic scenarios?

Individual Partners

The clinical assessment also includes individual sessions to determine level of desire, extent of sexual thoughts and fantasies, solo sexual activity and related fantasies, desired forms of erotic stimulation, ease in articulating erotic desires, and fantasies that make the individual comfortable or uncomfortable. Individual sessions provide a forum for discussing secrets that can later be shared, unusual sexual preoccupations, or if there is an extramarital affair. The therapist also considers aspects of the HSDD that will require medical evaluation.

The Couple

Throughout the duration of the assessment process the therapist evaluates the couple's emotional contracts, styles of communication, level of discord, conflict resolution style, and ways of defining problems. Each partner's capacity for intimacy is another focal point of an ongoing dyadic assessment. Thus, sexual and nonsexual relational parameters are evaluated.

The Intergenerational System

Intergenerational factors are assessed through the use of a genogram, which examines different aspects of familial functioning (DeMaria, Weeks, & Hof, 1999). Also, the clinician evaluates for incest, parentification, triangulation, and other dysfunctional patterns of familial relating that impact intimacy and sexuality. As stated, sexual misinformation generated within the family of origin can negatively influence intellectual and emotional understanding of sexuality and interfere with the enjoyment of sexual intimacy in adult relationships.

Cognitive Considerations

Our theory is that the presence of negative cognitions (about, e.g., the self, the partner, and the relationship) will directly affect sexual desire. We also believe that the individual who is able to experience sexual desire is actually having sexual thoughts while the individual who lacks desire has an absence of sexual thoughts or has a number of negative sexual thoughts. From the onset of treatment, negative sexual cognitions are observed regarding, for example, the self, the partner, the relationship, and the family of origin. This aspect of the assessment helps to determine which of the thoughts can be changed through cognitive therapy techniques and to further gauge other problems in the relationship that must be addressed through couple therapy. We return to this issue in the treatment section.

Empirical Tools

The previously mentioned assessment procedures are all clinical in nature. The clinician or researcher who wishes to conduct an evaluation that includes psychometric devices may also use new instruments that have been empirically validated for female clients. For general sexual dysfunction, the clinician could use the Female Sexual Function Index (FSFI; Meston, 2003; Wiegel, Meston, & Rosen, 2005). A new inventory that has been developed to assess HSDD is the Sexual Interest and Desire Inventory-Female (SIDI-F; Clayton et al., 2007; Sills et al., 2005). An instrument shown to have validity and reliability has not been developed for men.

Favorable Conditions for Treatment

We expect that other individual and relational issues will surface during treatment because HSDD does not occur in a vacuum. Most concerns are treatable, although their position of importance may vary during the duration of treatment. Often, the clinician must balance the pressure to treat the HSDD against the obvious problems that must be addressed first. It is always important to elucidate the relationship between the HSDD and the other concerns to promote compliance. We consider the following conditions to be favorable for treatment:

- Partners have positive sex beliefs and want to experience desire again.
- Both partners are relatively free from psychiatric problems that can impede treatment.
- There is an inability to break the cycle of negative sexual cognitions and obsessive thoughts that interfere with building sexual desire.
- If a partner has withheld historical information about physical, sexual, or emotional abuse or sexual addiction and is willing to share and work on this information.
- Negative sexual attitudes based on religious beliefs, internalized negative sex messages from the family of origin, and the resulting sexual guilt.
- Stress from situational life stressors that affect one partner such as severe work stress or death of a loved one.
- Unrealistic expectations, the normal physiological changes of aging, and the willingness to accept accurate information.

- Treatable relational difficulties in negotiating issues of power, control, inclusion, and autonomy.
- The couple's sexual script has not been successfully negotiated, or the partners may have different preferences or misinformation.
- Treatable discord in other areas of the relationship, such as ineffective communication, unresolved anger, and unmet expectations.
- When HSDD can be related to other sexual difficulties in either partner such as erectile dysfunction, inhibited female orgasm, or vaginismus.
- The presence of response anxiety (discussed later in this chapter).

Contraindications for Couple Therapy

The systemic treatment for HSDD is not appropriate when in the following situations:

- The HSDD partner does not wish for or care about sexual desire or has sexual aversion.
- The problem is viewed as solely belonging to the partner who lacks desire and the other partner is unwilling to participate in the therapy.
- A great deal of untreatable discord or the inability to work together cooperatively.
- One or both partners are not committed to their relationship.
- A lack of commitment to treatment such as during an affair or active addiction in one or both parties.
- Presence of a significant psychopathology in either partner.

One couple presented for treatment of the husband's gradual lack of desire for his wife and avoidance of sexual relations over the past year. He complained that she was too thin and that she was overly involved with their children. She was concerned that he was acting depressed and that his behavior had changed recently. He left the home for unexplained reasons and became secretive in his use of the cell phone and computer. The wife eventually discovered evidence of an extramarital affair. The focal point of treatment rapidly changed to address the crisis. (See Weeks & Gambescia, 2003, for treatment of infidelity.)

Etiology

The systemic framework is used to assess the risk factors for HSDD arising from three major areas: (1) the individual partners; (2) families of origin (intergenerational); and (3) the couple's relationship (interactional).

Individual Risk Factors

Psychological risk factors in the individual partners can be expressed within the context of sexual intimacy, thus giving rise to the development of HSDD. These involve anxiety, depression, negative cognitive distortions, inaccurate beliefs about sex, poor body image, a tendency to fuse sex and affection, career overload, and related sexual problems. In such cases, the therapist may be tempted to turn the focus of treatment to the partner with the lack of desire, but it is imperative that a relational stance is maintained (Weeks & Gambescia, 2002).

Fears in one or both partners could place a couple at risk for the development of HSDD since emotional and physical intimacies are closely related. Working on sexual desire may be hampered by one partner's fear of intimacy, anger, rejection and abandonment, exposure, feelings, or dependency. As noted previously, psychiatric factors such as anxiety, depression, obsessive-compulsive disorder, and sexual orientation conflicts can contribute to the development of HSDD. Further, physical factors, sexual abuse, and emotional trauma can inhibit desire. It is important for the therapist to assess all of these areas.

Intergenerational Risk Factors

Many of the aforementioned risk factors, such as antisexual beliefs, are learned within the social and familial contexts of each partner. It is essential that the therapist explore intergenerational legacies and other environmental messages regarding sexual intimacy. In one example, the couple presented for treatment of the woman's lifelong HSDD. She was raised in an extremely religious household and learned that sex was for procreation and not personal enjoyment. Although she recognized that her beliefs did not make sense, she found it difficult to observe her own body, to engage in erotic thoughts or solo sex, and to enjoy sexual intimacy with her husband. Treatment required a flexible format of individual and conjoint sessions, psychoeducation, bibliography, correcting mythological cognitions, and ultimately acceptance of her right to enjoy all of the intimate benefits of marriage.

Interactional Risk Factors

Interactional risk factors might overshadow the course of treatment as research indicates that the extent to which each partner is satisfied with the marriage is related to one's sexual satisfaction (Morokoff & Gilliland, 1993). Specifically, problems related to dyadic adjustment and HSDD often coexist. For example, women with HSDD tend to report greater degrees of marital distress and less relational cohesion (Trudel, Ravart, & Matte, 1993). For women, sexual satisfaction is related to factors such as the manner in which sex was initiated, level of arousal, and the behaviors present in that interaction. Other relational risk factors include contemptuous feelings, criticism, defensiveness, power struggles, and toxic communication (Gottman, 1994). The etiological factors previously mentioned are presented in a highly compressed form. Readers interested in doing a thorough assessment should consult our text on this subject (Weeks & Gambescia, 2002).

Medical Aspects

Most therapists treating HSDD are not physicians, yet they must assess for physical conditions that could cause or contribute to the lack of desire. Often, a medical consultation is a necessary part of treatment. The therapist must be comfortable interfacing with medical care providers, collecting medical information, and working collaboratively with psychiatrists, urologists, and gynecologists. Also, the therapist must be familiar with the role of testosterone in sexual desire and the medical conditions that could create deficiencies of this and other hormones. Additionally, chronic medical conditions, normative physiological changes, and iatrogenic effects of medications can contribute to HSDD (see Crenshaw & Goldberg, 1996; Maurice, 2007; Weeks & Gambescia, 2002).

Basic Treatment Strategies

Addressing Pessimism and Skepticism

In most cases, our couples have struggled with HSDD for months or years before seeking treatment. Often, they have attempted to change the problem on their own, have failed, and then have resigned themselves to a passionless relationship. Consequently, they enter treatment with a sense of pessimism and skepticism because they cannot imagine how talking about a sexual problem could possibly alleviate it. Lack of sexual desire is a complex phenomenon and is difficult for a person to change. The couple's failed attempts should be normalized by explaining that pessimism is a natural response to a difficult situation. The therapist should support them for their efforts to correct the problem even if these strategies have failed.

Maintaining a Systemic Focus

HSDD couples often view the symptomatic partner as the one with the problem. They must be educated to think systemically. This involves helping them to recognize that HSDD is a relational problem. One systemic technique is the *therapeutic reframe* in which the therapist helps to conceptualize the HSDD in a different way (Weeks & Treat, 2001). The therapist reframes the HSDD by asking focused questions that become more and more directed to help the couple appreciate how relational problems contribute to the lack of desire. The therapist emphasizes that the couple struggles together and will need to work together to resolve the problem. For a more detailed discussion of reframing, the reader is directed to Weeks and Gambescia (2002).

Responsibility for Sexual Intimacy

Many of our clients feel powerless with respect to owning and controlling their sexual feelings. They believe that sexual gratification is something that happens to them. Throughout the process of therapy, couples gradually learn that sexual desire and satisfaction are created, fostered, practiced, and nurtured by the self and the partner (Gambescia & Weeks, 2006).

Sensate focus exercises (discussed in Chapter 15 in this volume) and other cognitive behavioral assignments promote responsibility for sensual and sexual enjoyment. Ultimately, our couples recognize that they have control over their feelings, behavior, and sexual satisfaction.

Setting Priorities

The systemic treatment of HSDD should not be generic or predetermined. Usually, the therapist commences by focusing on the presenting problem. During the course of treatment, however, other individual or relational issues might take precedence. These often include anxiety, anger, sexual ignorance, or lack of communication. The therapist prioritizes the order in which each issue is treated. Some problems may overlap or be addressed concurrently. Moreover, it is important for the couple to understand that the format must be flexible and that modifications do not indicate failure. In one instance, individual issues in the husband contributed to his lifelong HSDD. During treatment, he revealed that as a child he had been sexually abused; this fact surprised his wife of 20 years. The couple needed time to discuss and understand this aspect of his childhood experience and the impact of early trauma on adult sexual functioning. Then, the focus of treatment returned to the HSDD as the couple gained a better understanding of the genesis of the problem.

Establishing Treatment Goals

The fundamental goal of treatment is to restore sexual desire to the intimate relationship; however, other objectives can be accomplished in the process. A lack of sexual desire can be tied to other elements of the couple's relationship, specifically those that diminish the sexual experience such as anger, resentment, or poor communication. Thus, treatment of HSDD addresses relationship problems, thereby improving overall relationship satisfaction. Moreover, effectively working together to solve the couple's sexual problem will foster greater improvements in their overall emotional relationship.

Implementing Goals

Since the treatment of HSDD also addresses the relational problems, it is essential that the therapist is qualified and knowledgeable about couples and sex therapy techniques and knows the circumstances under which the techniques will be most effective. Furthermore, we suggest that couples must be active members in their treatment; thus, they should be aware of why a strategy is being used and what the outcome is expected to be. This collaborative effort will increase compliance.

Correcting Unrealistic Expectations

Couples enter a relationship with expectations of themselves, of each other, and of what it means to be in a loving relationship. The expectations are often unstated, and partners are left feeling disappointed upon the realization that hopes and dreams will not come to fruition. Some ideas are unrealistic from the start, such as believing that if your partner loved you, he or she would know automatically what you want. In cases where expectations are not met, one partner may misattribute this to his or her partner not caring about him or her enough and, as a result, may withhold sex or desire. The therapist should help the couple to develop realistic perceptions of themselves, what each can offer, and a reasonable perception of love and all that it involves.

Lowering Response Anxiety

In our clients, the low-desire partner continuously monitors and worries about the lack of sexual desire rather than enjoying sexual activity. People experience response anxiety when they believe they should enjoy more desire for their partner than they currently feel. The focal point of sexual intimacy turns into anxiety rather than pleasure. As response anxiety increases, the likelihood of desire decreases, thereby increasing anxiety, and so on.

One critical component to the treatment of HSDD is lowering the response anxiety, and we use several techniques. First, the therapist educates the couple by explaining the concept. Cognitive strategies such as thought-stopping and thought substitution are also useful (Beck, 1976, 1995). Another method is to confront irrational ideas that foster response anxiety, such as the equation of sex and intercourse. In this case, the definition of sex is broadened to include behaviors such as noncoital sexual touching that are less likely to cause response anxiety. The therapist familiar with systemic approaches can use *paradoxical intervention*, a technique in which a symptom is intentionally prescribed for the client to recognize that he or she has control over the symptom (Weeks & L'Abate, 1982).

Addressing Affect

Another focus of treatment is the emotional processes that occur within the session. As such, the couple will learn to communicate about feelings rather than staying fixed on content. The therapist will need to attend to the level of affect expressed by each partner. For instance, the lower-desire partner may appear to have a lack of motivation for sex and a lack of affect and may seem withdrawn, especially in the sexual area. Conversely, the higher-desire partner is often more emotional, frustrated, and pessimistic. In these instances, the therapist should help the partners attend to and discuss their style of expressing emotion. Also, they are helped to inquire rather than to ascribe motives for each other's feelings. This process helps the couple become more aware of themselves, their patterns of interactions, and the emotional barriers to feeling desire. This work is ongoing.

Cognitive Work

Cognitive therapy is indispensable in the treatment of HSDD. Negative cognitions about sexual intimacy, the self, and the partner directly contribute to the lack of desire by preventing the emergence of enjoyable sexual thoughts and fantasies. This cognitive mental mechanism is powerful; it has strong behavioral consequences. Further, couples develop interlocking sets of irrational beliefs that perpetuate sexual problems; these beliefs need to be explored, interrupted, and changed conjointly. A man with HSDD might think, "I'm just not interested in sex." His partner might also think, "He isn't interested in sex, so why initiate anything?" These two interlocking thoughts help to perpetuate sexual avoidance.

The partners are helped to identify interlocking irrational sexual beliefs and to replace them with more positive, factual cognitions. Also, they are encouraged to engage in erotic thoughts and fantasies to promote prosexual cognitions and feelings. Each partner learns to monitor his or her thoughts or behaviors to determine when the nonproductive thought has started again. It is stopped (thought-stopping) and consciously replaced (thought substitution) with an enjoyable idea. As such, the individual is mentally rehearsing or replaying a positive sexual encounter. This process creates a state of positive anticipation for the next experience. Eventually, erotic thoughts become more natural and automatic (Beck, 1976, 1995; Weeks & Hof, 1987, 1994).

Communication

Another aspect of treatment involves helping the couple to discuss their sexual needs, wishes, preferences, and concerns. Since most of our clients find it difficult to talk about sex, the therapist might start by fostering communication about less threatening topics and gradually move into sexual intimacy. Other areas of effective communication include using "I" statements, validating each other, listening reflectively, and learning to edit what one says (Weeks & Treat, 2001). In addition, Gottman (1994) recommends that a 5:1 ratio of positive to negative exchanges promotes relational satisfaction.

Psychoeducation

The therapist wants to correct as much misinformation as possible about sexual desire, the lack of desire, and sexuality in general. The revision of some misconceptions may take time and repeated discussions, whereas others seem to evaporate the moment the conversation is over. Some mythological beliefs are not revealed until they are uncovered through an individual discussion with the therapist. Bibliotherapy reinforces the psychoeducational process by providing accurate information about sexual structure and functioning. Also, we recommend readings that normalize aspects of sexual intimacy such as fantasy and solo sexual activity (Barbach, 1982; Comfort, 1994; Friday, 1998a, 1998b; Zilbergeld, 1992).

Systemic Homework

The therapist treating HSDD must play a directive role in session and beyond the therapy hour through the prudent use of assignments to be performed at home. Homework assignments address individual, relational, and inter-generational issues associated with the lack of sexual desire. For instance, homework for the individual partners includes prescriptions regarding physical exercise, guided imagery, gradual exposure to sexual material, directed masturbation, and exposure to fantasy through bibliotherapy or selected visual materials (Bright, 2000; Martin, 1997). Homework for the couple includes sensate focus, communicating sensual and sexual wishes and needs, and conflict resolution exercises (Barbach, 1982). The couple is also directed to explore intergenerational messages regarding sexual intimacy, pleasure, and entitlement to sexual satisfaction. Additionally, the continued use of homework assignments will promote compliance and will prevent relapse of the sexual symptoms, particularly with desire phase disorders (McCarthy, 1999).

Treating Other Sexual Dysfunctions

It is not unusual for an individual to have more than one sexual problem; thus, it is possible that HSDD might be related to another sexual difficulty such as physical discomfort during sex, erectile dysfunction, or trouble with orgasm. Sometimes, the higher-desire partner also has sexual difficulties that can make intercourse less desirable, such as erectile dysfunction, thereby increasing the possibility of HSDD. The role of the therapist is to educate the couple in how other sexual dysfunctions in either partner might contribute to the development and maintenance of HSDD. Further, the couple is encouraged to make a commitment to working on all elements of the dysfunction, not just the HSDD.

A couple, married for 30 years, sought treatment for the man's disinterest in sex for the past few years. The therapist learned that he had experienced erectile dysfunction (ED) for several years but that the couple managed to have noncoital sex on a regular basis. Assessment revealed that he engaged in masturbation and fantasy when alone, although his erections were not robust. The wife was unaware that he had any sexual desire for her, and she blamed herself for the couple's lack of sex. Each time she brought up the sexual issue for discussion, he would retreat. Finally, she insisted on treatment. The husband explained that the ED made penetration difficult or impossible and that he felt emasculated and embarrassed by his lack of performance. For him, it was easier to avoid sex altogether rather than anticipate a failure. Through psychoeducation, cognitive therapy, and behavioral homework, the couple gradually resumed sexual intimacy. In addition, they attended a urological consultation, and an oral medication was prescribed to promote more adequate erections.

Advanced Techniques

Promoting Sexual Intimacy

The topic of sexual intimacy is a central focus of systemic treatment of HSDD. The couple share their ideas about what it means to be intimate, identify discrepancies in their definitions, and work toward a common meaning (Weeks & Treat, 2001). Next, the therapist helps the couple to understand that intimacy and sex are not distinct entities. This concept is reinforced during the treatment as intimacy within their sexual relationship is encouraged. Additionally, the therapist works with the couple to expand their definition of sexuality to include other intimate sexual and nonerotic behaviors. Increasingly, the couple becomes aware of the ways they create obstacles to intimacy and how these barriers can inhibit sexual desire.

Working with Fears of Intimacy

Fears of intimacy and closeness, whether conscious or unconscious, are often exhibited through one's behavior. It is important to address this issue since, for many, the fear of intimacy compromises sexual desire. The therapist assumes that the fear of intimacy may be an unconscious motivator in cases of HSDD; thus, this position should be shared with the couple. Then the therapist helps the partners identify their fears through the use of a genogram focusing on elements of one's upbringing that have an effect on intimate behavior (DeMaria, Weeks, & Hof, 1999). Also, the therapist educates the couple about the many reasons why individuals might fear intimacy so that they understand the concepts and will be willing to discuss the related issues as they apply to them.

In HSDD cases, a few factors related to underlying fears of intimacy are seen more frequently. For example, the fear of losing control is sometimes manifested in relationships through a power imbalance that is so severe that one partner is perceived as a parent and the other as a child. This issue has the potential to make sex feel nearly incestuous (Weeks & Gambescia, 2002). The fear of losing oneself is another common presentation. It relates to HSDD in that desire is one aspect of the relationship that is in their control. One partner's fear that the other's ultimate goal is to control him or her is unconsciously reduced through the inhibition of sexual desire for the partner.

There are several guidelines for treating intimacy fears. First, it is important to identify the fear. Next, the therapist uses cognitive therapy to help neutralize the negative thoughts associated with the fear and then to replace them with appropriate and adaptive cognitions. The therapist and clients then work to disrupt the pattern of avoidance that results from the fear. It is important for each partner to validate the fearful partner's emotions without agreeing with him or her, as agreeing would lead to continued avoidance of the feared stimuli and, consequently, the behavior.

When the therapist is confident that the couple can directly tackle the fear, the suggestion should be made that the fear is threatening to the present relationship and serves little or no purpose. It is essential that the therapist and couple explore the ways each person in the relationship contributes to the problem rather than placing the blame solely on the person with the fear. The underlying fears of intimacy are usually deeply entrenched and require extended work ranging from cognitive therapy to intergenerational work.

Working with Conflict and Anger

Many of our HSDD couples have experienced anger and frustration over a protracted period of time. For some, the anger has become chronically suppressed or circumvented, making it very difficult to feel desire toward one's partner. Eventually, the couple avoids all emotional contact to avoid the unpleasant feelings. Additionally, sexual feelings become suppressed and fused with the noxious emotions of, for example, anger, frustration, disappointment, and helplessness. The couple must be helped to understand that anger, if expressed, need not destroy the partner or the relationship. A variety of techniques can be implemented to promote appropriate expression of anger (Weeks & Gambescia, 2002).

In one case, the wife, in her mid 30s, suffered from situational HSDD and avoidance of sex for a year after the birth of their first child. Her husband was frustrated and angry about her apparent lack of attention to him and the ailing sexual relationship. His anger was uncensored, which caused her to withdraw from him. The more he raged, the more unreceptive she became. By the time they presented for treatment, they were prepared for divorce. The therapist used immediate techniques to regulate affect of both partners. As the woman began to discuss her feelings of frustration, blame, and sadness, her husband was able to respond more empathically. He accepted her feelings; thus, she became interested in getting closer to him, and so on. The therapeutic outcome was positive after six months.

Medical Therapies

A variety of prosexual remedies is currently available to enhance the sexual appetite. Most of these preparations are nutritional supplements and remain unregulated by the U.S. Food and Drug Administration (FDA). Some prescription medications are used off-label for prosexual purposes. For example, bupropion sustained release (SR), an antidepressant, has been found to enhance desire in nondepressed women (Ashton, 2007; Segraves, Clayton, Croft, Wolf, & Warnock, 2004; Segraves et al., 2001).

The iatrogenic effects of many commonly used prescription medications can be another factor in HSDD (Ballon, 1999; Rosen, Lane, & Menza, 1999). Treatment strategies for overcoming the sexual side effects of medications include waiting to see if the symptoms remit, lowering the dose, substituting another antidepressant, adding a supplementary medicine to act as an antidote, or discontinuing the medication for brief periods (Fava et al., 1998). Bupropion SR is used to counteract HSDD caused by another group of commonly used antidepressants called selective serotonin reuptake inhibitors (SSRIs).

Testosterone is recognized as an important component of the sexual appetite in men and women as it promotes sexual desire, curiosity, fantasy, interest, and behavior (Crenshaw & Goldberg, 1996; Rako, 1996). Testosterone deficiency in men can be treated with an assortment of products and with varying results; however, testosterone deficiency in women remains untreated pharmacologically. Moreover, the relationship between testosterone and sexual desire in women is complicated. Davis, Davison, Donath, and Bell (2005) found that HSDD in women cannot be diagnosed through assessing the level of circulating sex hormones such as testosterone. Specifically, some women with low testosterone levels do not experience desire problems, and most women with HSDD have normal testosterone levels.

The medical and psychological treatments can work in combination as proposed in the intersystems model (Weeks & Gambescia, 2000, 2002). However, we do not believe that medications will override the effects of adverse relationship factors in HSDD but may prove useful where certain medical and drug side effects are present. A drug may eventually be developed that serves as a basic "energizer" of sexual desire, thus making it easier to experience desire when the suppressive individual, relational, and family-of-origin factors are worked through therapeutically.

Relapse Prevention

The therapist should help the couple to understand that sexual desire is maintained through active sensual and sexual contact with one another. Thus, the therapist assists the couple in relapse prevention by including strategies in the repertoire that involve sensual touching and caressing. These strategies are discussed in detail in Chapter 15 in this volume on sensate focus. The therapist must be mindful that relapse is to be expected, especially since conflicts and anger not related to sexuality can emerge during the sensate focus exercises. One of the signs that a couple is relapsing is their noncompletion of the homework assignments. Therefore, the couple is reminded to plan a schedule including sexual dates to spend with one another.

Paradoxical strategies can also prevent relapses (Weeks & Gambescia, 2002; Weeks & L'Abate, 1982). One strategy is to ask the couple to identify and predict the ways that they might sabotage their progress in therapy. Therapists can also ask the couple to predict the factors that might provoke the recurrence of inhibited desire. Asking the couple to think about these factors will increase the likelihood that these problems will not arise.

Conclusion

Treating HSDD can be complex, as it involves many factors related to the individual partners, to intergenerational influences, and to the couple's relationship. The intersystem approach can guide the therapist to decode and address many problem areas in couples presenting with this complex dilemma. The therapy is characterized by a number of apparent contradictions. First, although the symptoms are ostensibly expressed by one partner, HSDD is a relational problem. Next, HSDD is not simply a sexual problem; often, the lack of desire is a reflection of other problems in the relationship. Also, the HSDD partner may appear unemotional, yet the sexual symptom is often a way of indirectly expressing strong emotions related to the partner. The partner with HSDD might appear disinterested in sex. In effect, this individual wants to feel desire for his or her partner, yet this desire cannot be forced or it will further diminish the sexual appetite. The therapist must be equipped with a variety of techniques that are used judiciously; patience and flexibility are critical. Moreover, the therapeutic strategies must be shared with the partners to ensure their cooperation. As the intersystemic issues are addressed, often concurrently, sexual desire will gradually return to the relationship.

References

American Psychiatric Association (APA) (2000). *Diagnostic and statistical manual of mental disorders* (4th ed., text rev.). Washington, DC: Author.

Ashton, A. K. (2007). The new sexual pharmacology: A guide for the clinician. In S. R.Leiblum (Ed.), *Principles and practice of sex therapy* (4th ed., pp. 509–541). New York: Guilford Press.

Ballon, R. (1999). Sildenafil and sexual dysfunction associated with antidepressants. *Journal of Sex & Marital Therapy, 25*(4), 259–264.

Barbach, L. (1982). *For each other: Sharing sexual intimacy.* New York: Doubleday.

Basson, R. (2000). The female sexual response: A different model. *Journal of Sex and Marital Therapy, 26*, 51–65.

Basson, R. (2001a). Are the complexities of women's sexual function reflected in the new consensus definitions of dysfunction? *Journal of Sex & Marital Therapy, 27*, 105–112.

Basson, R. (2001b). Using a model for female sexual response to address women's problematic low sexual desire. *Journal of Sex & Marital Therapy, 27*, 295–403.

Basson, R. (2007). Sexual desire/arousal disorders in women. In S. R. Leiblum (Ed.), *Principles and practice of sex therapy* (4th ed., pp. 25–53). New York: Guilford Press.

Beck, A. T. (1976). *Cognitive therapy and the emotional disorders.* New York: International Universities Press.

Beck, J. (1995). *Cognitive therapy: Basics and beyond.* New York: Guilford.

Both, S. & Everaerd, W. (2002). Comment on the female sexual response: A different model. *Journal of Sex and Marital Therapy, 28*, 11–15.

Bright, S. (Ed). (2000). *Best American erotica 2000.* New York: Touchstone.

Clayton, A. H., Segraves, R. T., Leiblum, S., Basson, R., Pyke, R., Cotton, D., et al. (2007). Reliability and validity of the sexual interest and desire inventory-female (SIDI-F), a scale designed to measure severity of female hypoactive sexual desire disorder. *Journal of Sex & Marital Therapy, 32,* 115–135.

Comfort, A. (1994). *The new joy of sex: A gourmet guide to lovemaking in the nineties.* New York: Crown Publishing.

Crenshaw, T. & Goldberg, G. (1996). *Sexual pharmacology.* New York: W. W. Norton.

Davis, S., Davison, S., Donath, S., & Bell, R. (2005). Circulating androgen levels and self-reported sexual function in women. *Journal of the American Medical Association, 294*(1), 91–96.

DeMaria, R., Weeks, G., & Hof, L. (1999). *Focused genograms: Intergenerational assessment of individuals, couples, and families.* Philadelphia: Brunner/Mazel.

Fava, M., Rankin, M., Alpert, J., Nierenberg, A., & Worthington, J. (1998). An open trial of oralsidenafil in antidepressant-induced sexual dysfunction. *Psychotherapy and Psychosomatics, 67*(6), 328–331.

Friday, N. (1998a). *Forbidden flowers: More women's sexual fantasies.* New York: Pocket.

Friday, N. (1998b). *Men in love.* New York: Dell.

Gambescia, N. & Weeks, G. (2006). Sexual dysfunction. In N. Kazantzis & L. L'Abate (Eds.), *Handbook of homework assignments in psychotherapy: Research, practice, and prevention* (pp. 351–368). Norwell, MA: Kluwer Academic Publishers.

Gottman, J. (1994). *What predicts divorce: The relationship between marital processes and marital outcomes.* Hillsdale, NJ: Lawrence Erlbaum.

Heiman, J. R. (2002). Psychologic treatments for female sexual dysfunction: Are they effective and do we need them? *Archives of Sexual Behavior, 31*(5), 445–450.

Katz., R. C. & Jardine, D. (1999). The relationship between worry, sexual aversion, and low sexual desire. *Journal of Sex & Marital Therapy, 25,* 293–296.

Laumann, E. O., Palik, A., & Rosen, R. C. (1999). Sexual dysfunction in the United States: Prevalence and predictors. *Journal of the American Medical Association, 281,* 537–544.

Lerner-Goldhor, H. (1989). *The dance of anger.* New York: HarperCollins.

Martin, R. (Ed). (1997). *Dark eros: Black erotic writings.* New York: St. Martin.

Maurice, W. L. (2007). Sexual desire disorders in men. In S. R. Leiblum (Ed.), *Principles and practice of sex therapy* (4th ed., pp. 181–211). New York: Guilford Press.

McCarthy, B. W. (1999). Relapse prevention strategies and techniques for inhibited sexual desire. *Journal of Sex & Marital Therapy, 25,* 297–303.

Meston, C. M. (2003). Validation of the female sexual function index (FSFI) in women with female orgasmic disorder and in women with hypoactive sexual desire disorder. *Journal of Sex & Marital Therapy, 29,* 39–46.

Morokoff, P. & Gilliland, R. (1993). Stress, sexual functioning, and marital satisfaction. *Journal of Sex Research, 20,* 43–53.

Rako, S. (1996). *The hormone of desire: The truth about sexuality, menopause and testosterone.* New York: Haworth.

Rosen, R., Lane, R., & Menza, M. (1999). Effects of SSRIs on sexual function: A critical review. *Journal of Clinical Pharmacology, 19*(1), 67–85.

Segraves, K. & Segraves, R. (1991). Hypoactive sexual desire disorder: Prevalence and comorbidity in 906 subjects. *Journal of Sex & Marital Therapy, 17,* 55–58.

Segraves, R. T., Croft, H., Kavoussi, R., Ascher, J. A., Batey, S. R., Foster, V. J., et al. (2001). Bupropion sustained release (SR) for the treatment of hypoactive sexual desire disorder (HSDD) in nondepressed women. *Journal of Sex & Marital Therapy, 27,* 303–316.

Segraves, R. T., Clayton, A., Croft, H., Wolf, A., & Warnock, J. (2004). Bupropion sustained release for the treatment of hypoactive sexual desire disorder in premenopausal women. *Journal of Clinical Psychopharmacology, 24*(3), 339–342.

Sills, T., Wunderlich, G., Pyke, R., Segraves, R. T., Leiblum, S., Clayton, A., et al. (2005). The sexual interest and desire inventory-female (SIDI-F): Item response analyses of data from women diagnosed with hypoactive sexual desire disorder. *The Journal of Sexual Medicine, 2,* 801–818.

Trudel, G., Ravart, M., & Matte, B. (1993). The use of the mutliaxial diagnostic system for sexual dysfunctions in the assessment of hypoactive sexual desire. *Journal of Sex & Marital Therapy, 19,* 123–130.

Ullery, E. K., Millner V. S., & Willingham, H. A. (2002). The emergent care and treatment of women with hypoactive sexual desire disorder. *Family Journal: Counseling and Therapy for Couples and Families, 10*(3), 346–350.

Weeks, G. (1994). The intersystem model: An integrative approach to treatment. In G. Weeks & L. Hof (Eds.), *The marital-relationship casebook: Theory and application of the intersystem model* (pp. 3–34). New York: Brunner/Mazel.

Weeks, G. (2004). The emergence of a new paradigm in sex therapy: Integration. *Sexual and Relationship Therapy, 20*(1), 89–103.

Weeks, G. & Gambescia, N. (2000). *Erectile dysfunction: Integrating couple therapy, sex therapy, and medical treatment.* New York: W. W. Norton.

Weeks, G. & Gambescia, N. (2002). *Hypoactive sexual desire: Integrating sex and couple therapy.* New York: W. W. Norton.

Weeks, G. & Gambescia, N. (2003). *Treating infidelity: Therapeutic dilemmas and effective strategies.* New York: W. W. Norton.

Weeks, G. R. & Hof, L. (Eds.). (1987). *Integrating sex and marital therapy: A clinical guide.* New York: Brunner/Mazel.

Weeks, G. & Hof, L. (Eds.). (1994). *The marital-relationship therapy casebook.* New York: Brunner/Mazel.

Weeks, G. & L'Abate, L. (1982). *Paradoxical psychotherapy: Theory and practice with individuals, couples, and families.* New York: Brunner/Mazel.

Weeks, G. & Treat, S. (2001). *Couples in treatment: Techniques and approaches for effective practice* (rev. ed.). New York: Brunner/Mazel.

Wiegel, M., Meston, C., & Rosen, R. (2005). The female sexual function index (FSFI): Cross-validation and development of clinical cutoff scores. *Journal of Sex & Marital Therapy, 31,* 1–20.

Zilbergeld, B. (1992). *The new male sexuality.* New York: Bantam.

6

The Treatment of Erectile Dysfunction

Nancy Gambescia
Shelley K. Sendak
Gerald R. Weeks

Contents

Introduction

Erectile dysfunction (ED) is a common age-related sexual disorder affecting up to 30 million men in the United States (Saigal, Wessells, Pace, Schonlau, & Wilt, 2006). It is related to a variety of organic risk factors and thus can be a harbinger of cardiovascular disease in some men (Thompson et al., 2006). Additionally, ED is comorbid with psychogenic factors such as anxiety and relational conflict. Regardless of the etiology, ED adversely affects a man's self-esteem, his quality of life, his partner's enjoyment of sexual intimacy, and the overall interpersonal relationship (Chevret, Jaudinot, Sulllivan, Marrel, & Solesse de Gendre, 2004). The intersystems method, discussed throughout this text, is a comprehensive, intimacy-based, and integrative approach to assessing and treating ED. It addresses the biopsychosocial issues of each partner, relational dynamics, environmental factors, and intergenerational etiologies. The desired outcome of the intersystemic approach is the restoration of sexual satisfaction for the couple, not just erectile capacity.

Medical treatments for ED, specifically the oral agents, have become increasingly available and popular in recent years, yet focusing exclusively on medications is not a panacea. Defining and treating ED solely as a medical issue can circumvent or overlook underlying psychological and relational contributors. Too often, when couples use medications to promote erections, they are surprised and disappointed by the recognition of preexisting relational or sexual dysfunctions in the man or his partner (Weeks & Gambescia, 2000). The therapist must consider all factors that affect the man, his partner, and their intimate relationship to optimize physical intimacy.

Description

The *Diagnostic and Statistical Manual of Mental Disorders,* 4th ed., text revision (*DSM-IV-TR*) classifies male erectile disorder as the "persistent or recurrent inability to attain, or maintain, until completion of sexual activity, an adequate erection" (APA, 2000, p. 545). Moreover, to meet the criteria for this diagnosis, the disturbance must cause "marked distress or interpersonal difficulty" (ibid.). The diagnosis is unwarranted if another Axis I disorder better accounts for the dysfunction or if the dysfunction is a direct effect of a medication, a medical condition, or substance abuse. The classification is further clarified by qualifying erectile disorders according to duration, context, and severity.

In terms of duration, ED can be lifelong (primary) or acquired (secondary). Lifelong ED is an extremely rare presentation in which the man has always had ED. Acquired ED, which occurs in men who have previously had satisfactory erections, is more common. The onset of acquired ED can be gradual or sudden, but in either case men develop persistent difficulty in obtaining or maintaining an erection until the completion of sexual activity.

Another category, generalized or situational, clarifies the context of the ED. Generalized ED is a rarely reported variety that occurs in all situations, partnered or alone. Situational ED is more common and is usually psychogenic in etiology; in such cases, ED occurs only with certain partners or at certain times. Situational ED can present in various ways; sometimes erections are satisfactory during masturbation but not while engaging in partnered sexual activity. Other examples involve erectile difficulty with particular partners, under specific circumstances, and occasionally while alone.

ED presents with varying degrees of severity, ranging from mild to complete. In mild ED, erectile failure is infrequent or minimal but still distressing to the man and his partner. Even extremely mild erectile incapacity can produce performance anxiety that can precipitate more frequent and problematic ED. Moderate ED typically falls into one of two patterns: (1) the man can obtain only a partial erection; or (2) his erection fails before the completion of sexual activity. As with mild ED, moderate ED can provoke a great deal of performance anxiety, which may further disrupt erectile ability. In complete ED, the penis lacks sufficient tumescence for sustained, successful penetration, noncoital sexual activity, or satisfying solo sex.

Etiology

ED may have psychological, organic, or combined etiologies; however, the *DSM-IV-TR* (APA, 2000) recognizes only those cases of ED stemming from psychological factors or when medical conditions contribute to, but do not fully account for, the dysfunction.

Organic Etiology

Vascular, Hormonal, and Neurological Conditions
Organic etiologic factors can arise from the vascular, hormonal, and neurological systems (Porst, 2001; Stief, 2002), although vascular conditions are by far the most common, comprising nearly 70% of organic etiologies (Ghanem & Porst, 2006). Vascular problems interfere with circulation of blood to the penis. Neurological factors, such as stroke, Alzheimer's disease, spinal cord and pelvic injury, and Parkinson's disease impair the central nervous system processes needed to commence erection. There is either failure to initiate a nerve impulse or interrupted neural transmission (Porst & Sharlip, 2006). Hormonal factors, mainly hypogonadism (a condition in which the testes do not produce sufficient testosterone) or hyperprolactinemia (a rare condition involving the pituitary gland), may result in both a loss of libido and inadequate nitric oxide release needed for penile tumescence (Stief, 2002).

Other Medical Conditions
Other medical conditions that have been associated with organic ED include diabetes, prostate cancer and its treatment, Peyronie's disease (curvature of the penile shaft), thyroid problems, lung disease, brain trauma, and epilepsy (Gambescia & Weeks, 2006b). Medications that adversely affect the ability to obtain or maintain an erection include the classes of antihypertensives, hormonal agents, anticonvulsants, and antidepressants, especially selective serotonin reuptake inhibitors (SSRIs). For a full discussion of iatrogenic ED, see Chapter 14 on sexual pharmacology in this volume.

Modifiable Physical Risk Factors
Modifiable physical risk factors are also linked to ED. Smoking can damage the blood vessels needed for maintaining an erection (Bacon et al., 2003; Sullivan, Keoghane, & Miller, 2002). A diet high in cholesterol can harden, narrow, or block the arteries leading to the penis, resulting in ED (Bacon et al., 2003; Feldman, Goldstein, Hatzichristou, Krane, & McKinlay, 1994). Inactivity increases the risk of heart disease, circulatory problems, and ED (Derby et al., 2000). Recreational drugs and excessive alcohol use often decrease sexual performance (Bacon et al., 2003). Obesity is associated with increased risk of ED (Bacon et al., 2003; Saigal, 2004).

Since ED is often a sentinel symptom of medical conditions such as atherosclerosis, diabetes, and hypertension (Ghanem & Porst, 2006) it is important for therapists to assess for underlying medical and modifiable lifestyle conditions that can predispose the man to ED and to request an evaluation by a physician when necessary.

Psychogenic Etiology

A large number of ED cases have either a predominately psychological or mixed psychogenic and organic etiologies (Lewis, Rosen, & Goldstein, 2003; Peterson & Fuerst, 2007). The intersystemic model provides three categories for identifying the psychological etiology of ED:

1. Current personality and mental health factors, including performance anxiety and mental illness
2. Interpersonal factors between the partners
3. Intergenerational conditions, developmental vulnerabilities, and socio-economic factors

Individual Factors
The individual's psychological issues and personality factors may negatively impact erectile functioning. Mental illnesses, such as schizophrenia and bipolar disorder, can make it difficult to sustain feelings of sexual desire and to focus behavior sufficiently to achieve satisfactory erections. However, it is more frequently the case that depression, anger, low self-esteem, poor body image, and adherence to rigid gender ideals impair erectile capacity. Although much more research needs to be conducted on how psychological factors contribute to ED, evidence exists for a bidirectional causal relationship between ED and anxiety, negative affect, and

depression (Fisher, Rosen, Mellon, et al., 2005). This recent research supports our clinical observations that negative cognitions and performance anxiety are major contributors to, as well as consequences of, ED.

Performance anxiety is the anxiety a man experiences when he perceives that he is not getting an erection fast enough, that the erection is not firm enough, or that it does not seem to last long enough. Once a man experiences even a single case of ED, a vicious cycle may become established whereby anxiety about a repeated episode of unsatisfactory erections is experienced whenever the man commences or even thinks about sexual activity. He anticipates erectile problems, fixating on performance rather than the pleasurable aspects of sexual arousal. In such instances, an individual's ability to relax is hampered, increasing the amount of negative self-talk and skewing perceptions of self-worth and partner attributes (Dean et al., 2006).

Relational Factors
In general, a lack of sexual attraction and satisfaction can contribute to ED. Thus, those elements that lower satisfaction, such as incompatible sexual belief systems or a sexually dysfunctional partner, may contribute to the development or maintenance of ED. Relationship issues such as communication problems, power struggles, ineffective problem solving or unmet intimacy needs can contribute to the progression of ED and can interfere with seeking treatment (Althof, 2002). Also, ED may occur in response to conscious or unrecognized fears of intimacy, dependency, rejection, or being controlled (Weeks & Gambescia, 2000). In a relational dynamic, ED can be a contributor to and consequence of infidelity, a lack of partner trust, and changes in perception of partner's physical attractiveness.

Intergenerational Factors
Negative or traumatic sexual socialization can contribute to the development of negative sexual self-schemas, thereby increasing the likelihood of ED. More frequently, men may have learned from their families of origin and early socialization to understand and experience sexuality in ways that negatively impact personal perceptions and their sense of sexual adequacy. For example, familial and social messages connecting masculinity to physical perfection can exacerbate body image concerns, fears of aging, and feelings of inadequacy. These feelings then increase apprehension about physical desirability, which then increases performance anxiety (McCabe, 2005).

Sociointergenerational factors such as socioeconomic class and life cycle changes have been linked to ED; Laumann, Paik, and Rosen (1999) noted a strong correlation between low economic standing and men's sexual dysfunction. It may be that poverty is a threat to the masculine role of economic provider, with perceptions of lessened masculinity impinging upon perceptions of sexual adequacy. Family life cycle changes such as fertility problems, having a baby, retirement, children leaving home, and improvements in partner's earnings can also place sufficient stress on the relationship and the individual, contributing to erectile problems.

Mixed Etiology

Emphasis on mixed etiology has grown as many recognize a false dichotomy between psychogenic and organic causes (Wincze & Carey, 2001). ED as a result of medications and other substances may impact the man, his partner, and their relationship just as negatively as dysfunctions that meet diagnostic criteria stipulated in the *DSM-IV-TR* (APA, 2000). Additionally, even in clearly organic ED cases, secondary psychogenic problems frequently develop, including performance anxiety, avoidance of intimacy, or relational disengagement. Treating only the organic problem will leave the performance anxiety or relational disengagement unattended, resulting in continued couple distress and "solutions" that only worsen the couple's well-being.

Although etiology is important for understanding the range of treatment options, therapists may want to focus on the level of distress and interpersonal difficulty caused by the ED when developing an intersystemic treatment plan. There is growing evidence that ED is a dysfunction that presents along with or serves to mask other sexual dysfunctions in the man and in his partner (Althof, 2002; Fisher, Rosen, Eardley, Sand, & Goldstein, 2005; Weeks & Gambescia, 2000, 2002). Relational comorbidity is evidenced in situations where ED may be a response to a partner's sexual difficulties or to conflict within the partnership (Althof, 2002).

Intersystemic Assessment

Assessment in the intersystemic approach focuses on both the individual and relational aspects of ED. A thorough intake should begin with review of each partner's medical, psychosocial, and sexual histories, followed by an assessment of the couple's relationship status and current sexual dynamics.

The goals of this assessment strategy are to establish etiology and, moreover, to generate a shared understanding of the meaning of the ED, its impact on the man and his relationship, and appropriate treatment options.

Individual Assessment

Medical History

As stated previously, a recent thorough medical history is important in assessing etiology, determining risk factors, and developing a treatment plan. The therapist must discern those organic conditions that are known risk factors for ED or may adversely impact treatment (discussed previously). All prescribed or recreational medications taken, the dose, and duration should be noted. If necessary, the man should be referred for a physical examination by an internist to determine the general state of health or illness. Sometimes it is necessary to refer to a urologist, who might conduct a number of blood studies and other tests to determine the cause and extent of the man's ED. Current medical consensus suggests using specialized tests only in a stepwise fashion, after a general history, a focused physical examination, and routine blood screening (Padma-Nathan, 2006).

Psychosocial History

The intersystemic model incorporates a psychological assessment of cognitions, behaviors, and affect at the individual, relational, and intergenerational levels. It is important to investigate the aforementioned individual psychological risk factors and to assess levels of sexual awareness and performance anxiety. Often, men may be inclined to dismiss psychological explanations for their ED or to attribute their ED to temporary situations or life stressors (Perelman, Shabsigh, Seftel, Althof, & Lockhart, 2005). With popular culture's conflation of erection and masculinity, attempts to connect ED to emotional or mental states may be construed as attempts at emasculation. Here, joining with the client is imperative in the successful completion of a psychosocial history.

When assessing cognition, the overall theme is to look for evidence of unrealistic sexual expectations, cognitive distortions, and lack of sexual knowledge. What are the man's thoughts regarding sexuality, relationships, and masculinity? How does the man understand his current sexual situation? In addition to body image and aging concerns, there may be anxiety about the size and function of the penis and general physical attractiveness.

Behavioral and emotional assessment should focus on anxiety and styles of stress management in the context of his social environment. How does the man express or display emotions? How does he translate internal states into behaviors? How does he display self-esteem? It is important to investigate the man's degree of emotional or physical stress. About what does the man worry? How does anxiety manifest (e.g., insomnia, anger)? What does the man do for stress reduction (e.g., positive recreation, such as meditation and exercise or maladaptive overeating or use of drugs or alcohol)? Answers to these questions must be considered in the larger context of the man's life, including life stage and cultural injunctions or social prescriptions for masculine behavior. The therapist must inquire about socialization patterns and current relationships with friends, family, and authority figures. Is the man experiencing any significant life cycle changes? Have there been any changes in his or his partner's employment or finances, home environment, legal issues, or household composition? How has the man experienced and responded to these?

Intergenerational History

Family-of-origin messages may provide important information about both the course of the ED, its relational dynamics, and expectations for treatment. It is important to note how the intergenerational messages influence cognitions, behaviors, and emotional states. Asking how affection was expressed in the family of origin, the degree of physical contact permitted among family members, and the meanings of physical expression within the family will ensure greater therapist understanding of the ED from an intersystemic perspective.

Many mid-life and older men may have learned from their families of origin and socioreligious upbringing not to discuss sexual matters and that being a man means silencing their feelings and fears. Sexual scripts may have developed that put older men in a double bind when admitting to a sexual dysfunction: They may fear being seen as "dirty old men" if they admit to being sexual, and they may fear being seen as "less of a man" if they admit they are not able to obtain or sustain an erection.

Sexual History

It is important to evaluate the level of sexual functioning, past and current levels of sexual activity and satisfaction, and any history of abuse or trauma. Queries about sexual functioning may be the easiest way to commence, as they are the most matter of fact. It will also be of importance to discuss the degree of distress experienced by the man or his partner.

Discuss the man's perceptions of what may be causing the ED and the details of the problem:

- How long has he had problems with erections?
- Was the onset of problems sudden or gradual?
- Does he have erections in the morning or during sleep?
- Does he have erectile difficulties more often when alone or with a partner?
- Can he obtain and maintain an erection with sufficient sexual stimulation? When?
- If he attempts penetration, how often is he successful?
- During penetration, how difficult is it to maintain the erection to completion?

Also, it is helpful to ask about what measures the couple has taken to correct the situation on their own.

With any sex history, it is important not to privilege sexual intercourse as the hallmark of successful sexual experiences or to assume a specific gender of the partner. Married or other heterosexual-identified men may seek treatment for ED that occurs only with a male partner or during certain acts, such as fellatio or anal penetration, which would be missed if an exclusive focus on coitus were maintained by the therapist.

Relational Assessment

It is not useful to consider an individual's erectile difficulties without considering the context of the intimate relationship in which sexual activity takes place (Dean et al., 2006; Weeks & Treat, 2001). The therapist should be observant about the overall relationship dynamics, as each partnership is a unique, interlocking system with its own rules and regulating mechanisms. One partner's behavior influences the other; a difficulty in one affects the other. Initial relational questions should include those about length of relationship, offspring, and relevant extended family members, which will help place the couple in their family context.

The therapist should also assess the couple's degree of cohesion, empathy, and commitment and level of autonomy. What are the man's and his partner's level of sexual satisfaction and activity? How is sexual activity negotiated? What are the couple's current, previous, and optimal levels of sexual functioning? In examining communication styles, the patterns of interaction and how conflict is resolved should be noted. Are any nonsexual dyadic issues magnified or obstructed by the sexual problems? What is shared in terms of emotional intimacy? Are there worries about lack of desirability within either partner? Are there deeper feelings of inferiority predating the relationship that are triggered by the ED? Importantly, ask what other problems might surface if the ED were to disappear suddenly or as if by magic.

In examining the relational components, it is important to remember that many mid-life and older women may have received the messages that they should not want or enjoy sex, so admitting dissatisfaction may be problematic. Note if there is a history of sexual abuse or relational problems in the partner. At a minimum, questions should address the adequacy of sexual stimulation and level of satisfaction for the man and his partner, with a focus on the typical patterns of initiation of sexual activity and how sexual desire is shared. The therapist should assess for other interpersonal aspects of lovemaking, such as skill deficits and sexual myths from early sexual development, which can be later addressed through conjoint psychoeducation.

Typically, there is a great deal of anxiety from both partners during the sexual assessment process. The man with the ED may be anxious about his performance, whereas his partner may assume the blame for the ED. Such a dynamic will certainly complicate the couple's formulation of and reaction to the ED. The therapist should work toward de-escalation and recommend a period of individual sessions until the tension is resolved. Additionally, assessment of couple dynamics may involve secrets that will not be revealed in the presence of a partner. Utilizing individual sessions allows an opportunity for disclosure of any secrets or concerns that the partners cannot express in the presence of the other. In the case of secrets, such as infidelity, treatment of the ED must be delayed temporarily. The goal then becomes to work with the couple to gain treatment readiness.

The therapist must be mindful of the negative effects of pessimism. The couple have struggled together, have attempted to treat the problem on their own, and may feel skeptical about correcting the situation. The therapist must acknowledge the impact the ED has had on each partner and the relationship, must applaud the couple's efforts, and must note the progress they have already made. Not only is this validating and reinforcing of treatment seeking, but the couple's responses to the therapist's praise may also indicate further the relational issues that underlie or are currently being unaddressed through the focus on the ED.

Treatment

Couples are often motivated to seek treatment for ED because they fear that the relationship may be suffering or that the man's partner is not satisfied (Weeks & Meana, 2006). The intersystemic treatment of ED, therefore, involves clarification of the meaning of the dysfunction for the couple, expansion of sexual pleasure beyond coitus, and promoting or restoring erectile capacity. For many couples, the primary treatment goal entails preparing the couple for a return to sexual activity after a period of abstinence (Fagan, 2004). In such instances, the couple must be given the opportunity to process thoughts about past sexual experiences as well as apprehension about their future. Realistically however, sex therapy today for ED often requires dealing with the effects and effectiveness of medical treatments in addition to psychotherapeutic interventions. When medical options are less effective or undesirable, the therapist helps the couple to expand their definition of sex and intimacy and to establish a wider repertoire of sexually pleasurable activity. Most importantly, there is no generic treatment plan for ED because each situation is unique.

Medical Treatments

There are a number of established medical treatments for ED, and the therapist is responsible for understanding their limits and benefits. Additionally, psychotherapists must have a good working relationship with several reputable physicians to make timely referrals and to ensure coordination of care.

Oral Agents

The most common medical treatment for ED is the use of oral agents, namely, the phosphodiesterase type 5 (PDE5) inhibitors. In this class of medications, toxicity, efficacy, and tolerance are roughly similar; however, the duration of action varies among the three (Porst, 2001; Wright, 2006). Sildenafil and vardenafil are effective for up to 4 hours whereas the duration of action for tadalafil is up to 36 hours. Common side effects of the PDE5 inhibitors include the perception of a blue aura and enhanced brightness (especially for sildenafil), headache, flushing, dyspepsia, and rhinitis (Lue et al., 2004). All PDE5 inhibitors are contraindicated if using medicines containing organic nitrates or nitric oxide because the interactive effect can reduce the blood pressure to dangerous levels. PDE5 inhibitors are also contraindicated in persons with retinitis pigmentosa, a recent stroke, myocardial infarction, excessively low or high blood pressure, unstable angina, severe liver impairment, or anyone who is too physically debilitated to have sexual relations (Wright, 2006).

Oral agents may be effective as one aspect of a comprehensive treatment plan, but caveats abound. Most importantly, the couple must understand that PDE5 inhibitors are not aphrodisiacs; erections occur only in the presence of desire for sexual activity. Also, taking a pill for sex may set up unrealistic expectations for the man and his partner about frequency and duration of sexual episodes (Rosen et al., 2006). Another limitation is that in some persons, PDE5 inhibitors lose efficacy with continued use, which may result in discontinuance and pessimism (Rosen, 2007). Sometimes, the use of PDE5 inhibitors as a tool to restore confidence may actually be counterproductive, promoting fears that the man may be unable to perform without the medication (Swindle, Cameron, Lockhart, & Rosen, 2004).

Penile Suppositories and Injections
The intraurethral suppository contains a vasoactive medication that is directly inserted into the penile urethra via an applicator, promoting erection. The efficacy of this method is weak. With the intracavernous injection, a vasoactive liquid medication or combination of vasodilators is injected into the corpus cavernosum of the penis, promoting erection. Each method is considered generally safe if used properly. Nonetheless, use is tempered by problems with administration, a need for extensive patient and partner education, and side effects that can include prolonged erections (priapism) and fibrosis of the cavernous tissue (Hatzimouratidis & Hatzichristou, 2004; Porst & Adaikan, 2006).

Devices and Prosthesis
A vacuum constriction device (VCD) provides a noninvasive medical option for the treatment of ED with proven efficacy and safety. The VCD is an acrylic cylinder used with a vacuum pump. This device promotes erection through creation of a vacuum; a hand- or battery-operated pump draws air from a cylinder into which the penis has been inserted. Reduced air pressure within the cylinder allows increased blood flow to the penis, causing an erection. Blood is trapped through the use of the tourniquet applied around the base of the penis that is removed after sexual relations (Gambescia & Weeks, 2006b). Preference for this mode is limited because

of the inconvenience of using such a device during sexual intimacy (Peterson & Fuerst, 2007).

As a last option, a variety of penile prostheses are available to those who do not respond to other medical treatments. Prostheses involve invasive and irreversible surgery that may result in scarring or infection and frequently do not meet partner or client expectations (Lewis et al., 2003).

Addressing Modifiable Risk Factors

Therapists today must also address the physiological and behavioral aspects of ED through modification of the identifiable risk factors discussed earlier. Basic psychoeducation is useful in explaining the relationship between modifiable risk factors and disease processes, specifically when encouraging the reduction of smoking and alcohol consumption and establishing healthful exercise and eating patterns. The therapist must help the man and his partner establish and work toward goals that promote physical health and sexual functioning (McCarthy & Fucito, 2005; Moyad et al., 2004; Weeks & Gambescia, 2000).

Relational Psychotherapy

Restructure Cognitions

Increasingly, ED treatment methods involve cognitive restructuring, specifically setting realistic and positive expectations for sexual function and frequency, reeducating the couple that enjoyable sex does not necessarily involve intercourse, and promoting full-body, reciprocal pleasure (McCarthy & Fucito, 2005; Rosen, 2007). At its best, treatment for ED will result in enhanced sexual satisfaction and relationship well-being, regardless of erectile capacity (Tiefer, 2006).

The therapist also utilizes other cognitive techniques to identify negative, inaccurate, or self-defeating thoughts and to help the couple recognize how these thoughts can influence feelings and behaviors. The therapist coaches partners to stop negative cognitions and to substitute positive, reality-based thoughts. These processes require a great deal of monitoring and reinforcement throughout the duration of treatment.

Additionally, it is critical to validate the distress the couple are experiencing and to empathize with the toll the ED has taken on the man, his partner, and the relationship. It is important to convey to the couple that while biological factors may cause or contribute to ED, the matter is not simply physical. The couple must be helped to understand that an erect penis is not the hallmark of physical, mental, or sexual health or masculinity.

Enhance Communication Skills
The imprecision of sexual colloquialisms and euphemisms can lead to confusion, miscommunication, and discord. Couples can become frustrated and apprehensive when they experience difficulty in discussing sexual matters. The therapist normalizes ubiquitous problems in discussing sexual issues and encourages clear and precise communication by clarifying terms the couple may use. Accurate, matter-of-fact language will improve communication in the therapist–couple relationship, will provide a model for the couple to emulate, and will promote the couple's comfort when discussing sexual issues outside of treatment.

With specific relevance to ED, many factors can potentially interfere with communication. Some of these include embarrassment, fear of making the ED worse, the ability to deny a problem due to the intermittent nature of mild or moderate ED, and the belief that a physician should be consulted first (Fisher, Rosen, Eardley, et al., 2005). The couple must be commended that they have taken an important step through their willingness to discuss sexual concerns during therapy sessions and that continued discussions on their own can help to address and resolve their sexual problems.

Correct Misattributions
Even when partners agree on the meaning of certain terms and have become comfortable discussing ED, they may misinterpret each other's communication. Often, men misperceive that their female partners are not emotionally supportive enough about the ED; this attribution inaccuracy can cause the woman to feel misunderstood and emotionally disconnected from her partner (Weeks & Meana, 2006). Additionally, Fisher, Rosen, Mellen, et al. (2005) noted that men may construe genuine support from their partners as humiliating and as evidence that they have a profound problem. Further, many men minimize episodes of ED; their partners can misinterpret this minimization as the men being disinterested in the sexual relationship. Female partners are likely to believe that his ED is due to sexual boredom, relationship problems, and his lack of sexual attraction to her; such misattributions can be extremely upsetting to both partners. Further, they may be inaccurate as a female partner's sexual attractiveness is typically not high on a man's list of attributions for ED (Fisher, Meryn, Sand, Brandenburg, Buvat, & Mendive, 2005; Fisher, Meryn, Sand, Brandenburg, Buvat, Mendive, et al., 2005). The therapist's

role is to correct such misattributions, noting that motivations and intentions are frequently misunderstood, especially in sexual matters.

Promote Systemic Thinking

The therapist must reframe ED as the couple's problem, with significant impact to both partners and to the relationship, regardless of the originating cause (Weeks & Gambescia, 2000). This strategy will help to provide an intersystemic framework from which to view and treat the ED. The therapist should engage the couple in discussions about their understanding of sexual satisfaction and relational well-being, how they define and negotiate intimacy, and the meaning of the ED to their present relationship. These strategies will allow more opportunities to see how the ED may stem from relational causes not previously considered. In addition, the couple will learn that sexual problems sometimes arise as a way to avoid other relational problems. The therapist should explain how relational issues become linked with ED and can impact a couple's relationship in a variety of ways. Then the couple will be encouraged to entertain connections between the ED and other relationship problems they may not have considered when they first entered treatment.

Additionally, the couple must be helped to comprehend the role of the partner in the development and maintenance of the ED. Specifically, the therapist should discuss with the couple that sometimes preexisting sexual problems or those in response to the ED, such as the lack of sexual desire, may surface during treatment. The couple is helped to discuss how they felt about their sexual relationship prior to and during the emergence of ED, the concerns that they may currently have, and other expectations. Our clinical observations are supported by research findings that, despite seeking treatment to improve sexual functioning, 23% of men who discontinued PDE5 inhibitor therapy reported that partners expressed no interest in sex (Klotz, Mathers, & Sommer, 2005).

Foster Realistic Expectations

Once an intersystemic understanding of ED is developed, establishing realistic treatment goals and expectations ensures better outcomes and prevents relapse. Realistic expectations are vital, especially since in the era of medical remedies even short-term sex therapy may seem too long. Men with ED usually have been dealing with the problem unsuccessfully for a considerable amount of time. Frequently, the couple has avoided physical intimacy for months or years. They may have tried to remedy the difficulty on their own, hoped that it would go away, and found that the more they tried the more they failed. The man and his partner often share feelings of pessimism and a sense of urgency to correct the situation. The therapist must instill optimism and utilize techniques that result in measurable and steady progress (Weeks & Gambescia, 2000).

One way to promote realistic expectations is to help the couple recall when they believed they were at their sexual best. Here, the detailed sexual history taken in the assessment phase can help to bring to mind past satisfying sexual episodes, incorporating as much sensory details as possible. Then, the therapist can lead them to construct realistic expectations of sexual enjoyment given their preferences, ages, and physical ability. This process is interactive and ongoing with the therapist offering accurate information and data about normative sexuality.

Correct Sexual Myths

Commonly, we find that couples are uninformed about normative sexual functioning, sexuality and aging, and sexual anatomy. Often they fail to challenge intergenerational misconceptions and mythology. Sexual ignorance fuels ambivalence, fears about intimacy, and problems in communication. Breaking the cycle necessitates exploring and dispelling sexual myths and providing accurate information. We have had success when assigning selected bibliotherapy such as the first half of Zilbergeld's (1992) *New Male Sexuality* or discussing recently published data regarding sexuality (see, e.g., Lindau et al., 2007). Information of this nature provides accurate data and challenges inaccuracies such as the equation of erection with self-worth (Althof & Weider, 2004). The therapist is responsible for reading and reviewing the assigned material with the couple and for exploring their reactions and ideas in subsequent sessions (see Gambescia & Weeks, 2006b). To be effective, cognitive and educational interventions need to respect the couple's religious or moral sensibilities, life stage, physical abilities, and cultural beliefs.

Reduce Performance Anxiety

Treatment of performance anxiety may focus on cognitive restructuring, biofeedback, relaxation techniques, and development of a wider repertoire of sexual activities beyond intercourse. We recommend a relational context in which the partners can help to identify and correct anxiety provoking thought processes, such as all-or-nothing thinking. Moreover, the couple, rather than the man alone, can best redefine sexual activity. Overall, the therapist prescribes and promotes conditions that focus on relaxing, enjoying pleasurable sensations, and eliminating anxiety. Given typical relationship dynamics, this will involve encouraging the man's partner to relax as well.

Behavioral Assignments

Sensate focus is a key technique in the relational treatment of ED. This discussion reviews some of the salient features in the treatment of ED. The reader is encouraged to review Chapter 15 on sensate focus in this volume for a detailed presentation of the principles and procedures.

Sensate focus exercises are progressive, nondemanding physical home-work exercises commonly used as a component of the treatment of ED. The exercises are reciprocal (each partner gives and then receives sensual pleasure) and also incremental (small steps are taken to ensure success). Each step desensitizes the couple to sexual anxiety and, therefore, is built on the successes achieved in the previous attempts. The primary objective of sensate focus is for each partner to become more aware of his or her own physical sensations. This is paramount because typically the couple enters treatment concentrating on sexual performance, not sensuality. For couples struggling with ED, sexuality becomes laden with anxiety; sensate focus helps to reduce the anxiety that ensues when a man and his partner fear the repetition of erectile failure he experienced previously (Weeks & Gambescia, 2000). Additionally, couples with sexual dysfunctions gradu-ally avoid physical and sexual contact over time; thus, sensate focus enables them to reconnect slowly in a mutually satisfying manner.

The therapist describes the nature and purpose of sensate focus home-work, attending to detail, to promote understanding of the assignment and overall compliance. Couples we have treated are grateful for expla-nations about the rationale and pacing of the exercises. The couple must comprehend that numerous homework trials are necessary and that physi-cal intimacy is reintroduced in small, safe, graduated increments. Thus, exercises are crafted to fit the couple rather than trying to fit the couple to the exercises. The therapist provides the general structure and facilitates feedback from the couple about the activities that were successful and what they wish to do next. The feedback from each task serves as the foundation for the next exercise (Gambescia & Weeks, 2006b).

Initially, the couple and therapist decide about the degree of sensual touch that they can tolerate. Any sexual contact, especially intercourse, is prohibited. Proscribing intercourse helps to create a nondemand situation, removes performance pressure, and promotes relaxation.

The partners are reminded to focus on what they are feeling and to stop any thoughts that can interfere with their experience of sensual pleasure.

At each progression in the exercises, the therapist reminds the couple to ask each other consistently if the action is pleasurable. This will allow each to concentrate on pleasure and not performance, to become attuned to the sensations in the partner, and to constantly generate feedback that prevents performance anxiety.

When the couple is ready, sensate focus exercises gradually progress to full-body nongenital massage. Gradually, the scope of the sensate focus exercises expands, allowing the partners to experience genital sensations in an anxiety-free environment. Each partner is advised to let the genital sensations build to whatever level is desirable, including—but not necessarily—having an orgasm.

The physical homework gradually evolves to include intercourse, if desired. The act of coitus, like the other forms of sensual touch, must also be nondemanding. Nondemand intercourse does not require any particular type of performance; thus, if a partner desires intercourse without orgasm, it is acceptable (Weeks & Gambescia, 2000). The therapist must recognize that transitioning to intercourse may be difficult because of unrealistic expectations associated with it. If intercourse is not desired, the couple can enjoy noncoital pleasuring. If the couple decides to have intercourse, they should be instructed to focus on the pleasurable sensations and thoughts. The therapist should normalize that levels of desire may vary and do not have to be synchronous.

Stop–start technique is another behavioral homework prescription in the treatment of ED. The therapist instructs the man to stimulate himself or have his partner stimulate him until he can achieve an erection and then let it abate. This technique is performed several times before any further sexual activity. The man learns to control erections by deliberately deciding that he will let the erection go and get it back again. This technique usually helps the man regain lost confidence and a sense of control. When performed as a couple, this homework also ensures that the couple reengage in sexual play, allowing them to establish new patterns of being sexual without pressure on either of them to see the goal as coitus.

Once ED is no longer a problem, the therapist should ensure that co-occurring sexual and relational dysfunctions are addressed. At this point, the therapist can also ask about optimizing the sexual relationship. This might involve exploration of other erotic activities, techniques, and communications that will strengthen the couple's sexual relationship and will prevent relapse or the development of other dysfunctions.

Relapse Prevention
Resistance to treatment and relapse may be signs of other sexual dysfunctions in the couple such as hypoactive sexual desire disorder (HSDD), problems with communication, or relationship conflict (Weeks & Gambescia, 2002). The therapist should anticipate and predict that relapses can occur and are a normative part of treatment. This will help the couple to remain optimistic in the presence of a setback. They can be reminded to use the cognitive-behavioral skills they have acquired previously (McCarthy & Fucito, 2005) while the therapist works to uncover other issues that might be triggering relapse.

Research and Future Directions

Current medical remedies have changed the treatment format for ED. It is expected that medical advances will continue to evolve; on the horizon are therapies to improve function at the cellular or enzymatic levels and tissue engineering that may allow for organ replacement (Hellstrom, 2006). Even as medical advances continue, the need for effective psychotherapy remains (see Melnick & Abdo, 2005, for a review). Currently, the most effective treatments combine medical and psychological therapies (Althof, Rosen, Rubio-Aurioles, Earle, & Chevret-Measson, 2006; Perelman, 2005)—that is, a method remarkably akin to our intersystemic approach. Future psychotherapy should continue to provide clinically viable, empirically tested approaches that address the biological, psychological, interpersonal, and social systems in which men and their partners experience ED. Since increasing sexual and relational satisfaction is the goal of the intersystemic treatment of ED, restoring erectile capacity is a means, not an end. Focusing on anything less than sexual satisfaction in the context of the couples relationship ensures less than optimal outcomes.

For a more detailed discussion of the intersystemic treatment of erectile dysfunction, see Gambescia and Weeks (2006a, 2006b) and Weeks and Gambescia (2000).

References

Althof, S. (2002). When an erection alone is not enough: Biopsychosocial obstacles to lovemaking. *International Journal of Impotence Research, 14*(Suppl. 1), 99–104.

Althof, S., Rosen, R., Rubio-Aurioles, E., Earle, C., & Chevret-Measson, M. (2006). Psychologic and interpersonal aspects and their management. In H. Porst & J. Buvat (Eds.), *Standard practice in sexual medicine* (pp. 18–30). Malden, MA: Blackwell Publishing.

Althof, S. & Wieder, M. (2004). Psychotherapy for erectile dysfunction. *Endocrine, 23*,131–134.

American Psychiatric Association (APA) (2000). *Diagnostic and statistical manual of mental disorders* (4th ed., text revision). Arlington, VA: American Psychiatric Association.

Bacon, C., Mittleman, M., Kawachi, I., Giovannucci, E., Glasser, D., & Rimm, E. (2003). Sexual function in men older than 50 years of age: Results from the Health Professionals Follow-up Study. *Annals of Internal Medicine, 139*(3), 161–168.

Chevret, M., Jaudinot, E., Sullivan, K., Marrel, A., & Solesse de Gendre, A. (2004). Impact of erectile dysfunction (ED) on sexual life of female partners: Assessment with the Index of Sexual Life (ISL) questionnaire. *Journal of Sex & Marital Therapy, 30*, 152–172.

Dean, J., deBoer, B., Graziottin, A., Hatzichristou, D., Heaton, J., & Tailor, A. (2006). Partner satisfaction and successful treatment outcomes for men with erectile dysfunction. *European Urology Supplements, 5*, 779–785.

Derby, C., Mohr, B., Goldstein, I., Feldman, H., Johannes, C., & McKinley, J. (2000). Modifiable risk factors and erectile dysfunction: Can lifestyle changes modify risk? *Urology, 56*(2), 302–306.

Fagan, P. (2004). *Sexual disorders: Perspectives on diagnosis and treatment.* Baltimore, MD: John Hopkins University Press.

Feldman, H., Goldstein, I., Hatzichristou, G., Krane, R. J., & McKinlay, J. (1994). Impotence and its medical and psychosocial correlates: Results of the Massachusetts Male Aging Study. *Journal of Urology, 151*, 54–61.

Fisher, W., Meryn, S., Sand, M., Brandenburg, U., Buvat, J., & Mendive, J. (2005). Communications about erectile dysfunction among men with ED, partners of men with ED, and physicians: The Strike Up a Conversation Study (part I). *Journal of Men's Health and Gender, 2*(1), 64–78.

Fisher, W., Meryn, S., Sand, M., Brandenburg, U., Buvat, J., Mendive, J., et al. (2005). Communications about erectile dysfunction among men with ED, partners of men with ED, and physicians: The Strike Up a Conversation Study (part II). *Journal of Men's Health and Gender, 2*(3), 309.e301–309.e312.

Fisher, W., Rosen, R., Eardley, I., Sand, M., & Goldstein, I. (2005). Sexual experience of female partners of men with erectile dysfunction: The Female Experience of Men's Attitudes to Life Events and Sexuality (FEMALES) study. *Journal of Sexual Medicine, 2*, 675–684.

Fisher, W., Rosen, R., Mellen, M., Brock, G., Karlin, G., Pommerville, P., et al. (2005). Improving the sexual quality of life of couples affected by erectile dysfunction. *Journal of Sexual Medicine, 2*, 699–708.

Gambescia, N. & Weeks, G. (2006a). Erectile dysfunction. In J. Fisher & W. O'Donohue (Eds.), *Practitioner's guide to evidence based psychotherapy* (pp. 284–290). New York: Springer.

Gambescia, N. & Weeks, G. (2006b). Sexual dysfunction. In N. Kazantzis & L. L'Abate (Eds.), *Handbook of homework assignments in psychotherapy: Research, practice, and prevention* (pp. 351–368). Norwell, MA: Kluwer Academic Publishers.

Ghanem, H. & Porst, H. (2006). Etiology and risk factors of erectile dysfunction. In H. Porst & J. Buvat (Eds.), *Standard practice in sexual medicine.* Malden, MA: Blackwell Publishing.

Hatzimouratidis, K. & Hatzichristou, D. (2004). Treatment options for erectile dysfunction in patients failing oral drug therapy. *EAU Update Series, 2,* 75–83.

Hellstrom, W. (2006). Future treatment aspects of erectile dysfunction: Gene therapy and tissue engineering. In H. Porst & J. Buvat (Eds.), *Standard practice in sexual medicine* (pp. 115–120). Malden, MA: Blackwell Publishing.

Klotz, T., Mathers, M., & Sommer, F. (2005). Why do patients with erectile dysfunction abandon effective therapy with sildenafil (Viagra)? *International Journal of Impotence Research, 17,* 2–4.

Laumann, E., Paik, A., & Rosen, R. (1999). Sexual dysfunction in the United States: Prevalence and predictors. *Journal of the American Medical Association, 281,* 537–544.

Lewis, J., Rosen, R., & Goldstein, I. (2003). Erectile dysfunction in primary care. *Nurse Practitioner, 29*(12), 48–57.

Lindau, S., Schumm, P., Laumann, E., Levinson, W., O'Muircheartaigh, C., & Waite, L. (2007). A study of sexuality and health among older adults in the United States. *New England Journal of Medicine, 357,* 762–774.

Lue, T., Giuliano, F., Montorsi, F., Rosen, R., Anderson, K., Althof, S., et al. (2004). Summary of recommendations on sexual dysfunctions in men. *Journal of Sexual Medicine, 1,* 6–23.

McCabe, M. (2005). The role of performance anxiety in the development and maintenance of sexual dysfunction. *International Journal of Stress Management, 12,* 379–388.

McCarthy, B. & Fucito, L. (2005). Integrating medication, realistic expectations and therapeutic interventions in the treatment of male sexual dysfunction. *Journal of Sex & Marital Therapy, 31,* 319–328.

Melnick, T. & Abdo, C. (2005). Psychogenic erectile dysfunction: Comparative study of three therapeutic approaches. *Journal of Sex & Marital Therapy, 31,* 243–255.

Moyad, M., Barada, J., Lue, T., Mulhall, J., Goldstein, I., & Fawzy, A. (2004). Prevention and treatment of erectile dysfunction using lifestyle changes and dietary supplements: What works and what is worthless, part I. *Urology Clinics of North America, 31,* 249–257.

Padma-Nathan, H. (2006). Sildenafil citrate (Viagra) treatment for erectile dysfunction: An updated profile of response and effectiveness. *International Journal of Impotence Research, 18*, 423–431.

Perelman, M. (2005). Psychosocial evaluation and combination treatment of men with erectile dysfunction. *Urologic Clinics of North America, 32*, 431–445.

Perelman, M., Shabsigh, R., Seftel, A., Althof, S., & Lockhart, D. (2005). Attitudes of men with erectile dysfunction: A cross-national survey. *Journal of Sexual Medicine, 2*, 397–406.

Peterson, F. & Fuerst, D. (2007). Assessment and treatment of erectile dysfunction. In L. VanderCreek, F. Peterson, & J. Bley (Eds.), *Innovations in clinical practice: Focus on sexual health.* Sarasota, FL: Professional Resource Press.

Porst, H. (2001, October). *Expanding treatment options for erectile dysfunction.* Paper presented at the 4th Congress of the European Society for Sexual and Impotence Research, Rome, Italy.

Porst, H. & Adaikan, G. (2006). Self-injection, trans-urethral and topical therapy in erectile dysfunction. In H. Porst & J. Buvat (Eds.), *Standard practice in sexual medicine* (pp. 94–108). Malden, MA: Blackwell Publishing.

Porst, H. & Sharlip, I. (2006). History and epidemiology of male sexual dysfunction. In H. Porst & J. Buvat (Eds.), *Standard practice in sexual medicine* (pp. 43–48). Malden, MA: Blackwell Publishing.

Rosen, R. C. (2007). Erectile dysfunction: Integration of medical and psychological approaches. In S. R. Leiblum (Ed.), *Principles and practice of sex therapy* (4th ed., pp. 277–312). New York: Guilford Press.

Rosen, R., Janssen, E., Wiegel, M., Bancroft, J., Althof, S., Wincze, J., et al. (2006). Pscyhological and interpersonal correlates in men with erectile dysfunction and their partners. *Journal of Sex & Marital Therapy, 32*, 215–234.

Saigal, C. S. (2004). Obesity and erectile dysfunction: Common problems, common solution? *Journal of the American Medical Association, 291*, 3011–3012.

Saigal, C., Wessells, H., Pace, J., Schonlau, M., & Wilt, T. (2006). Predictors and prevalence of erectile dysfunction in a racially diverse population. *Archives of Internal Medicine, 16*, 207–212.

Stief, C. (2002). Is there a common pathophysiology for erectile dysfunction and how does this relate to the new pharmacotherapies? *International Journal of Impotence Research, 14*(Suppl. 1), 11–16.

Sullivan, M. E., Keoghane, S. R., & Miller, M. A. (2002). Vascular risk factors and erectile dysfunction. *British Journal of Urology International, 87*(9), 838–845.

Swindle, R., Cameron, A., Lockhart, D., & Rosen, R. (2004). The Psychological & Interpersonal Relationship Scales: Assessing psychological and relationship outcomes associated with erectile dysfunction and its treatment. *Archives of Sexual Behavior, 33*, 19–30.

Thompson, I., Tangen, C., Goodman, P., Probstfield, J., Moinpour, C., & Coltman, C. (2006). Erectile dysfunction and subsequent cardiovascular disease. *Journal of the American Medical Association, 294*(23), 2996–3002.

Tiefer, L. (2006). The Viagra phenomenon. *Sexualities, 9,* 273–294.

Weeks, G. & Gambescia, N. (2000). *Erectile dysfunction: Integrating couple therapy, sex therapy and medical treatment.* New York: W. W. Norton.

Weeks, G. & Gambescia, N. (2002). *Hypoactive sexual desire: Integrating sex and couple therapy.* New York: W. W. Norton.

Weeks, G. & Meana, M. (2006). *Perception of erectile dysfunction and its treatment in affected men and their partners.* Unpublished research findings.

Weeks, G. & Treat, S. (2001). *Couples in treatment* (2nd ed.). Philadelphia, PA: Brunner-Routledge.

Wincze, J. & Carey, M. (2001). *Sexual dysfunction: A guide for assessment and treatment* (2nd ed.). New York: Guilford Press.

Wright, P. (2006). Comparison of phosphodiesterase type 5 (PDE5) inhibitors. *International Journal of Clinical Practice, 60,* 967–975.

Zilbergeld, B. (1992). *The new male sexuality.* New York: Bantam Books.

7

Premature Ejaculation
An Integrative, Intersystems Approach for Couples
Stephen J. Betchen

Contents

PE Defined

Premature ejaculation (PE), sometimes known as rapid ejaculation (RE), is widely believed to be the most common male sexual problem, averaging between 20% and 30% prevalence (Althof, 2007). Studies utilizing data from the Global Study of Sexual Attitudes and Behaviors (GSSAB) also found that about one third of the men surveyed reported PE (Laumann et al., 2005; Montorsi, Sotomayor, & Sharlip, 2005).

Masters and Johnson (1970) diagnosed a man with PE if he could not delay ejaculation long enough for his partner to reach orgasm 50% of the time. Most contemporary sex therapists see this definition as somewhat flawed. Polonsky (2000), for example, pointed out that women on average take longer than men to orgasm. Moreover, he reported that 30% to 40% of women cannot achieve intravaginal orgasms—a challenge to Freud's (1905/1953) coital/transfer theory, which postulated that women who could not achieve coital orgasm were neurotic and immature.

Requiring a man to control himself during the sexual process for what could be an inordinate amount of time might indeed be an unrealistic expectation for both partners. Most sex therapists feel that a more prudent objective would be that a man have enough control over his ejaculatory process to reasonably determine when he wishes to ejaculate and that his partner's needs be taken into consideration. In most cases, this will entail the man learning how to last long enough to please both he and his partner; in others, it may also include meeting the partner's needs prior to intercourse.

While there is no laboratory test for PE, many sexologists have resorted to measuring the number of intravaginal thrusts to define the disorder. Others have employed a stopwatch to measure the intravaginal ejaculatory latency time (IELT), or the time between the start of vaginal penetration and the onset of intravaginal ejaculation (Waldinger, Hengeveld, Zwinderman, & Olivier, 1998). The criteria used most often by clinicians to assess PE (Metz, Pryor, Nesvacil, Abuzzahab, & Koznar, 1997), however, and those used herein are taken from the *Diagnostic and Statistical Manual of Manual Disorders*, 4th ed., text revision (*DSM-IV-TR*) (APA, 2000). It is believed that the *DSM-IV-TR* is an appropriate reference for clinicians, particularly those who work with couples, because "it calls for judgment regarding lack of control of ejaculation and interpersonal difficulties" (Symonds, Roblin, Hart, & Althof, 2003, p. 362). Specifically, the manual states that the "essential feature of Premature Ejaculation is the persistent or recurrent onset of orgasm and ejaculation with minimal sexual stimulation before, on, or shortly after penetration and before a person wishes it" (APA, 2000, p. 552). Further distinctions are made between lifelong (primary) and acquired (secondary) types, generalized and situational types, and due to psychological or combined factors (psychological and medical). The idiosyncratic nature of the sexual partner, age, context, and the frequency of sexual activity are also considered factors.

A formal definition for PE is certainly helpful to the clinician; however, couples present the disorder on a wide continuum. The majority report that the man ejaculates immediately after penetration. Others claim that the man ejaculates during foreplay or just prior to vaginal penetration. Because of this variation, and because it is common for partners to disagree as to the extent of their problem, it is vital for the clinician to obtain the couple's definition of their problem.

Etiology of PE

PE is considered a disorder of the orgasm phase of the male sexual response cycle. Masters and Johnson (1966) found that during the first phase of this cycle, referred to as the sexual arousal or excitement phase, vasoconstriction occurs (i.e., increased blood in the tissues of the genitals) and culminates in an erection (Kaplan, 1979, 1995, later added that a desire stage precedes this phase). A plateau phase follows in which arousal basically intensifies and a peaking of sexual pleasure and a release of sexual tension and rhythmic contraction of the perineal muscles and reproductive organs leads to a sense of "ejaculatory inevitability." The orgasm phase quickly follows and is characterized by a release of semen. A state of resolution completes the cycle. When a male cannot sustain a long-enough period of time engaged on the plateau stage, PE is the result.

Individual Biological/Physiological

The origin of PE can sometimes be attributed to an individual man's unique physiological structure. Waldinger et al. (1998) discovered that a range exists among men in their ejaculatory speed—as if ejaculatory time existed on a continuum. The authors found that some men ejaculated very rapidly, some at an average speed, others slowly, and some not at all. They also discovered that 91% of men with lifelong PE had a first relative with lifelong PE. Neurological studies have indicated that ejaculation is mediated in the brain; neurotransmitters transfer messages from one nerve to another (Waldinger, 2002). Serotonin (i.e., 5-HT) has long been felt to be the primary transmitter regulating ejaculation. There is evidence that lifelong PE is related to decreased central serotonergic neurotransmission, 5-HT_{2C} receptor hyposensitivity, or 5-HT_{1A} hypersensitivity (Waldinger, 2003).

Physical illnesses attributed to PE include arteriosclerosis, diabetes, endocrine irregularities, epilepsy, multiple sclerosis, and other degenerative neurological disorders. Urological problems such as urinary tract infections and prostatitis or prostate infection, which is perhaps the most common cause, have also been found to result in the disorder (Metz & Pryor, 2000; Metz et al., 1997). Temporary or permanent physical injury such as pelvic fractures can also cause PE (Metz & McCarthy, 2003; Metz et al., 1997).

Pharmacologic side effect PE is a distinct form of premature ejaculation that can result from the chronic use of or withdrawal from certain drugs, particularly opioids such as heroin (Barada & McCullough, 2004; Segraves & Balon, 2003). There is, however, some evidence that opioid use can correct a previous premature ejaculation problem (Palha & Esteves, 2002). Certain tranquilizers as well as over-the-counter cold medications such as pseudophedrine, or Sudafed (McNeil-PPC, Inc., New Brunswick, New Jersey) can also cause PE (Metz & McCarthy, 2003). Men who chronically use or abuse alcohol can develop PE upon withdrawal because they may have relied too heavily on the alcohol to delay their ejaculation rather than having learned appropriate behavioral strategies (APA, 2000) (see the case-study section in this chapter).

Individual Psychological

PE can also be caused by individually oriented emotional issues. Anger, frustration, low self-confidence, mistrust, negative body image, and psychosocial stress associated with financial difficulties, occupational problems, and the death of a significant other may be factors (Metz & McCarthy, 2003; Metz & Pryor, 2000). A man in his middle 20s presented with acquired PE. Although he apparently never experienced this problem in previous relationships, he claimed that he lacked confidence that he would be able to please his new, experienced girlfriend whom he saw as "special." He maintained this notion about himself even though his girl-friend did little to warrant his concern. She was gentle and supportive of him, particularly when it came to sex.

Chronic psychological disorders such as bipolar disorder, dysthymic disorder, generalized anxiety disorder, obsessive-compulsive disorder, and posttraumatic stress disorder can produce PE. Temporary psychological difficulties like adjustment disorders with anxiety or depression can result in the disorder as well (Metz & McCarthy, 2003).

Some clients who suffer from other sexual disorders, most notably erectile disorder, can eventually develop PE. Out of fear of losing their erections, these individuals "stuff" their penises inside their partners and try to ejaculate as soon as possible (before they lose their erections). The origin of the erection problem may be physiological or psychological or both.

Masters and Johnson (1970) recognized the role psychosexual skills played in the development of ejaculatory control. The sex researchers wrote that coital encounters in "semiprivate situations under the pressure inherent in dual concern for surprise or observation" (p. 88) encouraged premature ejaculation. They specifically cited sexual encounters in the back seats of cars and the practice of the "withdrawal technique" in which the man withdraws from intercourse before he reaches the stage of ejaculatory inevitability.

Cognitive-behavioral sexologists support behavioral and social learning perspectives. Metz and Pryor (2000), for example, reported that men with psychosexual skill deficit tend to be lacking in dating and interpersonal skills. As a result, they might "experience a lack of awareness of body management techniques, such as the pubococcygeal muscle in ejaculatory management" (p. 302). A high school senior convinced his parents to allow him to seek treatment after an embarrassing experience he had with PE on his first date ever. Apparently, he was so excited that he ejaculated within seconds after his date began kissing him. The date also complained that he kissed like a "fish" and was too rough when feeling her breasts. The young man was so horrified with his performance that he considered never dating again.

Psychoanalytic theory views premature ejaculation as a neurotic symptom representative of a man's unresolved ambivalence toward women (Kaplan, 1974). This ambivalence or conflict is anchored in an unconscious struggle against remaining dependent on his mother; it manifests in a desire to give the woman something of himself that he values (i.e., his semen) but a need to exact revenge (i.e., PE) "for the disappointments of love to which as a child his mother subjected him, and which he finds repeated again in later years" (Abraham, 1917/1949, p. 297).

Couple/Dyadic Factors

Systemic therapists, whether predominantly cognitive-behavioral or psychodynamic, believe that PE can be symptomatic of relationship issues. Power or control struggles, fear of commitment, fear of intimacy, and unrealistic expectations about sexual performance generated by the demands of a partner are thought to be causal factors of PE to which both partners contribute (Betchen, 2001; Metz & McCarthy, 2003).

Poor couple communication can cause sexual problems for a couple according to Gottman (1994). Moreover, it is a good predictor of divorce. Following a passionate, prolonged bout of foreplay, the wife of a man with PE would mount him and have intercourse at a frenzied pace—usually a process that her husband could only withstand for seconds until he ejaculated. The wife, a virgin when she married, believed that this was the way to truly please her husband—she never thought to ask if this assumption was true. Not wanting to hurt his wife's feelings as well as accept the fact that he could not keep up with her, the husband refrained from requesting to either reduce the foreplay period or to pace the intercourse in a more manageable way conducive to pleasing both he and his wife. It was only when the couple began to communicate more effectively that they were able to compromise and alleviate the man's PE.

Sex is a common context for power and control struggles in couples (Betchen, 2001, 2006). This is true in part because partners need to cooperate with one another to create a healthy sex life. When one partner wants something one way and the other a different way, struggles often ensue. For example, a young man and his girlfriend agreed that he lasted through approximately 15 minutes of continuous thrusting, but the girlfriend desired 30 minutes of intercourse at a rapid pace. But, when the young man would slow down to preserve himself his girlfriend would become frustrated and speed the pace up by thrusting into him harder and faster. Although bothered by his girlfriend's behavior, the young man perceived himself as having PE and requested that he get help in learning to last 45 minutes. This dynamic exemplified a power and control struggle as well as unrealistic expectations in the bedroom.

It is nearly impossible to have a fear of intimacy without a fear of commitment. Couples can certainly commit to cohabitate, but if there is an aversion to intimacy they will most likely find a way to distance within the relationship to gain much needed space or to sabotage in an effort to achieve complete freedom. A commitment under such conditions would thus be considered a physical one at best, not necessarily an emotional one. Given the correlation of sex with such powerful relational concepts as attraction, desire, and love, sexual dysfunction can be enlisted—consciously or unconsciously—as a representative of these fears.

A middle-aged man's acquired PE was found to be symptomatic of his unconscious desire to end his long-term marriage—a desire that was too painful for him to admit to himself given the guilt he would experience over putting his three young children through a divorce. Rather than separate, this man attempted to satisfy his immediate sexual needs by ejaculating quickly in his wife without demonstrating any concern for her needs. It was his way of communicating to her that he was no longer committed to the relationship. It was also eventually revealed that the man preferred that his wife end the relationship, thereby sparing him the pain of having to face his children. He eventually achieved his goal.

Family-of-Origin Factors

Sexual disorders, PE included, can be symptomatic of psychological conflicts emanating from the family of origin (Betchen, 2001, 2005). Once these conflicts are internalized they can be passed down from generation to generation and manifest into the same or different symptoms. Bowen (1978) referred to this process as the *multigenerational transmission process*. He postulated that the greater the influence that the family of origin had on the individual, the lower the individual's *differentiation of self* and, hence, the greater the odds of the individual being symptomatic. Bowen recommended the genogram as a tool to assess family-of-origin influences; DeMaria, Weeks, and Hof (1999) contended the genogram could also be used to assess sexual influences (see "Assessment: Constructing the Sexual Genogram" later in this chapter).

A newly married man reported with acquired PE that developed soon after he married. By examining the man's family of origin, it was determined that the PE symptom was a direct result of the severe parentification he had experienced as a child. Once the man married, he began to feel burdened or reparentified by his new responsibilities. He also perceived his new wife as more demanding of him than she was prior to their marriage. The man's PE symptom was a metaphor for his feelings of burden.

He was exhibiting the following message through his disorder: "I want to get my needs met for once, without having to worry about anybody else." This reaction was an artifact of his family of origin.

Sociocultural Factors

Kaplan (1974) wrote that the factors that damage our sexuality are rooted in our families and the association between sex and sin promoted by Judeo-Christian religions. According to Klein (2006), our society now enables a renaissance of the blurring of church and state that has contributed to a backlash against sexual freedom. Mirrored by many families, this development has helped to produce or exacerbate sexual conflict and dysfunction.

It still holds true that growing up in a home with rigid religious values or a strict moral code can produce conflict about satisfying one's sexual urges. Receiving negative messages about sex (e.g., "Sex is dirty") can do the same. Thus, when an attempt is made to quell these urges via masturbation or otherwise, feelings of anxiety, guilt, and shame may be evoked (Betchen, 1991; Kaplan, 1974; Metz & McCarthy, 2003). More than one man with this type of upbringing has presented to me with PE. These men believed it was acceptable to have sex, particularly with their spouses, but not to enjoy the sexual process. As a compromise, they did their manly duty as quickly as possible while numbing themselves to the pleasure of the orgasmic experience.

Even religious groups that encourage sex between spouses can, because of their laws, create sexual skill deficits leading to PE and other sexual disorders. In treating Hassidic Jews, I found the concept of refraining from premarital sex in conjunction with isolating from the popular culture/media to be important factors in their erectile difficulty and their inability to control the ejaculatory reflex. Because of inexperience, some of these men demonstrated little knowledge about the general mechanics of intercourse.

Ethnic and cultural influences can be factors in determining PE. According to Montorsi et al. (2005), men of southeast Asia who follow the Kama Sutra and Latin American men who are more accepting of female sexuality may be more concerned with female orgasm and thus more likely to report a problem with PE. Conversely, men in countries who do not concern themselves as much with pleasing women may be more prone to develop PE but not necessarily to define it as a problem. This supports the belief that clinicians need to consider cultural differences and should always ask clients what their definition of the problem is.

A Systemic Treatment Model for Couples with PE

The model offered is primarily for those clinicians who work with couples and believe that sexual disorders are often intricately linked to the nonsexual dynamics or symptoms in a relationship. A systemic model can be used with couples who present with a wide variety of symptoms, and it has been found to be particularly effective with those who suffer from sexual disorders such as PE (Betchen, 2001, 2005), erectile disorders (Weeks & Gambescia, 2000), and hypoactive sexual desire (Weeks & Gambescia, 2002).

The proposed model combines aspects of psychoanalytic conflict theory (Freud, 1910/1957) and psychodynamic family-of-origin work (Bowen, 1978) with basic sex therapy principles and exercises (Kaplan, 1974, 1989). Medical needs are addressed as well. The specific psychotherapeutic objective is for each partner to work toward uncovering and resolving any unconscious conflicts that are rooted in the family of origin. These conflicts can be responsible for many deleterious dynamics or symptoms (sexual and nonsexual) presented.

Kaplan (1974) was less than optimistic about the prognosis of a sexual symptom treated primarily via psychoanalytic and psychodynamic therapies. She therefore advocated for the use of psychodynamic interventions if and when behavioral interventions/sexual exercises were first met with overwhelming resistance. In the model presented, behavioral exercises are employed; however, the application of any exercise is left to the discretion of the clinician. Exercises may be assigned simultaneously with the psychodynamic work, and other times the psychodynamic work is at the forefront of the treatment. A medical evaluation is mandatory.

The Therapeutic Process

Structuring the Treatment
The clinician must control the structure of the treatment process, or the couple will endlessly play out in the session the dynamics that they play at home (Weeks, Odell, & Methven, 2005). Because this is a conjoint model, both partners are urged to attend the first session. This allows the clinician to quickly evaluate each partner as an individual and in the context of the interaction between the partners. Berman (1982) contended that seeing both partners together serves to balance the treatment, helps to ensure that the therapist is viewed as neutral, and increases the chance that the

couple will envision their problem as systemic rather than the sole responsibility of one partner.

Following the first session, each partner is seen individually for the
next two consecutive sessions. Other individual sessions are added at the
discretion of the clinician. Individual sessions may be useful in conjoint
treatment to resolve certain therapeutic blocks. These may occur when
the clinician feels that vital information is being withheld (e.g., an affair)
or when a sexual history or sexual disorder proves too embarrassing to
discuss in conjoint mode, when countertransference issues must be processed, or when internalized conflicts result in an especially rigid relational system (Berman, 1982; Weeks, Gambescia, & Jenkins, 2003).

Assessment: Constructing the Sexual Genogram

The sexual life of an adult is greatly impacted by family history and,
in turn, plays a major role in the life of a couple (DeMaria et al., 1999).
Incorporated into the genogram process is a sexual examination replete
with questions regarding each partner's sexual history and current sexual status. Many of these questions are based on Kaplan's (1983) assessment procedure listed in her book *The Evaluation of Sexual Disorders:
Psychological and Medical Aspects.* Kaplan's overriding objective in the
evaluation stage is to achieve an accurate diagnosis of the sexual problem
presented, to determine the origin of the problem, and to set up an effi-
cient and effective treatment plan. The evaluation herein usually can be
completed in one or two sessions, depending on the complexity and cooperation of the couple. However, the genogram process is ongoing as the
clinician can, at any time, add new information or make adjustments to
his or her initial hypotheses.

Medical Treatment

Segraves and Balon (2003) wrote, "Treatment of premature ejaculation
with pharmacological agents is feasible, practical, and well tolerated" (p.
281). After the assessment is completed, it is recommended that the man be
immediately referred for a complete physical examination (if he has not had
one recently), preferably by a urologist with a background in working with
sexual dysfunctions. Although there are no pharmacological agents currently approved to treat PE, selective serotonin reuptake inhibitors (SSRIs)
such as paroxetine (Paxil; GlaxoSmithKline, Philadelphia, Pennsylvania),
sertraline (Zoloft; Pfizer, New York), and fluoxetine (Prozac; Eli Lilly and
Company, Indianapolis, Indiana) have been found to be significantly
effective in the off-label treatment of PE. Paxil was found to produce

the strongest ejaculatory delay (Waldinger, Zwinderman, Schweitzer, & Olivier, 2004).

SSRIs do, however, possess numerous drawbacks. There is a required chronic dosing that lasts only when the drug is in the body, the therapeutic response is unpredictable, and they have a delayed onset of action and a long half-life. Side effects may include diminished libido, drowsiness, fatigue, nausea, diarrhea, headaches, and dry mouth (Barada & McCullough, 2004).

Off-label use of other antidepressants such as monoamine oxidase inhibitors (MAOIs) and tricyclic antidepressants (TCAs), particularly clomipramine (Anafranil; Novartis Pharmaceuticals, East Hanover, New Jersey) have also been proven effective (Waldinger et al., 2004). Clomipramine, however, can completely interfere with orgasm during sexual activity; it has also been found to produce such side effects as lightheadedness, sleepiness, nausea, dry mouth, and vision problems (Strassberg, de Gouveia Brazao, Rowland, Tan, & Slob, 1999).

Neurololeptics, α-blockers, β-blockers, anxiolytics, smooth muscle relaxants, topical anesthesia (e.g., prilocaine-lidocaine cream), and oral phosphodiesterase type 5 (PDE5) inhibitor agents such as sildenafil citrate (Viagra; Pfizer, New York) have also been used to treat PE (Symonds et al., 2003). Some individuals believe that the success PDE5 agents have produced may have more to do with reducing performance anxiety than treating the PE per se. Topical creams, although effective, interfere with sexual spontaneity, can cause significant penile hypoesthesia and transvaginal absorption (which, unless used with a condom, can lead to genital numbness in the man and his partner), female anorgasmia, and an undesired loss of erection after 30–45 minutes (Atikeler, Gecit, & Senol, 2002; Montorsi et al., 2005).

Though few men refuse to obtain a medical evaluation, many will reject medication, particularly when it is prescribed in the absence of an organic problem. This may be a convenient way to block treatment success and should be dealt with as resistance; other men may be realistically concerned about the side effects of medication or may prefer to deal with the problem via psychotherapy. Additionally, if the man is in a relationship, his partner should be included in this and any treatment discussions. When medications are considered, the clinician should correspond with the consulting physician in an attempt to comfort the man and to find the most effective medication with the least deleterious side effects. The man should be made aware that the body sometimes adjusts to medication or that a spontaneous remission of any drug-related sexual problems may occur. This may be the case for SSRIs and MAOIs but not TCAs; apparently, the anorgasmia that TCAs produce does not remit spontaneously (Komisaruk, Beyer-Flores, & Whipple, 2006). Nevertheless, if the man still refuses medical treatment and there is no organic basis for the problem the clinician can work with him and his partner. If there is an organic problem the man should be urged to follow up with the physician. While psychotherapeutic gains might be limited, the couple can benefit from modified prescriptions and opportunities to discuss their issues.

PE Exercises

The clinician may assign sex therapy exercises if he or she feels the underlying relationship dynamics will allow for success. The basic tenet of treatment is to help the man learn to tolerate increasing levels of stimulation while in control of his ejaculatory reflex. This is accomplished through incremental exercises that allow him to tolerate more stimulation, to become aware of his premonitory ejaculatory sensations or the sensations prior to the point of ejaculatory inevitability, and to learn to pace himself and to have intercourse in a way that minimizes friction or stimulation of the penis until he is ready to ejaculate.

If the couple proves ready, sensate focus exercises are initially assigned (Masters & Johnson, 1970) because they tend to create a more intimate atmosphere for the couple and to help to reduce any anxiety that may be associated with the couple's sexual process (see chapter 15 in this volume on sensate focus). If, however, a couple is not in need of such a preliminary experience, more sophisticated exercises specifically designed for PE are immediately offered. In this model, the stop–start method (Semans, 1956) as applied by Kaplan (1974, 1989) is the exercise method of choice.

The stop–start method will specifically allow the male to become aware of his premonitory sensations so that he can control ejaculatory latency while enjoying the sexual process; numbing either emotionally or physically to prolong ejaculation is considered counterproductive. Toward this end, in the first exercise the man is asked to lie on his back and have his partner stroke his penis with a dry hand while he pays attention to the erotic feelings in his penis. When he feels near orgasm, but before the point of ejaculatory inevitability, the partner is to stop stroking and allow the man's erotic feelings to dissipate (but not long enough for him to lose his erection). If the man does not have a partner, he can practice the stop–start technique on his own.

Couples are to do the stop–start exercises three to five times per week. When the man achieves enough control that he only has to stop two to three times in a 10-minute period, the couple may move on to the next exercise. The second exercise entails repeating the first exercise, only this time the partner is to stroke the male using a water-based lubricant; the lubricant serves to increase the level of sensitivity and to further prepare the male for intercourse. As an adjunct exercise, during the week the man is to practice Kegel exercises by contracting his pelvic floor muscles at the point before ejaculatory inevitability—this may result in better ejaculatory control (Kegel, 1952).

The third exercise is called slow–fast penile stimulation. The man is to have his partner stroke him until he reaches a high level of sexual excitement and then to slow down rather than come to a complete stop. The fourth exercise entails the partner stroking the man at a high level of arousal continuously without stopping. During the fifth exercise the partner is to mount the man (female superior position) and use the man's penis to caress her vagina; the partner stops caressing just before the point of ejaculation. The female superior position allows the man to relax his lower body muscles and to better concentrate on the point of ejaculatory inevitability.

In the sixth exercise, the partner, still on top, inserts the man's penis but only moves to maintain the orgasm (quiet vagina or nondemand coitus). This can be repeated as a seventh exercise with partners lying side by side. In the eighth and final exercise the man mounts his partner (male superior position) and practices speeding up and slowing down his thrusting (as opposed to stopping it altogether)—this better simulates intercourse (gay couples can adapt all exercises accordingly).

Some couples insist on exercises for PE even if the clinician feels they are in too much conflict to complete them successfully. The clinician can first warn the couple that they should wait, but if he or she senses that the couple will prematurely terminate the treatment unless exercises are immediately prescribed, it is recommended that sensate focus exercises be assigned because they will usually do little damage if unsuccessful. If the couple is not ready for exercises they will rarely get through sensate focus and will return to treatment with the realization that they have problems (e.g., relationship issues) that need to be addressed before their sexual symptom can be alleviated. Other couples will collude in using their failure to prematurely end treatment.

Even when couples seem ready for exercises, it is quite common for one or both partners to sabotage them (e.g., engaging in a fight right before the exercises are to begin), thus indicating ambivalence about solving their problem. Some couples engage in control struggles about when to do the exercises or disagree about who should initiate them. Others insist on improvising or fail to follow the clinician's instructions. The clinician should be as clear and detailed as possible about the exercises assigned. For example, insisting that the couple agree on the time, place, and frequency of the assignments helps to ensure success. It is also important to agree on who will initiate the exercises (one or both partners) and how long they should last. Oftentimes the partner will feel taken advantage of in the exercise process. The clinician can discuss whether the partner wishes to have her needs met prior to beginning each exercise and how the couple can accomplish this objective (noncoital stimulation performed on the partner may be a solution).

The clinician may find it useful to supply the couple with handouts detailing all exercises. However, because couples differ in introspective ability, motivation, levels of resistance, degree of experience, and degree of sexual difficulty, the exercise regimen should be considered by the clinician to be a general framework for treatment and not one automatically applied to all couples. As previously noted, the definition of PE is dependent to a great deal on what the couple brings to the clinician. This specific definition will in turn help to determine how PE exercises, if any, are utilized.

A couple presented with great motivation to conquer their problem with PE as quickly as possible. During sexual activity, the man ejaculated within three minutes of penetration; however, his wife could achieve a vaginal orgasm within five minutes of intercourse. The couple decided to learn how to stretch their lovemaking a little longer for optimum satisfaction. No psychodynamic work was required in this case, and there was no need to assign sensate focus exercises. Because the man could last as long as he wanted via manual and oral sex, the couple chose to proceed right to the sixth exercise (i.e., stop–start with penile insertion) with great success. As noted, a couple with more anxiety and a penchant for resistance may need to delay exercises until a sufficient amount of psychotherapy has taken place.

Exposing Conflicts and Facilitating Differentiation
While the exercises are in progress, the clinician helps each partner to uncover any individual conflicts that may be responsible for the PE symptom. Unveiling and working on these conflicts contributes to an increased level of differentiation from the family of origin. This in turn allows for a resolution of the conflicts and a reduction in both sexual and nonsexual dynamics or in symptoms presented by the couple. To uncover these conflicts, the clinician must recognize any relevant patterns of behavior put forth and must interpret any contradictions that the couple exhibits.

Uncovering Conflicts on the Interactional Level

On this level the clinician observes the couple's interactional style and looks for patterns and contradictions that represent conflicts and collusions that may be responsible for their sexual symptom. These may show themselves in a sexual and nonsexual context. For example, a wife may complain vociferously that her husband never initiates a conversation about their relationship issues. But, when he does open his mouth, the clinician notices that she dominates the interaction with a lecture. This demonstrates an interactional conflict or contradiction on the wife's part: She claims to desire verbal interaction with her husband but blocks it from occurring. The husband demonstrates his conflict about wanting a voice in the relationship as well as his collusiveness in the relational dynamic by failing to stop his wife from interrupting him.

Sex therapy exercises will also allow the clinician to identify interactional conflicts and contradictions in the sexual context of the couple. For example, a husband may claim to want to alleviate his PE symptom but may find numerous excuses to avoid doing his sex exercises. If and when he does embark on these exercises his wife may start an argument with him, thereby sabotaging them. It might be helpful if the clinician discusses some of the potential difficulties that may impede the exercises. These can be based in part on the clinician's knowledge of the couple and their potential for control struggles. The couple is helped to understand how their struggles may represent unconscious conflicts that can sabotage their stated treatment goals.

The couple's interactional style will also show itself in contexts other than the one presented in therapy. If a couple grasps this concept, they may be better able to see that their problem might not be limited to their specific sexual symptom. A PE sufferer who has avoided treatment, for example, may have trouble giving others what they want in general; his wife may have difficulty getting what she wants in other contexts as well. To expand the process in this case, the clinician can explore these issues to see if there is a pattern correlated to the marital and sexual dynamics.

Uncovering Conflicts on the Psychodynamic Level

While some couples may be aware their interactional style is contributing to their PE symptom, they are almost never aware of the underlying psychodynamic contributions to the problem. The clinician may use the genogram to help each partner become conscious of these conflicts by probing each partner's family of origin with a series of questions. The objective is to make the connection between the conflicts, interactions, and the PE symptom. As noted, this procedure should continue throughout treatment.

The genogram of a man with PE revealed that he was engaged in a lifelong struggle for independence from the women in his life, dating back to his dominant mother. His conflict was that he needed a woman, but he also struggled against becoming too dependent on one. His PE served as a vehicle to create a control struggle that allowed him to be partially committed; this bought him the tolerable amount of space and closeness he needed to be in the relationship. His partner experienced a distant father and a history of dating distant men. Her conflict was that she longed for a loyal, loving man in her life but feared that if she became too close to one she might reexperience abandonment; she thus chose men who were ambivalent about committing to her.

The clinician can see this conflict in the man's family of origin and dating history, and can explore with him how his unconscious conflict is in charge of his interactional relationships with women and his PE symptom. The clinician can ask what it feels like for him to be dominated by women and can explore how this might have been related to his PE. The partner can be led to explore her fear of abandonment and can be asked what it feels like to not be fully committed to and how these issues might be related to her marital dynamic.

Crucial to therapy is helping partners move away from mutual "blame mode." The clinician can use the uncovered conflicts to show them that they are complementary, not necessarily "opposites." In the preceding example, both partners had a conflict with giving and getting and, in turn, an issue with intimacy. To foster mutual empathy the clinician can frame this in the following manner: "While your individual conflicts manifest somewhat differently, neither of you trusts that you will be reciprocated if you give of yourselves."

Resolving Conflicts and Increasing Differentiation

The major difficulty with resolving conflicts lies in the fact that real solution of a conflict involves the frustration of both sides of a conflict. Simply put, gain on one side entails a loss on the other. Partners do not seem to accept this notion and will spend inordinate amounts of energy trying to find a way to "have it all," even after their conflicts are made clear to them. They are afraid that changing will make things worse. The ability to choose a different way of life most often depends on the degree of anxiety partners can tolerate and their ability to bear frustration.

The man with PE who struggled over independence–dependence issues with women had to come to the realization that he could not maintain his relationship with his partner at a safe distance; it was symptomatic of a lack of differentiation from his mother, was responsible for his negative projections onto his female partner, and was symptomatic of his PE. He had to decide whether he wanted to tackle the anxiety that came with taking the risk of giving up some of his freedom in a relationship with a woman. If he did so, he might achieve intimacy and sexual health, but he might lose the degree of control and independence he had fought for most of his life.

The man's partner had to differentiate from her distant father and decide whether she could take the risk of allowing a man to want her to see if she was really lovable. It would have been necessary for her to give up on her father, but in the process she could discover that she really was worthy of love. Both partners, of course, could choose not to do the work and either stay in their same dilemma or terminate the relationship. Ultimately it is the couple's choice as to whether they want change—the therapist's main job is to show them the conflicts and to help them to explore their options.

Termination

Treatment success is predicated on the alleviation of the PE symptom; the timeline for this success varies. While improved individual differentiation and a more functional couple interactional style are often prerequisites for success, if the PE is found to be solely organic in origin and is treated successfully with medication, treatment will obviously be brief. In most cases, however, the PE symptom will not dissipate until psychodynamic conflicts have improved—this often takes longer. In other instances, the PE symptom is alleviated, but the underlying conflicts produce another symptom (i.e., symptom replacement); in this situation, the clinician should warn the couple that their underlying problem lives and should gently encourage them to continue treatment. They should also know that their PE symptom could return if they end prematurely.

Generally, the termination of a case is a decision made by the couple and the clinician together. The termination process may take one or several sessions to accomplish. The couple can be told that booster sessions will be available given the chances of relapse (Metz & McCarthy, 2003). This gesture often eases the separation process.

Case Study

Dave and Roselyn were married and in their early 50s. Dave presented with acquired, specific PE, but during the evaluation process he admitted that he may have had the disorder his whole life but never realized it because he usually had a drink or two to prepare him for intercourse. It is only with Roselyn that he became fully aware of his problem, in part because he stopped using alcohol to comfort him prior to having sex. A complete physical from his urologist prior to presenting for treatment cleared Dave of any organic problems.

Dave never experienced PE during oral and manual sex, but with intercourse he could only last a maximum of three thrusts (or a few seconds) before ejaculating. "There is something about intercourse that gives me problems," he said. Both partners were frustrated by this situation because Roselyn was capable of achieving intravaginal orgasms without a great deal of stimulation. Dave often brought her to orgasm prior to intercourse, but it was clear that both partners wanted intercourse to last longer.

The interactional style of the couple presented itself across a variety of contexts. Whether it was the way Dave dealt with his business colleagues or clients, friends, his ex-wife, or his children, he failed to set limits and was exploited—at times he failed to reach his goals. Roselyn's reaction was always the same—she would chastise Dave for not being able to stand up for himself and for proving to be incompetent. She also felt that Dave did not defend her against others. Roselyn's mantra to Dave was, "That was just stupid Dave, just plain stupid." Dave did not counter Roselyn's complaints; he too believed that something was wrong with him, and he wanted to grow stronger and be more successful. Neither partner initially realized that this issue was connected to their PE symptom.

During the course of the treatment it became obvious that Roselyn was right about Dave's behavior. For a bright man with a great deal of ambition, his judgment in certain situations and his lack of control demonstrated an emotional conflict about being successful that was at least partially responsible for his relationship and sexual symptom. Roselyn's interactional conflict manifested differently. She continuously stated how much she wanted a better life for her and Dave, but her overreaction to his behavior enabled her to feel miserable about her marriage and her life in general. She also claimed to want Dave to feel empowered and to stand up for himself, but her constant chastising reduced him and highlighted his incompetence.

Because the couple reported that affection and foreplay were not issues, the stop–start method was prescribed in the second session, and the couple progressed until it was time for Dave to penetrate Roselyn. Dave then began to sabotage, and, in turn, Roselyn began to punish him verbally. As their conflicts were revealed, however, Dave and Roselyn came to realize that they were similar in a very important way—they both had conflicts about being "big" (the couple's word for empowerment and success) that were anchored in the depreciative way their parents treated them in their respective families of origin. This insight helped them to empathize with one another and to decide "to be big" together—a sign of increased differentiation.

Although the couple colluded to sabotage several stop–start exercises (Dave was passive aggressive, and Roselyn cajoled), they eventually succeeded in eradicating their PE symptom. The treatment took approximately 14 months, addressing what Dave and Roselyn considered a long-range cure to their relationship and sexual problems.

Future Considerations

It is hopeful that medical science will someday offer a greater contribution to the alleviation of PE. Nevertheless, a primary concern for many sex therapists, particularly those who advocate the integration of couples and sex therapy, is that the treatment for PE, like erectile dysfunction (ED), will eventually become grossly skewed toward a medical solution. McCarthy (2001) wrote, "Both the general public and medical community now prefer use of a medical intervention first, and only if that is unsuccessful are psychological or sex therapy assessment and interventions considered" (p. 1).

Many physicians prescribe medications but fail to ask questions about their patients' relationships—they ignore any underlying psychological or systemic issues at play. Often, the partner is omitted from the decision to take medication. As a result, individuals continue to suffer from associated relationship dynamics—dynamics that may continue to plague the couple's sex life or other nonsexual areas. This shortsightedness also exists within the field of psychotherapy. Despite the evidence supporting the correlation between relationship and sexual problems, many professionals still look to the individual symptom bearer as the sole identified patient.

The model presented is comprehensive and systemic. It contends that exposing conflicts and differentiating from the negative effects of the family of origin leads to the resolution of these conflicts and any accompanying sexual symptoms. It is a complicated process with many skills required; eliminating one treatment option over another or simplifying the process either from a psychotherapeutic or medical perspective only deprives the couple of appropriate treatment (Althof, 2007; Barnes & Eardley, 2007; Perelman, 2006). Clinicians need to be broad-minded in the treatment of couples who present with sexual problems and should consider a myriad of factors to help the couple achieve a more prospering intimate relationship, free of sexual difficulty.

References

Abraham, K. (1917/1949). Ejaculatio praecox. In D. Bryan & A. Strachey (Trans.), *Selected papers of Karl Abraham, M.D.* (pp. 280–298). London: Hogarth Press and the Institute of Psychoanalysis.

Althof, S. (2007). Treatment of rapid ejaculation: Psychotherapy, pharmacotherapy, and combined therapy. In S. Leiblum (Ed.), *Principles and practice of sex therapy* (4th ed., pp. 212–240). New York: Guilford.

American Psychiatric Association (APA) (2000). *Diagnostic and statistical manual of mental disorders* (4th ed., text revision). Washington, DC: Author.

Atikeler, M. K., Gecit, I., & Senol, F. A. (2002). Optimum usage of prilocaine-lidocaine cream in premature ejaculation. *Andrologia, 34,* 356–359.

Barada, J. & McCullough, A. (2004). *Premature ejaculation: Increasing recognition and improving treatment (Archived Web Conference).* Retrieved August 12, 2006, from: http://www.medscape.com

Barnes, T. & Eardley, I. (2007). Premature ejaculation: The scope of the problem. *Journal of Sex & Marital Therapy, 33,* 151–170.

Berman, E. (1982). The individual interview as a treatment technique in conjoint therapy. *American Journal of Family Therapy, 10,* 27–37.

Betchen, S. (1991). Male masturbation as a vehicle for the pursuer/distancer relationship in marriage. *Journal of Sex & Marital Therapy, 17,* 269–278.

Betchen, S. (2001). Premature ejaculation as symptomatic of age difference in a husband and wife with underlying power and control conflicts. *Journal of Sex Education and Therapy, 26,* 34–44.

Betchen, S. (2005). *Intrusive partners-elusive mates: The pursuer-distancer dynamic in couples.* New York: Routledge.

Betchen, S. (2006). Husbands who use sexual dissatisfaction to balance the scales of power in their dual-career marriages. *Journal of Family Psychotherapy, 17,* 19–35.

Bowen, M. (1978). *Family therapy in clinical practice.* New York: Aronson.

DeMaria, R., Weeks, G., & Hof, L. (1999). *Focused genograms: Intergenerational assessment of individuals, couples, and families.* Philadelphia: Brunner/Mazel.

Freud, S. (1905/1953). Three essays on the theory of sexuality. In J. Strachey (Ed. and Trans.), *The standard edition of the complete psychological works of Sigmund Freud* (Vol. 7, pp. 125–245). London: Hogarth Press and the Institute of Psychoanalysis.

Freud, S. (1910/1957). Five lectures on psycho-analysis. In J. Strachey (Ed. and Trans.), *The standard edition of the complete psychological works of Sigmund Freud* (Vol. 11, pp. 9–55). London: Hogarth Press and the Institute of Psychoanalysis.

Gottman, J. (1994). *What predicts divorce? The relationship between marital processes and marital outcomes.* Hillsdale, NJ: Lawrence Erlbaum Associates.

Kaplan, H. S. (1974). *The new sex therapy: Active treatment of sexual dysfunctions.* New York: Times Books.

Kaplan, H. S. (1979). *Disorders of sexual desire.* New York: Brunner/Mazel.

Kaplan, H. S. (1983). *The evaluation of sexual disorders: Psychological and medical aspects.* New York: Brunner/Mazel.

Kaplan H. S. (1989). *PE: How to overcome premature ejaculation.* New York: Brunner/Mazel.

Kaplan, H. S. (1995). *The sexual desire disorders: Dysfunctional regulation of sexual motivation.* New York: Brunner/Mazel.

Kegel, A. (1952). Sexual functions of the pubococcygeus muscle. *Western Journal of Surgery in Obstetrics and Gynecology, 60,* 521–524.

Klein, M. (2006). *America's war on sex: The attack on law, lust and liberty.* Westport, CT: Praeger.

Komisaruk, B., Beyer-Flores, C., & Whipple, B. (2006). *The Science of Orgasm.* Baltimore, MD: Johns Hopkins Press.

Laumann, E. O., Nicolosi, A., Glasser, D. B., Palik, A., Gingell, C., Moreira, E., et al. (2005). Sexual problems among women and men aged 40–80 years: Prevalence and correlates identified in the Global Study of Sexual Attitudes and Behaviors. *International Journal of Impotence Research, 17,* 39–57.

Masters, W. & Johnson, V. (1966). *Human sexual response.* Boston: Little, Brown & Company.

Masters, W. & Johnson, V. (1970). *Human sexual inadequacy.* Boston: Little, Brown & Company.

McCarthy, B. (2001). Relapse prevention strategies and techniques with erectile dysfunction. *Journal of Sex & Marital Therapy, 27,* 1–8.

Metz, M. & McCarthy, B. (2003). *Coping with premature ejaculation: How to overcome PE, please your partner and have great sex.* Oakland, CA: New Harbinger Publications.

Metz, M. & Pryor, J. (2000). Premature ejaculation: A psychophysiological approach for assessment and management. *Journal of Sex & Marital Therapy, 26,* 293–320.

Metz, M., Pryor, J., Nesvacil, L., Abuzzahab, F., & Koznar, J. (1997). Premature ejaculation: A psychophysiological review. *Journal of Sex & Marital Therapy, 23,* 3–23.

Montorsi, F., Sotomayor, M., & Sharlip, I. (2005). *Premature ejaculation: Past, present, and future perspectives.* Retrieved August 12, 2006, from: http://www.medscape.com

Palha, A. P. & Esteves, M. (2002). A study of the sexual habits of opiate addicts. *Journal of Sex & Marital Therapy, 28,* 427–437.

Perelman, M. (2006). A new combination treatment for premature ejaculation: A sex therapist's perspective. *Journal of Sexual Medicine, 3,* 1004–1012.

Polonsky, D. (2000). Premature ejaculation. In S. Leiblum & R. Rosen (Eds.), *Principles and practice of sex therapy* (3rd ed., pp. 305–332). New York: Guilford.

Segraves, R. T. & Balon, R. (2003). *Sexual pharmacology: Fasts facts.* New York: Norton.

Semans, J. (1956). Premature ejaculation: A new approach. *Southern Medical Journal, 49,* 353–358.

Strassberg, D. S., de Gouveia Brazao, C., Rowland, D. L., Tan, P., & Slob, A. K. (1999). Clomipramine in the treatment of rapid (premature) ejaculation. *Journal of Sex & Marital Therapy, 25,* 89–101.

Symonds, T., Roblin, D., Hart., K., & Althof, S. (2003). How does premature ejaculation affect a man's life? *Journal of Sex & Marital Therapy, 29,* 361–370.

Waldinger, M. D. (2002). The neurobiological approach of premature ejaculation. *Journal of Urology, 168,* 2359–2367.

Waldinger, M. D. (2003). *Rapid ejaculation.* In S. Levine, C. Risen, & S. Althof (Eds.), *Handbook of clinical sexuality for mental health professionals* (pp. 257–274). New York: Brunner/Routledge.

Waldinger, M. D., Hengeveld, M. W., Zwinderman, A. H., & Olivier, B. (1998). An empirical operationalization study of DSM-IV diagnostic criteria for premature ejaculation. *International Journal of Psychiatry in Clinical Practice, 2,* 287.

Waldinger, M. D., Zwinderman, A. H., Schweitzer, D. H., & Olivier, B. (2004). Relevance of methodological design for the interpretation of efficacy of drug treatment of premature ejaculation: A systemic review and meta-analysis. *International Journal of Impotence Research, 16,* 369–381.

Weeks, G. & Gambescia, N. (2000). *Erectile dysfunction: Integrating couple therapy, sex therapy, and medical treatment.* New York: Norton.

Weeks, G. & Gambescia, N. (2002). *Hypoactive sexual desire: Integrating sex and couple therapy.* New York: Norton.

Weeks, G., Gambescia, N., & Jenkins, R. (2003). *Treating infidelity: Therapeutic dilemmas and effective strategies.* New York: Norton.

Weeks, G., Odell, M., & Methven, S. (2005). *If only I had known… Avoiding common mistakes in couples therapy.* New York: Norton.

8

The Complex Etiology of Delayed Ejaculation
Assessment and Treatment Implications

Sallie Foley

Contents

Defining Delayed Ejaculation

Delayed ejaculation is also referred to as inhibited ejaculation, retarded
ejaculation, ejaculatory incompetence, male orgasmic disorder, impaired

ejaculation, anejaculation, impaired orgasm, delayed orgasm, inhibited orgasm, and ejaculatory inhibition (Wincze & Carey, 2001). The numerous ways to refer to delayed ejaculation give some indication of the difficulties in coming to agreement about not only what it is but also how to effectively treat it (Richardson & Goldmeier, 2006). Of all the male sexual disorders, delayed ejaculation relies most on clinical and anecdotal observations for treatment. Virtually no empirical studies for treatment are available (Hartmann & Waldinger, 2007).

The *Diagnostic and Statistical Manual of Mental Disorders,* 4th ed., text revision (*DSM-IV-TR;* APA, 2000) defines delayed ejaculation under 302.74, Male Orgasmic Disorder. The diagnostic features described are "persistent or recurrent delay in, or absence of, orgasm following a normal sexual excitement phase during sexual activity that the clinician, taking into account the person's age, judges to be adequate in focus, intensity, and duration," and it causes "marked distress or interpersonal difficulty." The *DSM-IV-TR* goes on to suggest that it cannot be accounted for by other Axis I disorders and is not "exclusively the physiological result of a substance, either drug of abuse or medication, or due to a general medical condition." Finally, it is not caused by a medical condition and can be lifelong or acquired, generalized or situational, and due to psychological or combined factors (APA, 2000, p. 550).

From the description, one sees problems in diagnosis. The clinician is put in the position of having to judge whether technique is adequate, stimulation has been sufficient, and excitement has been normal. If delayed ejaculation is situational or intermittent—for instance, it only occurs in the presence of a partner when trying to have intercourse—the clinician is also going to address that partner's reactions to the problem as well as any interpersonal dynamics contributing to the delayed ejaculation (Hartmann & Waldinger, 2007). This may be further complicated by the pressure some couples feel in certain life circumstances, including concerns about conception or contraception (Metz & McCarthy, 2007; Perelman & Rowland, 2006). Intermittent delayed ejaculation increases in likelihood as men age (Blanker et al., 2001). Theoretically, the *DSM-IV-TR* has a separate classification for delayed ejaculation when it is caused by medication or drug abuse: substance-induced sexual dysfunction with impaired orgasm. In practice, many sex therapists use the term *delayed ejaculation* to refer to all male inhibited orgasmic disorders regardless of etiology and cause (Shull & Sprenkle, 1980). This ambiguity does not help clinicians sort orgasmic dysfunction from ejaculatory problems or more practically address the high prevalence of delayed ejaculation with mixed biopsychosocial features (Wincze & Carey, 2001). The European

Association of Urology (EAU; Colpi, Weidner, Jungwirth, Pomerol, Papp, Hargreave, & Dohle, 2004) makes a distinction between orgasm and ejaculation and defines delayed ejaculation as "the condition wherein abnormal stimulation of the erected penis is necessary to achieve orgasm with ejaculation." The EAU acknowledges that it is a form of anorgasmia and that both delayed ejaculation and anorgasmia may be present in the same person. This is an important educational point for both the clinician and the client. The pathways for orgasm and ejaculation are separate, involving different neural circuits (Waldinger & Schweitzer, 2005). The EAU also acknowledges that causes for delayed ejaculation can be psychological, organic, or due to medications like antidepressants, antihypertensives, or antipsychotics—in other words, a biopsychosocial approach (Colpi et al., 2004).

A contemporary approach to diagnosis that is more straightforward is the one developed by Metz and McCarthy (2007), who prefer the term *ejaculatory inhibition*. They suggest that proper diagnosis and treatment depends on knowledge of the 10 types of delayed ejaculation differentially caused by five physiological types of problems (i.e., physical system conditions, physical illness, physical injury, drug side effects, and lifestyle issues), four psychological types of problems (i.e., psychological system, psychological distress, relationships distress, and psychosexual skills deficits), and a 10th "mixed" type of problem where the delayed ejaculation co-occurs with another sexual dysfunction like low sexual desire or a partner's dyspareunia (Metz & McCarthy, 2007).

Clinicians treating delayed ejaculation will need to approach it as a couple's problem to solve (Apfelbaum, 2000), understanding that it will often be a mix of psychological and organic causes and that pharmacologic agents, like antidepressants and antihypertensives, often play an expanding role in the causes of delayed ejaculation (Perelman, 2003). The lack of empirical data, the varying theories about cause, and the different algorithms for treatment all point to a sexual dysfunction that is not well understood, requiring an eclectic approach to treatment (Richardson, Nalabada, & Goldmeier, 2006; Wincze & Carey, 2001). In many ways, it is the counterpart of inhibited sexual desire. Whereas some people cannot develop enough desire and interest to have sexual arousal, others—in biology, psychology, or both—cannot fully enjoy the sexual arousal they have (Perelman & Rowland, 2006). Ultimately, individuals with delayed ejaculation feel like the Rolling Stones' song: They "can't get no satisfaction." A good working definition of delayed ejaculation is that "a man finds it difficult or impossible to ejaculate despite the presence of adequate sexual stimulation, erection, and conscious desire to achieve orgasm" (Hartmann & Waldinger, 2007).

The problem of arousal without ejaculation is further complicated by two myths in dominant culture—one that frustrates the therapist, the other the client. The first myth is that many clinicians do not seek skill development in treating delayed ejaculation because they think that it is so unusual that they will rarely see it in their practices (Metz & McCarthy, 2007). Primary (lifelong) anejaculation is indeed rare, but delayed ejaculation is increasingly common due to medications (i.e., antidepressants) and because of an aging population (Perelman & Rowland, 2006). With aging there is often an increase in chronic illness: more changes in blood flow, neuroperception, and medication usage (Marumo & Murai, 2001). This may lead to intermittent delayed ejaculation or increasing difficulty with ejaculation associated with partner intimacy arousal. Situational delayed ejaculation may result from overreliance on the partner's arousal and resultant inability to describe one's own arousal trajectory or from an overreliance on a very specific, idiosyncratic masturbation pattern that must be followed inflexibly (Lipsith, McCann, & Goldmeier, 2003; Metz & McCarthy, 2007).

The other myth that bedevils clients more than therapists is the urban legend that in sexual interaction, the man who can "go longer" is the gold standard for sexual satisfaction. In fact, partners are usually dissatisfied and frustrated with delayed ejaculation and often feel personally rejected (Metz & McCarthy, 2007). For men with delayed ejaculation, there can be feelings of inadequacy both in sexual function and in self-image (Zilbergeld, 1999). Due to frustration and low self-esteem, a man may avoid intimate communication and sexual interaction rather than engage in problem solving with his partner. It is quite possible that many years may elapse before getting help (Apfelbaum, 2000).

To summarize, it is not easy to treat delayed ejaculation, and to ignore any part of the biopsychosocial interaction is a mistake. However, delayed ejaculation can be treated successfully for some and managed more hopefully for others. The sex therapist should expect treatment to be integrated, to involve individual, interactional, and intergenerational understandings, and to include both systemic and behavioral approaches.

Prevalence

In the United States, the prevalence of delayed ejaculation was reported in the National Health and Social Life Survey conducted by researchers at the University of Chicago (Laumann, Gagnon, Michael, & Michaels, 1994). When asked, 8% of men aged 18–59 reported they had an inability to achieve orgasm for at least two months in the last year. Delayed ejaculation may be underreported because it can co-occur with other sexual dysfunctions like erectile dysfunction or low sexual desire. Individuals presenting with delayed ejaculation considered within the context of other sexual dysfunctions, aging, or as a result of psychopharmocologic medications are seen in every sex therapist's practice (Perelman, 2001). Unfortunately, prevalence data vary and generally are in short supply, but it is estimated that 7% to 15% of men over the age of 50 will cope with secondary delayed ejaculation. This form of sexual dysfunction is characterized by intermittent problems and is correlated with aging (Perelman, 2004).

Prior and Current Treatments

Past therapies have included medications especially for selective serotonin reuptake inhibitor (SSRI)-induced delayed ejaculation. Richardson et al. (2006) reported that amantadine, cyproheptadine, yohimbine, bupropion, bethanechol, and buspirone have all been used with varying degrees of success, but none of the studies were placebo-controlled stopwatch studies.

In the past, psychological therapy has included meditative relaxation with psychotherapy (Delmonte, 1984), increased sexual play (Shaw, 1990), behavioral therapy with increased manual stimulation or vibratory stimulation to penis, and increased sensory awareness (Bancroft, 1989; Hawton, 1989; Wincze & Carey, 2001) and self-awareness and partner communication (Apfelbaum, 2000). The most current treatments available for delayed ejaculation are illustrated in the "sexual tipping point" devised by Perelman in the treatment of delayed ejaculation (Perelman & Rowland, 2006); in the use of integrated treatment combining systemic, psychodynamic, and cognitive-behavioral modalities described by Hartmann and Waldinger (2007); and in the integration of couples therapy and psychosexual skills training advocated by Metz and McCarthy (2007). There are no research studies comparing the use of medication treatment with the use of psychotherapy treatment in delayed ejaculation.

The Intersystem Approach to Treatment

The intersystem approach to treating sexual dysfunctions is useful in addressing the known or suspected causes and subsequent treatment of delayed ejaculation. Weeks (1994) described the intersystem approach as a framework with five components:

1. Individual/biological/medical
2. Individual/psychological
3. Dyadic relationship
4. Family of origin
5. Society/culture/history/religion

The therapist's case formulation includes information organized in all five components and treatment that encompasses the individual, interactional, and intergenerational aspects in each component. The intersystem approach is particularly useful in sex therapy because it is integrative, guards against the clinician's neglect of any component, and assures systematic formulation and interventions that are replicable and consistent. In fact, even when assessment points to only one causative agent (i.e., biological causes within the individual), all components must be explored with the client. There are too many times when a hasty conclusion prevents a full understanding of the person/dyad and also of the person's or couple's unique abilities to change based on the interaction of these systems (Weeks & Gambescia, 2000).

Individual Causes of Delayed Ejaculation— Physiological and Psychological

The etiology of delayed ejaculation is not well understood and is thought to be a complex mix of the individual/biological/psychological, interactional, and intergenerational (Metz & McCarthy, 2007). There are a number of possible biological causes for delayed ejaculation (Schuster & Ohl, 2002). Some researchers hypothesize that delayed ejaculation is caused, at least in part, by slower bulbocavernous reflexes (slower reflexes), less sensitivity in the penis, and a too-high penile sensory threshold (the opposite of premature ejaculation) (Bindley & Gillan, 1982; Lipsith et al., 2003). There may also be congenital abnormalities (Hendry, 1998; Perelman & Rowland, 2006; Schlegel, Shin, & Goldstein, 1996), or abnormalities due to pelvic trauma or surgery. Common surgical procedures that have been associated with delayed orgasm or ejaculation are radical prostatectomy, transurethral resection of the prostate, and bladder neck surgery

(Hendry, 1998). Medications are often associated with delayed ejaculation (Montejo-González et al., 1997; Munjack & Kanno, 1979; Segraves, 1995). Common medications that can cause delayed ejaculation include anticholinergics, antiadrenergics, antihypertensives, psychoactive drugs, SSRIs and other antidepressants, antipsychotics, and medications associated with the treatment of obsessive-compulsive disorder (Richardson et al., 2006; Segraves, 1995). Alcohol can also cause delayed ejaculation, although a review of research indicates that alcohol and delayed ejaculation have not been systematically studied (Richardson et al., 2006). Again, the clinician relies on clinical case reports since there is a lack of empirically based study of causation. Delayed ejaculation may also result from spinal cord injury, multiple sclerosis, and diabetes (DasGupta & Fowler, 2002; Lopicollo, 1994; Richardson et al., 2006).

Psychological causes are so varied that almost any psychological experience has been named the culprit for delayed ejaculation (Shull & Sprenkle, 1980). The client's history should include a thorough assessment of the individual's psychosocial development, major life events, cultural and religious beliefs related to sexual attitudes and functioning, body image, gender identity, general self-esteem, and history of relationships (Metz & McCarthy, 2007; Richardson et al., 2006). Additional hypotheses of causative factors include specific fears of being hurt, castration anxiety, fear of pregnancy or committing in a relationship, performance anxiety, religious proscriptions against sexual behavior, and anger at the self or the partner (Wincze & Carey, 2001).

The absence of carefully controlled research to understand psychological causes for delayed ejaculation has been documented (Hartmann & Waldinger, 2007). Apfelbaum (2000) theorized that delayed ejaculation results from an individual being out of touch with his own sensory experience in the presence of another person. He cannot "let go of control" and "selfishly" attend to his own pleasure. Further, there may be fears about being inadequate that lead to being overly goal directed. A man can objectify his penis and become driven by a compulsion to reach orgasm (Apfelbaum, 2001). Since lack of orgasm during intercourse is the most common type of delayed ejaculation, Apfelbaum (2000) also suggested that delayed ejaculation is really a form of a desire/arousal dysfunction—the man is not orgasmic with his partner but can self-stimulate to orgasm. He prefers his own autoarousal and is not able to fully relax and be reciprocal with his partner. He maintains an erection, but it is automatic and not pleasurable.

If a man has delayed ejaculation that is situational and he is able to masturbate to orgasm by himself but cannot orgasm with a partner, it is hypothesized that he may have difficulty with loss of control in front of another person or have fears of hurting or being hurt by the other (Hartmann & Waldinger, 2007). Delayed ejaculation leads to performance anxiety, thereby increasing the possibility of further sexual problems (Metz & McCarthy, 2007). Men with delayed ejaculation report feelings of shame, loss of control, and helplessness as a result of their problem (Zilbergeld, 1999). Perelman and Rowland (2006) observe that both idiosyncratic masturbatory styles and high-frequency masturbation may lead to difficulty in comfort or communication with a partner about the stimulation pattern needed for ejaculation.

Anxiety disorders present special challenges in sex and relationship therapies (Barlow, 2002). Bancroft and Janssen (2000) proposed a theory of erectile dysfunction related to centrally mediated anxiety in either the fear of performance or anxiety related to outcome of performance. The individual with delayed ejaculation may be similarly challenged, resulting in being overly controlling of either his sexual response or his relationship (Baucom, Stanton, & Epstein, 2003). A clinician must remember the role of anxiety in delayed ejaculation and question, "Is there underlying anxiety that may have been present well before the event of delayed ejaculation, or is there underlying anxiety that has been created by the event of delayed ejaculation?" Intermittent delayed ejaculation, often experienced by men over the age of 50, may cause increased anxiety and relationship stress (Foley, 2005).

Relational Causes of Delayed Ejaculation and Treatment Approaches

Relationship factors often play a role in both generalized and situational delayed ejaculation. Causative influences can include insufficient pleasure in the interaction, the man's holding back as a way of gaining power, ambivalence about commitment, being overly concerned about "pleasing the partner," difficulties the couple may have in facilitating his communicating of necessary and adequate stimulation, disparity between a fantasied partner and the real partner, and idiosyncratic masturbatory patterns that prevent arousal in partnership (Apfelbaum, 2000; Perelman & Rowland, 2006; Shull & Sprenkle, 1980; Wincze & Carey, 2001).

The partner of the man with delayed ejaculation often feels that she or he is to blame for not being attractive enough or skilled enough to facilitate ejaculation (Hartmann & Waldinger, 2007). There can be a degenerative, spiraling effect when both people experience feelings of failure and inadequacy, leading to a couple's avoidance of sex. Sometimes the man with delayed ejaculation will fake orgasms to please his partner. The sexual interaction thus becomes mechanical and disconnected, performance oriented without pleasure, serious not playful (McCarthy & McCarthy, 1998). Eroticism, sexual playfulness, intimacy, mutuality, and spontaneity—central to a couple's sexual pleasure—are usually absent.

Metz and McCarthy (2007) pointed out that delayed ejaculation often leads to reduced motivation and interest in sex, to lowered sexual desire, and to sexual avoidance. Secondary sexual dysfunction of inhibited sexual desire or erectile dysfunction can occur. Situational delayed ejaculation can result from relationship dissatisfaction and problems the couple are experiencing outside the bedroom. A man who is conflicted about his relationship may not experience pleasurable relaxation and sensation necessary for orgasm (Metz & McCarthy, 2007).

Intergenerational Causes of Delayed Ejaculation

Intergenerational causes include faulty or nonexistent sexual education and overly critical, strict religious orthodoxy (Wincze & Carey, 2001). Hypotheses about intergenerational influences abound, and there is no empirical data to support the theories (Hartmann & Waldinger, 2007). It is possible that early experiences of punitive shaming either if caught masturbating or being sexually curious can lead to difficulties with delayed ejaculation. Some men report feeling conflicted about aggression, either because of overly aggressive parental figures or because of severe restriction of any form of normal aggressive activity. These men may become anxious about showing "aggression" or "selfishness" during sexual activity with a partner (ibid.). Men may receive messages and sexual scripts that run the gamut from thinking that real men ejaculate easily and every time to thinking of sex as sport and that real men should be detached and not intimate. These messages coupled with a lack of sexual education can spell disaster for some men (Metz & McCarthy, 2007). A past history of trauma can also create conflicts that can manifest in delayed ejaculation (Lew, 1990), including the confusion of arousal and aggression or association of shame with pleasurable arousal.

Sociocultural Factors Affecting Delayed Ejaculation

Culture and socialization contribute to a person's formation of sexual identity and influence sexual functioning. In North America, men are taught
to be independent, self-sufficient, and protective of partner and family.
Advertising also has a stake in promoting this "mighty man" sexual performance image since it sells sexual enhancement products. Zilbergeld
(1999) called this predominant image of male sexuality the "fantasy
model," observing that North American culture views the penis as "two
feet long, hard as steel" and able to go all night. This prevalent cultural
model is constrictive and can make real men into anxious performers who
have difficulty staying connected with their own sensations, maintaining
partner intimacy, and keeping a realistic understanding of what sexual
responsivity looks and feels like (Apfelbaum, 2000; Kelly, 2003; Metz &
McCarthy, 2004). The cultural paradigm stressing these characteristics is
a potent socializer. Men may be hesitant to admit they have a problem
with delayed ejaculation and feel even more shame if they must seek help.

Assessment—Establishing Openness and Safety in Sex Therapy

Assessing delayed ejaculation may occur in individual or couples treatment. The process of asking questions and seeking information about the
problem will be interwoven with information that the therapist provides
to the client both about the processes and about the dynamics of interaction between the therapist and the client. At the beginning of treatment,
the therapist explains how the psychotherapy proceeds and gains the cli-
ent/couple's agreement to participate in this process. The assessment questions in Table 8.1 outline the process of assessing delayed ejaculation, but
the clinician must also be attuned to creating an environment of safety
and openness. In the absence of empirically based algorithms for treatment, the clinician must rely on skillful piecing together of individual,
couple, and intergenerational contributors to the problem. The client and
the therapist will collaborate in treatment planning and increasing the client's insight and awareness (Hartmann & Waldinger, 2007).

As the clinician moves through the assessment questions, the clinician
will clarify to the client what a sex therapist is—many people are referred
and have no idea what they will encounter when meeting a sex therapist or

TABLE 8.1   The Intersystem Assessment: Individual and Couple

Structure of Assessment Process: Couple Session, Individual Session with Each Partner, then Return to Couple Sessions

Couple, first session: Presenting problem/concern

- History of problem
- Precipitants
- Communication about problem to others, including partner and professionals
- Solutions previously tried

Individual and interactional information during couple session

- Age
- Developmental history and family of origin observations
- Social interests/friends
- Present home/family life
- Relationship status
- General capacity to experience pleasure in life
- Work and meaning of work to person
- Current partnership: length of relationship
- Past crises in the relationship and how the couple solved them
- How does the couple handle disagreements and anger
- How does the couple divide up work/ roles/financial responsibilities/parenting

Individual session, orientation/gender/ relationship history

- Sexual orientation
- Age of awareness of sexual orientation
- Shame about sexual orientation or sexual habits from earlier development?
- Gender—self-esteem and body image
- Relationships: length, satisfaction, changes over time, upsetting events in relationship

Individual session, sexual history with intergenerational and sociocultural focus

- Earliest remembered sexual experiences and general attitude about these experiences
- How learned about sex: What did family teach about male and female sexuality?
- What were the positive and negative, overt and covert messages received about sex?
- What cultural messages are believed about male sexuality? For instance, how would the client finish the phrase, "A real man should…."
- How would the client's father or grandfather have answered the above question?
- How was the client introduced to, or socialized to, these cultural messages?
- Childhood, adolescent, and early adult sexual development and sexual experiences
- Sexual mistreatment or trauma. Note: It is normal for people to initially downplay trauma history. Often a client will provide more detail about past history of trauma later in the session or later in sex therapy.

(continued)

TABLE 8.1   The Intersystem Assessment: Individual and Couple (continued)

Individual session, general

- Health data
- General health
- Relaxation/stress—self-awareness
- History of serious illness and family of origin history
- Current medications—this is especially important because of effect on delayed ejaculation
- Alcohol and substance use, including marijuana, cocaine—effect on delayed ejaculation
- Thought and mood (i.e., ruminations, anxiety, depression, obsessions/compulsions, thought disorders, prior mental health challenges—effect on delayed ejaculation)

Individual session, sexual history with individual focus

- Any difficulty with erections—important to differentiate from delayed ejaculation?
- Any pain during erection?
- When did difficulty with ejaculation begin?
- Does the person have retrograde ejaculation due to prior surgeries?
- Does the person experience orgasm even though they cannot experience ejaculation?
- Difficulty with infertility or having children
- If have children, how have children affected sense of sexual self and sex life?
- General current attitude about sex and its importance in life: What are beliefs about sex?
- Self-concept as a sexual person
- Is sexual behavior ever enjoyable? When?
- Decisions about safer sex and birth control
- Current feelings about masturbation and does masturbation lead to ejaculation?

Couples session, interactional information:

- What is this couple's history of sexual interaction together?
- How do they communicate about sex?
- What is their motivation for sexual interaction at this time?
- How frequent is sexual activity?
- Who initiates and what happens: What is their typical sexual pattern?
- Range of sexual behaviors and comfort level
- What is a typical situation where delayed ejaculation occurs?
- Are either aware if he is under pressure to perform, experiences "spectatoring," or is mechanical or detached in approach?
- When does he lose his erotic focus and feel pressure?
- Does the person with delayed ejaculation avoid intense sensory experience with his partner during sexual activity (i.e., avoid wetness in kissing or genital contact) or avoid increased sensory intensity like heavy breathing or moaning?

- If ejaculation occurs with masturbation, what are the specific actions, thoughts, fantasies that he relies on to assure ejaculation?
- Current feelings about partner initiating sex and how does he respond?

- Can he have a subjective feeling of pleasure, enjoy stimulation from his partner, and direct his partner in ways to stimulate him?
- Is he able to ejaculate to manual stimulation from his partner?
- How does the couple handle the partner's desire for orgasm?
- If the partner has an orgasm, does sexual interaction continue?
- Is either partner comfortable with masturbation in front of the other?
- How well do they know each other's bodies, and what "works" in sexual pleasure?
- What happens when things don't "work"? Does either partner get frustrated or accusatory? If so, how does the couple handle these difficulties?
- Does intercourse take place? If so, does he sometimes ejaculate during intercourse? How long does this take?

Discussion of sex therapy

- Assess their motivation for treatment.
- Are they able to plan sexual interactions?
- Do they hold the myth that good sex equals spontaneous sex?

what will happen in a sex therapy session (Wincze & Carey, 2001). The clinician then proceeds to ask how the individual or couple was referred for therapy, if either has ever sought sex therapy or psychotherapy before, and, if so, what that experience was like for him or them. Following the client's line of reasoning for choosing a specific therapist will provide information about how this client assesses his own situation, fantasies he may have about "instant cures" or pace of treatment, and general level of awareness of how psychotherapy works. It is useful to explore how long the client knew about the possibility of sex therapy but waited to begin.

It is important to discuss the gender of the therapist with the client and if this was an important consideration in selecting the therapist. If the client is assigned a therapist at a clinic and has not chosen the therapist, the therapist will need to ask the client how the client feels about having a same-gender or different-gender therapist. For some, the therapist's gender is not an important issue. But most clients will have feelings one way or the other about the effect their therapist's gender has on their comfort level in talking about sexual concerns (Maurice, 1999). Clients may feel strongly that they do not wish to discuss their sexual problems with a woman either due to embarrassment or due to feelings that she "could never understand" what he is going through. Conversely, the client may feel that talking to a woman is easier because a male therapist would make the client feel more inadequate or less masculine. In fact, in a research study involving 65 couples randomly assigned to a man, a woman, or a dual sex therapy team, there was no significant difference in treatment outcomes (LoPiccolo, Heiman, Hogan & Roberts, 1985).

The therapist may predict that at times the client/couple will feel frustrated or experience a loss of hope. The therapist may even request that if the client/couple becomes so frustrated that they are considering terminating that they will first come in and talk with the therapist before ending treatment. The therapist's prediction of frustration and despair and the invitation to discuss even matters of disappointment with the therapist serve as a parallel process mirroring the way that the couple will eventually learn to talk constructively with each other about disappointments without disengaging from sexual interaction. Finally, in the treatment of delayed ejaculation, it is especially important to discuss the need for an individualized treatment plan (Maurice, 1999). Some clients expect a standard protocol. It is useful to contrast physical therapy and psychotherapy (of which sex therapy is a subset) to highlight the differences in procedure in the two practices. In physical therapy, there is often a specific set of exercises set out in stepwise fashion. Physical therapy often uses a "carrot on a stick" approach—certain exercises will produce certain results. The therapist in sex therapy must create a tone of positive hope for improvement but cannot promise a specific outcome by following a stepwise program. However, sex therapy should make sense to clients, and time will be needed to explain interventions (Metz & McCarthy, 2007).

The assessment takes several sessions and usually includes one individual session with each partner. In individual sessions, a greater emphasis can be placed on developmental history, social, cultural, and religious influences and any concerns that may be difficult for the individual to address with the partner present.

Treatment of Delayed Ejaculation

Treatment of delayed ejaculation must proceed flexibly, integrating the individual, interactional, and intergenerational approaches characteristic of intersystem sex therapy.

Treatment techniques routinely rely on three things:

1. Cognitive-behavioral therapy (CBT), which implements homework (sometimes referred to as *homeplay*) assignments that increase competence.
2. Insight-oriented strategies, which reduce self-blame and judgment and increase feelings of self-acceptance.
3. Interactional strategies, which promote intimacy and mutuality as well as further sexuality education and positive sexual interaction for the couple.

Competence, self-acceptance, and furthering mutuality are the base for a more successful resolution to the problem of delayed ejaculation.

The treatment of delayed ejaculation may take only a few months when the problem is primarily the result of sexual misinformation and mild anxiety and the person is able to engage in specific behavior change—like more direct stimulation and personal focus on pleasure. However, delayed ejaculation is more often a treatment of behavior accommodation, where longer-term issues are uncovered and certain aspects of personality "are what they are," meaning resistant to change. Then ejaculation may be accomplished occasionally, but delayed ejaculation remains intermittently and must be accommodated and endured at least some of the time. In these situations, the couple will need to reinforce that their friendship and mutual acceptance are vital parts of their sexual life (Metz & McCarthy, 2007).

Medication/Biologic Approaches and the Individual

Individual approaches include a respect for possible biologic and genetic precursors of delayed ejaculation. At this time, there are no medications that specifically treat lifelong or acquired delayed ejaculation. In the future some medication may be developed that would involve stimulation of the dopamine, noradrenalin, and oxytocin receptors in the brain (Hartmann & Waldinger, 2007).

It is possible for some individuals, whose delayed ejaculation is associated with not reaching adequate sensory thresholds, to be helped by the use of vibratory stimulation. In one presentation of lifelong delayed ejaculation, the individual purchased a small battery-operated vibrator that he learned to use and found stimulation pleasurable against his upper inner thigh, on his perineum, and at the base of the shaft of his penis. He used the vibrator to successfully achieve sensory thresholds to orgasm while masturbating alone. He was not currently in a partnership so it is not possible to tell if he was able to successfully ejaculate with a partner. He was cautioned by the sex therapist about "idiosyncratic masturbation" and learned to masturbate to ejaculation without the vibrator.

If the individual is taking any medication that may contribute to delayed ejaculation, it is recommended that the clinician work with the treating physician to alleviate medication interference whenever possible (Segraves, 1995). This may include, for instance in the case of some SSRIs, the possibility of reducing the dosage, switching to another medication with fewer side effects or possibly adding a medication (e.g., buproprion) where appropriate. Explaining to the client that medication dosing, switching, or adding will require teamwork, an inquisitive attitude, and patience is important in the client's tolerance of this sometimes long and frustrating road of treatment.

It is often possible that an individual with delayed ejaculation develops erectile dysfunction. In these cases, the person may be helped by treatment with sildenafil.

Some clients do not have erectile dysfunction but experience a positive placebo effect from taking sildenafil while treating delayed ejaculation. Developing patience in treatment is not easy for clients, and some clients respond more positively when they feel they are "doing something." The benefits of this must always be weighed against the drawbacks that may include the client thinking that medicines are the preferred route of treatment, a commonly held belief in the United States.

Sensory Defensiveness or Anxiety Treatments and the Individual

Having noted the central role that anxiety or obsessiveness plays either in helping to create or to further problems of delayed ejaculation, the introduction of anxiety-reduction techniques is a significant part of sex therapy for delayed ejaculation. These techniques are essentially cognitive-behavioral techniques and begin with teaching the individual mindfulness and breathing techniques, progressive relaxation, and increasing sensory tolerance (Metz & McCarthy, 2007).

For many individuals with delayed ejaculation, there may be problems with sensory defensiveness—a condition in which normal sensory input, like certain smells, tastes, sounds, or touch, may be experienced as overwhelming and anxiety producing by a person with sensory defensiveness (Curtis, 2001). For instance, an individual who is mucus averse and dislikes open-mouth kissing or the sensation of vulvovaginal "wetness" may have difficulty reaching the necessary sensory threshold for ejaculation in the presence of a partner because the normal wetness or slipperiness of sex is uncomfortable for the individual. In these situations, it is necessary to teach techniques of increasing sensory tolerance through progressive desensitization not only to touch and wetness but also to the amount or intensity of the experience, focusing on intimacy and closeness rather than on performance (Metz & McCarthy, 2007). A client may select the homework assignment of exploring different types of kissing without further sexual demand (often referred to in sex therapy as *nondemand*), increasing tolerance for open-mouth kissing and tongue exploration. Or a client who is unable to ejaculate during intercourse may experiment with the sensation of nondemand "wetness" and "closeness" by taking showers with a partner and learning to explore genitals, to use lubrications, and even to rub his penis against his partner's body while they are both "wet all over" in the shower.

Masturbation Flexibility and the Individual

Many individuals with delayed ejaculation have strong idiosyncratic masturbation patterns that have been in place a long time. Using an educational approach, the sex therapist encourages the individual to reconsider the inflexible masturbation pattern and to begin to slowly branch out both in stimulation (i.e., by using different positions and different intensities of touch when self-stimulating) and by using different fantasies or visualizations when self-stimulating. The technique is especially useful when the delayed ejaculation is situational and involves a partner but is not present when the person is masturbating alone. The sex therapist explains to the individual that increasing his flexibility in masturbation will translate into being more capable of openness to partner touch and flexible response to arousal in partnership.

Resistance is a therapeutic term indicating that the client is avoiding insight, behavior change, or communication change with partner (Goldstein, 1995). Resistance to changing—or, more accurately, *trying* to change idiosyncratic masturbation patterns—should be pointed out to the client. The client's resistance to trying new things needs to be explored with the client so that he can use insight into his own behavior as a part of his treatment.

Resistance is correctly interpreted by some clients to be a way of really staying in place with his partner. Clinicians often observe that a client may become aware that he does not like his partner and is using delayed ejaculation to get his body to speak for him. In some cases, this has been the beginning of the end for the relationship and has led the client to explain he has no real sexual interest in the partner, which has, in turn, led to the couple's decision to separate. However, other couples have used this awareness to address the reasons why there is no sexual interest and to rededicate themselves to creating a positive and playful relationship with the hope that this will lead to more positive interactions in the sexual relationship. For many with motivation and mutual generosity, this is the case.

Increasing Awareness of Outside Influences

Sex therapy often reduces anxiety and self-criticism by exploring the sources of external messages that have influenced the client and encouraging new perspectives about the meanings of those messages. Often a process of reframing takes place. Weeks (1994) pointed out that exploring the real intentions and realistic assessment of behavior can help the client reach different conclusions about the meaning of a sexual behavior like delayed ejaculation. If he has considered himself to be "inadequate," "withholding," "uncaring," or "over the hill," it will be helpful to explore with this individual the other meanings that delayed ejaculation can carry. Notably, a therapist can remind the client that many individuals with delayed ejaculation are very caring and are actually being overly responsive or attentive to their partners. They are committed to not being aggressive, selfish, or overwhelming their partner with their own sexual needs. They may suffer from a lack of sex education and are self-conscious about sexuality information. And they may just be trying too hard, not having pleasure, pressing on because they feel the demand to perform.

Hopefully, the client can begin to see the ways he has been burdened by these negative beliefs that often stem from either faulty intergenerational messages or social expectations he has inculcated. He may advance this insight orientation by using the therapy to understand the background family history that helped create those intergenerational messages about sexuality that were so negative about sexual involvement. Some clients realize that early messages about sex being dirty, immoral, or shameful have contributed to anxiety in sexual interaction. At times, the insight may include a memory of having been caught masturbating as a child—memories that are inevitably connected with having displeased the adult and memories that led to negative feelings about sexual pleasure. A client may also reflect on the cultural messages he learned about his own sexuality and sexual performance, on messages from television, magazines, and the Internet that stress performance not pleasure, and on disconnection of the man from his penis and his partner. He may also recognize that he was socialized not to seek help from others for his problems.

Finally, sex therapy may stimulate awareness of grief and loss for the individual who has struggled with the problem. Understanding that he has a right to grieve and that sexual dysfunction is a loss that "no one brings over a casserole for" can create an environment of openness and therapeutic alliance. The very process of talking in sex therapy, of grieving, and of gaining new information about sexual function can lead to decreased performance anxiety and increased self-esteem.

Interactional Techniques

If a client with delayed ejaculation has a partner, it is crucial to include that person in the treatment if at all possible. The partner will need an opportunity to dispel myths, to grieve the presence of the problem, and to engage positively in finding more successful ways to interact. The couple will be helped through increasing psychosexual skills with graduated homework assignments, through decreasing performance pressure, and through increasing comfort and playfulness (Metz & McCarthy, 2007). Couples who are capable of relaxing and playing together may be helped by the therapist introducing the concept of *borrowing competencies* from other parts of their relationship. The therapist asks the couple to discuss when and how they relax and play together. For instance, if this couple enjoys playing cards, hiking together, or any other shared activity, the therapist can point out that the couple knows how to experience pleasure and playfulness that can be borrowed over into the now "too serious" sex life. This can contribute to a more comfortable focus on nondemand physical playfulness including nongenital massage (i.e., touch that is not sexually or genitally focused). The therapist continues to point out that playfulness requires a focus on one's own sensory experience, that is, being selfish at the same time one is engaged in partnership.

Treatment is often linear, beginning with nondemand playfulness, building pleasurable experiences and then proceeding on to nondemand physical playfulness and sensate focus exercises. The couple learns to increase comfort with increased erotic stimulation, thereby decreasing self-consciousness. Couples need to be reminded that trust in being physical, erotic, and sensual takes time.

The therapist may find that there is disappointment on the partner's part to the "slow" pace of therapy or therapeutic interventions. It is important to "hear the partner out" when concerns arise as well as continue to assess how the couple sustain friendship and intimacy. The therapist encourages the partner and person with delayed ejaculation to see themselves as a team engaging in desensitizing techniques, in reducing performance anxiety, and in increasing sensuality. The partner may need to be encouraged to continue to understand her or his own sexual response as separate and important.

Work with couples should include intergenerational messages about sexuality for both individuals. When suggesting the couple try any technique, it is important that the couple feels they have the choice to do the assignment. The sex therapist can offer a range of two or three different possible assignments, thereby allowing the couple to make the decision as to which one they will try. The couple should also decide who will be in charge of initiating homework and may need to establish day, time, and place for the homework. Grieving the idealization that sex should be spontaneous may be a part of the treatment for the couple as well.

In addition, couples can each create their own "desire" checklist of behaviors or interactions that they enjoy. They can work together to create pleasant and pleasurable places in which to enjoy sex (Foley, 2005). Some couples have sexual scripts of how they want sexual interaction to proceed, and these scripts may need discussion and modification in sex therapy. Establishing the expectation that sexual interaction will be about mutual pleasure while decreasing the focus on perfect performance is an important part of modifying sexual scripts (Foley, Kope, & Sugrue, 2002). Some couples need to work on reading each other's body cues and to use massage, dance, or exercises to learn to mirror each other's movements, increasing comfort in being together.

If an individual with delayed ejaculation has avoided intercourse for some time and is partnered to a postmenopausal woman, she may have some vaginal atrophy if she has not been engaging in penetrative sex (Foley,

2005). If intercourse is resumed after a time of no sex, a woman may have dyspareunia (Foley et al., 2002). She may need to investigate the use of a localized estrogen replacement (e.g., Vagifem [Novo Nordisk, Princeton, NJ]; Estrace vaginal cream (Warner Chilcott, Rockaway, NJ); Estring (Pfizer, New York), as well as to practice penetration with fingers, a penis-shaped vibrator, or vaginal dilators (vaginal inserters) before resuming sexual intercourse. Discussion of lubrications should be included in the sex therapy as well (Foley, 2005).

Intersystems Approaches in Three Therapeutic Situations

If a man with delayed ejaculation does not have a partner, the sex therapist might recommend that he use a vibrator with masturbation, might encourage further sexuality education, might increase his understanding about intergenerational messages from his childhood, and might recommend flexibility in masturbation techniques so that the client does not become overly dependent on one way. Clients can also learn to pleasure to arousal for 10 or 15 minutes without focusing on or attempting orgasm, followed by shifting their focus to other things and allowing arousal and erection to abate. Practicing this emphasis on pleasure over performance often helps with intermittent delayed ejaculation and spectatoring.

If a client with delayed ejaculation also has anxiety or sensory defensiveness with his partner, the sex therapist will need to predict a longer course of treatment, addressing the client's tendency to retreat to self-stimulation, educate about the role of anxiety and sensory defensiveness, and help his partner to address reactivity or disappointment in sexual situations. Encouraging nondemand pleasurable touch, increasing intimacy behaviors and language, and encouraging focus on the couple's friendship and other resiliencies may provide the necessary ingredients for change. This approach may also work for couples with the intermittent delayed ejaculation that many men experience with aging.

In more complex presentations, especially for those clients who must overcome trauma or untangle pleasurable responses from fear or anxiety about intimacy, therapy will assist the couple in gaining understanding about physiological reactivity post-trauma or anxiety and its effect on sexual functioning. A therapist may need to flexibly provide some individual treatment if a client is experiencing flashbacks or triggers when sexually active. Sometimes, the client may need his or her own individual sex therapy to work through past traumatic experiences. In these situations, the therapist will need to help the couple understand how histories of child-hood neglect or past trauma are affecting the couple in their attempts to engage sexually. The therapist can help the couple stay positively engaged in their therapy, address feelings of anxiety, frustration, or shame, and minimize blaming. Homework assignments must be flexible and slowly paced. A coherent narrative of the trauma experience may need to be developed piece by piece (Naperstek, 2004; Scaer, 2001; Solomon & Siegel, 2003). Finally, the couple will need to be reminded to reduce idealizations of "perfect sex" and to become more accepting of sex that is "good enough" most of the time (Metz & McCarthy, 2007).

Future Directions

The diagnosis and treatment of delayed ejaculation is an area that needs further study and collaboration between disciplines to develop a more definitive diagnosis—even if it is a complex diagnosis. The diagnosis of delayed ejaculation will be affected by both the rising numbers of aging men in the boomer generation and the increasing numbers of men using medications that may affect ejaculation and orgasm. This will add pressure to look for better ways to research the treatment of delayed ejaculation, both medically and psychologically. The intersystem treatment approach is currently viewed as the most relevant. Continued research is needed about the effectiveness of this treatment technique and the characteristics of clients who tend to benefit from this approach. At this time, there is no medical treatment for delayed ejaculation. In fact, it responds best to intersystems approaches combined with motivation, flexibility, and patience on the part of both the client and the sex therapist.

References

American Psychiatric Association (APA) (2000). *Diagnostic and statistical manual of mental disorders* (4th ed., text revision). Washington, DC: Author.
Apfelbaum, B. (2000). Retarded ejaculation: A much misunderstood syndrome. In S. Leiblum & R. Rosen (Eds.), *Principles and practice of sex therapy* (3rd ed., pp. 205–241). New York: Guilford Press.
Apfelbaum, B. (2001). What the sex therapies tell us about sex. In P. Kleinplatz (Ed.), *New directions in sex therapy: Innovations and alternatives* (pp. 5–28). New York: Brunner-Routledge.

Bancroft, J. (1989). *Human sexuality and its problems* (2nd ed.). Edinburgh: Churchill Livingstone.

Bancroft, J. & Janssen, E. (2000). The dual control model of male sexual response: A theoretical approach to centrally mediated erectile dysfunction. *Neuroscience and Biobehavioral Reviews, 24,* 571–579.

Barlow, D. H. (2002). *Anxiety and its disorders: The nature and treatment of anxiety and panic.* New York: Guilford Press.

Baucom, D. H., Stanton, S., & Epstein, N. B. (2003). Anxiety disorders. In D. K. Snyder & M. A. Whisman (Eds.), *Treating difficult couples: Helping clients with co-existing mental and relationship disorders* (pp. 57–87). New York: Guilford Press.

Bindley, G. S. & Gillan, P. (1982). Men and women who do not have orgasms. *British Journal of Psychiatry, 140,* 351–356.

Blanker, M. H., Ruud Bosch, J. L. H., Groeneveld, F. P. M. J., Bohnen, A. M., Prins, A. D., Thomas, S., et al. (2001). Erectile and ejaculatory dysfunction in a community-based sample of men 50 to 78 years old: Prevalence, concerns, and relation to sexual activity. *Urology, 57*(4), 763–768.

Colpi, G., Weidner, W., Jungwirth, A., Pomerol, J., Papp, G., Hargreave, T., & Dohle, G. (2004). EAU Guidelines on Ejaculatory Dysfunction. *European Urology, 46,* 555–558.

Curtis, V. (2001). Dirt, disgust, and disease: Is hygiene in our genes? *Perspectives in Biology and Medicine, 44*(1), 17–31.

DasGupta, R. & Fowler, C.J. (2002). Sexual and urological dysfunction in multiple sclerosis: Better understanding and improved therapies. *Current Opinion Neurology, 5,* 271–278.

Delmonte, M. M. (1984). Case reports on the use of meditative relaxation as an intervention strategy with retarded ejaculation. *Biofeedback & Self Regulation, 9,* 209–214.

Foley, S. (1994). Psychogenic sexual dysfunction. In R. Lechtenberg & D. Ohl (Eds.), *Sexual dysfunction: Neurologic, urologic, and gynecologic aspects* (pp. 189–211). Philadelphia: Lea & Febiger.

Foley, S. (2005). *Sex and love for grownups: A no-nonsense guide to a life of passion.* New York: Sterling.

Foley, S., Kope, S. A., & Sugrue, D. (2002). *Sex matters for women: A complete guide to taking care of your sexual self.* New York: Guilford Press.

Goldstein, E. G. (1995). *Ego psychology and social work practice.* New York: Free Press.

Hartmann, U. & Waldinger, M. (2007). Treatment of delayed ejaculation. In S. Leiblum & R. Rosen (Eds.), *Principles and practice of sex therapy* (4th ed., pp. 241–276). New York: Guilford Press.

Hawton, K. (1989). *Sex therapy: A practical guide.* Oxford: University Press.

Hendry, W. F. (1998). Disorders of ejaculation: congenital, acquired and functional. *British Journal of Urology, 82,* 331–341.

Kelly, G. F. (2003). *Sexuality today: The human perspective.* New York: McGraw-Hill.

Laumann, E. O., Gagnon, J. H., Michael, R. T., & Michaels, S. (1994). *The social organization of sexuality: Sexual practices in the United States.* Chicago: University of Chicago Press.

Lew, M. (1990). *Victims no longer: Men recovering from incest and other sexual child abuse.* New York: Harper and Row.

Lipsith, J., McCann, D., & Goldmeier, D. (2003). Male psychogenic sexual dysfunction: The role of masturbation. *Sexual and Relationship Therapy, 18*(4), 447–471.

LoPiccolo, J., Heiman, J. R., Hogan, D. R., & Roberts, C. W. (1985). Effectiveness of single therapists versus cotherapy teams in sex therapy. *Journal of Consulting Clinical Psychology, 53,* 287–294.

Lopicollo, T. A. (1994). Sexual function in persons with diabetes: Issues in research, treatment and education. *Clinical Psychology Review, 14,* 1–86.

Marumo, K. & Murai, M. (2001). Aging and erectile dysfunction: The role of aging and concomitant chronic illness. *International Journal of Urology, 8*(8), 550–557.

Maurice, W. L. (1999). *Sexual medicine in primary care.* St. Louis, MO: Mosby.

McCarthy, B. & McCarthy, E. (1998). *Male sexual awareness.* New York: Carroll & Graf.

Metz, M. E. & McCarthy, B. W. (2004). *Coping with erectile dysfunction: How to regain confidence and enjoy great sex.* Oakland, CA: New Harbinger Publications.

Metz, M. E. & McCarthy, B. W. (2007). Ejaculatory problems. In L. Vandecreek, F. L. Peterson, & J. W. Bley (Eds.), *Innovations in clinical practice: Focus on sexual health* (pp. 135–155). Sarasota, FL: Professional Resource Press.

Montejo-González, A. L., Llorca, G., Izquierdo, J. A., Ledesma, A., Bousoño, M., Calcedo, A., et al. (1997). SSRI induced sexual dysfunction: Fluoxetine, paroxetine, sertraline and fluvoxamine in a prospective, multicentre and descriptive clinical study of 344 patients. *Journal of Sex and Marital Therapy, 23,* 176–194.

Munjack, D. J. & Kanno, P. H. (1979). Retarded ejaculation: A review. *Archives of Sexual Behavior, 8,* 139–150.

Naparstek, B. (2004). *Invisible Heroes: Survivors of trauma and how they heal.* New York: Bantam.

Perelman, M. (2001). Sildenafil, sex therapy, and retarded ejaculation. *Journal of Sex Education and Therapy, 26,* 13–21.

Perelman, M. (2003, July–August). Regarding ejaculation, delayed and otherwise. [Letter to the editor]. *Journal of Andrology, 24*(4), 496.

Perelman, M. (2004). Evaluation and treatment of the ejaculatory disorders. In T. Lui (Ed.), *Atlas of male sexual dysfunction.* Philadelphia, PA: Current Medicine.

Perelman, M. A. & Rowland, D. L. (2006). Retarded ejaculation. *World Journal of Urology, 24*(6), 645–652.

Richardson, D. & Goldmeier, D. (2006). Recommendations for the management of retarded ejaculation: BASHH special interest group for sexual dysfunction. *International Journal of STD and AIDS 2006, 17,* 7–13.

Richardson, D., Nalabanda, A., & Goldmeier, D. (2006). Retarded ejaculation—A review. *International Journal of STD & AIDS 2006, 17,* 143–150.

Scaer, R. (2001). *The body bears the burden: Trauma, dissociation, and disease.* New York: Haworth.

Schlegel, P. N., Shin, D., & Goldstein, M. (1996). Urological anomalies in men with congenital absence of the vas deferens. *Journal of Urology, 155,* 1644–1648.

Schuster, T. G. & Ohl, D. A. (2002). Diagnosis and treatment of ejaculatory dysfunction. *Urologic Clinics of North America, 29,* 939–948.

Segraves, R. T. (1995). Antidepressant induced orgasm disorder. *Journal of Sex and Marital Therapy, 21,* 192–201.

Shaw, J. (1990). Play therapy with the sexual workhorse: Successful treatment with twelve cases of inhibited ejaculation. *Journal of Sex and Marital Therapy, 16,* 159–164.

Shull, G. R. & Sprenkle, D. H. (1980). Retarded ejaculation: Reconceptualization and implications for treatment. *Journal of Sex and Marital Therapy, 6,* 234–246.

Solomon, M. & Siegel, D. (2003). *Healing Trauma: Attachment, mind, body, and brain.* New York: Norton.

Waldinger, M. D. & Schweitzer, D. H. (2005). Retarded ejaculation in men: An overview of psychological and neurobiological insights. *World Journal of Urology, 23,* 76–81.

Weeks, G. (1994). The intersystem model: An integrative approach to treatment. In G. Weeks & L. Hof (Eds.), *The marital-relationship therapy casebook: Theory and application of the intersystem model* (pp. 3–34). New York: Brunner/Mazel.

Weeks, G. & Gambescia, N. (2000). *Erectile dysfunction: Integrating couple therapy, sex therapy, and medical treatment.* New York: W. W. Norton.

Wincze, J. P. & Carey, M. P. (2001). *Sexual dysfunction: A guide for assessment and treatment* (2nd ed.). New York: Guilford Press.

Zilbergeld, B. (1999). *The new male sexuality.* New York: Bantam.

9

Inhibited Arousal in Women

Kevan R. Wylie
Ruth Hallam-Jones

Contents

Introduction

Female sexual arousal disorder (FSAD) is a common condition in women
that frequently copresents with hypoactive sexual desire disorder (HSDD).
In all circumstances a careful sexual history must be taken to identify
whether the arousal disorder has come about as a consequence of HSDD or

whether any desire disorder has come about secondary to FSAD. Although some of the principles and practice within clinical management of these two conditions is similar, it is essential that as accurate a diagnosis as possible is made to clarify the thinking and formulation of the problems for the clinician, woman, or her partner.

The current epidemiological data indicate that around 40% of adult women and around 30% of adult men have at least one sexual dysfunction (Lewis et al., 2004). Nicolosi et al. (2004) found that for sexually active women, the most common problems were a lack of sexual interest (21%), lubrication difficulties (16%), and an inability to reach orgasm (16%).

The definitions for FSAD are best found within the *Diagnostic and Statistical Manual of Mental Disorders,* 4th ed., text revision (*DSM-IV-TR*) classification system (APA, 2000). The following criteria must be met:

1. Persistent or recurrent inability to attain or to maintain until completion of the sexual activity an adequate lubrication-swelling response of sexual excitement. The disturbance causes marked distress or interpersonal difficulty.
2. The sexual dysfunction is not better accounted for by another Axis I disorder (except another sexual dysfunction) and is not due exclusively to the direct physiological effects of a substance (e.g., drug abuse, medication) or a general medical condition.

Specify type: Lifelong type or acquired type
Specify type: Generalized type or situational type
Specify type: Due to psychological factors or due to combined factors

The *DSM-IV-TR* (APA, 2000) classification of sexual disorder is derived from phases of a linear sexual response cycle first described by Masters and Johnson (1966) and then Kaplan (1979). Laan and Both (2005) argued a number of serious problems with the classification criteria of *DSM-IV-TR*. The complexity of establishing "adequacy of sexual stimulation" is difficult to quantify. Clarity and evidence of normal arousal from sufficient sexual stimulation based on age, life circumstances, and sexual experience is lacking. In addition, each of the four primary *DSM-IV-TR* diagnoses are not necessarily independent. Finally, there is increasing evidence that physiological response does not necessarily coincide with subject experience. The revision by the International Committee of the American Foundation of Urological Disease (Basson, Berman, & Bernett, 2000) incorporates medical risk factors and divides arousal disorders into primary, secondary, and situational, as well as including the concept of personal distress.

Increases in blood flow through both the clitoral and vaginal tissues can bring about significant changes in the genitalia. Increases in blood flow through the middle wall of the vagina are what bring about transudate and lubrication. Increasing blood flow to the clitoral area leads to an increased prominence and fullness of the body of the clitoris, and an increase in the flow to the bulbs of the clitoris brings about other changes including swelling and sensory changes.

HSDD is defined as a persistent or recurrent deficiency or absence of sexual fantasies, thoughts, or desire for, or receptivity to, sexual activity, which causes personal distress. The absence of personal distress prevents the diagnosis being established (Basson et al., 2000). It is important to differentiate between it and related conditions such as sexual aversion, sexual anorexia, or sexual anhedonia (Boul, Hallam-Jones, & Wylie, submitted). The evolution and understanding of HSDD has been described recently by Segraves and Woodard (2006). It is important to distinguish between personal distress and interpersonal distress as the latter may involve criticism or complaints by the partner rather than the individual woman.

We wish to emphasize early on in our description that in addition to comorbidity between sexual problems, this condition may present in a number of additional ways. Sexual arousal has both psychological and physiological correlates. The emphasis of each of these, and in particular the individual clinician's determination of importance of these correlates, can have a profound impact on both the understanding and management of the condition. Many psychological components to sexual arousal can occur independently of genital arousal. Psychic excitation, sexual anticipation, emotional longing, and related anticipatory and preparatory sexual behaviors are just some of these. These must be differentiated from the lack of sexual fantasy and desire to engage in sexual activity seen with HSDD. The physiological correlates that accompany genital arousal can include genital swelling around the introitus, sensory change including tingling and heightened sensitivity, clitoral body prominence, protuberance and firmness, and a general awareness of moisture or actual oozing of fluid from the vagina. Genital arousal is a combination of increased blood flow both in the vagina (causing the transudate of lubrication) and the clitoral bulbs and body (which brings about many of the other signs and experiences).

FSAD, like so many other sexual problems, can have a negative impact on the general well-being and emotional well-being of the woman. This can affect her overall quality of life and have a substantial impact on the relationship with her partner. A number of important comorbid conditions may be associated with this condition, and it is likely that there are common risk-factor categories associated for sexual dysfunctions of arousal in both men and women (Lewis et al., 2004). The principal areas of concern involve cardiovascular status, neurological conditions, and psychiatric conditions. One of the commonest cardiovascular conditions is diabetes mellitus, which is increasingly regarded to have a similar impact on genital blood flow in women as in men. Other conditions including hypertension, dyslipidemia, and smoking cigarettes are also risk factors (ibid.).

Endocrinological contributions toward FSAD include conditions bringing about the hypo-oestrogenism states natural menopause and surgically induced menopause. The contribution of reduced androgens is less clear but is considered by many as a contributory factor. Neurological conditions include multiple sclerosis and conditions that bring about autonomic neuropathy. Common psychiatric conditions include anxiety, depression, and anorexia nervosa (Maurice, 2003). Women who are prescribed medications for cardiovascular or psychiatric conditions are particularly prone to the sexual side effects secondary to these conditions.

In summary, physiological changes of FSAD include damage or disease of the blood vessels of the pelvic region or nerves of the pelvic region and generalized vascular disease (e.g., peripheral vascular disease, hypertension, diabetes mellitus). Medical conditions may bring about hormonal change such as hypothyroidism, hypo-oestrogenism, and hypoandrogenism (e.g., menopause), as may the effect of prescribed medications. Psychological causes include anxiety, depression, the consequences of sexual trauma and abuse, bereavement, relational problems, and major psychiatric conditions (e.g., posttraumatic stress disorder, major depression, psychosis).

In addition to the medical factors just described, interrelational and intraemotional (e.g., intracognitive and intrapsychodynamic) factors can further impact and contribute toward sexual function or dysfunction. As such, it is important that the psychosexual therapist and sexual medicine clinician undertakes a thorough assessment of each of these components. Whether these are addressed either by one or both of the cotherapists or by an assisting general medical practitioner or physician will depend on local policy. Treatment models that focus on identified symptoms, "diseased end organs," or identified partners often fail to provide a holistic and integrative understanding of the various contributory factors. It is our belief that such treatment plans that remain grounded in this individualist and end organ perspective are both inadequate and less helpful than viewing matters in a more holistic and systemic way by identifying how the physical, psychological, and interrelational problems affect the woman, the couple, and their general well-being and relatedness. The precise relationship between sexual satisfaction and relationship satisfaction remains disputed and hard to measure. In general the literature suggests that individuals with greater relationship satisfaction may also report improved sexual satisfaction (Byers, 2005; Yeh, Lorenz, Wickrama, Conger, & Elder, 2006).

Assessment of FSAD

Nearly half of men and women in a survey done in 2005 had experienced at least one sexual problem but only 19% sought help from their physicians (Moreira et al., 2005). It should be emphasized again that FSAD must have a thorough assessment, particularly as the detail given by the referrer may be minimal or misleading. However, the complexity and associated comorbidity of the individual and the partner found in FSAD means that the therapists must repeatedly review the state and progress of assessment. Therapeutic interventions may also act as diagnostic tools to demonstrate ongoing assessment needs. As such, there may be a blurred distinction between when assessment ends and treatment begins. For many couples, sensate focus has served this dual purpose.

Our preferred approach to dealing with problems presenting as FSAD is one of an intersystem approach with five different components (Weeks, 2004). The first of these is to understand what the woman brings into the relationship as well as what her partner (if present) brings into the couple. Each will have his or her own physiological perspective, and it is important to remember that the man or lesbian partner may have his or her own contributory causes of dysfunction. The second component is the woman's psychological makeup. This component is almost certainly the individual's psychological makeup, which is something that incorporates the individual's values, attitudes, opinions, general intelligence, general upbringing, and any psychopathology, however "soft" that may be. This is important for assessing any woman with FSAD. The third component is the interrelational aspects of the couple, and for this to be dealt with adequately a systemic perspective must be taken. The fourth element deals with family of origin for both individuals in the relationship, since both families and upbringing within particular environments (e.g., education, religion, society, culture) can all have an impact on individuals' perspective of sexuality. The final component in the intersystem model is how the environmental, societal, cultural, religious, and historical factors seem to have a marked influence on both decision making and judgments.

As part of the initial assessment in our clinic, a brief questionnaire is sent to patients that collects the epidemiological data and brief outline of their previous medical and psychosexual history. Obtaining this information in advance saves time during the therapeutic sessions and to a degree ameliorates the possibility of one person being presented as the specific person holding the problem (and so meriting referral). Both partners are invited to complete and return the questionnaire in advance of their appointment, which needs to accommodate the needs of both partners so that both members of the couple are able to attend together from the outset. This can then be perused by both clinicians and any supervising team so that some basic information, at least according to the reality of the individual completing the form, is obtained. Initial hypotheses and formulations can therefore be established (see http://www.porterbrook-clinic.org.uk/publicdocs/CouplesQ.pdf for the questionnaire).

Part of working systemically is to be engrossed in what is happening in the session and in the current reality of the couple rather than being allowed to be "indoctrinated" with the "story according to" either or both partners who attempt to assist the clinician in understanding the basis of a problem. We recognize and appreciate the importance of establishing any organic contribution toward the problem. This is crucial because not only can steps be taken to prevent deterioration of any biological processes, but also any litigious issues that may follow a failure to diagnose such issues is addressed. Notwithstanding this, as explained already, a number of factors must be addressed in any attempt to understand the individual and couple issues. We cannot stress enough that an initial perusal of these completed comprehensive forms is often extremely revealing and helps the cotherapist and supervisory team to make a formulation and progress in the first therapeutic session thereafter.

Preliminary Assessment

The intersystem approach developed by Weeks (1994) pertaining to individual interactional and intergenerational components is extremely helpful in resolving couples-related problems. One of the difficult decisions for clinicians is whether to proceed with sessions when one partner fails to appear. This is particularly complicated during the preliminary assessments. Our approach is to meet with the individual attending the appointment for just three to four minutes and explain our way of working. We then ask the individual to bring his or her partner next time and write to both parties explaining how important it is for us to be able to see them both together. If one partner refuses to attend, then we will of course see the individual person (usually the person with a presenting problem)—but in a separate appointment that does not involve the support of a clinical supervisory observation team. This approach is not always entirely understandable or even acceptable in a publicly funded health service system, but with adequate documentation and advance information it is important to maintain boundaries within a systemic environment. Although we maintain confidentiality, it is not possible in couples work to have information from an individual that is not shared with the partner.

When an individual woman attends alone, a different approach may be used where a full psychosexual, psychosocial, and medical history can be taken from the woman over one or two 45- to 60-minute assessment appointments. This can then be used to assess and provide for sexual education needs at the same time. The use of questionnaires has been recommended and may be used in couples sessions as well. One such is the Sexual Interest and Desire Inventory-Female (SIDI-F; Sills et al., 2005). The Profile of Female Sexual Function (PFSF) is specifically for women with suspected HSDD in postmenopausal women (Derogatis et al., 2004). The Female Sexual Function Index (FSFI) is established for self-report and can discriminate between clinical and nonclinical populations (Rosen et al., 2000). It has been specifically validated in women with HSDD and orgasmic disorders (Meston, 2003).

Key Area of Questions

One of the key issues to address is the extent of the relational etiology in causing this disorder. The vital question when working with couples is who (the woman or her partner) is distressed about the inhibited arousal and what they are distressed about. This question needs asking and reviewing as the therapeutic relationship develops with the woman. Why has she sought help?

If the arousal difficulties have meant that the woman experiences no sexual satisfaction and a secondary desire disorder has developed, then why would the woman seek assistance to improve something that is now so unsatisfying? The usual answer is to retain the relationship due to her partner's distress. Recent work by Dennerstein (2006) reported similar findings. This is a difficult starting point for a therapy that needs motivation to succeed. If the woman has the need to establish motivation for sexual activity, then this is the key not only to the therapeutic approach but also to the possible outcome. Exploring relational issues leads to understanding the possibility of change both in the woman's sexual attitude and behavior and in the adaptability of the couple relationship to other styles of behavior. For example, if her loss of arousal or desire is linked to a very different sexual timetable with her partner and the partner is not able to change his cycle of need for sexual activity, then this may prevent any therapeutic work, despite the woman's actual motivation to change herself. A variety of specific assessment activities can be used with a couple to try to help them understand how they function together at a sexual level and some of the reasons. These activities can be part of the session work (structured intervention), or they may be set as tasks (strategic intervention) for the couple to carry out at home to bring back to a later session. Systemically, activities rather than "heavy discussion" are often more useful, acting as creative interventions, than mere reflection or reviewing of the past.

A decision as to whether the woman can be offered a physical treatment without going through an extended assessment may happen when there is a clear temporal recollection of physical symptoms that precedes other complaints or difficulties (Althof, Dean, Derogatis, Rosen, & Sisson, 2005.)

Sex Therapy Assessment Activities

We have chosen to describe a horticultural view of therapy, with the goal of a *green, organic garden* being representational of the healthy couple relationship (Table 9.1, Box 9.1). We have therefore described the process in a gardening concept to draw on this easily understood and commonly appreciated metaphor. For example, the woman with a physical etiology may need to nurture the garden plants already growing by pruning, feeding, and strengthening her arousal skills that are still functioning. The concept of sexual activity being considered natural only if it is spontaneous is usually unhelpful. Activity can be reframed as needing to be chosen, grown, nurtured, and worked for by the individual and couple and is used through our assessment and thereafter within the treatment options. A number of these assessment activities can be carried out during the session together or may be given to carry out at home as a task. The following concepts of therapeutic

TABLE 9.1 Horticultural View of Couple Therapy

Issue	Activity	Results Possible
Initial review of motivation to grow	Is there desire to change and grow? Small tasks/activities set.	This may aid the couple to break out of the status quo or become a diagnostic tool for the therapist to demonstrate the difficulty in moving and suggest why this may be. For example, a couple may be unable to set a time to regularly give each other a listening opportunity. Success in carrying this out may improve the communication, but failure may demonstrate any of the problems of lack of time, different priorities for time, anxiety about becoming more attached, fear of sharing and being vulnerable or other relevant issues, or of regaining hope only to find it failing again.
Diagnostic introductory check of ability to grow	Assess individual goals and priority areas of the relationship.	Realistic discussion of the inability of the couple's relationship to meet the desired goals for each partner may be a vital component.
Complex tools to measure or assess garden growth	Assess satisfaction and confidence in each individual and level of inhibition and behavioral skills—using worksheets, exercises, and self-assessment tools.	*Tree climbing.* How strong and brave are they in achieving tasks when they work together? *Reviewing the relational roots.* This involves looking at past events and experiences in their sexual and relationship history. These activities need to be done by each individual and then shared together as a couple would do so to explain their different experiences in the past for learning. This is not approached as dynamic therapy but with an intended plan as to how they will work together given their different skills/models of working. *Genogram of growth.* A genogram is extremely useful to look at who talked to them about sex and what those comments and events and learning experiences were (Hof & Berman, 1986). This can be linked to a full-family genogram to find out who didn't talk about matters such as sex or who modeled different sexual behaviors and interests. You can ask the questions: Who talked in your family about sex? What did they tell you? Did you believe it, and was it right? This work may be given as a verbal task to be carried out on an audio recorder as an alternative to drawing it all on paper.

(continued)

TABLE 9.1   Horticultural View of Couple Therapy (continued)

Issue	Activity	Results Possible
		Body image or plant diagrams. This activity is linked to body image. Body image is an important area to understand with women suffering with this condition because the therapist needs to link their ability and experience of sexual arousal with how they view the rest of their body. The standard statements used are: You won't want to encourage anyone else to help your body get aroused if you don't actually like your own body; or You have to like your own body before you can allow another permission to arouse your body. This foundation attitude is key to what the therapist is assessing. For example, it is often quite helpful to get the individuals in the relationship to draw their body and then to color the different areas of the body with either green (i.e., acceptable; I enjoy this part of my body, I think it looks okay), yellow (i.e., I tolerate this part of my body; I think it is necessary but I don't particularly give it much attention), or red (i.e., I don't enjoy this part of my body; I don't like it being touched, I don't myself give this area any care or attention, other than what is required to keep it clean and dressed). Changes can then occur through reframing and new learned experiences of behavioral tasks.
		Beliefs about sexual issues and reasons for healthy growth. This activity that we have found to be very helpful is designed to aid the therapist to understand the couples' beliefs about sexual issues. This is achieved by giving an individual or couples a list of sexual myths and asking them to add to it the myths that they grew up with. This can explore false beliefs and also how many of the current statements and myths they still hold on to. Obviously this requires the couple to feel free in the therapeutic relationship and to be honest about what they have changed in their attitudes.
		Reviewing past storm damage. An assessment checklist that can be useful to explore includes asking them to write down any past, bad, or

Issue	Activity	Results Possible

negative experiences of sexual activity that they do remember and to make sure that they include (if necessary) their own experiences of touching themselves, which they may see as having been bad or negative. This again may link into messages the therapist got from the body image assessment, which will give the therapist further evidence of possible past history of difficult events causing poor body image. It is always worth giving more time to explore this, particularly with the potential links with sexual abuse in the past. The therapist may even find that they have talked about the body image issues without discussing abuse, but when asked about them specifically for negative and bad issues, rather than abuse issues, they may then own problems that they would not have put under the title of abuse but that the therapist might perceive as being abusive. For example, one woman presented with a piece of work she had done at home looking at her body image where her hair was colored red as were her thighs and her hands. It was not until we had looked at the bad experiences in the past that she did not see herself as having been abused, but she had a brother who had sexual activity with her, using her hair as an object of his sexual arousal, and had on occasions masturbated between her thighs using her hands to touch his penis. The link became quite clear between body image and bad experiences, and as soon as she was permitted the space to connect it, she herself wondered why she had not seen it earlier. While collecting bad experiences do not forget also to include experiences of friends and siblings that may have been highly important in shaping what the woman regards as her sexual understandings. For example, if a sibling was sent away from home because she was pregnant and she was pressured into having the baby adopted at birth, the patient may not have had any bad experiences, but her siblings' experiences will be absolutely crucial to her attitude.

(continued)

TABLE 9.1   Horticultural View of Couple Therapy (continued)

Issue	Activity	Results Possible
		Knowledge of gardening. In terms of assessing knowledge base and need for sexual education, sometimes the most useful ways of establishing how much sex education the individual or couple need and their knowledge base is to assess the issue in the session. This can be done by either helping the woman understand and share a common language (see http://www.porterbrookclinic. org.uk/publicdocs/Language.pdf) or by using written materials. One of our big failures in society is that a large percentage of our patient group have very poor sexual education and a very limited repertoire of sexual activity and very little understanding of sexual language. Giving the couple written material can be helpful as it gives them an opportunity to think the issues through while reading the book. They can then come back and discuss it with the therapist in detail. The couple takes some responsibility of raising the areas of difficulty and conflict. Examples of the books we might suggest are given in Box 9.1, and we suggest that the therapist should read these in advance before making a recommendation. Any woman with inhibited arousal should be encouraged to look at these in detail and then review the material with their therapist.
		Relooking at the flowerbed. Here, activities that are useful to help establish how the current relationship works and how it has developed are introduced. Start by looking at the value of exploring the priorities for each of them as individuals: What are their priorities for a relationship? How much does the current relationship meet these priorities? A suitable tool is at http://www.porterbrookclinic.org. uk/publicdocs/Priorities.pdf. The concept of "are they fair" and "is the relationship fair" comes from *Equal Partners—Good Friends* (Rabin, 1996).

BOX 9.1   Patient Educational Material

Title	Author	Publisher
New Male Sexuality	Bernie Zilbergeld	Bantam 1999 ISBN 0553 38042-7
Perfectly Normal	Sandra Perfot	Rodale 2005
She Comes First	Ian Kerner	PerfectBound 2004 ISBN 0060729678
Becoming Orgasmic	Julia Heiman and Joseph LoPiccolo	Platkins 1999
The Mirror Within	Anne Dickson	Quartet Books 1999 ISBN 0704 33474-7

---

tools available to therapists for use can be viewed as helping the woman to nurture any available sexual arousal that is still present or to develop and grow new arousal ability where she has not experienced it before.

Diagnostic Check of the Garden's Ability to Grow
This introductory work may benefit by checking the different individual goals held, and this can be linked to level of priorities for other areas of the relationship that appear to need work or change.

Complex Tools to Measure Garden Growth
We need to ascertain the changes of growth, which means using adequate outcome measures to see changes in relational and sexual activity in terms of satisfaction and confidence for each individual and also how they decrease couple inhibition and behavioral skills.

All of these activities and topics may be vital to explore and investigate to ascertain some of the reasons why the couple has come and to identify their individual motivation for improving arousal issues in the relationship. However, after the initial issues other problems may be identified that may be more complex or deep-seated.

Case Example (Assessment)

Alice, age 36, with two children ages 7 and 5, attended a couples therapy session and was obviously distressed by the situation she had described on her assessment sheet as relationship deterioration due to her problems with lack of excitement and sensation and now lack of desire as well. She discussed this more fully in the session, especially the anxiety that she had about the relationship that in the past had also been a problem for her, resulting in separation from her first husband. Only a year ago Alice and her partner, Andrew, had separated for a month. The issue that led to repeated friction was usually her low desire for sexual activity, lack of satisfaction with any activity she engaged in, and her unhappiness at her genitalia being so unresponsive because they were dry and often sore after any lovemaking with Andrew.

Alice felt the problem had been present since the birth of her second child, who was now age 5. The low desire seemed continuous since that time; however, there seemed to have been a five-year history of poor arousal with very little evidence of physical arousal on stimulation. She could recall two occasions when she had experienced sexual interest and had initiated sexual activity with Andrew, but with little sexual satisfaction. Therefore, this had not led to an increase in desire but had caused confusion, and she often reviewed these two occasions, trying to find the clue to what had gone wrong. On exploring more closely her reason for her attending the appointment, it became clear that her motivation for attending was not straightforward. She felt well in herself, and she would be quite happy to never engage in a sexual relationship again. However, although she was sad at her partner's distress over this last dimension of their lives, she did not appear to wish to improve her sexual activity just for his benefit. Alice said that she had tried often to do this, and it just upset her more as she was so dry and unsatisfied. As the therapist's understanding of the woman deepened, the therapist realized that the woman's main aim was to correct the poor couple image that her daughters were receiving from them: "They never see us being warm," she commented. "They don't know how parents should be. They are getting old enough to comment on couple behavior on TV and compare it with their experience at home." All of her children's attitudes seemed to reflect what was not normal in her relationship and what she was failing as a mother to do in giving them better guidelines and standards.

The therapeutic work remained difficult even when the patient had high motivation, but Alice was not aware of any personal reason for her to engage in the therapy. Alice appeared willing to work at improving the arousal disorder to give her children a better appreciation of couples relationships. Her priority was to give the best to her children. The main gain for her was to know that her children see both her and Andrew as a more warm and affectionate couple and to experience an ability to include affection as a family activity.

Physical Examination

A general examination of the cardiovascular, neurovascular and endocrine status should be carried out. A focussed physical examination of the gynecological system includes examination of the external genitalia. This will include looking at skin turgor and thickness and any abnormalities in the distribution and amount of pubic hair, which may all signify a degree of atrophy. The vaginal mucosa on inspection and the pH may change with atrophic changes, and other pathologies may be identified. The physical examination will often provide the opportunity for the physician to educate the patient about anatomy and sexual function.

Physiological Assessments (Specialist Tests)

To assess genital arousal, several options are possible, including intravaginal photoplesmography, the Gold Sheffield Electrode, and measurement of labial temperature (Goldstein, Meston, Davis, & Traish, 2006). Doppler ultrasonography is a further investigation that may be useful to assess clitoral blood flow. Sexual synergy during intercourse has been noted as an important factor in sexual arousal for both men and women. Using Doppler ultrasonography, the vascular responses of clitoral arteries to vaginal pressure stimulation in 10 volunteer women found that pressure stimulation along the lower third of the vagina increased blood velocity and flow into the clitoral arteries in 9 of 10 women. Blood flow increases at 4 to 11 times baseline prestimulation level were noted (Lavoisier, Aloui, Schmidt, & Watrelot).

The role of hormonal effects on sexual arousal remains controversial. The oral administration of dehydroepiandrosterone (DHEA) at a dose of 300 mg increased the concentration of dehydroepiandrosterone sulfate (DHEAS) by two- to fivefold, with greater mental and physical sexual arousal to erotic video when compared with placebo. The vaginal pulse amplitude (VPA) and vaginal blood volume (VBV) demonstrated significant increase between neutral and erotic film segments within both conditions but of nondifferentiated drug conditions (Hackbert & Heiman, 2002). However, in premenopausal women, although there was a significant increase in blood levels of DHEAS 30 minutes following drug administration, there was no significant effect on either VPA or subjective response to erotic films (Meston & Heiman, 2002).

A recent report of 20 healthy women and 20 women with vulvar vestibulitis syndrome (VVS) who underwent both genital and nongenital sensory testing at baseline and in response to erotic and neutral stimuli films was considered. Sexual arousal was assessed by measurement of surface skin temperature change of the labia minora. Touch and pain thresholds were assessed at the vulval vestibule inside the labia minora and on the surface of the forearm. Erotic stimuli brought about a significant increase in physiological sexual arousal and vulval sensitivity in both groups, although women with VVS reported a significantly lower desire to engage in intercourse after viewing the erotic film and reported lower levels of desire and arousal on questionnaire measures. The VVS women also exhibited significantly more genital and nongenital pain sensitivity and catastrophized. The women were more hypervigilant and expressed fear of pain. Physiological sexual arousal occurred with an increase of vulval sensation in contrast to previous findings (Payne et al., 2005). Laan and Both (2005) advocated for psychophysiological assessment of genital arousal response in reaching the diagnosis of FSAD as part of the overall clarification of the actiology of arousal problems. They described sexual arousal as an emotional response generating a subjective feeling into which explicit memory is necessary for sexual feelings to be experienced.

Treatment Options in Couples Sex Therapy

These can be summarized as reducing response anxiety; reframing the problem to become couple oriented rather than specific end organ focused; attending to any comorbid affective, cognitive, emotional, and behavioral aspects of FSAD, including those that may be exacerbated by the response and behavior of the partner; normalizing the commonality of the condition.

Though we may advocate a multifactorial and interdisciplinary approach to dealing with any problems of FSAD that may be multietiological in causation, it is important to try to present this to the individual and to the couple as succinctly and as simply as possible. By doing so, the likelihood of instilling faith and confidence will be improved. Identifying treatment priorities and making incremental and gradual changes are beneficial. Most of the work is done in a strategic sense insofar as therapeutic interventions suggest out with the session (i.e., maneuvers and exercises outside of the therapeutic session rather than within ["structural"]).

Sexual intimacy is promoted in four stages (see Weeks et al., 2008). In addition, the inevitability of "disaster days" and "relapse inevitability" must be addressed. We encourage the couple to define the problem in simple terms and by identifying these specific concerns and breaking down the components into their most reducible and definable form. The aim should be to provide the opportunity for the couple to explore these without any immediacy or threat of scrutiny by focusing not just on these intensely investigated sequences of the courtship ritual. We strongly encourage couples to become as intimate as they feel comfortable, and, if necessary, we will encourage them to find ways of deepening their relationship, starting initially with the sensate focus program and encouraging regularity of the process on the basis that "practice makes perfect." Fears of intimacy, the consequences of sexual activity (e.g., pregnancy, infection), and the need to ensure commitment to a prolonged (yet fruitful) relationship together may need substantial exploration.

Some simple maneuvers that are important in the early stages include ensuring adequate education about sexual response and setting boundaries for what is acceptable and unacceptable behavior, whether this is arguments between the couple or sexual activities with the interpartner relationship. We always encourage couples to have time together, including quality time in the evening where child-care facilities may be necessary.

It is our belief that treatment is most effective and efficacious in terms of time and therapist–patient involvement if an intersystem approach is used for the management of this complex and often difficult-to-treat clinical scenario. Time spent during the initial assessment can glean valuable information that allows for a substantial collection of information about the woman and, where relevant, her partner or partners. By offering an inclusive assessment that asks about physical, psychological, and relationship issues, the woman will be afforded the opportunity to reflect on the importance of why each of these areas is being examined and why information is being gathered as part of the holistic assessment. It should therefore be much less of a surprise when a package of care and intervention is presented that has more than one treatment modality.

Early on in therapy, we want to understand clearly what it is that both partners are hoping to achieve while attending the clinical service. For some, this is no more than a restoration of clinical function, and any attempt to identify psychological or "head-originated" issues will be rejected, sometimes forcefully by one or both partners. Some example tools are listed in Table 9.2, Table 9.3, and Table 9.4.

TABLE 9.2   Couples Sex Therapy Treatment Tools (1)

Objectives	Activities
Behavioral	
This can be viewed as the patient pruning and training the plants to grow in the chosen direction. Need to understand the couple changes needed and see why and what training is required. Often the initial training needed is sexual education physical, anatomy and physiology, and psychological and cognitive and emotional education, which may take longer to absorb and to understand the complex issues.	It may be useful to make a list of the changes needed in the order of difficulty. Then, starting with the priorities at the lowest level of difficulty, work toward changing the behavior that is relevant to the sexual dysfunction. This may utilize an individual sexual growth program and may use the *Becoming Orgasmic* focus (Heiman & LoPiccolo, 1999). For example, for Alice and Andrew the level of physical intimacy was experienced as limited so the list of suitable physical contacts was made. The easiest was set first, to regularly increase physical intimacy. This is vital to improve the physical contact needs to begin to gain physical and psychological arousal. Newly gained behavioral skills must be rehearsed regularly, and the skills must continue to be developed to prevent the skills stagnating again.
Systemic 1. Multiple nutrients	
The interdependence of the (garden) couple means that by changing the interdependence of plant nutrients and feed material (i.e., hormonal chemical intake) the structure can be altered.	Medication prescribed is not only a sexual medicine issue; it may also be a systemic intervention as one change (e.g., resolving an anemic state) may bring about becoming more alert, energized, and so more interested to work and improve her ability for physical arousal.
Systemic 2. Breaking the weed power chain	
This can be achieved by regular weeding, reviewing, decreasing, and removing couple problem areas, friction, and misunderstanding or by keeping the area full, growing other plants (e.g., more couple time together, more opportunity to feed back and review events together).	This may involve the use of sensate focus as a means of encouraging intimacy but without allowing the problem areas of higher arousal (later stages). Banning this higher level of arousal to prevent anxiety and failure may, of course, systemically produce more desire and even activity from them both. This stage involves keeping the watering system functioning, the need to ensure the "love" water barrels are kept topped off, and the need to assist the couple and ensure that they supply and obtain adequate love and support from the partner and their friends, often not from the family. This adequate supply enables them to share warmth, support, and encouragement with each other—love tanks.

Objectives	Activities
Systemic 3. Complex integration work	Growth in different areas needs to be achieved. Options for treatment are often more successful, particularly in the short term, if a behavioral systemic integrated approach is used. Behavioral work can include sex education by adding an increased range of possible sexual behaviors or by altering the attitude of the couples to differing acceptability behavior. The therapist will need to establish a directory of what activities the couple find more helpful and how they want to reengage in intimacy. So what choices do couples often make for treatment?
Systemic 4. Replanting the healthy growth	Couple activities that she is working on with her partner are encouraged. Because Alice had chosen this combined integrated approach there was of necessity a very important need for communication between the different clinicians involved. The couples therapist, for example, needed to understand what physical treatment options were being utilized and when changes in treatment occurred.

TABLE 9.3   Couples Sex Therapy Treatments (2)

Systemic 5. Retraining the vine—package of individual sexual growth (ISG) program	At this point other activities will be important to begin to integrate into this pattern using the body (color) mapping discussed earlier in the assessment. This now becomes part of the individual sexual growth (ISG) program where we look at the areas that were seen as green and acceptable and encourage more personal time and attention to be lavished on those areas while moving into the yellow areas to allow these areas more opportunity to be sensuous and acceptable to the individual. As time progresses and these areas are covered and improved, the therapist will suggest a move toward including the least red of the red areas (i.e., the least difficult) and gradually then move toward the more difficult areas, which tend to be either areas of high sexual connotation or areas linked to abuse or negative experience.

(continued)

TABLE 9.3   Couples Sex Therapy Treatments (2) (continued)

Systemic 6. Replanning the touch—vulval massage and desensitization of the vulval area	What is meant by vulval massage? The concept of touching the genitalia can have been a negative experience; for instance, all touch of the vulval area may have been viewed as a painful experience, preventing the patient being open to refocusing on sexual touch. By increasing touch of sexual tissue via a clinical exercise the therapist can help to open up alternative ways of experiencing touch—this may not rapidly move the sensations from negative to positive, but, for example, the use of vulval massage may initially just provide the patient with a system to allow a small area of vulval tissue to be touched without discomfort. This neutral experience can be increased in area, frequency, and intensity to hopefully work toward altering one's beliefs about the impossibility of touch being a positive activity and to allow experimentation of possible tissue arousal.
Systemic 7. Wake up the new growth buds—versatile vibrators	This area of new growth of arousal may lead to the possibility of using specific appropriate sexual toys and aids to increase sensitivity and variety of sensation to improve arousal. The new highly versatile vibrators can be very successful at providing alternative stimulation of the nervous systems' responsiveness. This also needs to be linked to the use of an adequate lubrication to ensure that the new growth of sensitive tissues is encouraged with this protective aid.
Systemic 8. Connecting the vines together—sensate focus (SF0 and ISG)	These areas then become integrated as they are more sensually perceived into the sensate focus with the partner so the process is desensitizing the areas, moving them into the individual sexual growth program and then moving them into the sensate focus. This is a complicated piece of work made more difficult by the fact that one continually needs to look not only at the patients needs but also at the needs of the partner, including the sexual needs of the partner. He or she is not a mere bystander but is actively involved in this and may need to be helped to support his partner and needs to feel that his own issues are regularly reviewed and supported. Time needs to be given to helping him engage in his own sexual satisfaction, either by him or

with his partner's support, and this can be helped by a variety of ways.

Systemic 9a. Feeding both plants—couple-related activities

It is important to give plenty of support to the couple as they learn more about their sexual needs. By helping Andrew to be able to voice his sexual needs and to say how he would like them met adds balance to the work carried out. This raises the huge issue of allowing space for the partner as well as encouragement and a chance to develop their own sexual and masturbation practices. This needs to be seen by the couple as part of the learning experience of the couple, and the therapist will be working toward helping the couple understand and accept the need for Andrew to have a much wider repertoire of sexual activity and to understand his own body better. This will need to be worked within the context of the individual and couple's religious, ethnic, and cultural beliefs and lifestyle.

Systemic 9b. Feeding both plants—male-related activities

Finding what Andrew's other needs are is important, and ensuring that in the concentration on sexual issues we have not colluded with Alice to ignore these needs such as social time with his own peers and other activities that enhance his lifestyle. This is a period of intense growth for both partners in the relationship, and the therapist will be working hard with the couple, holding them emotionally as they try these new tasks. Often this can be difficult as their lifestyle will still have other stressors that may occur and may appear to be taking priority again.

Systemic 9c. Feeding both plants—family-related activities

In addition, often couples systemically hold to the stuck position by bringing in new stressors so as to prevent the changes from occurring. An example of this would be a couple that start therapy and then decide they want to do the kitchen extension. It is important to discuss before commencing and during therapy the need for this to be a priority area, and the building projects, for example, need to be allowed to wait until therapy has achieved its goals. Other members of the family, including the children, may also join in this prevention of movement and maintenance of the status quo by creating their own crises so as "to help" the parents to remain the same.

TABLE 9.4   Couples Sex Therapy Treatments (3)

Systemic 10. Attaching the walkways or talking to flowers	All of these discussions on therapy issues are going to raise the therapist and couple's awareness of any communication issues that exist between them. Any changes that a couple make in their relationship also demonstrate, because of the possible friction involved, the weak spots in terms of how well they explain what they want, how well they listen to each other, and how well they are able to adapt their thinking to new ideas. It is therefore vital that this part of the therapy assesses and provides treatment options to improve communication skills. These communication skills can be taught during therapy or may, again, be set as activities that can be carried out at home (see Crowe & Ridley, 2000).
	Nonverbal communication may also be important, and this is not only touch (SFO and ISG). For example, a positive effect of male fragrance on genital arousal during erotic fantasy was noted in one study but only during the follicular phase (Graham, Janssen, & Sanders, 2000) with the effect not being mediated by any effects of fragrance on mood.
Systemic 11. Reestablishing the plants	Sex growth in individuals cannot occur without permission given to change. Not changing and staying with the status quo is usually much easier. Some individuals can use self-motivation and insight to aid the growth and rerooting in new behaviors, but often it requires partner encouragement, which is difficult to achieve when they are trapped in the same cycles. The couples therapist may be used or seen as an agent for change and reestablishment of the plant by "giving permission" to move or to alter growth. Giving suggestions of possible growth behavior, prescribing changed activities, or modeling acceptance of new actions, roles, and diversity may all be useful and may help to decrease the power of previous familial models (e.g., by parents and family) of unhelpful patterns of relating and arousal.
Systemic 12. Limiting movement—restricting the sexual activity	Constricting or preventing movement may help to encourage or strengthen growth. Often the systemic action of restricting the couples' sexual activity may increase their confidence in the area they are already inhabiting or using, but it could lead to the combining of the couple's energy to resist the constriction and to more powerful couple strength to resist the therapist's ideas and to become more independent. By placing a ban on arousal may make her more relaxed about it occurring or may make her more determined to work at experiencing it again.

Systemic 13. Prescribing or alternating symptoms	Giving one individual the chance to live with, to practice, and to gain understanding on how it is to live with the other partner's symptoms can be helpful to both members of the couple relationship. For instance, having no desire or experiencing jealousy can isolate and prevent understanding or support from a partner as they are often reactive to those situations. Imagining experiencing the "other's symptoms" of inhibited arousal for a short period of time may be helpful. How much more quickly can a patient gain insight into a partner's response once they have felt the reality of the symptoms?
Systemic 14. Spelling out the cost of no growth	Growth takes effort and time, and couples who put in the energy or cost to enable them to reframe or change will need to give rewards to each other for that change to occur. However, no growth or change also has a more negative cost to the system. Restricting or preventing progress or seeking help for arousal desire can enable a stuck system to be reviewed to see the cost of divorce, separation, or remaining in an entrenched stance.
Systemic 15. Reversing plant positions—roles	The situations we occupy allow for our view of the present situation—changing positions in the plot allows a couple to see the world from a different (partner's) perspective—tasks swapped can allow a different appreciation of the role taken in the relationship and the pressures and lack of support that may be available for that role. Giving Andrew the role for a week of never achieving arousal made him feel left out and deprived. This helped him afterward to spend time and effort to include Alice in differing ways of experiencing warmth.
Systemic 16. Accepting the stunted plant—adapting to reality or loss—or using it as a new focus	The inability to change may be the focus for anger and sadness, but a reframe, if considered, can allow this stuckness to be a new stability to base other change on. For example, Alice may not experience high levels of sexual arousal, but she can learn not to worry about arousal and work on her ability to relax and enjoy the time we give to lovemaking as valuable couple space. A more common difficulty experienced with women with inhibited arousal is that their motivation for intimacy may come from a very different source then their partners. The concept of differing sexual languages and differing intimacy languages is probably important to explain why men with their activity-orientated language demonstrate their love by being sexual (e.g., "I care about you. The proof that I care about you is that I physically desire you and initiate sexual activity toward you"). The

(continued)

TABLE 9.4   Couples Sex Therapy Treatments (3) (continued)

woman's language may be much more emotional and verbal and says, "Because I care about you and I love you I then am willing to be sexual as evidence of my emotion." This is difficult because when the woman does not choose to be sexual, the result may be a perception by the male partner that she does not love him. It is difficult for a man in such a situation to understand that his partner does not necessarily link her ability to be sexual with her ability to show love. This can be divisive and a source of confusion for many couples. It can become the cause of secondary desire disorder because a woman who does not wish to be sexual may still want the intimacy of cuddles and hugs and may want to know that it will not lead any further so she won't need to be worried about the consequences. However, the male activity language may suggest, "If I can't do it properly, it is better not to start," and therefore the couple's inability to carry out the concept of a full sexual range of behaviors may mean his withdrawal and lack of intimacy. The woman with "desire disorder" may actually crave intimacy yet not "desire" penetrative sexual activity. This can make the diagnosis even more difficult, as she may express distress at the lack of intimacy and no distress at the lack of sexual activity.

Case Example—Continued (Treatment)

Physical treatment and couples sex therapy were offered in an integrated manner (Daines & Hallam-Jones, 2007). What did Alice and Andrew choose? Alice initially appeared to be more interested in the assessment process than the treatment. She was keen to find out what had caused the problem and to understand it. However, as the sessions progressed and she realized that there were a variety of causes and treatment options, she shared that she had previously expected that there would be no actual successful treatment. She had felt that, by coming to the clinic, the most useful thing she would achieve was a chance to talk about it and to share how difficult it had been. By being given the option of discussing physical treatments she became much more interested in the possibility of there being real choices to make. She did want to discuss the problems that she and Andrew were having in further detail and valued the opportunity to choose couples therapy. At the same time she wanted to be assessed for whether any physical treatment options were suitable or available for her. Alice had her blood hormone levels measured, which revealed borderline testosterone levels. However, Alice was eager to try an unlicensed medical option concurrent with the couples therapy.

In couples therapy, the sensate focus is used not only as a diagnostic tool but also as a treatment option. Often the therapist will integrate into the couple's behavioral work an individual sexual growth program as a separate individual piece, and a series of exercises that the patient can commit to that will aid the other behavioral activities can be introduced.

To assess these issues, the therapist has to understand the differing languages the couple are using and help them to understand their different meanings. The therapist should help the couple identify what intimacy means to them and what it is that they have lost or want to regain. This can be achieved from a behavioral standpoint by asking the couple to list the 10 things that they would want to regain in the relationship and then to systematically work through how to achieve those in the therapy program. From a systemic point of view, the therapist could look at how the couple can break the current stuck pattern of nonintimacy by inducing intimacy from a different standpoint and seeing whether this had any effect of changing the whole of the intimacy relationship—for example, "I don't want sex but I do want a holiday in April. I will have sex three times in March and we will then have a holiday in April." The concept of female plasticity may be useful for women to understand that women can change their minds and enjoy different sexual activities if they allow a positive attitude to accompany the new experiences (see Baumeister, 2001).

Finally, to understand the whole system before commencing a therapy program it is vital that the therapist spend adequate time assessing which sexual activities this couple have actually carried out between sessions. It is hard to have sexual desire if you have only ever learned to do one kind of sexual activity in one particular way and that particular way is now removed from you due to illness or body discomfort or change in situations. An example of this is the couple that have only ever had limited foreplay and sex in the missionary position, which becomes impossible if the position becomes too painful for an individual. Adaptability is fairly difficult to achieve with no alternatives; therefore, assessment includes ascertaining exactly which behaviors they use, have tried, and have found helpful in the past. This may give some excellent starting points or clues as to how to progress in therapy and some insight into possible outcome levels.

Physical Treatments

Laan and Both (2005) described the treatment process to include both psychological treatments, particularly around sensate focus exercises and masturbation training as well as use of the EROS-CTD (clitoral therapy device). Pharmacologically they suggest possible agents to include phosphodiesterase inhibitors, prostaglandins, phentolamine, dopamine agonists, and androgens.

In contrast, Basson (2007), in describing the overlap of the phases of the sex response, especially those of arousal and desire, had a more detailed approach to the psychological assessment and treatment of the condition. This involves assessing the couple's emotional intimacy (e.g., the ability to trust one another, mental health issues, and the context of the couple's usual sexual activities) and assessing the thoughts during sexual interaction. The biological contribution toward the treatment in this combined diagnosis approach is much less biological and is much more about the loss of libido.

Linking a trial of a physical agent (e.g., phosphodiesterase type 5 [PDE5] inhibitor) with a new experience or using the EROS-CTD may help both interventions to be more successful. In Billup et al. (2001), women were shown to have an 80% improvement in lubrication after using the EROS-CTD. However, the women need to buy their own device and need to have the time and motivation to use it every day for 15 to 30 minutes. It may take up to six weeks for results to develop. It appears to work better if it is integrated into other treatments (e.g., sexual growth programs) and is clearly explained with information sheets and the opportunity to watch an instructional DVD. It is difficult for a woman to initially identify the agent bringing about change, but she will continue to use whatever will help her best in the future.

One of the issues often addressed early in therapy is the need to find (or at least the request to find) a physical treatment for the presenting symptoms. There is evidence of nitric oxide PDE5 inhibitors pathways existing in women in a similar manner to that found in men with erectile dysfunction (Angulo et al., 2003). Women's partial response in clinical trails for sildenafil has been demonstrated (Caruso, Intelisano, Lupo, & Agnello, 2001). In addition, the importance and contribution of androgens or other substances that may affect the dopamine receptors may need increasing attention (Walsh & Berman, 2004). In those patients where pharmacological agents are recommended (or even chosen by the woman), sildenafil was found to be effective in enhancing vaginal engorgement during erotic stimuli conditions in healthy women without sexual dysfunction (Laan et al., 2002). In addition, the effects of yohimbine plus L-arginine glutamate on sexual arousal in postmenopausal women with sexual arousal disorder was found to include VPA responses to erotic films at 60 minutes postdrug and menstruation compared with placebo (Meston & Worcel, 2002).

The efficacy and safety of Zestra (Zestra Laboratories, Charleston, SC) for women with FSAD was reported by Ferguson et al. (2003). When applied to the vulva, both normal women and women with FSAD showed statistically significant improvements relative to the placebo. The agents in Zestra are listed as dietary supplements in the United States. Sublingual administration of apomorphine in doses of 2 mcg and 3 mcg allows rapid uptake, an absence of serious side effects, and the possibility of an improvement in sexual symptomatology (Russell et al., 2002). Estrogen delivered locally into the vagina as low-dose natural estrogens (estradiol tablet or ring or estradiol pessaries) improves both menopausal vaginal atrophy and symptoms of dryness, pain, and discomfort (Simunic et al., 2003).

A study showed that tibolone was associated with significant improvement in sexual function in postmenopausal women, which was thought to reflect the estrogenic and androgenic properties of the compound. Significant increase in vaginal blood flow in response to erotic fantasy but not to visual material suggests two possible pathways of female sexual response (Laan, Van Lunsen, and Everaerd, 2001). This follows previous work by Laan, Everaerd, Van Bellen, and Hanewald (1994) showing that the largest contribution to female sexual excitement resulted in the processing of stimulus content and stimulus meaning in video material—especially when the film was made by women, since those made by men evoked more feelings of shame, guilt, and aversion. Sexuality around menopause is an area that needs much more attention, for there is considerable ignorance both at clinician and patient level. This matter is addressed further by Wylie (2006b) and Wylie et al. (2007). In addition, the need to optimize clinical interventions for sexual difficulties of any type, including FSAD, within a relationship may require considerable psychosexual and psychological maneuvers (Wylie, 2006a).

Prognostic Planning

Before concluding, we need to consider prognostic factors that may be positive for therapy to be experienced as supportive, the primary of which must be the intention to experience positive sexual arousal. This may be inhibited or ameliorated by patients who have a number of comorbid conditions—particularly patients with psychiatric conditions. Reduced situational life stresses are inevitably a positive indicator of success of any type of intervention, whether this is physiological or pharmacological or psychological. Of primary importance is ensuring that any anxiety that may be present, however real to the individual or couple, is addressed and that suitable maneuvers to manage this are established early on. In addition, sharing the problem and accepting and recognizing as well as acknowledging this to be the case is important. Exploring these problems, including any intergenerational legacies and environmental messages that may affect or interfere with sexual intimacy, may well improve the likelihood of positive response to any subsequent therapeutic exercises.

Conclusion

We emphasize that the complexity of this disorder requires a thorough assessment to identify the possible multiple issues that are contributing to the etiology. However, the patient can expect the therapists to have an array of tools to use for these issues and, where necessary, to integrate the physical, relational, and psychological interventions into the change process and growth work that the couple are encouraged to commence. Regulatory acceptance of the validity of this diagnosis will limit both available and concurrent treatment options.

References

Althof, S. E., Dean, J., Derogatis, L. R., Rosen, R. C., & Sisson, M. (2005). Current perspectives on the clinical assessment and diagnosis of female sexual dysfunction and clinical studies of potential therapies: A statement of concern. *Journal of Sexual Medicine, 2*(S3), 146–153.

American Psychiatric Association (2000). *Diagnostic and statistical manual of mental disorders* (4th ed., text revised). Washington, DC: Author.

Basson, R., Berman, J., & Bernett, A. (2000). Report of the international consensus development conference on female sexual dysfunction: Definitions and classifications. *Journal of Urology 163*(3), 888–893.

Basson, R. (2007) Sexual desire/arousal disorders in women. In S. R. Leiblum (Ed.), *Principles and practice of sex therapy* (pp. 25–53). New York: Guilford.

Baumeister, R. (2001). *Social psychology and human sexuality*. Philadelphia, PA: Psychology Press (Taylor & Francis).

Boul, L., Hallam-Jones, R., & Wylie, K. R. Submitted.

Byers, E. S. (2005). Relationship satisfaction and sexual satisfaction: A longitudinal study of individuals in long-term relationships. *Journal of Sex Research, 42*, 113–118.

Caruso, S., Intelisano, G., Lupo, L., & Agnello, C. (2001). Pre-menopausal women affected by sexual arousal disorder treated with sildenafil: A double-blind cross-over, placebo-controlled study. *British Journal of Obstetrics and Gynaecology, 108*(6), 623–628.

Crowe, M. & Ridley, J. (2000). *A behavioural-systems approach to couple relationship and sexual problems: Therapy with Couples*. Oxford: Blackwell Publishing Limited.

Dennerstein, L. (2006). *Journal of Sexual Medicine*.

Derogatis, L., Rust, J., Golombok, S., Bouchard, C., Nachtigall, L., Rodenberg, C., et al. (2004). Validation of the profile of Female Sexual Function (PFSF) in surgically and naturally menopausal women. *Journal of Sex and Marital Therapy, 30*, 25–36.

Goldstein, I., Meston, C. M., Davis, S. R., & Traish, M. A. (2006). *Women's sexual function and dysfunction*. Philadelphia, PA: Taylor & Francis.

Graham, C. A., Janssen, E., & Sanders, S. A. (2000). Effects of fragrance on female sexual arousal and mood across the menstrual cycle. *Psychophysiology, 37*(1), 76–84.

Hackbert, L. & Heiman, J. R. (2002). Acute dehydroepiandrosterone (DHEA) effects on sexual arousal in postmenopausal women. *Journal of Women's Health and Gender-Based Medicine, 11*(2), 155–162.

Heiman, J. & LoPiccolo, J. (1999). *Becoming orgasmic*. London: Piatkus Books.

Hof, L. & Berman, J. (1986). The sexual genogram. *Journal of Marital & Family Therapy, 12*(1), 39–47.

Laan, E., Everaerd, W., Van Bellen, G., & Hanewald, G. (1994). Women's sexual and emotional responses to male and female-produced erotica. *Archive of Sexual Behaviour, 23*(2), 153–169.

Laan, E., Van Lunsen, R. H., & Everaerd, W. (2001). The effects of tibolone on vaginal blood flow, sexual desire and arousability in postmenopausal women. *Climacteric, 4*(1), 28–41.

Laan, E., Van Lunsen, R. H., Everaerd, W., Riley, A., Scott, E., & Boolell, M. (2002). The enhancement of vaginal vasocongestion by sildenafil in healthy premenopausal women. *Journal of Women's Health and Gender-Based Medicine, 11*(4), 357–365.

Laan, E. W. & Both, S. (2005). Female sexual arousal disorder. In R. Balon & R. T. Segraves (Eds.), *Handbook of sexual dysfunction* (pp. 123–154). Boca Raton, FL: Taylor & Francis.

Lavoisier, P., Aloui, R., Schmidt, M., & Watrelot, A. Clitoral blood flow increases following vaginal pressure stimulation. *Archives of Sexual Behavior, 24,* 37–45.

Lewis, R. W., Fugl-Meyer, K. S., Bosch, R., Fugl-Meyer, A. R., Laumann, E. O., Lizza, E., et al. (2004). Epidemiology/risk factors of sexual dysfunction. *Journal of Sexual Medicine 1*(1), 35–39.

Masters, W. H. & Johnson, V. E. (1966). *Human sexual response.* Boston: Little, Brown.

Maurice, W. L. (2003). Sexual medicine, mental illness and mental health profession. *Sexual and Relationship Therapy, 18,* 7–12.

Meston, C. M. (2003). Validation of the Female Sexual Function Index (FSFI) in women with female orgasmic disorder and in women with hypoactive sexual desire disorder. *Journal of Sex and Marital Therapy, 29,* 39–46.

Meston, C. M. & Heiman, J. R. (2002). Acute dehydroepiandrosterone effects on sexual arousal in premenopausal women. *Journal of Sex Marital Therapy, 28*(1), 53–60.

Meston, C. M. & Worcel, M. (2002). The effects of yohimbine plus L-arginine glutamate on sexual arousal in postmenopausal women with sexual arousal disorder. *Archives of Sexual Behaviour, 31*(4), 323–332.

Moreira, E. D. Jr., Brock, G., Glasser, D. B., Nicolosi, A., Laumann, E. O., Paik, A., et al. (2005). Help seeking behaviour for sexual problems: The global study of sexual attitudes and behaviors. *International Journal of Clinical Practice 59*(1), 6–16.

Nicolosi, A., Laumann, E. O., Glasser, D. B., Moreira, E. D. Jr., Paik, A., & Gingell, C. (2004). Sexual behaviour and sexual dysfunction after age 40: The global study of sexual attitudes and behaviours. *Urology 64*(5), 991–997.

Payne et al. Archives of Sexual Behaviour. Advice online.

Rabin, C. (1996). *Equal partners—Good friends.* London: Routledge.

Rosen, R., Brown, C., Heiman, J., Leiblum, S., Meston, C., Shabsigh, R., et al. (2000). The Female Sexual Function Index (FSFI): A multidimensional self-reported instrument for the assessment of female sexual function. *Journal of Sex and Marital Therapy, 26,* 191–208.

Segraves, R. & Woodard, T. (2006). Female hypoactive sexual desire disorder: History and current status. *Journal of Sexual Medicine 3*(3), 408–418.

Sills, T., Wunderlich, G., Pyke, R., Segraves, R. T., Leiblum, S., Clayton, A., et al. (2005). The Sexual Interest and Desire Inventory-Female (SIDI-F): Item response analyses of data from women diagnosed with hypoactive sexual desire disorder. *Journal of Sexual Medicine 2,* 801–818.

Simunic, V., Banovic, I., Ciglar, S., Jeren, L., Pavicic Baldani, D., & Sprem, M. (2003). Local oestrogen treatment in patients with urogenital symptoms. *International Journal of Gynaecology and Obstetrics, 82*(2), 187–197.

Walsh, K. E. & Berman, J. R. (2004). Sexual dysfunction in the older woman: An overview of the current understanding and management. *Drugs Aging, 21*(10), 655–675.

Weeks, G. (1994). The intersystem model: An integrative approach to treatment. In G. Weeks & L. Hof (Eds.), *The marital-relationship casebook: Theory and application of the intersystem model* (pp. 3–34). New York: Brunner/Mazel.

Weeks, G. (2004). The emergence of a new paradigm in sex therapy: Integration. *Sexual and Relationship Therapy, 20*(1), 89–103.

Wylie, K. R. (2006a). Optimising clinical interventions for sexual difficulties within a relationship. *Journal of Men's Health & Gender 4,* 650–355.

Wylie, K. R. (2006b). Sexuality and the menopause. *Journal of the British Menopause Society, 12*(4), 149–152.

Wylie, K. R. (2007). Loss of sexual desire in the postmenopausal woman. *Journal of Sexual Medicine, 4,* 395–405.

Yeh, H. C., Lorenz, F. O., Wickrama, K. A., Conger, R. D., & Elder, G. H. Jr. (2006). Relationships among sexual satisfaction, marital quality and marital instability at midlife. *Journal of Family Psychology, 20,* 339–343.

10

Anorgasmia in Women

Marita P. McCabe

Contents

Definition and Description of Disorder

Current diagnostic criteria of female sexual dysfunction (FSD) vary across diagnostic categories. The *Diagnostic and Statistical Manual of Mental Disorders,* 4th ed., text revision (*DSM-IV-TR*; APA, 2000) categories are limited to psychiatric disorders and reflect the traditional linear models of sexual response (Kaplan, 1979; Masters & Johnson, 1966). The *DSM-IV-TR* classifies orgasmic disorders as one of a number of sexual dysfunctions for women. This diagnostic category is further specified as lifelong or acquired, generalized or situational, and attributable to either psychological or combined psychological and medical factors. Additional criteria require that the dysfunction causes the subjective experience of marked distress and interpersonal difficulty. However, specification of the occurrence of the dysfunctional (i.e., frequency, settings, activities, encounters) is not taken into account (McCabe, 2001).

Inhibited female orgasm is defined as "persistent or recurrent delay in, or absence of, orgasm in a female following a normal sexual excitement phase during sexual activity that the clinician judges to be adequate in focus, intensity and duration" (APA, 2000, p. 549). More recently, Basson (2001) highlighted the overlapping nature of the different phases of the female sexual response cycle among women. A review of clinical and empirical research has indicated that women may experience orgasm before maximum arousal or during peak arousal and that further orgasms may occur during the gradual resolution phase of sexual arousal (Basson, 2005).

This overlap between the sexual response phases has implications for treatment, which are discussed later in this chapter. However, the previous discussion suggests that many of the same strategies that are useful for treating arousal disorders would also aid treatment of orgasmic disorder.

Intersystemic Etiology

A broad range of factors has been related to the development of anorgasmia in women. McCabe (1991) developed a model of sexual dysfunction that incorporated factors from intergenerational, individual, and relationship influences. The contribution of these factors to anorgasmia is outlined in the following sections.

Intergenerational Influences

Difficulties in the process of socialization during childhood have been considered an important predictor of adult sexual dysfunction. The development of misconceptions about sex, negative attitudes toward sexual pleasure, and problems with sexual orientation or gender identity may result from the family of origin and may negatively influence sexual functioning in adulthood (Basson, Althop, et al., 2004; Graziottin & Leiblum, 2005). Such historical factors are particularly salient in the development of lifelong sexual problems (Basson, Leiblum, et al., 2004). Hof and Berman (1986) also attributed adult attitudes and behaviors to sexual scripts that are developed during childhood as a result of parental attitudes toward sex. In reviews of the literature, it has been claimed that one of the causes of sexual dysfunction in adulthood is sexual abuse during childhood (Chaill, Llewelyn, & Pearson, 1991; Talmadge & Wallace, 1991). However, both these reviews based their conclusions on studies that were largely clinical explorations, with little or no attempt to sample representative groups of adults. Although these studies have demonstrated that a large proportion of dysfunctional adults have experienced sexual abuse during childhood, without corresponding data from nondysfunctional samples, causative statements cannot be made.

The contribution of experiences or attitudes during adolescence to adult sexual dysfunction has received little attention. Heiman, Gladue, Roberts, and LoPiccolo (1986) found that the type of relationship in which first intercourse occurred had an impact on adult sexual functioning for women but not for men. However, Leitenberg, Greenwald, and Tarran (1989) found that the frequency of sexual experiences during adolescence had no impact on adult levels of sexual satisfaction, sexual arousal, or sexual dysfunction.

It is difficult from the literature on intergenerational factors to determine the manner in which they may impact female anorgasmia. Much of the literature talks about links between events in childhood and adolescence and overall levels of sexual dysfunction in adulthood, without specifying exact sexual dysfunctions. Further research, with the inclusion of a range of sexual dysfunctions as well as a control group, is necessary to better understand the impact on sexual functioning of events in childhood. Given the overlapping nature of sexual disorders among women that was discussed earlier, it is likely that childhood events that negatively impact on one phase of the sexual response cycle are also likely to have a negative impact on other phases.

Individual Influences

There has been little investigation of the individual factors that are associated with female anorgasmia. Obstfeld, Lupfer, and Lupfer (1985) found that sexual identity had no impact on sexual functioning, but the influence of lifestyle factors as well as sexual attitudes on sexual dysfunction—in particular, female anorgasmia—requires further exploration. It has been suggested that stress, levels of fatigue, sexual identity, health, and other individual attributes and experiences may alter sexual desire or response. Morokoff and Gillilland (1993) investigated the impact of life stressors (e.g., unemployment, stressful life events, daily hassles) on sexual functioning. Unemployment was shown to predict lower levels of sexual desire. Women with mood disorders have been shown to consistently demonstrate lower levels of sexual functioning in all phases of the sexual response cycle compared with normal controls (e.g., Clayton, McGavery, Clavet, & Piazza, 1997; Cyranowski, Frank, Cherry, Houck, & Kupfer, 2004). However, McCabe (2005) demonstrated that performance anxiety was associated with high levels of anorgasmia. This would suggest that the more a woman focuses on and becomes anxious about her arousal levels and whether she is likely to experience an orgasm, the less likely she is to be orgasmic. Further research is necessary to explore the role of individual influences in the development and maintenance of anorgasmia in women.

Relationship Factors

A substantial body of research has explored the contribution of relationship factors to sexual functioning. These studies have focused on the role of the quality of the relationship on the sexual functioning of the partners. Snyder and Berg (1983) found that the major causes of sexual problems in men and women related to their interactions with their partner. The general level of enjoyment of sexual activities as well as satisfaction with the frequency of sexual activities were associated with sexual distress. Lack of affection for the partner was also an important predictor of sexual satisfaction.

Communication between partners seems to play an important part both in the quality of the marital relationship and level of sexual dysfunction. A general lack of communication and difficulty in communicating preferences for various types of sexual interactions has been demonstrated among sexually dysfunctional couples (McCabe, 1999; Pietropinto, 1986). Empirical studies have consistently demonstrated that anorgasmic women reported experiencing significantly greater discomfort with communication about sexual activities (Kelly, Strassberg, & Kircher, 1990; Kelly, Strassberg, & Turner, 2004). Roffe and Britt (1981) found evidence of high levels of hostility among couples seeking sexual dysfunction therapy. However, they also found that a lack of expressiveness and low levels of affection within the relationship contributed to sexual dysfunction. Hulbert (1991) found that sexually assertive women were more likely to experience high sexual desire, arousal, and sexual satisfaction. On the other hand, Heiman et al. (1986) found no difference in the communication patterns of sexually functional and dysfunctional couples. It is difficult to interpret these conflicting results. Perhaps it is the way the sexual interaction and lack of communication within the relationship is viewed that relates to sexual dysfunction rather than the objective interaction and communication patterns.

McCabe and Cobain (1998) found that relationship factors were strongly associated with sexual dysfunction for women but not as strongly for men. Global deficits in the current relationship (e.g., relationship quality) as well as lower levels of sexual experience were more likely to occur among sexually dysfunctional women. Whether the sexual dysfunction led to relationship difficulties or vice versa is not clear. Regardless of which set of problems occurred first, both were now in place. Surprisingly, there were no differences between the functional and dysfunctional groups in their levels of communication, sexual communication, or arguments. But this does not mean that the relationships of the sexually dysfunctional responders were of the same quality as those of the functional respondents; women who have poor relationships, and who are unable to communicate, may express their lack of satisfaction with their relationship by avoiding sexual interactions with their partner and so restrict their range of sexual experiences. Levels of sexual satisfaction showed a particular deterioration among the anorgasmic groups (McCabe & Cobain, 1998). Examining the data from a different perspective, it may be that the negative attitudes toward sex impede the development of sexual intimacy, causing not only sexual dysfunction but also a breakdown in other aspects of the relationship. According to Travis and Travis (1986), intimacy is developed through a range of sexual and sensual contracts. Discomfort with non-genital and genital touching impedes the development of intimacy, which in turn leads to a breakdown in relationship functioning and eventually to sexual dysfunction in one or both partners.

Assessment

Intersystemic evaluation of anorgasmia in women should include a detailed psychological, relational, and social, and medical history (Walsh & Berman, 2004). For treatment approaches to address the psychological factors that contribute to anorgasmia, it is important to have a clear understanding of the manner in which they contribute to this sexual dysfunction. There have been major changes in the treatment of female sexual dysfunction in the last 10 years, with an increase in the use of centrally acting (e.g., serotonin agonists) to peripheral localized treatment (e.g., vaso-dilating creams) (ibid.). However, these medical approaches are not based on a clear physiological cause for these disorders and have been shown to be largely ineffective. The following discussion considers the factors that need to be evaluated among women with anorgasmia prior to treatment.

It is important to evaluate the role of intergenerational, individual, and relationship factors that may have precipitated or be maintaining the sexual dysfunction. These factors are likely to vary from one woman to another. However, it seems that a central factor to the development of anorgasmia needing to be evaluated is the nature of communication in the relationship. Kelly, Strassberg, and Turner (2006) found that there were behaviorally assessable differences in the communication pattern of couples experiencing female anorgasmia when compared with functional couples, specifically the negative interactional dynamics of blame and lack of receptivity to interactions by their partner.

It is also important that the clinician has a clear understanding of the nature of the sexual dysfunction. To this end, the clinician needs to assess the frequency of orgasm, the situation in which anorgasmia occurs, whether anorgasmia is primary or secondary, if anorgasmia is partial or complete, and the length of time the problem has been in place. An additional piece of information that I have found useful in therapy is to determine if other events occurred at the time the anorgasmia developed. It is also useful to question the woman and her partner on why she is seeking treatment at this point in time and what expectations or goals she has for therapy.

Treatment

Treatment programs for sexual dysfunction frequently lack adequate research methodology, which makes it difficult to evaluate their effectiveness:

- There is often no clear definition of the problem.
- The target variables for treatment are not clearly specified, so evaluation of treatment success is inadequate.
- There are no pre- and postmeasures of target variables.
- Outcome measures, if used, are lacking in adequate information on their psychometric properties.
- The treatment program is not clearly described.
- Sample sizes are too small for adequate statistical analysis.

These flaws make it difficult to evaluate which treatment programs for female anorgasmia are most successful and cost effective (O'Donohue, Dopke, & Swingen, 1997; O'Donahue, Swingen, Dopke, & Roger, 1999).

A further factor that may relate to the success of therapy is the length of time the problem has been in place. When a problem has been present for an extended period of time, it may have become incorporated into the person's self-view, and the relationship may have adjusted to incorporate the dysfunction. As a result, a number of changes need to occur if the dysfunction is no longer present, so the person with the dysfunction or the partner may be resistant to these changes.

Some educational content would appear to be useful for women with anorgasmia. Teaching effective techniques of stimulation may well improve the orgasmic response of anorgasmic women. However, the transfer of the ability to reach orgasm through masturbation to an ability to reach orgasm in intercourse is problematic. Directed masturbation has been shown to be an effective strategy for women with primary anorgasmia (Heiman & Meston, 1997). This process involves providing education to the woman about the ways to achieve orgasm and then providing her with strategies and permission to explore her body. This process of self-exploration allows the woman to discover what is sexually arousing for her, what feels pleasant, and what is difficult or unpleasant. The woman is encouraged to use a mirror to examine her genitals in the early stages of this exercise. She is also encouraged to tune in to her sensations, to alter her cognitions regarding masturbation, and to use sexual fantasies to enhance her sexual response (Heiman, 2007).

Directed masturbation has been shown to be particularly effective among women who experience primary anorgasmia, with a success rate reported of between 80% and 90% (LoPiccolo & Stock, 1986; Riley & Riley, 1978). For women with secondary anorgasmia, the directed masturbation appears to be less effective, with success rates of 10% to 75% being reported (Kilmann, Boland, Norton, Davidson, & Caid, 1986; Kuriansky, Sharp, & O'Connor, 1982).

For a woman to transfer her orgasmic response in masturbation to sexual interaction with her partner, she and her partner may need to use additional stimulation of the woman's genitals during sexual intercourse. The woman needs to learn to communicate her sexual needs to her partner and to guide the partner on how to stimulate her. During sexual intercourse, it is important that the *coital alignment technique* (Heiman, 2007) is used, which increases the level of clitoral contact as well as the orgasmic frequency among women with secondary anorgasmia (Heiman, 2007).

The previous discussion demonstrates the difficulties encountered in comparing studies designed to increase sexual education regarding treating secondary anorgasmia. Nontreatment control groups are rarely included; outcome measures are not clearly defined (and may be unrealistic); and the differential effect of sex education is difficult to isolate due to combination treatment strategies. However, it seems that ignorance of the best techniques, reluctance about using them, and an inability to communicate preferences for sexual stimulation to the partner contribute to low orgasmic frequency during sexual interaction.

Medical treatment strategies for anorgasmia are not considered in detail in this chapter. This is primarily because the focus is on psychological interventions but also because hormone replacement and other pharmaceutical approaches have not been shown to be effective in the treatment of this dysfunction (see Kope, 2007 for a summary of medical approaches to the treatment of anorgasmia).

Studies seem to demonstrate that psychological interventions for anorgasmia are most effective if they utilize cognitive and behavioral strategies and focus on intergenerational, intrapersonal, and interpersonal factors that may contribute to the women's sexual dysfunction. Heiman (2007) reviewed a range of treatment approaches for anorgasmia in women, including pharmacotherapy, psychoanalytic, cognitive-behavioral, and systems theory. She noted that research studies support the adoption of cognitive-behavioral approaches, although the strategies employed in systems approaches in sex therapy may be useful. However, these approaches have yet to be adequately evaluated in research studies.

McCabe (2001) implemented a psychologically focused treatment program for 95 sexually dysfunctional men and 54 sexually dysfunctional women, 36 of whom experienced anorgasmia. The treatment program was based on cognitive-behavioral principles. It was a 10-session program that focused on enhancing communication between the partners, increasing sexual skills, and lowering sexual anxiety and performance anxiety. Both cognitions and behaviors that impeded functioning in these areas were addressed. Homework exercises comprised sensate focus exercises and cognitive strategies and behavioral exercises to enhance communication between partners. During therapy sessions, there was discussion of blocks to sexual performance, and strategies to overcome these blocks were developed by addressing cognitions and behaviors that impeded sexual performance and enjoyment of sexual activities. The first two therapy sessions occurred weekly, and the subsequent sessions occurred fortnightly.

Therapy was successful for 44.4% of women and was most likely to be effective for women who experienced anorgasmia and sexual arousal disorder; it was least effective among women who experienced a lack of sexual interest. In fact, of the 36 women who presented with anorgasmia pretherapy, only 6 women experienced problems in this area posttherapy. A more detailed description of this treatment program is presented later in this chapter.

The results of this study demonstrated that a large proportion of participants experienced sexual dysfunction less frequently posttherapy, but many of them still experienced some level of sexual dysfunction. Does this constitute successful therapy, or does successful therapy only entail a complete absence of sexual dysfunction posttherapy? This dilemma demonstrates the difficulty of defining success in therapy and the importance of a complete description of pretherapy and posttherapy levels of sexual dysfunction as well as other associated measures of sexual functioning.

Effective Strategies from Previous Research

As noted earlier, research examining the effectiveness of treatment strategies for anorgasmia is limited. However, levels of both communication and performance anxiety appear to be important factors to address in the treatment of this sexual dysfunction.

Communication

A lack of communication between partners about their sexual relationship appears to be a factor related to anorgasmia in women. Everaerd and Dekker (1982) compared the relative effectiveness of sex therapy and communication skills training on the treatment of secondary orgasmic dysfunction. Both therapies were assessed as equally effective in improving orgasmic experience, although the extent of the improvement was not reported. In this study, sex therapy consisted of sensate focus and sexual stimulation exercises, with a ban on intercourse. The communication training included exercises for active and passive listening, verbalization and reflection of feelings, productive conflict management, and assertive behavior.

Both communication and sexual skills training, together with measures to reduce anxiety, were used in the treatment of primary and secondary anorgasmia by McGovern, McMullen, and LoPiccolo (1978). Women with primary anorgasmia improved markedly in orgasmic responsiveness, whereas the women with secondary anorgasmia did not. This led the researchers to suggest that marital therapy might be more appropriate for the latter, since these women reported more dissatisfaction with their marital relationships than did the women experiencing primary anorgasmia.

More recently, Weeks (1994, 2004) developed the intersystem approach to the treatment of sexual problems. This approach focuses on the couple in the resolution of sexual problems and the dynamic that operates in the couple relationship. Although Weeks develops strategies to work with the genetic makeup, values, family of origin, and cultural setting within which the dysfunction occurs, an overriding systemic approach to the resolution of the problem means that effective communication patterns are central to the resolution of the sexual dysfunction.

Performance Anxiety

Performance anxiety can arise from various sources. A woman's past failure to achieve orgasm can elicit in her self-defeating and distracting thoughts about whether she will be able to achieve orgasm this time. The enthusiasm of an insecure partner, who regards her orgasmic response as an assurance of his or her own competence, can be perceived by the woman as a pressure on her to achieve orgasm. Fear of rejection or feelings of obligation toward the partner may lead her to accept her partner's sexual overtures, despite apprehension about her ability or desire to respond fully. As sexual activity continues, she tries to will her response, wanting to become so aroused that orgasm will be triggered but afraid she might "turn off" or that her partner might become impatient or irritated at her slowness. She mentally monitors her own and her partner's response, unable to allow herself to relax and enjoy the sexual stimulation for its own sake. She can no longer trust her own natural sexual responsitivity to maintain and intensify the arousal process through to orgasm but, rather, as spectator, demands her body's response. At the same time, her partner is also a spectator as he or she physically attempts to bring her to orgasm, wondering what he or she is doing wrong when she does not respond (Masters & Johnson, 1970). This view is reinforced by Kaplan (1974, 1983), who regarded obsessive self-observation arising out of fear of failure to be the single most immediate cause of female anorgasmia.

The original proponents of performance anxiety, Masters and Johnson (1970) attempted to deal with this problem by counseling couples on the nature of performance anxiety and by temporarily placing a ban on orgasm and intercourse until permitted by their sensate focus program. The partners engaged in a graduated series of tasks from general body massage through to intercourse. Although this program purported to address performance anxiety, it also involved assertion training, modeling, behavioral rehearsal, and education. By focusing on sexual activities other than intercourse, subjects explored a wide range of sexual activities; this process may well have lengthened the time involved in sexual play before intercourse occurred. Elements of this program are still evident in treatment programs for anorgasmia and are an essential element in the program described next.

Systemic Treatment Framework
As noted at various points of this chapter, female anorgasmia is likely to be caused, precipitated, and maintained from a range of intergenerational, individual, and relationship factors. After an adequate assessment of the nature of the anorgasmia and the factors that relate to this sexual dysfunction, it is important that treatment address the multitude of factors that currently maintain this dysfunction. Consistent with the systemic treatment framework, the following program has been implemented for the sexual dysfunction of women with anorgasmia (McCabe & Delaney, 1991; Purcell & McCabe, 1992). We have found that these aims are best addressed in therapy by the use of three interrelated treatment strategies: communication exercises, sensate focus exercises, and guided fantasy.

Communication Exercises.   Communication exercises were devised both to improve the quality of the marital relationship and to develop and explore emotional responses of the woman. Questions were developed that were designed to address all aspects of the relationship, both sexual and non-sexual. Both partners were instructed to share their feelings with their partner about a particular issue. Each day a different issue was discussed, and feelings were expressed. Examples of early questions were:

- What do I like best about us as partners, and how does that make me feel?
- How do I feel about differences between us in desire for sexual contact?

As other aspects of the treatment program were pursued, the communication exercises continued to encourage the development of the emotional side of the woman by exploring her reaction to the program and sharing this reaction with her partner. For example, when partners were physically exploring their responses to body massage and genital stimulation, one of the communication questions was, "How do I feel when you caress me intimately? What body feelings occur?"

Sensate Focus Exercises
The Masters and Johnson (1970) sensate focus program was outlined in therapy and implemented at home by the client. The program was commenced two weeks after the commencement of therapy. These exercises comprised nongenital and then genital pleasuring and, finally, intercourse in a graduated pattern. A detailed description of sensate focus strategies is outline in Chapter 15 of this volume.

Fantasy
We have found that the use of sexual fantasy is an important aspect of therapy. The purpose of sexual fantasy seems to be different for men and women. Some women may have difficulty accepting themselves as sexual persons and may experience a high level of guilt in association with their sexual functioning. Therefore, they may experience difficulties in accepting the physical aspects of the sexual encounter. Men may also experience guilt in association with sexual expression, but this guilt is accompanied by a lack of emotional involvement in the actual relationship. Therefore, fantasies need to be aimed at enhancing the acceptance of oneself as a sexual person. Sexual fantasies are also very useful for women experiencing anorgasmia to distract them from their actual performance and therefore lower levels of performance anxiety. Early fantasies employed in the program described by McCabe and Delaney (1991) for anorgasmia emphasized the romantic, interpersonal aspects of the relationship. This allowed for sexual arousal within a romantic setting. Once arousal in this

setting was tolerated and then enjoyed, the fantasies used during progressive therapy sessions became more sexually implicit to counteract the feelings of guilt associated with the experience of physical sexual pleasure and to enhance the acceptance of oneself as a sexual being. Within these fantasies both the emotional and physical aspects of sex were presented so that the development of both types of involvement could be explored to foster sexual functioning.

Research and Future Directions

Further research is required on the development and evaluation of integrated treatment programs for anorgasmia in women. A combination of both psychotherapy and pharmacotherapy should also be evaluated in future research. With the advent of readily available medications for erectile disorder in men, combination therapies may also be shown to be effective for females. Future research, therefore, needs to focus on whether outcomes are improved by the use of more focused integrated psychological interventions or combination therapies. In this way the most efficacious treatment for anorgasmia can be determined.

In a paper that provided a comprehensive review of pharmacotherapy for sexual dysfunction in women, Basson (2004) proposed that there is still too little known about the mode of action, effectiveness, and long-term consequences of utilizing medical interventions for female sexual dysfunction, particularly anorgasmia. It is likely that there will continue to be research studies to attempt to isolate a safe, effective medical intervention for sexual dysfunction in women. However, given the nature of the factors that contribute to sexual dysfunction in women, it is unlikely that a medical intervention alone is likely to be effective. It is possible that, as for a number of sexual dysfunctions in men, a combined psychological and medical approach to sexual dysfunction in women may be the treatment of choice in the next 10 years.

Case Study

Client

A husband and wife, aged 31 and 29 years, respectively, were referred by a family planning agency. They had been married for 18 months and had lived together for 12 months prior to the marriage. Both college-educated professional people, they had met while working together and had become friends. The wife at this time was just emerging from a broken first marriage and subsequent divorce. The sexual relationship in her first marriage was not good, but she had had several affairs in which she had enjoyed sex, experiencing orgasm during sexual interaction but not during intercourse. Currently she still enjoyed sex and became sexually aroused, but her frequency of orgasm was reported as having fallen to 25% during sexual activity. She had not experienced orgasm during intercourse at all. As a consequence, she claimed that she was beginning to lose interest in sex and came to therapy looking for more enjoyment. She reported her loss of interest in sex as beginning when she and her now-husband had begun living together. Up until then, their sexual relationship had been good from both their points of view. She also reported no anxiety about sex and a rather neutral attitude toward it in the original family home.

The husband, who came from a very religious background, described family attitudes as neutral toward sex. He reported no other sexual relationships, either past or present. There was a concern about premature ejaculation, but questioning revealed his concern to be unfounded. He enjoyed sex and seemed to function well. There was no admission of any anxiety about sex—just enthusiasm for his wife to enjoy it more and experience orgasm during intercourse. Both husband and wife were currently working in demanding jobs. In the coming months they planned to start a family.

Treatment Program

The program involved nine sessions with the therapist.

Session 1
In pretherapy, specific information was given about the program. Both partners were present, with joint and separate interviews being conducted. This was followed by the counseling of both partners together on the nature of secondary orgasmic difficulties. The concept of performance anxiety was introduced, and its effects on the sexual response of both men and women were explained. The cooperation of the male partner in being neither too enthusiastic nor ambivalent about his wife's sexual response was elicited. A temporary ban on any sexual activity, until allowed by the

therapist in the context of the sensate focus program, was prescribed. The communication exercises were introduced, and the time commitment required by these and the sensate focus program were made clear. The format of the individual therapy sessions was briefly outlined as (1) review of the preceding week; (2) relaxation with guided imagery based on each phase of the sensate focus program; and (3) brief discussion of how the guided imagery was experienced.

Important features that emerged in this session with the couple were that both lived busy professional lives, often with meetings for further study outside working hours. They did not think of themselves as having a sexual problem in their relationship but thought that the wife's diminishing enjoyment of sex could become a problem if not addressed. Their main aim in coming to therapy was to increase the wife's enjoyment. She currently experienced orgasm during 25% of their sexual interactions but had never experienced it during intercourse either in this or in previous relationships. Also noted was the husband's enthusiasm for his wife to enjoy sex more and his disappointment that he would not be coming to all the sessions with her. Both partners commented that their sexual relationship had been very good and nonproblematic before they began living together. Both partners admitted to having difficulty resolving conflict and to being more likely to withdraw into silence rather than express feelings. The husband also expressed some concern about the possibility that he was ejaculating too early during intercourse. Further inquiry into what was happening enabled the therapist to reassure him that he was not a premature ejaculator.

Both husband and wife came from similar lower-middle-class socioeconomic backgrounds. Both had grown up in intact families with one or more siblings of the opposite sex. Religion was an important factor in the early life of both partners. The wife's religious background was Protestant and the husband's was Catholic. In both homes, as children they were allowed to ask questions and talk about sex, but discussion was not encouraged and parental attitudes were described as neutral. There was no display of physical affection either to spouse or children in either household.

The wife had a steady boyfriend at 17 years of age, and this developed into a sexual relationship, although she felt both guilt and anxiety about intercourse and regarded it as unpleasant. Otherwise, there were no other unpleasant or traumatic sexual experiences during this time. She was sexually responsive and orgasmic with her present partner before they formed a permanent relationship. Currently, she felt negative about sexual fantasy, sexual secretions, and masturbation but positive about foreplay

and manual orgasms. She also regarded sex as important in their relationship and looked for a certain equality in both sexual and nonsexual
activities. Within this present relationship, however, there were conflicts
not satisfactorily resolved about the division of household labor and time
spent at the work place. Concerning her present problem, she thought that
previous negative experiences and lack of sexual knowledge had contributed to it. She also recognized that fatigue, mood, and duration of foreplay
influenced her ability to become aroused.

Sessions 2–7: Therapy

These sessions were for the woman alone and occurred at weekly inter-
vals, except for a two-week break between sessions 5 and 6. In session 6 it
was necessary to repeat much of the content of the previous session since
the home assignments had been somewhat neglected in the interval. The
first half of each session was devoted to a review of the past week and
its prescribed activities. It included counseling on any relationship and
sexual issues that had surfaced as a result of the communication or sensate
focus homework. Ways of dealing with self-monitoring and performance
concerns were described: thought-stopping; focusing on bodily sensations and feelings; and incorporating the latter into concurrent fantasies,
either self-generated or based on the fantasy imagery presented during
the therapy sessions. The experiences that were brought to therapy were
used to discuss cognitive, behavioral, and relationship-enhancing strategies to address any negative thoughts or responses. Only one fantasy
was presented in each session. The fantasy was presented following brief
relaxation instructions. Fantasies were drawn from Nin's (1978, 1979)
book of fantasies. At the conclusion, the woman was invited to talk of her
response—of aspects she found sexually arousing or maybe troubling in
some way. Progressively each of the stages of sensate focus was introduced
during these six sessions.

Session 2

The communication exercises were reported as going well, with additional
relationship issues being spontaneously raised. One such issue concerned
working late; that is, whereas it was accepted that the husband worked late,
it was not acceptable to him that the wife would. All but two of the communication questions were completed. The guided imagery session was
found enjoyable, relaxing, and nonthreatening. During this session the
woman was encouraged to explore her own body by herself at home. She
was told to use a mirror to help her examine her genitals and to touch her

breasts and genitals while engaging in sexual fantasy to see what types of touching she found pleasurable.

Session 3

The communication exercises continued to bring forward issues for discussion that had not been broached by the couple before. All the questions were tackled. The importance of the wife's work to her had been clarified between them. The couple found that listening to each other's expression of feeling, with no attempt to problem solve, was a new and refreshing experience. During the session, the communication of sexual feelings in a positive and nonrejecting way was discussed, with some modeling by the therapist in the use of appropriate phrases. The women revealed anxiety both about undressing in front of her male partner and about being aware of his sexual arousal. She was encouraged to explore, at home, in fantasy and in practice, aspects of undressing she might find sexually arousing to herself. She was also encouraged to explore her own body and, when she felt comfortable, to masturbate using a vibrator to enhance her sexual pleasure and to become familiar with the types of stimulation that she found pleasurable. These techniques were important for her to experience sexual arousal and also to discover how to guide her husband in techniques to increase her arousal and orgasmic response.

Session 4

The sensate focus sessions prescribed for the previous week had at first been just relaxing, but now the woman was finding them sexually arousing as well. Her husband reported finding the massage enjoyable. The communication exercises continued to open up discussion between the couple in such a way that they were able to resolve misunderstandings that had arisen. They had come to realize that the woman liked to plan ahead whereas her husband preferred more spontaneous activities. An association between her tendency to plan ahead and her sexual difficulties was explored and found relevant. At the same time, it was also recognized that the therapy program necessitated some planning of sexual activity that would work against the desired spontaneity of normal sexual activity even to the extent of inducing anticipatory performance anxiety. Another issue arising through the communication questions concerned the woman's poor body image. It was suggested that she ask her husband what he liked about her body as he massaged her and that later she would repeat these phrases to herself while standing naked in front of a mirror.

Session 5

By using the sensate focus exercises they had been discovering enjoyable ways of touching each other. The husband was encouraged to respond to the guidance provided by his wife in terms of what she found pleasurable in both general as well as genital body pleasure. In particular, the wife needed to provide guidance on pleasurable techniques for clitoral stimulation. Despite this, the woman said she was beginning to feel like she was under some pressure from the program and from the expectation that she should enjoy the activities, and she proceeded to describe sensitivity to being touched on the nipples or clitoris. This called for reassurance that the aim of the sensate focus exercises was to explore different ways of touching and being touched and that sometimes only a very gentle indirect approach might be pleasurable—or it might not. There seemed to be no pattern of masturbation at all, so it was suggested that she might like to explore herself what she found pleasurable then she could guide her husband's touch when they were together. She was encouraged to engage in the suggested activities out of a sense of curiosity and desire to know her own body, and then only when she was ready. At no time was anything to be tried just because she felt she "had" to because of the program.

Session 6

Career issues continued to be a focus of discussion for the couple. The husband had been able to voice his concern that, because she went to evening committee meetings of a professional nature, this might indicate she did not need him. Another area of concern was the woman's plans for improving the house. Her husband was not able to tell her that he found this prospect of more work at home a real burden. Through the communication exercises the role expectations that the couple had of husband and wife were now emerging and being discussed and negotiated. With the sensate focus, the woman was finding a reawakening of her sexual feelings and was discovering there was very little she did not enjoy. She was even discovering that being touched around the nipple area could be pleasurable. Her use of fantasy during sexual interaction was only occasional, and it was used to ward off distracting thoughts. However, she had been reading erotic stories to "get in the mood" before their mutual sexual activities.

Session 7

Their commitment to the communication exercises was evident again, with five of the seven questions being completed, with seemingly a good level of self-disclosure on both sides. With the allowance of nondemand intercourse, old anxieties returned as the woman felt under pressure to perform on the two occasions that the couple had intercourse. She did not like manual concurrent stimulation of her clitoris, finding it almost painful. Again she was encouraged to explore this more slowly, at first on her own and then guiding her partner's hand in any way that she found pleasurable.

In the preceding week the use of fantasy had not been sufficient to allay her anxieties. The woman was encouraged to continue with the nonde-mand (i.e., nonorgasmic) intercourse phase of the program, putting no pressure on herself to be orgasmic but focusing on any pleasurable sensations that arose. Only when she could relax and enjoy this, she was advised, should she allow the possibility of orgasm. A further therapy session was considered but was decided against. The couple seemed to need time to assimilate what had been happening and to explore the new techniques in their own time, without the pressure of reporting back to the therapist.

Session 8

The aim of this session was to review progress and problems and to assess the readiness to terminate therapy or the need to extend it. An appointment was made for a follow-up session two months later. This session reviewed the influence of the program both on sexual activity and the overall relationship. In the preceding week, the communication question on clitoral stimulation had provoked discussion between the partners and came up again in this session. It was explained by the therapist that this form of stimulation during intercourse was, for many women, the only way they were able to experience orgasm during intercourse. Husband and wife differed over the idea of self-stimulation and compromises were discussed.

During the joint session the woman made a connection between her ambivalence about expressing her own sexuality and her sexual difficulties and said this was something she planned to work on. She said she felt more relaxed about their sexual relationship but was finding that constantly having to decide what she did or did not like during their sexual activity was a distraction. This suggested that she was still feeling some performance pressure from the program.

In a separate interview the woman again reported little use of fantasy. She was disappointed she had not accomplished more during the program and reported that orgasm happened on less than 25% of their sexual encounters. However, she was finding sex more relaxing and enjoyable and felt hopeful of future improvement. She expressed some concern that her husband seemed depressed but that she did not know why.

In the interview with the husband it became clear that for him the relationship had reached a crisis point over the issue of beginning a family and that his wife was unaware of this. He had been unable to share with her his feelings of inadequacy about supporting her and a child. Indeed, these feelings had affected his commitment to the program, fearing the possibility of impregnating his wife each time they had intercourse. He was encouraged to raise this issue as a communication question in the following week, the urgency of doing so being stressed.

Session 9

In a follow-up two months later, the aim of this session was primarily a review of what had been happening since the couple had attended the posttherapy session and to note any changes that had occurred since that time. The issue of parenting had been raised and some resolution reached. The woman had been surprised at her husband's concern and ambivalence about becoming a father. The husband had now become more amenable to the idea and even talked of some positive aspects of having a child. The relationship seemed to have stabilized at a new level of understanding. Both husband and wife, when asked separately, commented that everything was going well. The partners seemed to have confronted and come to terms with some of the role pressures each was facing.

The woman remarked on feeling much more relaxed and happy about their relationship and about her own sexuality. She said they had bought two popular sex manuals and that she was reading and enjoying the stories of Anais Nin. She was also now finding fantasy useful and enjoyable, both before and during lovemaking. She was experiencing orgasm more often—about 50% of the time but not during intercourse.

Telephone Follow-Up (Six Months Posttherapy)

The woman reported that the improvement in their sexual relationship had been maintained and that she was experiencing orgasm in about 50% of sexual interactions, but not during intercourse.

Discussion

The eventual increase in the woman's orgasmic frequency from 25% to 50%, combined with a fall in performance anxiety and the overall rise in sexual satisfaction for the woman, suggests that the therapeutic focus on performance anxiety was appropriate. The finding that the effects of

therapy were not fully realized until after the end of therapy gave cre-
dence to the client's comment that therapy was itself perceived as impos-
ing performance demands. The focus on sexual arousal led to uncovering
areas of anxiety about particular sexual activities and to a deeper ambivalence about female sexuality. This, in turn, led to the recognition that
both sexual anxiety and performance anxiety can coexist in the one client, expressing both the demand to be nonsexual and the demand to be
orgasmically sexual. On the behavioral level, these demands can make a
woman reluctant to express her sexual preferences. On the other hand,
they can lead to performance pressures, with associated fears of failure,
from both the woman and her spouse to experience orgasm more often.
All the components of therapy—counseling, the use of fantasy, sensate
focus, and communication exercises—were too well integrated to allow
any assessment of individual contributions. The communication exercises
were found invaluable in allowing marital issues to surface and find some
resolution. Had this not happened, marital therapy may have replaced sex
therapy so that the problems in the relationship that were impacting on
the sexual problems could be addressed.

The goal of the program was remission of the symptoms of secondary orgasmic dysfunction by reducing performance anxiety and intensi-
fying sexual arousal. For the woman in this case study, some symptom
remission was achieved in conjunction with a reduction in performance
anxiety. Whether there was intensification of arousal is unclear. However,
there appeared to be an increase in sexual communication and a decrease
in performance anxiety, which seemed to be associated with an increase
in relationship factors, sexual satisfaction, and orgasmic response. Sexual
anxiety, as measured by the questionnaire, persisted at a relatively low
but stable level. However, anxiety about particular sexual activities and
female sexuality did surface during therapy sessions. Some attitudinal
change toward various sexual activities was achieved, along with reports
of increased sexual enjoyment and feelings of relaxation about sex.

References

American Psychiatric Association (APA) (2000). *Diagnostic and statistical manual
of mental disorders* (4th ed., text revision). Washington, DC: Author.
Basson, R. (2001). Female sexual response: The role of drugs in the management of
sexual dysfunction. *Journal of Obstetrics and Gynaecology, 98,* 350–353.

Basson, R. (2004). Pharmacotherapy for sexual dysfunction in women. *Expert Opinion on Pharmacotherapy, 5,* 1045–1059.

Basson, R. (2005). Women's sexual dysfunction: Revised and expanded definitions. *Canadian Medical Association Journal, 172,* 1327–1333.

Basson, R., Althop, S., Davis, S., Fugl-Meyer, K., Goldstein, I., Leiblum, S., et al. (2004). Summary of recommendations on sexual dysfunction in women. *Journal of Sexual Medicine, 1,* 24–34.

Basson, R., Leiblum, S., Brotto, L., Derogatis, L., Fourcoy, J., Fugl-Meyer, K., et al. (2004). Revised definitions of women's sexual dysfunction. *Journal of Sexual Medicine, 1,* 40–48.

Chaill, C., Llewelyn, S. P., & Pearson, C. (1991). Long term of sexual abuse which occurred in childhood: A review. *British Journal of Clinical Psychology, 30,* 117–130.

Clayton, A. H., McGarvey, E. L., Clavet, G. J., & Piazza, L. (1997). Comparison of sexual functioning in clinical and nonclinical population using the Changes in Sexual Functioning Questionnaire (CSFQ). *Psychopharmacology Bulletin, 33,* 747–753.

Cyranowski, J. M., Frank, E., Cherry, C., Houck, P., & Kupfer, D. J. (2004). Prospective assessment of sexual function in women treated for recurrent major depression. *Journal of Psychiatric Research, 38,* 267–273.

De Bruijn, G. (1982). From masturbating to orgasm with a partner: How some women bridge the gap—and why others don't. *Journal of Sex and Marital Therapy, 8,* 151–167.

Delaney, S. & McCabe, M. P. (1988). Secondary inorgasmia in women: A treatment program and case study. *Sexual and Marital Therapy, 3,* 151–167.

Everaerd, W. & Dekker, J. (1982). Treatment of secondary orgasmic dysfunction: A comparison of systematic desensitization and sex therapy. *Behaviour Research and Therapy, 20,* 269–274.

Graziottin, A. & Leiblum, S. R. (2005). Biological and psychosocial pathophysiology of female sexual dysfunction during the menopausal transition. *Journal of Sexual Medicine, 2*(Suppl 35), 133–145.

Heiman, J. R. (2007) Orgasmic disorders in women. In S. R. Leiblum (Ed.), *Principles and practice of sex therapy* (4th ed., pp. 84–123). New York: Guilford Press.

Heiman, J. R., Gladue, B. A., Roberts, C. W., & LoPiccolo, J. (1986). Historical and current factors discriminating sexually functional from sexually dysfunctional married couples. *Journal of Marital and Family Therapy, 12,* 163–174.

Heiman, J. R. & LoPiccolo, J. (1983) Clinical outcome of sex therapy: Effects of daily v. weekly treatment. *Archives of General Psychiatry, 30,* 443–449.

Heiman, J. R. & Meston, M. (1997). Empirically validated treatment for sexual dysfunction. *Annual Review of Sex Research, 8,* 148–194.

Hof, L. & Berman, E. (1986). The sexual genogram. *Journal of Marital and Family Therapy, 12,* 39–47.

Hulbert, S. F. (1991). The role of assertiveness in female sexuality: A comparative study between sexually assertive and sexually non-assertive women. *Journal of Sex and Marital Therapy, 17*, 183–190.

Kaplan, H. S. (1974). *The new sex therapy: Active treatment of sexual dysfunctions.* New York: Brunner/Mazel.

Kaplan, H. S. (1979). *Disorders of sexual desire.* New York: Brunner/Mazel.

Kaplan, H. S. (1983). *The evaluation of sexual disorders: Psychological and medical aspect.* New York: Brunner/Mazel.

Kelly, M. P., Strassberg, D. S., & Kircher, J. R. (1990). Attitudinal and experimental correlates of anorgasmia. *Archives of Sexual Behavior, 19*, 165–177.

Kelly, M. P., Strassberg, D. S., & Turner, C. M. (2004). Communication and associated relationship issues in female anorgasmia. *Journal of Sex and Marital Therapy, 30*, 263–276.

Kelly, M. P., Strassberg, D. S., & Turner, C. M. (2006). Behavioral assessment of couples' communication in female orgasmic disorder. *Journal of Sex and Marital Therapy, 32*, 81–95.

Kilmann, P. R., Boland, J. P., Norton, S. P., Davidson, E., & Caid, C. (1986). Perspectives of sex therapy outcome: A survey of AASECT providers. *Journal of Sex and Marital Therapy, 12*, 116–138.

Komisaruk, B.R., Beyer-Flores, C., & Whipple, B. (2006). *The science of orgasm.* Baltimore: John Hopkins University Press.

Kope, S. A. (2007) Female sexual arousal and orgasm: Pleasures and problems. In L. VanderCreek, F. Peterson, & J. Bley (Eds.), *Innovations in clinical practices: Focus on sexual health* (pp. 93–106). Sarasota, FL: Professional Resource Press.

Kuriansky, J. B., Sharp, L., & O'Connor, D. (1982). The treatment of anorgasmia: Long-term effectiveness of a short-term behavioral group intervention. *Journal of Sex and Marital Therapy, 8,* 29–43.

Leitenberg, H., Greenwald, E., & Tarran, M. J. (1989). The relation between sexual activity among children during preadolescence and/or early adolescence and sexual behavior and sexual adjustment in young adulthood. *Archives of Sexual Behavior, 18*, 299–313.

LoPiccolo, J., Heiman, J. R., Hogan, D. R., & Roberts, C. W. (1985). Effectiveness of single therapists versus co-therapy teams in sex therapy. *Journal of Consulting and Clinical Psychology, 53*, 287–294.

LoPiccolo, J. & Lobitz, W. C. (1972) The role of masturbation in the treatment of orgasmic dysfunction. *Archives of Sexual Behavior, 2*, 163–171.

LoPiccolo, J. & LoPiccolo, L. (1978). *Handbook of sex therapy.* New York: Plenum Press.

LoPiccolo, J. & Stock, W. E. (1986). Treatment of sexual dysfunction, *Journal of Consulting and Clinical Psychology, 54*, 158–167.

Masters, W. H. & Johnson, V. (1966). *Human sexual response.* Oxford, England: Little, Brown.

Masters, W. H. & Johnson, V. (1970). *Human sexual inadequacy.* Boston: Little, Brown.

McCabe, M. P. (1991). The development and maintenance of sexual dysfunction: An explanation based on cognitive theory. *Sexual and Marital Therapy, 6,* 245–260.

McCabe, M. P. (1999). The interrelationship between intimacy, relationship functioning, and sexuality among men and women in committed relationships. *Canadian Journal of Human Sexuality, 8,* 31–38.

McCabe, M. P. (2001). De we need a classification system for female sexual dysfunction? A comment on the 1999 Consensus Classification System. *Journal of Sex and Marital Therapy, 27,* 175–178.

McCabe, M. P. (2005). The role of performance anxiety in the development and maintenance of sexual dysfunction in men and women. *International Journal of Stress Management, 12,* 379–388.

McCabe, M. P. & Cobain, M. (1998). The impact of individual and relationship factors on sexual dysfunction among males and females. *Sexual and Marital Therapy, 13,* 131–143.

McCabe, M. P. & Delaney, S. M. (1991). An evaluation of therapeutic programs for the treatment of secondary inorgasmia in women. *Archives of Sexual Behavior, 21,* 69–89.

McGovern, K. B., McMullen, R. S., & LoPiccolo, J. (1978). Secondary orgasmic dysfunction. 1. Analysis and strategies for treatment. In J. LoPiccolo & L. LoPiccolo (Eds.), *Handbook of sex therapy.* New York: Plenum Press.

Morokoff, P. J. & Gillilland, R. (1993). Stress, sexual functioning and sexual satisfaction. *Journal of Sex Research, 30,* 43–53.

Nin, A. (1978). *Delta of venus.* London: Allen.

Nin, A. (1979). *Little birds.* London: Allen.

Obstfeld, L. S., Lupfer, M. B., & Lupfer, S. L. (1985). Exploring the relationship between gender identity and sexual functioning. *Journal of Sex and Marital Therapy, 11,* 248–258.

O'Donohue, W. T., Dopke, C. A., & Swingen, D. N. (1997). Psychotherapy for female sexual dysfunction: A review. *Clinical Psychiatry Review, 17,* 537–566.

O'Donahue, W. T., Swingen, D. N., Dopke, C. A., & Roger, L. G. (1999). Psychotherapy for male sexual dysfunction. *Clinical Psychiatry Review, 19,* 591–630.

Pietropinto, A. (1986). Male contribution to female sexual dysfunction. *Medical Aspects of Human Sexuality, 20,* 84–91.

Purcell, C. & McCabe, M. P. (1992). The impact of imagery type and imagery training on the subjective sexual arousal of women. *Sexual and Marital Therapy, 7,* 251–250.

Riley, A. I. & Riley, E. J. (1978). A controlled study to evaluate directed masturbation in the management of primary orgasmic failure in women. *British Journal of Psychiatry, 133,* 404–409.

Roffe, M. W. & Britt, B. C. (1981). A typology of marital interaction for sexually dysfunctional couples. *Journal of Sex and Marital Therapy, 7*, 207–222.

Snyder, D. K. & Berg, P. (1983). Determinants of sexual dissatisfaction in sexually distressed couples. *Archives of Sexual Behavior, 12*, 237–246.

Talmadge, L. D. & Wallace, S. C. (1991). Reclaiming sexuality in female incest survivors. *Journal of Sex and Marital Therapy, 17*, 163–182.

Taublieb, A. B. & Lick, J. R. (1986). Female orgasm via penile stimulation: A criterion of adequate sexual functioning? *Journal of Sex and Marital Therapy, 12*, 60–64.

Travis, R. P. & Travis, P. Y. (1986). Intimacy based sex therapy. *Journal of Sex Education and Therapy, 12*, 21–27.

Walsh, K. E. & Berman, J. R. (2004). Sexual dysfunction in the older woman—An overview of the current understanding and management. *Drugs & Aging, 21*, 655–675.

Weeks, G. (1994). The intersystem model: An integrative approach to treatment, In G. Weeks & L. Hof (Eds.), *The marital relationship casebook: Theory and application of the intersystem model* (pp. 3–34). New York: Brunner/Mazel.

Weeks, G. (2004). The emergence of a new paradigm in sex therapy: Integration. *Sexual and Relationship Therapy, 20*, 89–103.

11

Painful Intercourse
Dyspareunia and Vaginismus

Marta Meana

Contents

Introduction

Dyspareunia and vaginismus are disorders involving pain and sex. The pain wreaks havoc on the sex. It sets the stage for the development or reinforcement of comorbid sexual dysfunctions, negative sexual attitudes, avoidant and damaging behaviors, relationship discord, and declines in self-esteem and mood. These in turn augment the experience of pain. Despite significant overlap, pain may require certain interventions, while sexual problems may require others. An intersystem or integrative approach (Weeks, 2005) is thus the way to maximize effectiveness in the treatment of dyspareunia and vaginismus. In fact, a sex therapist alone is unlikely to properly assess or treat the painful intercourse without the collaboration of one or more other health professionals. A sex therapist, however, may be ideally suited to coordinate the effort if he or she has an understanding of the multidimensionality involved. The effort is a considerable one, as dyspareunia and vaginismus are difficult sexual problems to resolve.

Definition and Description

Dyspareunia is currently defined in the *Diagnostic and Statistical Manual of Mental Disorders,* 4th ed., text revision (*DSM-IV-TR*; APA, 2000) as recurrent or persistent genital pain associated with sexual intercourse that is not caused exclusively by vaginismus or lack of lubrication. Women presenting with dyspareunia will generally complain of significant pain during penile–vaginal intercourse. If prompted, they are likely to also report pain with other types of penetration such as finger insertion, tampons, and gynecological examinations. The prevalence of dyspareunia in women has been estimated at approximately 14%, with significant variation across the lifespan (Laumann, Gagnon, Michael, & Michaels, 1994). The highest prevalence is found in women 18–24 years of age, despite a persistent belief that dyspareunia is mostly associated with menopausal changes in vaginal elasticity and lubrication. Pain with intercourse can occur in men but is relatively rare, with a North American prevalence rate of 3% (ibid.). Higher rates have been reported in men who engage in receptive anal intercourse (Rosser, Metz, Bockting, & Buroker, 1997). Overall, however, dyspareunia is considered primarily a female sexual dysfunction.

Recently, some researchers and clinicians have been debating whether dyspareunia is a sexual dysfunction at all. They have proposed that it might be better characterized as a pain syndrome that interferes with sexual functioning only incidentally, much as back pain or a headache might (Binik, Meana, Berkley, & Khalife 1999; Meana, Binik, Khalife, & Cohen, 1997b). There has even been an appeal to remove dyspareunia from the sexual dysfunction section of future editions of the DSM (Binik, 2005). It is important for the clinician to be aware of this debate, as it underlines the multiplicity of dyspareunia. Classification issues aside, it remains important not to privilege the sex over the pain or vice versa in the treatment of dyspareunia (Meana, 2005).

Vaginismus is diagnosed when difficulty with vaginal penetration is attributed to a recurrent or persistent involuntary spasm of the musculature of the outer third of the vagina (APA, 2000). It is difficult to distinguish vaginismus from dyspareunia, since both involve pain and, often, hypertonicity (excess muscle tone) of pelvic floor musculature. Some have suggested that vaginismus might simply be the severe, phobic end of the dyspareunia continuum (Meana & Binik, 1994; Reissing, Binik, Khalife, Cohen, & Amsel, 2004). The one feature that seems unique to vaginismus, however, is a fear of penetration that can rise to the level of a phobia, both behaviorally and cognitively (Reissing et al., 2004). Women often report that sexual intercourse is nearly impossible, if not completely so. Vaginismus is much rarer than dyspareunia, with population-based estimates of 1% or less (Fugl-Meyer & Sjogren Fugl-Meyer, 1999).

Marked personal distress or interpersonal difficulty is a diagnostic criterion for both dyspareunia and vaginismus. They also share exclusion criteria that stipulate that both disorders be neither better accounted for by another Axis I disorder nor the direct product of a substance or general

medical condition. The etiology, assessment, and treatment of dyspareunia and vaginismus are relatively undifferentiated. Both disorders are
thus covered simultaneously for the rest of this chapter. Distinctions are
made when relevant.

Etiology

Individual Physiological Factors

A number of physiological factors can result in pain with intercourse.
Congenital malformations of the genital tract, such as a deviated vaginal
septum, are rare but need to be ruled out. Acute and chronic diseases, such
as urinary tract or yeast infections or dermatosis, are frequently reported
and have been linked to dyspareunia (Meana & Binik, 1994). Nerve dysfunction processes, such as those implicated in provoked vestibulodynia
(formerly vulvar vestibulitis), are currently believed to be the most common cause of premenopausal dyspareunia (Bergeron, Binik, Khalife, &
Pagidas, 1997). Provoked vestibulodynia is believed to be characterized by
excessive sensitivity or overgrowth of the nerve fibers in the vestibule area
where the vulva meets the vagina. This results in hyperalgesia (extreme
sensitivity) at the entry of the vagina, which is consequently painfully stimulated and irritated by most types of vaginal penetration. Postmenopausal
decreases in estrogen and its purported effects on the structure and tissues of the vaginal canal have long been associated with intercourse difficulties. Iatrogenic damage from episiotomies or other genital surgeries or
procedures can also result in painful intercourse (Meana & Binik, 1994).
In addition, women with vaginismus and vestibulodynia appear to have
chronic pelvic floor musculature hypertonicity (Reissing, Brown, Lord,
Binik, & Khalife, 2005). It is unclear whether this muscle tension is a cause
or a consequence of painful intercourse, but the hypertonicity is significantly implicated in the maintenance of the pain experience.

Individual Psychological Factors

Most pain experiences are impacted by expectancies and mood. Although
negative expectations and anxiety alone are unlikely to cause pain, their
mediating effect is sufficiently substantial to consider them the equivalent
of etiologic factors. The expectation and catastrophization of pain during

intercourse is likely to impact the experience negatively, as has been found in women with vestibulodynia (Pukall, Baron, Amsel, Khalife, & Binik, 2006). Anxiety about the situation can also further complicate the interaction (Payne, Binik, Amsel, & Khalife, 2005). There is, however, little support for any one psychological etiology in the development of painful intercourse. Most women with dyspareunia do not differ from controls on psychological factors, with the possible exception of a hypersensitivity and hypervigilance to pain in general. Some studies have found childhood sexual abuse and trauma to be more frequently reported by women with provoked vestibulodynia and vaginismus (Harlow & Stewart, 2005; Reissing, Binik, Khalife, Cohen, & Amsel, 2003), whereas others have found no difference between women with dyspareunia and no-pain controls (Meana, Binik, Khalife, & Cohen, 1997a). Other suggested etiologic factors in the development of painful intercourse include negative sexual attitudes and lack of sex education.

Interactional/Couple Factors

There is no doubt that painful intercourse has a significant impact on sexual relationships. It is common to see couples seeking sex therapy because the painful sex has become highly problematic—maybe even a relationship deal-breaker. It is also relatively clear that what transpires in these relationships can have a significant impact on the experience of pain. A partner who interprets the pain and sex-avoidant behavior as an indication of lack of interest, attraction, or commitment is likely to be upset and either to exert pressure or withdraw. Both of these reactions can exacerbate the situation. Relationship issues do not need to be directly responsible for the origin of the problem to be considered important contributing factors in these disorders. Not much research has been conducted on the impact of relationship factors on intercourse pain. One study, however, found that lower dyadic adjustment predicted higher pain intensity scores in women with dyspareunia (Meana, Binik, Khalife, & Cohen, 1998).

Intergenerational Factors

There is no research directly investigating family-of-origin factors related to the onset of painful intercourse. On the other hand, the implication of negative sexual attitudes and childhood sexual abuse or victimization as possible risk factors for sexual pain indirectly points to the family of origin. Lack of education about sexuality may also emanate from a particularly restrictive upbringing or one in which sexuality was considered a taboo subject. In terms of the pain experience, there are not sufficient data to indicate that the sexual pain disorders have a familial component. However, some research has indicated that individuals with families that have extensive pain histories are more likely to also experience pain themselves, especially women (Edwards, Zeichner, Kuczmierczyk, & Boczkowski, 1985; Lester, Lefebvre, & Keefe, 1994).

Societal/Cultural Factors

It is difficult to determine empirically the impact of societal/cultural factors on painful intercourse. Cross-cultural data are not available, although there is some suggestion that religious orthodoxy may be a risk factor for the development of vaginismus (Binik, Bergeron, & Khalife, 2007). More generally, women continue to be sociopolitically disempowered compared with men, and their sexuality remains central to their socioculturally defined sense of worth. This can translate into the stigmatization of women who encounter problems with their sexual function. Historically, women who have resisted sexual activity for one reason or another have been denigrated and had their femininity questioned. Against this backdrop, it is not surprising that many women with dyspareunia or vaginismus experience a heightened sense of inadequacy and an unrelenting, unspoken pressure to comply with their partners' desires, despite excruciating pain. This societal overlay on a distressing set of symptoms can contribute to their exacerbation.

Assessment

Although dyspareunia and vaginismus are often considered women's problems, they are essentially couple problems. Sometimes the couple will present for therapy. More often, women assume they will be engaging in individual therapy. They believe they are the ones with "the problem." Correcting this perception is the first important therapeutic intervention. Most partners can be persuaded to participate, as they are generally motivated to resolve the sexual dilemma. There are, however, exceptions, and the therapist has to do his or her best under the circumstances.

Involving a gynecologist is essential but will require therapists to identify gynecologists in their community who have a special interest and expertise in vulvar and pelvic pain. Women with these problems have traditionally been considered difficult patients because of the elusiveness of a cure; thus some physicians are reluctant to treat them. The involvement of a gynecologist who is interested and invested in both assessment and treatment of painful intercourse can be an important factor in the outcome. Some women with vaginismus will never have had a gynecological examination and believe that it is not possible. However, gynecologists familiar with this disorder usually succeed in performing the examination. It may require therapists to be present to help the client with relaxation.

Finally, it is not unusual for primary presenting problems to end up being secondary to more serious ones that are disclosed or discovered well after the initial intake. This is especially true in intersystem therapy, as the interactions between the systems may take a long time to reveal themselves clearly. It is thus essential that the therapist retain a hypothesis-testing attitude throughout the treatment, integrate assessment at all stages, and not become overly attached to initial case conceptualizations. This attitude also requires that the therapist have the flexibility to change treatment course, if ongoing assessment indicates a redirection in treatment.

Preliminary Assessment and Consultation

Pain is the primary presenting complaint in dyspareunia and in many cases of vaginismus, and, thus, pain should be assessed first. Essential questions include the following:

- Where exactly does it hurt when you have or attempt sexual intercourse? (A diagram or model of the genital and pelvic region will be very helpful here.)
- Describe the pain in terms of intensity (1–10 scale) and quality (descriptors like "burning" or "tearing").
- When does the pain start (before, during, or after penetration)?
- How long does the pain last?
- Do you always have pain with intercourse, or does it depend on certain conditions (e.g., fatigue, menstrual cycle, level of arousal)?
- Do you have genital or pelvic pain with other sexual or nonsexual stimulation (e.g., finger insertion, oral sex, tampon insertion, gynecological exam)?

- Do you ever have genital or pelvic pain spontaneously, without any stimulation?
- In your lifetime, when did you start having pain with intercourse (from the first time you had intercourse, or did it start later)?

This pain assessment should also be followed up with a referral to a gynecologist who can investigate the location of the pain with a vulvar cotton swab test and digital exploration. The gynecologist needs to assess if the client has any of the physiological risk factors covered in the physiological etiology section of this chapter. The therapist should ask the client to obtain a release of information from the gynecologist to facilitate consultation.

The sexual function of both the client and her partner should be the immediate next target of assessment. Most important to cover are the perceived impact of the pain on their sexual life (i.e., frequency of intercourse and other sexual activity, desire, arousal, orgasm, satisfaction) as well as the existence of comorbid sexual dysfunctions. For the purposes of the latter, it may be expedient to administer the Female Sexual Function Index (FSFI; Rosen et al., 2002) to women and the International Index of Erectile Function (IIEF; Rosen et al., 1997) to men. Treatment may need to address multiple sexual problems simultaneously. For therapists interested in developing a client-administered assessment protocol as an adjunct to the clinical interview, Meana, Binik, and Thaler (2008) provide a comprehensive review of the most psychometrically sound measures of sexual dysfunction.

The cognitive and coping styles of both partners are also important to assess. Why do they think they have this problem? What do they fear? What do they think it means, if anything? How do they cope with it? Personal theories about the cause of intercourse pain have been found to be more predictive of psychological adjustment than gynecological findings (Meana, Binik, Khalife, & Cohen, 1999). An investigation of cognitive and coping styles will very quickly reveal the extent of relationship distress around this issue and in general. It is imperative that the temperature of the relationship be taken at this stage, in part because treatment will rely to a great extent on the ability of the relationship to navigate the challenges of treatment. Finally, it is important to assess the existence of other Axis I and Axis II disorders. These are likely to have an impact on the disorder as well as on the course of therapy.

Treatment-Integrated Assessment

The intersystem approach places a significant burden on assessment, as it broadens the playing field substantially. It is neither reasonable nor productive to attempt to assess all possible contributors to the problem before starting treatment. The preliminary assessment provides a current snapshot of pain, sexual function, coping style, and relationship distress. There is some urgency, though, for treatment to commence. Further assessment can be integrated throughout the treatment. Sexual history, developmental and familial factors of relevance, general ideology about sexuality and gender, and the role that the pain problem plays in the relationship will more slowly become manifest as trust and rapport between the therapist and the couple grow. The treatment itself will raise issues of which clients were unaware at intake. That is how assessment and treatment are inseparable in an intersystem approach to dyspareunia and vaginismus.

Treatment

Initial Stage: Education, Goal Setting, Anxiety Reduction

Education is an integral part of the initial stage of therapy. Most clients will know close to nothing about dyspareunia and vaginismus and even less about their treatment. It is essential that the therapist be well versed in the outcome research on medications and procedures, which may include antifungals, antiallergens, topical estrogen, topical steroids, serotonin inhibitors, or even the recommendation of surgery. In addition to imparting their knowledge, therapists can provide clients with reading materials, as appropriate.

In the context of the initial assessment and gynecological findings, it is time to calibrate expectations and to set reasonable treatment goals. At the beginning of therapy, clients are often filled with hope that this problem will finally be resolved. The literature, however, indicates that the complete resolution of genital pain is difficult to attain. Even more elusive is the reestablishment of a level of sexual activity that satisfies both partners (Bergeron et al., 2001). Although hope is integral to treatment, expectations also need to be realistic. Aligning client expectations with the empirical data and setting goals that aim at pain reduction and increases in sexual function and satisfaction are central to the therapeutic effort.

Although most clients are hopeful as they start therapy, they are also understandably anxious. They believe treatment will be focused on the one activity they have been avoiding or fearing for a long time. It is also the activity that has often resulted in arguments, fears of abandonment, and feelings of inadequacy. The therapist can help allay the anxiety in the initial stage of therapy by starting to address some of the less threatening aspects of the pain problem. The following are a number of techniques that can be instrumental in the first stages of therapy:

1. Reinforcing help-seeking: The client and her partner should be commended for addressing the problem. They should be informed that failing to address the issue would likely only have made it further degenerate—that confronting the pain problem indicates strength and will, both of which auger well for treatment outcome.

2. Validating experience of pain: Many women experiencing pain with intercourse have been told that the pain is "in their heads" or a somatic manifestation of intrapsychic or relational conflict. Emphasizing that their pain is real is crucial. It is also important to explain that the exploration of well-being, sexual function, and their relationship reflects an understanding that these issues can have an impact on the pain and not that they are the "real" problem.

3. Demystifying pain: Even seemingly inexplicable pain has its patterns. One way of transforming the pain from a mysterious tormentor to a more controllable force is to train the client to explore the conditions under which the pain is minimized and maximized. A pain diary can be very helpful in this regard, as clients monitor conditions when the pain occurred (e.g., emotions, thoughts, behaviors, arousal level, relationship interactions that preceded and followed the pain). For women who have stopped attempting sexual intercourse, this demystification may simply involve a retrospective analysis of factors that made it worse or better.

4. Demystifying anxiety: Anxiety is not an inevitable reaction to the pain problem. It can be targeted and reduced or eradicated. Starting to do so using relaxation therapy techniques (e.g., imaging, breathing exercises, progressive muscle relaxation), cognitive restructuring, and decatastrophization can be important steps.

5. Genital self-exploration: Many women who experience intercourse pain have developed an avoidance of their genitalia. They usually have not tried to explore and locate where it hurts. Getting women reacquainted with their genitalia can be useful for a number of reasons:

   They can locate painful areas.
   They can experiment with muscle exercises.

They develop self-efficacy, whereby they come to control certain aspects of their genitalia (muscle flexing).

6. Deemphasizing intercourse: Letting the client know that much of the work ahead will focus on increasing desire, arousal, and relational connectedness rather than on increasing intercourse frequency will relieve anxiety. Discouraging or even banning intercourse until a later stage in the treatment may be indicated. Clients often experience these interventions as significant stress reducers that help them concentrate on other aspects of the treatment.

7. Emphasizing affection and sensuality: Directing clients to increase their nonsexual demonstrations of physical affection is an important step. It is common for couples who have stopped having sex or have greatly curtailed it to avoid all forms of physical contact. This damages their connectedness and alienates them from each other, both psychologically and physically.

Core Stage of Treatment: Connecting the Dots of Pain, Sex, Self, and Partner

The treatment of dyspareunia and vaginismus targets the interrelated domains of pain, sex, individual factors, and couple dynamics concurrently. This does not necessarily mean that every session has to cover these four domains. Some sessions will focus more on the sexual aspects than on the relational ones. Other sessions might fall exclusively into the domain of individual beliefs. That is perfectly natural and desirable. Treatment plans need to be responsive to snags along the way, as well as to the primacy of one domain over others in contributing to the disorder. But pain, sex, individual concerns, and couple dynamics all need to be juggled throughout the treatment. The neglect of any one of them can impact outcome negatively.

Pain and Physiological Processes

Addressing the Gynecological Consult

If the gynecologist consult has resulted in a recommendation for either a medical or surgical treatment component, sex therapists are well advised to further familiarize themselves with the details of that recommendation. There is controversy about some of the medical and surgical options, and clients may not know this. Therapists are well positioned to educate clients about these treatment options so that they can make an informed decision. If a client chooses to undergo a certain procedure or medical regimen, the therapist can also help the client adhere to the treatment and adjust to its effects.

Coordinating with Physical Therapy
Following the gynecological consult, it is often appropriate for the client to be assessed and treated by a physical therapist who specializes in pelvic floor dysfunction (Rosenbaum, 2007). Such physical therapists can be found by accessing the national database of the American Physical Therapy Association (http://www.apta.org). Individual states also have their own physical therapy association with referral directories. The number of physical therapy sessions can vary from a couple to several, and they focus on education about musculature and its role, manual therapy, and home exercises. Physical therapy can also include pelvic floor biofeedback and electrical stimulation. Rosenbaum provides a detailed description of the physical therapy regimen.

Ideally, the sex therapist collaborates with the physical therapist, especially in the planning and execution of vaginal dilatation. Vaginal dilatation is, in part, a form of systematic desensitization whereby the woman is instructed to insert dilators of increasing size into her vagina over a period of time. These dilators can be bought from a number of sources easily accessible through the Internet. For many years, vaginal dilatation and Kegel exercises were home exercises assigned by sex therapists. It is now thought that without the instruction of a physical therapist these exercises may be counterproductive for some women. Although the involvement of a physical therapist is optimal, circumstances (e.g., financial difficulty, lack of local professionals) can sometimes preclude this team approach. In those cases, carefully guided vaginal dilatation exercises are still worth attempting, even without physical therapy involvement. When the woman moves beyond her own insertion of the dilators to penile insertion, it is also important that the woman initially be in charge of the rate, extent, and movement during these first penile penetration attempts.

Addressing Influences on Pain
In the initial stage of therapy, women are asked to monitor influences on the pain experience, using a pain diary. This identification of exacerbating and alleviating factors can then be translated into specific interventions to improve the conditions under which sex takes place. The point is to learn

from the diary and then to try to instate the best possible conditions for sexual interactions—conditions that minimize the pain experience.

Sexual Interactions

Making Quality Time

Even couples who are not dealing with painful sex often fall into the trap of neglecting their sexual life. The multiple demands of busy professional lives and a laundry list of child-care activities can easily push couple-focused activities to the very bottom of the priority list. Many couples present to therapy saying that by the time they get to bed after a long day of obligations, they are exhausted. The result is that they either do not have sex at all or they have a routine, disengaged, and uninspired version of it. If pain is added to this scenario, the situation worsens considerably. Thus, the first change the couple needs to enact is to reserve quality time for sexual interactions. Some couples find it useful to set aside special times during the week for their sexual encounters. Other couples find this overly staged and lacking in spontaneity. Scheduled or not, sex cannot be neglected. It requires quality time and attention.

Building Desire and Arousal

It is well known that painful intercourse impacts all stages of the sexual response: desire, arousal, and orgasm. It is difficult for a woman to desire what hurts or to get aroused when she is anticipating pain. It may also be challenging for her partner to feel desire and become or stay aroused to an activity he or she knows the woman finds aversive. Difficulties with desire and arousal may also predate the onset of the pain. In most cases, reinstating desire and arousal is likely to be an essential part of any treatment plan for dyspareunia and vaginismus. There are a number of ways to target desire and arousal. The following are some suggested strategies, although not all of these will be appropriate for all clients and their partners:

1. Enhancing self-perceptions of desirability: For most women to feel sexy, they have to believe in their own desirability. They have to find themselves attractive before they believe anybody else's assessment. Partner compliments about physical attractiveness are often dismissed as thinly veiled attempts to get sex. It is thus important to build a woman's sense of her own attractiveness. This can be a challenge considering the idealized images of beauty with which the media bombards us. The therapist can, however,

work individually with each woman to heighten her sense of desirability, both cognitively and behaviorally. Most women have ideas about realistic things they can do to make themselves feel more attractive.

2. Use of erotica (books or videos): These materials can be used in anticipation of a sexual interaction, as part of one, or privately by the woman alone. They are "getting in the mood" strategies that can be instrumental, as long as the client chooses materials that are tasteful to her.

3. Directed solitary masturbation: Women who experience pain with intercourse have often stopped engaging in any sexual activity, even masturbation. Reintroducing masturbation may be useful to build desire and arousal as well as to reacquaint the client with her genitalia. Some women will never have masturbated at all, and a discussion about their desire to do so is indicated.

4. Heightening awareness of arousal: Because arousal is a relatively concealed phenomenon in women, many fail to attend to its physiological signs, such as lubrication and genital swelling. Heightening their awareness of these signs can serve two functions. First, the physiological feedback may increase subjective arousal. Second, since intercourse is likely to be less painful when aroused, it is useful for the woman (and her partner) to recognize the signs of arousal so that intercourse is not attempted until these signs are present.

5. Expanding the sexual repertoire: Many people define sex exclusively as intercourse. The rest is considered foreplay and consequently demoted to the status of preparations for the main event. It is thus not surprising that when couples have difficulties with intercourse, they have a tendency to drop all sexual interactions. What is the point of preparing for something that is not going to happen or that is going to feel bad anyway? Changing that focus is a good strategy for all couples and is essential for couples who have painful intercourse. Sex includes many acts that provide intense pleasure and orgasm. A couple who deprives themselves of these experiences because intercourse is problematic is missing out on a potentially very satisfying sex life. Furthermore, increasing the emphasis on nonintercourse sexual acts can also have the effect of raising arousal levels, which in turn decreases the intensity of pain. Finally, expanding the repertoire can also result in more exciting and less mechanistic sex. Rather than playing out the same script every time in the same order, sex can be open to variations and spontaneity. The expansion of the sexual repertoire has traditionally been implemented through sensate focus exercises designed to shift the attention from the performance of intercourse and its attendant anxiety to the experience of sensual pleasure (see Chapter 3 in this volume). But expanding the sexual repertoire is also about branching out in terms of locations and situations. Sex does not always have to happen in the bedroom with the

lights out at 11 p.m. It can happen in the kitchen, fully clothed at 2 p.m.! This may be challenging for some couples with children and hectic work schedules, but arrangements can be made to facilitate these interludes if the couple has the will. They should be encouraged to think outside their box to the extent they find acceptable. There are a number of books that couples may find helpful in their attempts to expand their sexual repertoire. Two of these are *The Guide to Getting It On* (Joannides, 2006) and *The Good Vibrations Guide to Sex: The Most Complete Sex Manual Ever Written* (Winks & Semans, 2002).

Communicating Preferences and Corrective Feedback

Even couples who claim to be very connected emotionally will often report that communicating directly about sex is difficult. They struggle with the best way to say things and are afraid to hurt each other's feelings, more so than in other aspects of their shared lives. The unfortunate result of this can be enduring unpleasant sexual experiences and missing out on others that could easily be introduced or increased. Couples can be taught to communicate about sex in nonhurtful, productive ways. Many are uncomfortable vocalizing preferences during sex, but there are other ways to communicate. They can do so verbally after sex, and they can do so with their bodies during sex. Following are three strategies, although the therapist should ask couples directly if they have any other ideas about how they can communicate sexual preferences in ways that are acceptable to them. When on task, couples can be quite creative in their problem solving about these matters:

1. Corrective feedback: After a sexual interaction, each person can identify two things the partner did that were real "turn-ons" and two things that were less than desirable. Requiring that both of them engage in this exercise removes the feared elements of blame and hurt. This feedback will then be incorporated into the next lovemaking session to enhance the next experience.
2. Body shifts: The body can be a terrific communicator if the partner is "listening." Often, a very minor shift or repositioning in one direction or another can be just the adjustment to enhance pleasure or to communicate that something does not feel good.
3. Hand-guiding: Another technique is for one person to gently take his or her partner's hand and to model for the partner the stimulation desired. This can be done quite seamlessly as part of the lovemaking. It can also be very arousing as both partners' hands together make the same motion.

Introducing Levity into Sex

For the couple who wants to maintain a sexual connection, sex needs to be taken seriously enough to prioritize it and to work on maintaining its vibrancy. On the other hand, many couples take what happens in any one sexual episode far too seriously. Clumsy attempts at arousing the partner are interpreted as reflections of personal inadequacy. Failure to "perform," as in the case in dyspareunia and vaginismus, is often considered a disastrous event. Introducing a healthy sense of lightness and even humor into sex can be very liberating, as it relieves pressure and can also increase intimacy. Even highly satisfied couples report frequent episodes when the sex did not rock anybody's world. These less than perfect interactions do not have to signal doom. They can be opportunities to laugh and to feel close in these valiant but not always spectacular attempts.

Individual Proclivities

Challenging Sexual and Relationship Schema

Each member of the couple comes to therapy with a set of beliefs or schema about pain, sex, and relationships. These beliefs may have their origins in personal experiences, familial upbringing, religion, culture of origin, or broad societal messages about sexuality and gender. It is not uncommon to find generally sex-negative beliefs or specific beliefs about painful intercourse that are rooted in sexist notions of femininity as intrinsically linked to receptivity. Though some of these beliefs need to be respected, others may be open to discussion and challenge. The therapist needs to explore which are which. Sometimes, clients are eager to be disabused of certain notions they find repressive, even when they have lived with them since childhood. Other clients are resistant to belief challenges. In every case, therapists need to remain sensitive to cultural values and not impose their worldview on clients. Even within very restrictive sexual and relationship schema, the creative and culturally competent therapist can usually find room to work and to improve the couple's situation.

Cognitive Reframing

Two cognitive styles have been empirically identified in women who experience pain with intercourse: hypervigilance and catastrophization (Payne et al., 2005). In relation to painful intercourse, hypervigilance refers to a cognitive style in which there is acute attention to and monitoring of pain cues and of sensation in the genitalia that could signal the onset of pain.

Catastrophization refers to a cognitive style that infers the worst possible outcome (Sullivan, Lynch, & Clark, 2005). A minor discomfort becomes an indication of irreversible physical damage. An insignificant argument signals the end of the relationship. The magnification characteristic of both hypervigilance and catastrophization makes the problem of painful intercourse much worse than it is. Challenging these distortions is an important part of therapy for women who experience painful intercourse. This can be accomplished with the following:

1. Education about the actual physiological consequences of pain with intercourse.
2. Reality testing with the partner and the therapist.
3. Exercises in which the client lists the evidence that supports and does not support her thoughts regarding what might happen when she has these sensations.

Coping Reconstruction

Ineffective coping strategies also tend to be either avoidant or emotionally based. Avoidance is a dead end. It entails either denial of the problem or resignation to it. Although seeking therapy signals that the client has decided to address the problem, the therapist needs to keep in mind that the partner may have insisted on the therapy or that the client will resist subsequent treatment steps as she approaches the feared stimulus. Using a lay explanation of a classical conditioning paradigm, the therapist can explain why avoidance is highly reinforcing yet ultimately counterproductive. The problem will not fix itself without direct confrontation. In fact, there is a very good chance that it will worsen. If resistance arises at different points in the treatment (and it usually does), it may be helpful to remind the client about the seductiveness and self-destructiveness of avoidance.

The emotionally focused coping of many women who experience pain with intercourse (and their partners) can result in anger, hostility, depression, anxiety, shame, and sexual aversion. These emotional states damage clients' (and their partners') well-being and their relationship. However, these destructive emotional states are not inevitable, even when the pain persists. Therapists can teach their clients how to regulate emotions. The client can learn that pain does not have to result in an emotional reaction, especially considering that the emotional reaction is likely to increase pain. Emotional regulation involves the following realizations:

1. Emotional reactions are often within a person's control—one can decide to submit to a feeling or not.
2. Feeling something does not make it true.
3. It is not always useful to give free reign to a feeling.
4. One can choose to feel something slightly different and more constructive.

Emotional regulation is not about emotional repression. It is about not giving emotions more than their due.

Relationship Dynamics

Bridging Sexual and Relationship Schemas

Most individuals are unaware that they have sexual and relationship schema. It is thus not surprising that couples rarely discuss their respective sexual and relationship belief differences about sex, gender, and relationships. The therapist can facilitate this discussion. Often couples are surprised to discover that they are working under substantially different assumptions. In the process of therapy, a wife may discover that her husband's beliefs about masculinity include the imperative to sexually satisfy his wife and that the dyspareunia feels emasculating to him. A husband may discover that his wife believes the pain is some kind of divine retribution for past "promiscuity." Although the aim of this exploration is not necessarily to change anybody's views in particular, the discovery of different worldviews and their familial or cultural origins can help depersonalize conflicts and to contextualize differences. This depersonalization and contextualization can also soften worldviews and can make room for compromise positions and the discovery of common ground.

Encouraging Individuation

In a relationship, it can sometimes be difficult to distinguish an individual problem from a relational one. Yet it might be the single most important skill to learn, both in terms of individual well-being and relationship adjustment. From the perspective of object relations theory, the goal is individuation—a state in which we have a sense of our autonomy and the autonomy of our partner as well as a secure attachment (the assumption that abandonment is not imminent) to this partner. Our partners should be wanted, loved, desired, but not needed for us to feel whole and to function. The purpose of a partner is to enrich our life rather than to fill the missing piece in a fragile construction of self. In other words, only whole people can have whole relationships. If we depend on our partner to make us feel whole and to soothe our own existential anxieties, then any problem our partner has will necessarily feel threatening, even if it has nothing to do with us. According to Schnarch (1991), who popularized this theory for couples, that state of affairs can be the death of intimacy—after all, how can you tell your partner all of your concerns and fears if you think he or she will interpret these to be threats to the relationship or to him or her personally? The main message of interventions targeting individuation is, "It's not about you."

Individuation is very relevant to couples dealing with painful intercourse. It is common for partners to present with concerns about what the pain means about the client's attraction or commitment to them or for women to worry about how the pain makes their partners feel. This is a major stumbling block. It turns the pain into a symbol of relationship dysfunction when it most often is not, even if relationship dysfunction is present. An important component in therapy for dyspareunia and vaginismus is the desymbolization of the pain. The pain is the pain. It does not reflect negatively on the woman experiencing it, and it does not reflect negatively on her partner. Any other interpretation is likely to make matters worse and to impede progress. It is thus important for the therapist to encourage individuation and to identify enmeshment when members of the couple interpret pain as a reflection of their own deficiencies.

Enhancing Communication
The communication of sexual preferences has already been covered in this chapter, but it is central to also investigate and treat general communication deficits. If communication failures exist in other aspects of the relationship, they are likely to result in relationship conflict, which will inevitably trickle down to sexual interactions. If these sexual interactions are already complicated by pain, the result can be very damaging. Following are some transitions the therapist is encouraged to urge clients to make:

1. From mind reading to asking: Individuals in romantic or marital relationships often engage in the dangerous practice of guessing what their partners are thinking or feeling. It is dangerous because it is often wrong, yet consequent behaviors are predicated on these faulty assumptions. A woman who experiences painful intercourse may be assuming that her partner is angry or hurt and act accordingly. Asking him how he or she feels may reveal a completely different set of emotions. It is easy to see how this misperception could confuse and create conflict. A simple

question might have resulted in a more positive outcome or in conflict that is at least centered on reality rather than on erroneous preconceived notions. Clients often do not realize they do this and can easily be persuaded to desist, with immediately positive results.

2. From expecting mind reading to requesting: The corollary of mind reading a partner's thoughts and feelings is the expectation that he or she can read ours. It is very common to hear clients say, "If he really knew me or cared, he would know what I really wanted." It is simply not reasonable to expect others to know what we want when often we do not even know ourselves. The tendency to expect that our partners be good mind readers rather than to request of them what we want reflects an idealization of intimacy as a state of pure, telepathic empathy. Individuals often report that they would have gladly granted a partner's request. Instead, their partners had assumed that they had passive-aggressively noted the desire and had refused to comply. Teaching clients to make requests is relatively easy and effective. It is, however, dependent on an honest answer.

3. From lying to tactful truth telling. The cessation of mind reading is partially contingent on one partner feeling that the other will tell him or her the truth. Many individuals are afraid to tell the truth to their partners for fear of hurting their feelings. The repression of these truths, however, often results in more distress as they tend to seep out in unexpected, equally hurtful ways or in even more damaging outbursts in which the truth is exaggerated by its long suffering repression. Couples struggling with painful intercourse often engage in this cycle of repression and aggression. A therapist can be instrumental in educating clients about the hazards of supposed repression and about how to speak a truth in tactful and constructive ways.

4. From character defamation to expressing how a behavior makes you feel: Confronting a partner about behaviors that are hurtful is always difficult. That is the origin of most arguments and couple conflict. Although nothing makes this type of interaction pleasant, some communication patterns definitely make it worse. A common destructive pattern is to say insulting things about the partner's character. For example, a husband who is very hurt by the facial expression of disgust made by his wife during intercourse might lash out and say, "You are so mean trying to make me feel terrible when we have intercourse, making those faces." It is easy to see how this would escalate. A much more constructive alternative would be something like, "I know that intercourse is difficult for you, but when you make faces indicating disgust, it makes me feel terrible inside." That statement is much more likely to be heard rather than defended against.

Reestablishing a Sexual Connection
As previously mentioned, it is very easy for couples struggling with painful intercourse to stop relating to each other sexually. Intercourse becomes increasingly problematic over time, and the sexual connection starts to fade. Although deemphasizing intercourse and focusing on sensuality are useful tools on the road back to sexuality, they remain confined to discrete sexual episodes. Ideally, reestablishing a sexual connection can be greatly facilitated by infusing sexiness into the everyday. This can be a French kiss as you go out the door on your way to work or a neck massage from behind when you are chopping onions for dinner. Even when sexual intercourse happens at the end of the day, the foreplay starts the moment both partners wake up. Satisfying sex tends to be preceded by sexy ways of relating to each other, even if there is no physical contact. Flirting should not just be reserved for strangers and acquaintances. Couples who have been together for a long time have a tendency to drop those sexy personas with each other. If sex has become problematic, as in the case of dyspareunia or vaginismus, flirting can even be experienced as pressure to have sex. Therapists can help here; by positioning the infusion of sexiness within the context of intercourse deemphasis, they can divest this quotidian sexiness of its performance threat.

Addressing the Function of Pain in the Relationship
A crucial systems intervention in the treatment of dyspareunia and vaginismus is to address the function of pain in the couple dynamic. Clients will easily list all the ways the pain has negatively impacted their relationship. Much more difficult to face, however, are the ways an improvement in symptoms may be threatening. It is critical to identify these potential threats, as they will likely be a significant source of treatment resistance. Questions of relevance to both partners would be the following:

- How would your life change if you (she) no longer had pain with intercourse?
- Do you have fears about what might happen if the pain went away or improved?
- Can you think of any negative consequences to the resolution of symptoms?

A woman who is not attracted to her partner may fear that once the pain subsides, she loses her "legitimate" excuse for avoiding sex. An insecurely attached male partner may worry that once the problem resolves, his partner may leave him. He may need her to be "damaged" so that she does not turn elsewhere for partnership. Sometimes clients can directly answer these function questions, and sometimes they cannot. The function of pain often becomes apparent when clients resist treatment components or demonstrate surprisingly little joy in significant improvements.

Challenges to Therapy

There are many challenges in the treatment of dyspareunia and vaginismus. Perhaps the greatest of these is the coordination of multiple health professionals in the treatment plan (Bley, 2007). This coordination can be complicated by the availability of such professionals, interdisciplinary communication, and financial burden on the client. Clearly, treatment has to adapt to the constraints of any one case, but the optimal strategy is multidisciplinary. Another challenge is balancing people's beliefs in the importance of spontaneity in sex with the structured nature of the assigned exercises. The therapist must tread lightly here and resist the temptation to schedule sexual interactions. Sex cannot become homework—there is nothing sexy about homework. In addition, treatment for painful intercourse is often characterized by the "exhilaration/disappointment roller coaster." The hope at the start of therapy and early gains can engender unbounded optimism about the eradication of symptoms. However, setbacks occur, improvements are adapted to, and the expectation of further improvement can rise substantially, sometimes unrealistically so. This can lead to feelings of disappointment and even to resignation. It is wise for the therapist to be proactive and to warn clients about this variable treatment course. The final challenge is the definition of treatment success. Although goals may be set at the start of therapy, clients will be secretly or openly revising these as they go through treatment. One member of the couple may consider lack of pain to be the end, whereas another may consider the treatment goal to be a certain intercourse frequency. Checking in with the expectations of both members of the couple can be helpful, although it does not always result in agreement.

Research and Future Directions

The last decade has witnessed an unprecedented level of clinical and research attention to dyspareunia and vaginismus. After half a century of assumptions about the symbolic aspect of pain with intercourse, we are finally taking the pain seriously and investigating its properties and multiple etiologies. This shift in attention toward pain has been tremendously validating for women who suffer from these disorders and has been highly productive from a basic science, etiologic perspective. We cannot, however, forget that this is a very special type of pain. Unlike most pains, it happens as a result of an interpersonal interaction. It also happens in the context of a gendered and socioculturally valued activity—sexual intercourse. This pain is thus necessarily complicated by questions of relationships, sexual politics, and femininity ideology (Tolman & Porche, 2000). The current research initiative runs the risk of focusing on physiology to the exclusion of interpersonal dynamics and social construction (Meana, 2005). A serious consideration of all factors is necessary in the treatment of dyspareunia and vaginismus.

One important future direction for research and clinical practice in regard to painful sex is the consideration of pain during same-sex sex. The general assumption has been that these problems are exclusively heterosexual. However, penetration is also a component of lesbian and gay sex. Little research exists on painful penetration in these contexts. Recently, some studies have examined anodyspareunia in gay men (Damon & Rosser, 2005), but more work needs to be done to understand the sexual function problems of sexual minorities. Individuals with disabilities are another minority group that needs more research and clinical attention. A number of chronic illnesses and their treatments can result in painful sex. The current momentum to enhance our understanding and treatment of dyspareunia and vaginismus is long overdue and promising. We must now ensure that the effort remains systems focused and inclusive.

References

American Psychiatric Association (APA) (2000). *Diagnostic and Statistical Manual of Mental Disorders* (4th ed., text revision). Washington, DC: Author.

Bergeron, S., Binik, Y. M., Khalife, S., & Pagidas, K. (1997). Vulvar vestibulitis syndrome: A critical review. *Clinical Journal of Pain, 13,* 27–42.

Bergeron, S., Binik, Y. M., Khalife, S., Pagidas, K., Glazer, H., Meana, M., et al. (2001). A randomized comparison of groups cognitive-behavioral therapy, surface electromyographic biofeedback, and vestibulectomy in the treatment of dyspareunia resulting from vulvar vestibulitis. *Pain, 91,* 297–306.

Binik, Y. M. (2005). Should dyspareunia be retained as a sexual dysfunction in DSM-V? A painful classification decision. *Archives of Sexual Behavior, 34*, 11–21.

Binik, Y. M., Bergeron, S., & Khalife, S. (2007). Dyspareunia and vaginismus: So-called sexual pain. In S. R. Leiblum (Ed.), *Principles and practice of sex therapy* (4th ed., pp. 124–156). New York: Guilford Press.

Binik, Y. M., Meana, M., Berkley, K., & Khalife, S. (1999). The sexual pain disorders: Is the pain sexual or the sex painful? *Annual Review of Sex Research, 10*, 210–235.

Bley, J. W. (2007). Female genital pain: Vaginismus and dyspareunia. In L. VandeCreek, F. L. Peterson, Jr. & J. W. Bley (Eds.), *Innovations in clinical practice: Focus on sexual health*. Sarasota, FL: Professional Resource Press.

Damon, W. & Rosser, B. R. (2005). Anosdyspareunia in men who have sex with men: Prevalence, predictors, consequences and the development of DSM diagnostic criteria. *Journal of Sex and Marital Therapy, 31*, 129–141.

Edwards, P. W., Zeichner, A., Kuczmierczyk, A. R., & Boczkowski, J. A. (1985). Familial pain models. The relationship between family history of pain and current pain experience. *Pain, 21*, 379–384.

Harlow, B. L. & Stewart, E. G. (2005). Adult-onset vulvodynia in relation to childhood victimization. *American Journal of Epidemiology, 161*, 871–880.

Fugl-Meyer, A. R. & Sjrogen Fugl-Meyer, K. (1999). Sexual disabilities, problems and satisfaction in 18-74 year old Swedes. *Scandinavian Journal of Sexology, 3*, 79–105.

Joannides, P. (2006). *The guide to getting it on* (5th ed.). Waldport, OR: Goofy Foot Press.

Laumann, E. O., Gagnon, J. H., Michael, R. T., & Michaels, S. (1994). *The social organization of sexuality: Sexual practices in the United States*. Chicago: University of Chicago Press.

Lester, N., Lefebvre, J. C., & Keefe, F. J. (1994). Pain in young adults: I. Relationship to gender and family pain history. *Clinical Journal of Pain, 10*, 282–289.

Meana, M. (2005). Teasing apart the pain from the sex: Is the pendulum swinging too far? *Archives of Sexual Behavior, 34*, 42–44.

Meana, M. & Binik, Y. M. (1994). Painful coitus: A review of female dyspareunia. *Journal of Nervous and Mental Disease, 182*, 264–272.

Meana, M., Binik, Y.M., Khalife, S., & Cohen, D. (1997a). Biopsychosocial profile of women with dyspareunia: Searching for etiological hypotheses. *Obstetrics and Gynecology, 90*, 583–589.

Meana, M., Binik, Y. M., Khalife, S., & Cohen, D. (1997b). Dyspareunia: Sexual dysfunction or pain syndrome? *Journal of Nervous and Mental Disease, 185*, 561–569.

Meana, M., Binik, Y. M., Khalife, S., & Cohen, D. (1998). Affect and marital adjustment in women's rating of dyspareunic pain. *Canadian Journal of Psychiatry, 43*, 381–385.

Meana, M., Binik, Y. M., Khalife, S., & Cohen, D. (1999). Psychosocial correlates of pain attributions in women with dyspareunia. *Psychosomatics, 40*, 497–502.

Meana, M., Binik, Y. M., & Thaler, L. (2008). Assessment of sexual dysfunction. In J. Hunsley & E. J. Mash (Eds.), *A guide to assessments that work* (pp. 464–487). New York: Oxford University Press.

Payne, K. A., Binik, Y. M., Amsel, R., & Khalife, S. (2005). When sex hurts, anxiety and fear orient toward pain. *European Journal of Pain, 9,* 427–436.

Pukall, C. F., Baron, M., Amsel, R., Khalife, S., & Binik, Y. M. (2006). Tender point examination in women with vulvar vestibulitis syndrome. *Clinical Journal of Pain, 22,* 601–609.

Reissing, E. D., Binik, Y. M., Khalife, S, Cohen, D, & Amsel, R. (2003). Etiological correlates of vaginismus: Sexual and physical abuse, sexual knowledge, sexual self-schema and relationship adjustment. *Journal of Sex and Marital Therapy, 29,* 47–59.

Reissing, E. D., Binik, Y. M., Khalife, S., Cohen, D., & Amsel, R. (2004). Vaginal spasm, pain, and behavior: An empirical investigation of the diagnosis of vaginismus. *Archives of Sexual Behavior, 33,* 5–17.

Reissing, E. D., Brown, C., Lord, M. J., Binik, Y. M., & Khalife, S. (2005). Pelvic floor muscle functioning in women with vulvar vestibulitis syndrome. *Journal of Psychosomatic Obstetrics and Gynecology, 26,* 107–113.

Rosen, R., Brown, C., Heiman, J., Leiblum, S., Meston, C., Shabsigh, R., et al. (2000). The Female Sexual Function Index (FSFI): A multidimensional self-report instrument for the assessment of female sexual function. *Journal of Sex and Marital Therapy, 26,* 191–208.

Rosen, R. C., Riley, A., Wagner, G., Osterloh, I. H., Kirkpatrick, J., & Mishra, A. (1997).The International Index of Erectile Function (IIEF): A multidimensional scale for assessment of erectile dysfunction. *Urology, 49,* 822–830.

Rosenbaum, T. Y. (2007). Physical therapy management and treatment of sexual pain disorders. In S. R. Leiblum (Ed.), *Principles and practice of sex therapy* (4th ed., pp. 157–177). New York: Guilford Press.

Rosser, B. R., Metz, M. E., Bockting, W. O., & Buroker, T. (1997). Sexual difficulties, concerns, and satisfaction in homosexual men: An empirical study with implications for HIV prevention. *Journal of Sex and Marital Therapy, 23,* 61–73.

Schnarch, D. M. (1991). Constructing the sexual crucible: An integration of sexual and marital therapy. New York: Norton.

Sullivan, M. J. L., Lynch, M. E., & Clark, A. J. (2005). Dimensions of catastrophic thinking associated with pain experience and disability in patients with neuropathic pain conditions. *Pain, 113,* 310–315.

Tolman, D. L. & Porche, M. V. (2000). The adolescent femininity scale. *Psychology of Women Quarterly, 24,* 365–376.

Weeks, G. R. (2005). The emergence of a new paradigm in sex therapy: Integration. *Sexual and Relationship Therapy, 20,* 89–103.

Winks, C. & Semans, A. (2002). *The good vibrations guide to sex: The most complete sex manual ever written* (3rd ed.). San Francisco: Cleiss Press.

12

Uncovering and Treating Sex Addiction in Couples Therapy

Martha Turner

Contents

Introduction

Sex addiction is elusive and is often undetected in couples therapy. Typically, other problems such as discord, infidelity, or generic sexual difficulties are presented before sex addiction surfaces, thereby obscuring an accurate assessment. Also, sex addiction can be the unknown force behind previous failed attempts at treatment. The nonaddicted partner might be suspicious yet not consciously aware of living with an addiction; in other instances, lying, secrets, and emotional distance become intolerable. As a rule, however, couples are reluctant to talk about it. Therapists need to be well versed in the many presentations of sex addiction to avoid overlooking it or discovering it after irreversible damage has occurred.

Sex addiction, though not as obvious as addiction to alcohol or drugs, can be just as lethal. Its onset is typically early adolescence, prior to the emergence of substance abuse. The family history of a sex addict frequently reflects little intimacy, inconsistent rules, inadequate supervision, high expectations, and an intergenerational history of addictions. In such families, children are often neglected, mistreated, or exploited; thus, they are vulnerable to sexual and other kinds of abuse by those within or outside of the family. They inadvertently discover addiction as a means to cope with their physical and emotional wounds.

Sex addiction is more prevalent than one would expect; possibly 4 of 10 adults in our culture may be sexually addicted (Carnes, 1991). Though the majority of sex addicts are men, increasing numbers of women are exploring and becoming "hooked" on cybersex and other hidden forms of sex addiction in the safety of their homes.

What Is Sex Addiction?

Sex addicts in search of recovery had few options for treatment until the past few decades. In the late 1970s sex addicts observed that Alcoholics Anonymous (AA) worked for alcoholics. Consequently, they started "Sexaholic" groups, based on the 12-step AA model, to formulate their own set of guiding principles for recovery. A landmark text, *Out of the Shadows: Understanding Sexual Addiction,* brought this topic to the forefront (Carnes, 1983). For the first time, an organized picture of sex addiction was composed. This was a remarkable feat considering the lack of clinical research available. Patrick Carnes, an internationally renowned speaker, researcher, and prolific writer on sex addiction and recovery, instituted specific treatment facilities for sex addiction. As a result, numerous individuals have sought help, and professionals are being trained to identify and treat sexual addiction. To date, a diagnostic category for sex addiction is not included in the *Diagnostic and Statistical Manual of*

Mental Disorders, 4th ed., text revision (*DSM IV-TR;* APA, 2000). Many therapists involved in addictions treatment have proposed diagnostic criteria to reduce the confusion about sex addiction and to facilitate proper treatment (see, e.g., Goodman, 2001). Nonetheless, there is much resistance, mostly from fear and misunderstanding, to accepting sex addiction as a disorder.

One of the problems in diagnosing sex addiction is that, clinically, it appears like other psychiatric disorders (e.g., anxiety, depression, pathologic lying, sociopathy, narcissism, obsessive compulsive disorder, posttraumatic stress disorder). In fact, many psychiatric disorders may coexist with sex addiction; thus, the diagnosis may be difficult to determine. When the diagnosis of sex addiction can be made, order tends to come to the chaos presented, and a clear direction for treatment is possible.

Etiology

Sex addiction is uniquely insidious; it starts earlier in the lifespan and lasts longer than most other addictions before it is addressed. For the majority, sex is usually the primary addiction; other addictions are secondary and are often used to augment sexual activity. Thus, cross-addiction and substituting addictions is common. For example, when one stops drinking, sex addiction may escalate. Unfortunately, other addictions are often treated first even when sex addiction is primary. In facilities that only treat chemical addictions, undiagnosed sex or other addictions are often a factor in recidivism.

Intergenerational Factors

Sex addicts and their partners share commonalities in their upbringing. In most instances, they grew up in families replete with neglect, abuse, poor boundaries, and the absence of healthy courtship modeling. Without intervention, myths, wounds, and role distortions are passed on to the next generation. Further, children in such families may experience subtle manifestations of covert or emotional incest, an emotional boundary violation in which the unsuspecting child is endowed with a status of being special to a parent. In exchange for feeling special, the child assumes responsibility for the emotional well-being of the parent. The child is unaware of the price being paid to future relationships, self-esteem, passion for life, and normal sexuality; all are eclipsed because of the loyalty bond (Adams, 2007; Love, 1990). When the original caregiver is also an abuser, the template for future relationships often becomes one of abuse.

Sex Addiction and the Couple

Considering the complementary intergenerational blueprints of sex addicts and their partners, it is understandable that they attract each other (Carnes, 1991; Turner, 1995). Unfortunately, because of their individual vulnerabilities, sex addicted relationships are usually disastrous. Although longing to be loved and feel normal, both have developed skewed thinking about love that translates into wanting power over others. The need to prevail in adult relationships is a result of suffering profound powerlessness from childhood and subsequent immense amounts of shame. The sex addict uses adult sexuality as a main coping mechanism, unaware of its conscious connection to childhood events. While sex addiction may have saved the sanity of the young person, it becomes seriously maladaptive in adulthood, destroying and exploiting relationships in its wake (Carnes, 1991). Partners of addicts cope by taking charge of others and forgetting themselves in the process. As a consequence, healthy courtship is not possible for someone with sex addiction or his or her partner.

Carnes (2001) poignantly demonstrated the maladaptive relational patterns of sex addicts and their partners by comparing their relational dynamics with healthy courtships (Table 12.1). For the vast majority of sex addicts and their partners, huge distortions exist relating to others socially and in meaningful reciprocal intimate partnerships. Their relationships

TABLE 12.1 Components of a Healthy Relationship

Component	Describes the Ability to ...	During This Phase ...
Noticing	Become aware and to discern the attractive or unattractive traits in others	• Each partner considers if he or she wishes to discover more about the other
Attraction	Feel physically drawn toward another and imagine carrying out those feelings	• Patterns are formed that will enhance one's arousal template • Curiosity, spontaneity, fantasy, and play are experienced as enjoyable attributes to sexual arousal

Component	Describes the Ability to...	During This Phase...
Flirtation	Make playfully romantic or sexual overtures to another person	• Each partner sends and receives signals of interest
Demonstration	Show off the pleasure of having a potential sexual partner while being aware of the appropriateness of the context and the other person's response	• May involve athletic prowess, dress, and other skills that may enhance the other person's interest • One must be who he or she is purporting to be • This is the first test of one's honesty and integrity
Romance	Experience, express, and receive passion	• Feelings of attraction, vulnerability, and risk in conjunction with the ability to express these feelings • Differentiating true feelings from projections both to and from the other and respecting boundaries
Individuation	Separate from one's partner and remain true to one's self	• Truth, trust, and full disclosure are necessary components • One does not operate out of fear of disapproval or control by the other
Intimacy	Respect the "otherness" of the individual despite shortcomings	• Partners enter an "attachment" phase that deepens the meaning of the forming relationship bond • Trust and integrity nurture the relationship, and each partner is able to experience a deeper vulnerability
Touching	Feel valued	• Healthy touch is given with permission and is respectful of the situation, boundaries, and timing • Can be healing; involves trust and judgment
Foreplay	Lead to genital sexuality	• Use all above steps
Intercourse	Experience passion; give up control and expectations of each other	• Trust • Both an emotional and spiritual connection
Commitment	Bond to another and stay attached despite difficulties that may unfold	• Each person matters and deserves to be honored by faithfulness and the willingness to keep the relationship honest, safe, and vital over time
Renewal	Continue to courtship	• Both partners participate in problem solving

are distorted in all of the areas critical for the development of healthy relationships. There is no sequence of normalcy in proceeding through the typical stages: Some are skipped; others are exaggerated. As such, relationships with a sex addict lack, for example, intimacy, respect, and individuation. Sadly, the problematic relational styles of the parents become intergenerational legacies for their children.

The complementary yet different relational dynamics of sex addicts and their partners are reflected in their core beliefs. According to Kasl (1989), sex addicts use sex to escape, to numb their feelings, and to exercise power. They use relationships to have sex. Fundamentally, sex addicts feel flawed and constantly defend against feelings of insecurity by believing that they do not need anyone, they do not care about anyone, and they believe that neediness is not okay. Their basic drive is for power. In contrast, partners of sex addicts use sex to attract a partner and to prevent abandonment. They feel powerful when being pursued or by handling crises (Carnes, 1983, 1991). Their basic drive is for security. Partners of sex addicts believe myths such as, "If I am good enough..." and, "Someday my prince will come." For them, anger is not acceptable.

Consider the comparison of healthy courtship with sex addiction patterns of courting. A fantasy sex addict can notice and be attracted to another but uses the information for secret visual creations. The creations are not reality based and will not be acted on. In seductive role sex addiction, honest, genuine courtship phases (including attraction) are passed over; courtship is about conquests. Intrusive sex addicts have a false sense of entitlement and take from others without regard to their wishes. Actually, all of the behaviors of sexual addiction have exploitive aspects in the courtship sequence, depending on the style of behavior.

The sex addict is desperate for an encounter; thus, social skills such as respect, timing, consideration, accountability, and honesty are circumvented. The fix comes first. For partners, there is something familiar yet not entirely conscious about the addict's behavior. The translation is that somehow the addict is the right match and will provide security—a faulty notion. The partner, often a woman, probably came from a similar family type, where she learned to overlook her own needs and desires in an effort to preserve pretense and to "save" the family. Also, she may try to be sexier to satisfy her addict, betraying herself in the process. The couple may seem to have a reasonable fit, or equilibrium, until one of the behaviors deflates the projection bubble and reality comes crashing in.

Cultural Distortions

In two courageous texts, Rutter (1989, 1996) identified the impact of cultural myths on the development of the individual. He concentrated on the distortions of gender roles that occur insidiously through early socialization and that eventually become "wounds" in adult relationships. Often unspoken, mythological assumptions about the roles of men and women compromise adult relationships. When sex addiction is added to the mix, the result is a courtship disaster. In these texts, Rutter identified how sexual boundaries are transgressed in the workplace and how professional men take advantage of women who come to them for their expertise. Table 12.2 presents the myths, wounds, and distortions, often not conscious, that men and women carry in their psyches.

TABLE 12.2   The Impact of Cultural Myths on Development

	Myths	Wounds Caused by Myths
Male Development	Women are to defer to men.	The "macho" stance is valued.
	Women have special powers of nurturing and healing.	Men don't cry or ask for help.
	Women are dark and destructive (monsters) if they disappoint men.	Vulnerability is seen as weak or soft.
	Women are seen as "really wanting it" (sex).	Men depend too much on women for intimacy.
	Women who are interested in sex are disinterested in their partners.	Intimacy is equated with physical contact.
	It's a woman's job to please her man.	Male authority is more important than the truth.
	All men need a sexual release.	Men are encouraged to act on sexual tension.
Female Development	Women's self-esteem depends on men's approval.	The caretaker role is encouraged in girls.
	Men are guardians and saviors and are needed for recognition.	The invasion of boundaries from childhood is a norm.
	Feminine values are a liability in the workplace.	Neglect makes women needy.
	Women must look beautiful and sexy.	Male mentors are sought for recognition.
	Women must have children for worth.	Women's strengths are denied.
	Women must deny their strengths to please men.	Women's bodies must be beautiful (objectified).

Assessment of Sex Addiction

In our culture, sex is considered *essential* not only for procreation but, to most, also for pleasure: It is an indispensable part of life. Sex is also regarded as *powerful* for some. In times of feeling powerless, stressed, inadequate, or incompetent, the draw to sex for power can be enormous. Individuals are willing to pay large amounts of money to view, participate in, or create sex, sometimes at their own peril. Finally, sex can be *frightening*, particularly in circumstances of childhood sexual abuse, rapes, unwanted pregnancies, sexually transmitted infections (STIs), and crimes of passion.

Signs of Sex Addiction

Carnes (1983, 1991) described 10 signs of sex addiction, some of which correlate to other addictions:

1. A pattern of unmanageable behavior.
2. Severe negative consequences due to sexual behavior.
3. Ongoing desire or effort to limit sexual behavior.
4. Inability to discontinue the behaviors despite severe consequences.
5. Persistent quest for self-destructive or high-risk behaviors.
6. Sexual obsession and fantasy as a primary coping mechanism.
7. Tolerance or the need for increasing amounts and varieties of sexual experience to attain the desired effect.
8. Severe mood changes regarding sexual activity.
9. Inordinate amounts of time spent obtaining sex, being sexual, or recovering from sexual experiences.
10. Neglect of important social, occupational, or recreational activities because of sexual behaviors.

These signs appear gradually until the addict's life becomes one of desperation and recklessness. By the time the secret life is revealed, the addict, family, and others have been severely damaged.

General Categories of Sex Addiction

Sex addicts use creative energy to attain consistent levels of arousal, novel sources of stimulation, and a focused desperate drive to escape from reality. This process results in a multitude of sexual behaviors. Carnes (1983, 1991) organized more than 100 sexual behaviors into 11 general categories. It must be emphasized, however, that while ostensibly sexual, the behaviors in each category are more related to power than sex. Sex is the vehicle to feeling power and control. Most sex addicts engage in at least three preferred behaviors, one of which is usually compulsive masturbation enhanced by pornography or fantasy:

1. *Fantasy sex* addicts are preoccupied with dramas about seduction with meticulous emphasis on the details of each meeting. Fantasies do not necessarily materialize to actual encounters. They experience power through creating the scene and selecting the players. Consequently, fantasy sex addicts isolate from meaningful emotional intimacy and neglect self-care and obligations to others. Typically, they experience intolerable shame, loneliness, despair, and suicidal ideation. To escape these painful emotions, the fantasy cycle begins again.

2. *Seductive role sex* addicts pursue the beginnings of relationships and then exit once the object has responded; commitment is intolerable. The power for this form of sex addiction is in the conquest. These individuals target bars, clubs, and conferences for potential selections and attempt to fill their emptiness by flirting with or seducing others. Feeling sexual is equated with normalcy. Often, they suffer from STIs or unwanted pregnancies.

3. *Anonymous sex* addicts cruise public places for brief, nameless sexual encounters that are not intended for relationships. They strive for momentary approval and acceptance and derive power from an agreement to have sex. Time is wasted searching beaches, parks, restrooms, and baths. Sadly, they are often lonely and desperate, suffering arrests, illnesses, assaults, and death.

4. Addicts who *pay for sex* experience power in using money to obtain sex, thereby controlling the specifications of the activities. They will pay for experiences such as sexually explicit phone calls, prostitutes, and advertisements for sex partners. Usual consequences include STIs, arrests, and significant financial debt.

5. Addicts who *trade sex* experience a vigorous rush (and power) from the danger and risk involved in receiving money for sex, exchanging sex for drugs, making sexually explicit videos or photos, exhibiting for hire, and "pimping" sex for money (i.e., procuring prostitutes). The consequences include arrests and endangering the self and others.

6. *Voyeuristic sex* addicts derive power and sexual gratification from secretly observing or spying on the naked bodies or sexual acts of others. Voyeurs get pleasure from the risk of being discovered while invading the privacy of unsuspecting people. They frequent strip shows

and adult book stores and often use pornography. Also, they furtively observe unsuspecting victims while compulsively masturbating and chain smoking. They suffer repeated arrests.

7. *Exhibitionistic sex* addicts derive gratification from exposing themselves in public places such as homes or cars. They feel powerful through surprising and shocking unsuspecting victims. To "normalize" their behavior, they might dress in a provocative manner to be noticed or might join a nudist colony. Consequences are misdemeanor arrests and angry rejections.

8. *Intrusive sex* addicts cross boundaries with others by making physical or psychological sexual advances without permission. Usually they fondle, touch, and use sexually explicit comments at inappropriate times. Sometimes, the inappropriate touch is disguised (e.g., brushing against people in crowded places). They derive power from taking advantage of someone who is vulnerable. Examples include using a position of power to exploit or be sexual with another person with less power (Rutter, 1996) or forcing sex on another (spouse or partner included). Consequences include victimizing and deeply traumatizing others and legal consequences.

9. *Pain exchange* involves inflicting or receiving physical harm or pain to enhance sexual arousal. Generally there is a preference to be either the victim or the perpetrator. Often, chains, bonds, whips, and other aids may be used to add risk and excitement. The emotions of fear, peril, and danger are very mood altering. The threat of injury and death from going too far is real. In either role, the addict attempts to gain power by mastering unconscious trauma from childhood that has been sexualized in adulthood.

10. In *object sex*, sexual arousal is associated with objects, body parts, or situations rather than reciprocal affectionate sexual activity. The behaviors of choice are often fetishes, masturbation with objects, cross-dressing, and sex with animals.These addicts achieve a sense of power by controlling or scripting sex. For instance, cross-dressers rarely give up their fetishes and may join transvestite clubs to have a place to belong. The consequences are profound isolation, self-injury, and an inability to connect to a whole person as a sexual partner.

11. *Sex with children* involves exposing, forcing, discussing, or otherwise exploiting children through sexual means. Arousal through child pornography is also included in this category. Consequences to the child are devastating, and the addict, when discovered, faces imprisonment and isolation. The power achieved through this sort of destructive activity involves dominating a child, often in a way that acts out the addict's own sexual abuse in childhood.

Cybersex, or sexual activity or arousal through communication on the Internet, must be added to the aforementioned categories because the Internet has become an increasingly popular venue for sex addiction. Progressively more women turn to their computers for relational encounters while men typically view pornography, frequent chat rooms, and look for prostitutes. For both, cybersex provides a medium to engage in fantasy, projection, and creation of scripts that would not occur in ordinary social settings. The normal features of a healthy relationship cannot be experienced online; thus, there is a limited opportunity to assimilate social cues that would give significant information regarding safety, personality, genuineness, emotional availability, gender, and age. The truth can be easily distorted when the exchange is merely text. Cybersex activity rapidly becomes addictive, resulting in sleep deprivation, poor functioning, and neglect of family until confronted and discovered. Also, there can be disastrous financial and legal consequences such as victimization by predators. Cybersex addicts achieve power from the excitement of untamed sex/romance combined with the illusion of safety, anonymity, and fantasy (see, e.g., Carnes, Delmonico, & Griffin, 1991; Cooper, Delmonico, & Burg, 2000; Schneider & Weiss, 2001).

All of the previously mentioned behaviors (real or fantasized) are exploitive of others, yet they may not necessarily denote sexual addiction. Some are episodic. Others take place with mutually consenting adults. A number fall within the criminal category of sex "offending" behaviors, which are dealt with legally. Sex addiction involves these classic signs: out-of-control behavior, obsession, powerlessness, and using sex to relieve pain (Carnes, 1991).

Treatment

Sex addiction is entrenched in the fabric of the couple's intimate relationship. The partners struggle to maintain equilibrium as they painfully negotiate the factors that have gradually corrupted their relationship. Since the nonaddicted partner is an ingredient of the system within which the addiction operates, treatment must involve the couple. Furthermore, the tasks for recovery from sexual addiction are enormous. The maladaptive coping mechanisms used for survival (addictions and other destructive behaviors) must be stopped or transformed. Like any other significant life change, this process can leave a person feeling raw, extremely vulnerable, angry, resistant, and terrified.

For couples, the treatment of sex addiction is growth oriented; partners are helped not only to overcome their problems but also to optimize their relationship. The goal of treatment is healthy sexuality in a committed relationship and a quality of life that promotes thriving on all levels for both. Considering the damage already done, couples struggling with sex addiction face the overwhelming challenges of establishing trust, consistency, diligence, and willingness to heal. Additionally, they will need to mourn many losses and to negotiate remorse and forgiveness. The therapist must provide a safe environment and a nonjudgmental attitude with patience, gentleness, and good boundaries. Respect for those having survived such an unpleasant ordeal must be genuine and backed by knowledge of sex addiction. Psychotropic medication is often necessary in the early phase of treatment. Separate therapy groups for the addict and the partner are enormously helpful in providing a safe place for learning self-love, social skills, empathy for others, and healthy protesting. Alternative trauma therapies can be beneficial adjuncts to helping one move away from child victim/entitlement perceptions to the adult choices of safety, empowerment, and realistic responsibility. The rewards of recovery are wonderfully freeing and bring hope for interrupting the damage and abuse of children of sex addiction.

Early Recovery

Often sex addiction is uncovered during couples therapy. The discovery or disclosure necessitates a shift in treatment and an understanding that the process will be long. Of course, a prerequisite of this kind of work is the therapist's self-awareness regarding personal sexual issues and beliefs; it is imperative that unconscious concerns do not interfere with the therapeutic process. Therapists need to be accepting of the broad range of human sexual expression and must have strong professional boundaries. It is easy to identify with the betrayed partner, but doing so could alienate the addicted partner and result in premature termination of treatment.

The couple will need reminders that all behaviors will be disclosed in a timely manner. Some partners will obsessively want to know all the details of the betrayals, but the knowledge may be so damaging that they cannot stay in therapy or in the relationship. Timing and preparation are essential. Also, the therapist must not be unwittingly manipulated into keeping secrets. Doing so creates further betrayal, rage, threats, and damage. Safety and trust must be built into the therapeutic process for both partners (Schneider, 2004).

The primary concern of early recovery is addressing and stopping the most dangerous and risky addictions first and then moving gradually to other addictive behaviors. Couples therapy is insufficient for the task at this stage because the addictions are so powerful that specific help is needed as well as being with other recovering people for validation, support, and shame reduction. As stated earlier, both partners likely carry deep wounds from childhood that have been enacted through relationship struggles. Hence, they have too little strength and self-worth, respectively, to work as a couple effectively. They need support and encouragement to follow individual tracks of therapy. If the couple has any conjoint meetings in the early phases of recovery, the therapist should remain neutral and address only the most pressing relationship issues. In effect, couples therapy should emphasize their strengths, ground rules for better communicating, and parenting issues.

The therapist must carefully assess each partner's capacity for intimacy, resilience, giving and receiving pleasure, positive regard and feelings for the other, giving and receiving love, and handling disappointments as well as changes. Without judgment and with great sensitivity, the therapist should take a thorough sexual history assessing for abuse, neglect, family attitudes about sex, and preferences for being sexual with a partner. Sexual genograms are useful and provide an intergenerational context for the individual partners (Berman, 1999). The therapist should be alert for clues suggestive of sexual addiction in families—for example, unexplained job losses, abortions, arrests, never marrying, going into religious life, STIs, sex aversion (like teetotalers in alcoholic families), and sexual anorexia (the control side of addiction). At the appropriate time, inquiring about fantasies may provide clues to earlier trauma, the formation of one's sexual arousal template, as well as subsequent choices of sexual behaviors. The therapist should also assess for the presence of other sexual problems with physical etiologies (e.g., congenital deformities, hormonal imbalances) or relational origins (e.g., erectile dysfunction, lack of desire). The therapist must be alert for signs suggesting earlier forms of abuse (e.g., special relationships with priests, excessive tickling by a parent and consequent bed-wetting), taking care not to assume too much. Addicts and partners have learned to compensate for deep-seated shameful behaviors in themselves, in each other, and in families of origin. They often know how to look and sound normal, being exceptionally skilled at deception to hide their shame. In fact, they might be quite overtly successful. High-profile sex addicts are accustomed to having their way and manipulating others with their money and power status; hence, they are difficult to treat.

When sex addiction is discovered, the first form of treatment is individual therapy for each partner with additional group therapy tailored to the needs of the addict and codependent partner, respectively. In some instances, inpatient treatment geared to sexual dependency is necessary. Attendance in 12-step meetings for sexual dependency and codependency will augment treatment. The multiple layers of assistance diffuse the many needs of this couple and make available daily access for help and support.

The therapist of the couple still has a minor role in the early stages of recovery, providing an anchor, hope, and voice for the couple until later stages when each has more of a self to offer and is ready to focus on finer communication skills and healthy sexuality. Despite levels of education and success, the partners are not adept at relationship skills; they still need coaching on basic self-care, social skills, and problem solving. Homework between sessions is useful in developing relationship skills (Carnes, 2001). Given the multiple treatment modalities, therapists must have permission to talk to each other to provide the best level of care. The therapeutic work can be very labor-intensive, and some couples will not make it together. Divorce rates are high, especially if one member chooses not to be treated. Betrayed partners, needing to be right, can be more resistant to change than the addicts. Each having a sponsor tends to help protect the relationship from deteriorating. A support network, such as peer supervision, is also extremely helpful for the therapists.

Middle Recovery

When the worst behaviors have been arrested and the partners have embraced their respective recovering communities, they stabilize enough to begin the work of middle recovery. Talk therapy alone is generally insufficient. Group therapy helps recovering people modulate affect and develop social skills. They learn respect for appropriate boundaries for others. Alternative treatments facilitate resolution of trauma and the concurrent cognitive distortions. These may involve art therapy, eye movement desensitization and reprocessing (EMDR), emotional transformation therapy (ETT), and psychodrama. Psychotropic medication (e.g., antianxiety or antidepressant agents) is often useful to calm the hypervigilant state from its persistent survival mode. With sex addiction, progress, not perfection, is the goal.

Trauma work is a major component of middle recovery. Since addicts and partners were traumatized as children, they continue to experience intense posttraumatic stress disorder (PTSD) symptoms. Trauma work involves incremental discussion of distressing events and feelings combined with coaching to contain the emotions. Thus, the memory of the trauma remains, but the emotional experience is significantly reduced due to a shift to a more adult perspective from a child's experience frozen in the past. For example, the person might learn to say, "It happened and it was not my fault. I did everything I could." Without trauma resolution, full recovery does not happen.

Establishing safety is an integral component of recovery from trauma and a precursor to trauma work. The client is helped to create a real or imagined safe place where one can hide from the wounds of the past or PTSD symptoms triggered by something in the present. Previously, the response to trauma was regression and victimization. Safety is empowering because it provides a strategy to think about trauma without reenacting it. When needed, refuge can be taken in the established safe place.

Advanced Recovery

This phase is less intense and more rewarding for all involved. The skill of the couples therapist is most useful now. The couple has tenaciously worked to preserve a bond that is strong enough to endure life's challenges together. Now, each partner has a stronger sense of self, has taken responsibility for personal recovery, and is able to offer substantial contributions to the relationship and family. Treatment for the couple involves all of the typical strategies to facilitate communication, to resolve conflicts, and to negotiate differences. Sex addicted couples, however, do not know how to relate intimately or sexually, and a concentration of effort in these areas is necessary.

Bibliotherapy is a useful adjunct to the work of advanced recovery. Hastings (2000) wrote a primer on healthy sexuality, which acknowledges the "cross-wiring" of beliefs regarding sexual norms in our culture. In sex addiction, the couple engages in many sexual beliefs and behaviors that are on the fringes of normalcy. The couple is helped to begin with a basic understanding of mutually satisfying sex and build from there. Johnson (1983) describes how courtship consists of projected images of an idealized partner. As the real image of the person emerges, falling out of love occurs. Wholesome relationships seek to blend the mystery and excitement of knowing one's partner within a context of daily living, compromise, and clearing miscommunications. Robinson (2004) focuses on the neurophysiology of relationships by examining attachment styles, sexual arousal, and bonding. This book is replete with information about neurotransmitters, reward centers, dopamine surges, and other primitive brain activities. There is an emphasis on promoting low-key sex through stimulating oxytocin (the bonding hormone) and by cuddling, nonsexual affection, and dialogues. This is a challenge for sex addicts who are used to extremes in sexual behavior. This delightful book is most useful in later phases of recovery with a committed partnership.

Another 12-step program, particularly helpful in the final stages of recovery, is Recovering Couples Anonymous (RCA). This fellowship helps recovering couples to restore their relationships through sharing common problems and experiences. There is an emphasis on providing support and hope, promoting healthy communication, and finding greater joy and intimacy. It adds a third dimension of "we" to each partner's individual track. The only requirement for RCA membership is a desire to remain in a committed relationship.

Case Histories

Dan and Joan

Dan and Joan have been married 33 years, with three children from Joan's first marriage. He is a successful businessman and a sex addict; she is a talented artist and a sex and love addict. Dan's parents were well intended yet emotionally distant. His father, whom he idolized, was emotionally absent; he worked continually and focused attention on his clients. Dan's mother lacked empathy and nurturance. Only Dan's achievements were recognized by his parents. Sexuality was an unmentionable topic; thus, he knew little about his parents' attitudes or values. Dan learned that sex was something done in secret and that asexuality was a family norm. Having suffered emotional deprivation from childhood, it was impossible to have a normal interest in sex, the desire to be loved by a woman, and an expectation that a relationship can work.

Consequently, Dan learned to be hedonistic, narcissistic, and addicted to sex—all of which caused a deep sense of shame. Dan employed specific strategies to counteract his feelings of shame: excessive use of pornography, seducing women, engaging in fantasy regarding seduction and sex, and having continuous affairs during much of his marriage. His addiction was his priority around which he organized his life. He loved intensity and drank to augment his sexual experiences. Dan recoiled at any suggestion to change his destructive lifestyle.

Dan's job necessitated relocation away from his home. He was miserable apart from Joan and became quite depressed. Also, he felt completely abandoned. This low point in his life was actually the beginning of a process that would eventually address the addiction—but not for 12 years. He made several serious attempts at recovery, but each was met with inevitable failure. Dan recognized that he was addicted to "intensity" as much as to sex, which he could not relinquish. Finally, in 2002, when confronted, he was able to surrender the last of numerous affairs.

Joan is the middle of three daughters. Her father was prone to depression. When he was away, Joan slept with her mother; when he returned, she was abruptly relocated to another room. Although her mother was a nurse, no information about sexuality was imparted. However, with regard to relationships with boys, Joan's mother was hypervigilant, threatening to tell her father if Joan was caught with a boy. Sadly, Joan was sexually abused on several occasions by older men and was also set up by her older sister for abuse. Joan's mother did not protect her from abuse. Joan was married for the first time at age 19 to her childhood boyfriend. She was not sexually compatible with her husband, and she started having affairs, which she pursued to make herself feel powerful and wanted. Joan's sisters have had difficulties with relationships; her older sister has been married three times, and her younger sister was also unfaithful to her husband.

During their marriage, Joan was unable to become pregnant when Dan wanted a child. He then had an affair with a woman who became pregnant. When he told Joan, she gave him a choice to remain in the marriage or leave. He chose to stay, but Joan felt so rejected by his affair that she retaliated with an emotional affair to palliate feeling worthless and empty. Eventually, Dan resumed having affairs, but Joan felt too much emotional pain to seek out anyone else, so she shifted to being obsessed by Dan's addiction. She compulsively searched for evidence of infidelity by examining his clothes, wallet, and briefcase. Also, Joan secretly had Dan under surveillance, following him to see if he was meeting women.

Their compulsions went on for three more years. She would catch him and confront him, and he would promise not to do it again. Just as she was beginning to trust him, he would start the cycle again. By the time they presented for treatment, Joan was so devastated by Dan's affairs that she considered divorce. Since her codependency was such a prevailing issue within their relationship, it was decided that Joan would attend a treatment program. She found it to be one of the hardest things she has ever done and one of the best. During her course of treatment, Joan learned that she was also a sex and love addict, although her focus was on sexual codependence. Eventually, the couple stabilized, and both worked on their respective recoveries.

Recovery from sex addiction is often interrupted by setbacks; Dan is no exception. In 2002, the last affair was discovered. Joan was devastated and felt foolish that she had trusted Dan again. This time, however, he was ready to surrender. He committed to two skilled therapists, went regularly to 12-step meetings, stopped drinking, and ceased his sexually addictive behaviors. Trusting Dan again was difficult for Joan, and Dan struggled with the doubt that he could really change and be peaceful with himself.

In 2005, this couple began to attend RCA 12-step meetings, which added the vital "we" dimension to their relationship. Through the support of the group, Joan has learned that women could be friends, that it is normal to have feelings, and essential to have choices. She is learning to trust her intuition and not deny her reality. Also, Joan is discovering how to communicate without shaming, blaming, or bringing up past hurts. She began to forgive herself for wronging others and gained an inner peace that benefits her on all levels. Her healing at a spiritual level has been significant. Dan learned to identify feelings and to stop indulgences in fantasy. Also, he gave up treating women as objects to begin the essential work of inner healing. His trauma from childhood was finally recognized and addressed. Very slowly, he has found a peace, inconceivable to him before. Dan and Joan discovered richness in helping others rather than rescuing them. Now they can laugh at themselves and have empathy for those suffering the pain they used to feel during their active addictions. They believe they have achieved more intimacy and openness than most couples ever dream of having.

Jerry and Beth

Jerry, a successful businessman, is married to Beth, the mother of their four children. When he was 6 months old, Jerry's father was reported missing in action during World War II. Eventually, his father was discovered to be living with the Resistance. He finally returned from military duty, but for years his father would go back for more tours of duty. Understandably, Jerry's mother suffered much stress and worry and was unable to parent him for substantial periods of time. Other family members cared for

Jerry when his mother was unable. When his father came home to stay, he immediately began overworking and was still not available to the family.

Jerry always felt responsible for the stress in the family and valiantly took on the role of the surrogate father. He became an excellent student and athlete. There was no discussion of sex in the home; instead, he was given a book about sex at age 13 or 14. Jerry was painfully shy and did not date until 11th grade. Then he attended a competitive college to study engineering and earned straight A's. Jerry was socially and sexually inexperienced, as college was solely for fulfilling his need for perfection. His first sexual experience occurred just before his senior year, with his sister's friend. There were so many worries of consequences that sex was not satisfying. The next experience was with his prospective first wife; this time, sex was enjoyable. They married, but passion soon diminished and differences became more profound. They parted amicably after three years. There were no children. For several years, Jerry enjoyed many relationships and social interests, including drinking. Then he met his present wife, Beth.

Beth came from a family riddled with alcoholism. Her paternal great grandfather killed his wife with a frying pan while drunk. Her father, proud of his Polish heritage, was charming, a great dancer, intelligent, fluent in three languages, and graduated from college with top honors in three years. After his army assignment in Paris, he returned and married her mother. His unpleasant nature emerged periodically, a feature that was exaggerated when drunk.

Her maternal grandfather ran away from his family in Poland at age 14 and immigrated to the United States. He married a Polish woman who had also immigrated, by herself, at age 12. Beth's extended family was encumbered with sexual shame and alcoholism.

Although Beth's father was never physically violent, she was afraid of him, as was her mother. As his drinking increased, he began to lose jobs. Beth knew from her mother that he had "strange ideas about sex." When Beth was 10, her mother took the children and moved away but did not keep her daughters from visits with him. Beth was favored by her father; to date, she has guilt about this with regard to her sister, who is practically homeless. Also, Beth was forced to view inappropriate sexual photographs and to listen to sexual comments that created confusion; these actions were initiated by her father.

Since sex was never discussed at home, Beth received no education. Her mother did help her with her menstrual period and gave her a sex education book, without comment. In 4th grade, after her parents divorced, an adult male "friend" shared his pornography with Beth and masturbated in her presence, telling her he could not help himself because she was so pretty. He said he knew he could trust her not to tell anyone. When Beth was 16, the same person molested Beth after stalking her.

Her first intimate sexual relationship started in adolescence and lasted six years. They often fought, and neither was faithful. During adolescence, Beth had many partners, always while drinking. This activity stayed hidden. In public, she was a perfect girl, class scholar, and athlete.

In college, her drinking increased as she spent much time with her boyfriend rather than studying. Beth's third year was spent abroad with good grades and much sexual activity. In her senior year Beth was a "stellar student." Soon after graduation, she met and became engaged to Jerry. She viewed him as ethical and stable, unlike her family's male role models. Their relationship was replete with intense love, drinking, and drugging. Ultimately, however, Dan began to experience erectile dysfunction (ED) despite a pleasurable sex life. They blamed it on work stress, and, despite attempts to resolve the problem on their own, ED still occurred. They rarely discussed or sought help for the ED. Jerry was a compulsive worker, which allowed Beth to function independently, including raising the children and starting affairs.

They had enjoyable family vacations. Nonetheless, Jerry worked during most of his free time. They both drank often, but Jerry began to have episodes of drunkenness, which upset Beth. He went to AA meetings, which he found supportive and helpful, and eventually he stopped drinking entirely for 16 years. The compulsive working continued, however. Beth spent more time with friends, socializing and drinking. Feeling estranged, Jerry began to drink again so he could rejoin her.

A few years prior to treatment, while at home suffering from the flu, Jerry discovered Beth having sex with a neighbor in their basement. Beth apologized profusely, saying they drank too much. Slowly, the truth began to emerge about her affairs. Jerry was devastated, unable to function. He agreed to attend her psychotherapy, which had initiated six months prior, and learned about her childhood sexual abuse and subsequent sex addiction. Beth voluntarily entered a treatment facility for addictions; fortunately, she has been sober from alcohol and sex outside the marriage since then. Also, Beth receives ongoing support through individual and group psychotherapy, combined with 12-step meetings for alcoholics and sexual addicts.

Jerry also committed to recovery by joining a group for sexual codependents. He saw a psychiatrist for depression and anxiety and was prescribed a selective serotonin reuptake inhibitor (SSRI) for depression and an antianxiety agent. Additionally, Jerry attended group psychotherapy and benefited from the experience. Eventually, the couple began marital therapy, which helped them to be less enmeshed and to construct appropriate boundaries with each other. They cultivated communication skills, gained respect for each other, and strengthened their relationship bond. Also, in conjoint treatment, they examined some of intergenerational issues stemming from their families of origin; this process increased empathy and insight.

They now feel safe with each other and can discuss crucial issues such as sex, her anger, his drinking, his overworking, and their mutual miscommunications. Their commitment to each other and their children has provided the needed energy for recovery. Jerry and Beth realize that they must continue to discuss important topics and to spend time together to maintain their love and understanding. They are learning the pitfalls of overinvesting in children and in social commitments. They also realize the importance of a support system that will help them address difficult topics. Jerry and Beth feel optimistic about their future.

Conclusion

Since sex addiction is prevalent in our culture and in much of the world, people with this disorder and their partners are certain to appear in the offices of couples therapists. If the therapist is knowledgeable, committed, patient, and willing to use all modalities available, the gratification is great. Sex addiction is incredibly shame based and is difficult to treat. Restoration to health takes a long time. Addicts are exquisitely sensitive to criticism. However, if they feel safe they can respond well because they long to be restored to their values.

Complex individual and couple dynamics are plentiful. Additionally, sexual secrets from previous generations are usually present in both families of origin. Although the partners might appear quite different initially, they have similar wounds in need of healing, which are not apparent when they first meet. Treatment can be successful provided they have enough of a bond to tolerate the psychic pain of disclosure, accountability, and the ability to forgive. Further, interrupting the intergenerational patterns of abuse, shame, and the distortions of both intimacy and sexuality is a great contribution to society. Our children need and deserve this intervention for their protection and their future quality of life.

Research and Future Development

The Society for the Advancement of Sexual Health (SASH) is the organization that addresses sex addiction. SASH has an excellent journal dedicated to this topic, *Journal of Sexual Addiction and Compulsivity*, which is published quarterly by Taylor & Francis. Patrick Carnes continues to do clinical research on all sex addicts and partners who come to treatment at Pine Grove Behavioral Health and Addiction Services in Hattiesburg, Mississippi and encourages therapists treating this population to collect data. Related research on disorders of sexual desire is being conducted at the University of Pennsylvania by Anna Rose Childress using functional magnetic resonance imaging (fMRI). This "brain mapping" determines which parts of the brain are activated by different types of physical sensation or activity. Currently, Childress focuses primarily on substance abuse craving but hopes to expand to other addictions. Vanderbilt University also uses fMRI to study sexual arousal specifically in new addicts. Despite its prevalence, there is still not enough interest from the general public to support this kind of research. Those suffering from sexual addiction have been the real pioneers in reaching out for help and in teaching the professionals what they know. They deserve help not only for their own pain but also for the advancement of sexual health in our culture. This will result in better treatment of our children in the future. Moreover, healthy courtship and proper parenting should be required courses in educational institutions for children and adults.

References

American Psychiatric Association (APA) (2000). *Diagnostic and statistical manual of mental disorders* (4th ed., text revision). Washington, DC: Author.

Adams, K. M. (2007). *When he's married to mom: How to help mother-enmeshed men open their hearts to true love and commitment.* New York: Fireside.

Berman, E. (1999). Gender, sexuality, and romantic love genograms. In R. DeMaria, G. R. Weeks, & L. Hof (Eds.), *Focused genograms: Intergenerational assessment of individuals, couples and families* (pp. 145–176). Philadelphia, PA: Brunner/Mazel.

Carnes, P. (1983). *Out of the shadows: Understanding sexual addiction.* Center City, MN: Hazelden.

Carnes, P. (1991). *Don't call it love.* New York: Bantam Books.

Carnes, P. (2001). *Facing the shadow: Starting sexual and relationship recovery.* Wickenburg, AZ: Gentle Path Press.

Carnes, P., Delmonico, D., & Griffin, E. (2001). *In the shadows of the net: Breaking free of compulsive online sexual behavior.* Center City, MN: Hazelden.

Cooper, A., Delmonico, D., & Burg, R. (2000). Cybersex users, abusers, and compulsives: The dark side of the force. *Sexual Addiction and Compulsivity,* *7*(1–2), 5–30.

Goodman, A. (2001). What's in a name? Terminology for designating a syndrome of driven sexual behavior. *Sexual Addiction and Compulsivity, 8*(3–4), 191–213.

Hastings, A. S. (2000). *Discovering sexuality that will satisfy you both.* Gretna, LA: Wellness Institute.

Johnson, R. (1983). *We: Understanding the psychology of romantic love.* San Francisco: Harper and Row.

Kasl, C. D. (1989). *Women, sex, and addiction: A search for love and power.* New York: Ticknor & Fields.

Love, P. (1990). *The emotional incest syndrome: What to do when a parent's love rules your life.* New York: Bantam Books.

Robinson, M. (2004). *Peace between the sheets: Healing with sexual relationships.* Berkeley, CA: Frog Ltd.

Rutter, P. (1989). *Sex in the forbidden zone: When men in power—therapists, doctors, clergy, teachers and others—betray women's trust.* Los Angeles: Jeremy Tarcher, Inc.

Rutter, P. (1996). *Sex, power and boundaries.* New York: Bantam Books.

Schneider, J. & Weiss, R. (2001). *Cybersex exposed: Simple fantasy or obsession?* Center City, MN: Hazelden.

Schneider, J. (2004). *Sex, lies, and forgiveness: Couples speaking out on healing from sex addiction.* Tucson, AZ: Recovery Resources Press.

Turner, M. (1995). Addictions in marital/relationship therapy. In G. R. Weeks & L. Hof (Eds.), *Integrative solutions: Treating common problems in couples therapy* (pp. 124–147). New York: Brunner/Mazel.

13

An Integrative Approach to Infidelity Treatment

Katherine M. Hertlein
Gerald R. Weeks
Nancy Gambescia

Contents

Introduction

Infidelity is a leading presenting problem in relationship therapy, yet it is notoriously difficult to treat effectively. Discovery or disclosure of infidelity precipitates a crisis for the couple because previously held beliefs about fidelity, trust, and love are destabilized. Typically, the couple begins treatment in a state of shock, disbelief, anger, and denial, accompanied by feelings of skepticism and pessimism as the partners question if the relationship is irreparably damaged. The course of treatment is often protracted and characterized by periods of instability.

The clinical work can be arduous yet rewarding. Most therapists, however, feel emotionally, morally, and intellectually challenged by such conditions. They are acutely aware that the fragile relationship could easily deteriorate. Additionally, countertransference reactions, if not understood, can impede therapeutic effectiveness. The therapist must be balanced, ethical, nonjudgmental, flexible, and armed with a variety of strategies and interventions (Weeks, Gambescia, & Jenkins, 2003).

We know from our clinical experience in working with couples that infidelity is often a current or past issue for the couple and a concern within the family of origin. In fact, the incidence of infidelity is considerably high in clinical populations; more than 50% of clients seek help for affairs and other forms of infidelity (Humphrey, 1985). Prevalence statistics, however, are inconsistent, often reflecting the particular aspects under investigation rather than the actual frequency. In general, for married, heterosexual Americans, infidelity appears to occur in 25% or fewer couples (Blow & Hartnett, 2005); this percentage is slightly higher in cohabitating couples (Treas & Giesen, 2000). An unwavering reality is that infidelity damages individuals and relationships (Johnson, 2005). In addition to the psychological impacts of infidelity, the physiological consequences of stress, exhaustion, and chronic agitation are considerable (Spring, 1996).

Definitional Issues

Every couple is unique in their understanding of relational exclusivity. In infidelity cases, the partners often disagree about whether a violation of relational exclusivity has taken place. A major task in infidelity treatment, therefore, is for the therapist and partners to arrive at common understanding about the specific behaviors in question, the terms used to describe such behaviors, and the nature of the violation of relational exclusivity. One way to determine if a line has been crossed is to trace the onset of deceptive communication. Deception is intended to obscure the transgression and to confuse the betrayed partner (Pittman, 1989). Secrecy, lies, and other forms of dishonesty are harbingers of infidelity, even if no physical contact has occurred. When one partner systematically conceals thoughts, emotions, and behaviors from the other, a violation of the couple's intimacy contract has taken place (Lusterman, 1998).

Although infidelity might manifest itself physically, emotionally, or virtually, the bottom line is the amount of shared time between one partner and another individual outside of the marriage or committed relationship (Glass, personal communication, September 2002). One issue that becomes problematic for the couple is the time, energy, and resources that are spent to maintain another relationship. Another issue is the suffering caused by depriving the primary relationship of attention, intimacy, and energy (Moultrup, 1990).

The appropriate definition of infidelity has been a topic of research and clinical interest for more than two decades. Inconsistent definitions of infidelity have created mythological problems in understanding and treating this phenomenon (Blow & Hartnett, 2005). Some authors use a narrow definition that focuses on the degree of physical contact (Thompson, 1984). This sort of description does not provide an explanation for the emotional aspects of betrayal. Another definitional problem is the belief that infidelity solely occurs within the context of marriage rather than the larger category of committed relationships. This assumption is limiting because committed unmarried couples also report that they have experienced infidelity in their relationships, and the consequences are just as devastating (Drigotas, Safstrom, & Gentilia, 1999; Hansen, 1987; Weeks et al., 2003).

As a result of continued discussions in the field, we need to acknowledge a broadened definition of infidelity—one encompassing emotions and behaviors applicable to a variety of couple structures and organizations. We consider infidelity a "violation of the couple's assumed or stated contract regarding emotional and/or sexual exclusivity" (Weeks et al., 2003, p. xvii). As such, intimacy is diverted from the primary partnership and is expressed through other outlets or relationships without the partner's consent (Shaw, 1997). This classification includes emotional infidelity, cybersex, same-sex relationships, and long-term committed relationships. Therapists using this extensive description show respect for each couple's unique relationship contract and factors that constitute a breach in a couple's agreement regarding exclusivity (Hertlein, 2004).

Research

The extensive research literature on infidelity is replete with contradictions. Also, it raises as many questions as it answers. We will present a précis of some of the more salient findings and the related inconsistencies using categories described by Weeks and colleagues (2003). These categories explore specific risk factors on individual, relational, and intergenerational levels that might create vulnerability to infidelity.

Individual Variables

Demographics such as gender, age, level of education, and religiosity influence the likelihood of infidelity, but mediating variables also affect the results. For example, people with higher levels of education were found to be more unfaithful (Atkins, Baucom, & Jacobson, 2001); in other studies, education was a more significant correlate for women (Forste & Tanfer, 1996), but perhaps only to the degree that her level differs from that of her partner (Blow & Hartnett, 2005). Religiosity, as defined by church attendance, was found in one study to correlate negatively with infidelity (Atkins et al., 2001; Liu, 2000), especially for women (Hansen, 1987); however, another study (Blumstein & Schwartz, 1983) found the opposite. Choi, Catania, and Dolcini (1994) reported a negative correlation between religiosity and infidelity, but only for Blacks and Hispanics and not for

Whites. Clearly, it is difficult to obtain an accurate representation of the factors related to infidelity occurrence with such conflicting results.

Gender and age are mediating variables for infidelity; however, the data are again contradictory. Some research suggests that, compared with women, men are more likely to engage in infidelity (Allen & Baucom, 2004; Atkins et al., 2001), to have more partners outside of the primary relationship (Blumstein & Schwartz, 1983; Spanier & Margolis, 1983; Wiggins & Lederer, 1984), to have more permissive attitudes regarding sex outside the primary relationship (Lieberman, 1988; Thompson, 1984), and to have a stronger desire to engage in infidelity (Prins, Buunk, & Van Yperen, 1993).

Diagnosed or insidious psychiatric conditions, such as depression, can affect the way couples relate to each other and resolve problems. Other mediating variables such as physical illness, life stage, or age can be contributing factors in one's decision-making processes, reactions, impulsivity, and other emotional processes (Atwater, 1979; Weeks et al., 2003). Any of these demographic variables can become a potential risk factor for infidelity.

A permissive attitude toward infidelity has emerged as an important covariate in much of the research. Individuals with more permissive attitudes toward infidelity are more likely to be unfaithful (Glass & Wright, 1992; Thompson, 1983; Treas & Giesen, 2000) as well as those with a strong interest in sex (Liu, 2000). Prior sexual experiences have been positively correlated with infidelity; married and dating women with four or more sexual experiences prior to the primary relationship are more likely to become unfaithful (Treas & Giesen, 2000). For women, a liberal sexual attitude is the best predictor of infidelity engagement (Hansen, 1987).

Relational Variables

Numerous relational risk factors are reported in the infidelity literature. Cohabitating (rather than married) couples are somewhat more inclined to violate the exclusivity of the relationship (Forste & Tanfer, 1996; Treas & Giesen, 2000). Also, if the beginning of the relationship occurs when the partners are young (i.e., late adolescence) they are more likely to experience infidelity (Amato & Rogers, 1997). Although there is no direct correlation regarding number of children and infidelity, having children initially decreases relationship satisfaction and, thus, might predispose it to infidelity (Gottman & Notarius, 2000). Further, previous divorce

(Wiederman, 1997) and remarriage (Christopher & Sprecher, 2000) appear to strongly influence the likelihood of infidelity.

Marital and sexual dissatisfaction are strongly correlated with infidelity, particularly for women (Atkins et al., 2001; Glass & Wright, 1985; Liu, 2000; Prins et al., 1993; Thompson, 1983). Also, infidelity is more likely when partners feel deprived in their relationship (Walster, Traupmann, & Walster, 1978). Yet a percentage of participants in these studies did not need to be dissatisfied with their relationships to be unfaithful; many unfaithful partners act on opportunity rather than on dissatisfaction (Glass & Wright, 1992; Wiggins & Lederer, 1984). The association between relational dissatisfaction and infidelity is affected by mediating variables, such as religion, culture, and ethnicity (Atkins et al., 2001; Choi et al., 1994; Thompson, 1983). Moreover, mediating variables can confuse the picture because each can influence the other.

Intergenerational Factors

Most of the literature on infidelity does not show a direct relationship between parental infidelity and the likelihood of their children engaging in infidelity. In fact, the correlates of infidelity are exclusively emotional and relational (Glass & Wright, 1992; Treas & Giesen, 2000). We know from our clinical work that people learn how to behave in intimate relationships by observing interactions of parents and others within the family of origin. In addition, we have seen repeatedly that affairs often reflect an intergenerational legacy. There is a paucity of data about the numerous intergenerational influences on marital behaviors, values, and expectations.

Integration in Infidelity Treatment

The body of literature on infidelity abounds with numerous typologies that have increased our understanding of this phenomenon. Nonetheless, these approaches have failed to produce a coherent, integrated conceptual framework or consistent treatment method (Glass, 2002). For example, Brown's (1991) typology includes categories such as the conflict-avoidant and intimacy-avoidant affairs. Charny (1992) focused on the motivations for infidelity and relational dynamics that perpetuate it. Barton and

Alexander (1981) viewed infidelity through a functional family therapy perspective; infidelity provides a distancing function between partners. These are just a few of the multiple frameworks published. As a result of the multiplicity of frameworks, there is little consistency in treatment approaches (Hertlein & Weeks, in press).

Although each model makes sense in its own right, the published approaches are most commonly generated by individual scholars and do not necessarily overlap; they appear sporadic and isolated. Moreover, most theoretical formulations have little or no research support (Hertlein & Weeks, in press). Only a small number of studies investigated specific treatment approaches and the efficacy of therapy for infidelity (Atkins, Baucom, & Christensen, 2005; DuPree, White, Olsen, & Lafleur, 2007; Gordon, Baucom, & Snyder, 2005; Hertlein, 2004).

Our framework utilizes a coherent, theoretical approach that reflects a synthesis of clinical experience, theory building, and research regarding infidelity and forgiveness. This is a departure from other treatment techniques for infidelity in that it is truly integrative. Rather than relying on combining elements of a system in an eclectic manner (as is predominant in infidelity treatment), the intersystems approach allows for the therapist to operate from a coherent theoretical base. It incorporates all relevant systems in treatment: the individual partners, dyadic dynamics, and family-of-origin issues. Additionally, it attends to the ABCs of a client's experience: the affective, behavioral, and cognitive aspects of infidelity. The integrative method addresses the multiple dimensions of infidelity; biological, social, and psychological factors of each person in the systems; and therapeutic techniques for managing these issues. This approach is composed of three phases: assessment, treatment, and consolidation.

Assessment

During the assessment phase, risk factors for infidelity are investigated with respect to the individual partners, dyadic concerns, influences from intergenerational sources, social and environmental triggers, and other multiple dimensions of infidelity. Additionally, therapist factors are assessed since therapists must be vigilant about reactions within themselves, about maintaining balance, and about confidentiality concerns.

Individual Factors

Biology

Biological data (e.g., age, health, physical illness, prescription and recreational drug use) should always be included in the assessment because they can serve as risk factors for infidelity. These biological factors provide a physical backdrop for psychological triggers such as midlife crisis, infertility, menopause, and sexual problems (e.g., erectile dysfunction, lack of desire). In some instances, biological factors may trigger psychological crises, impulsivity, low self-esteem, emotional reactivity, or other emotional reactions that increase vulnerability to infidelity. In one case, during a business trip a 50-year-old married woman had a brief sexual affair that she related to anxiety about aging and desirability. Another example involved a 55-year-old married man with progressive erectile problems of mixed etiology. He had sex with a prostitute to test his erectile capacity.

Psychology

The therapist must assess for any psychological individual issues that could serve as a risk factor for infidelity such as anxiety, depression, cognitive distortions, personality disorders, or other psychiatric diagnoses. In some cases, such disorders may be reflected in the decision to engage in infidelity to distract oneself from unpleasant symptoms. For example, individuals with mood disorders such as bipolar disorder and major depressive disorder may engage in infidelity in an attempt to reduce their feelings of depression and boredom. In other cases, personality disorders can make an individual vulnerable to infidelity. For example, with dependent personality disorder, individuals might develop an outside relationship in an attempt to meet their perceived unmet emotional needs. Similarly, people with narcissistic personality disorders might believe that they are entitled to seek an outside relationship to receive the adoration that they believe they deserve (Weeks et al., 2003).

Another area of growing interest in its relation to infidelity is that of attachment theory. Attachment is the affectional tie that binds people together in enduring relationships. Attachment issues affect romantic relationships (Mikulincer & Shaver, 2005), stress tolerance (Collins & Feeney, 2000), and caregiving behavior (Rholes, Simpson, Campbell, & Grich, 2001). All of these features are present in intimate relationships. Certain attachment styles (i.e., dismissive, fearful, and preoccupied) have been related to the motivation for infidelity (Allen & Baucom, 2004). Also, people with an anxious attachment style, especially women, are more likely to engage in infidelity (Bogaert & Sadava, 2002). Assessment for attachment vulnerabilities can render information about susceptibility to infidelity within an individual.

Sociocultural

One must also consider the wider context of influences on someone's life in relation to infidelity. For example, infidelity is positively correlated with nontraditional gender role orientation for women (Blow & Hartnett, 2005). Women are also more likely to engage in infidelity if they know other women who were unfaithful, emphasizing the importance of social norms (Buunk, 1980). Factors affecting Hispanics' engagement in infidelity include gender roles (i.e., dominance of men over women), family loyalty, and expectation of male infidelity at some point over the course of the marriage (Weeks et al., 2003). For African Americans, contributing factors include history of slavery, past and present discrimination, higher levels of stress and relational distress, and financial problems (Penn, Hernandez, & Bermudez, 1997). Additionally, the unequal status of husbands to wives within Asian Americans affects the likelihood of engaging in infidelity (Penn, Hernandez, & Bermudez, 1997).

Relational Factors

The second component of the integrated assessment is the evaluation of the couple. Most therapists conceptualize that dissension within a relationship is a major risk factor for infidelity (Hertlein, 2004; Weeks et al., 2003). Accordingly, therapists should inquire about potential areas of relationship discord, conflict, and unresolved anger. A major area of relational conflict involves unmet expectations (assumed or expressed). The therapist, therefore, must consider the couple's emotional contract, styles of communication, and means of resolving conflict and how each defines problems. Resolving underlying conflicts increases the likelihood of experiencing greater levels of intimacy. In many cases, efficacy of infidelity treatment depends on the degree to which the couple wants to develop intimacy with one another.

Unresolved anger can also impact a couple's treatment for infidelity. Hidden anger can lead to resentment and, ultimately, to emotional distance between partners. The emotional distance can make a couple vulnerable to infidelity (Weeks et al., 2003). For example, Jean and David came to therapy to discuss David's frequent extramarital relationships. After several sessions, David admitted to the therapist and to Jean that he felt pressed to get married after they found out that Jean was pregnant. In the eight years they had been married, David felt that he became increasingly resentful toward Jean for this decision.

In the relational assessment stage, it is also appropriate for the therapist to explore each partner's relationship history as well as to include a history of infidelity. In many cases, couples seeking treatment for infidelity will report that one or both partners has experienced infidelity previously, either in the current or past relationship. As discussed already, some determinants of infidelity include number of prior sexual encounters (Treas & Giesen, 2000) and opportunity, particularly within the workplace (Atkins et al., 2001; Glass & Staehel, 2003).

Intergenerational Factors

Though the couple is typically the primary focus of treatment, certain intergenerational factors can contribute to one's likelihood of becoming involved in infidelity. From a demographic standpoint, parental divorce increases the odds of engaging in infidelity (Amato & Rogers, 1997). More directly, some patterns of infidelity exist across generations. In such families, individuals may unconsciously maintain an intergenerational legacy by engaging in infidelity (Weeks et al., 2003). Other family-of-origin factors can serve as precursors to infidelity. These include learned patterns of emotional management. For example, an individual can learn to regulate conflict or anxiety within the relationship by triangulating or placing emotional energy into an outside source. Triangulation is, in many cases, at the core of the infidelity experience (Friedman, 1991). Through triangulation, the level of intimate involvement between partners is controlled. Emotionally involvement with an outside relationship limits the intimate investment with the primary partner.

Moultrup (1990) and others (Brown, 1991; Spring, 1996) also discussed the intergenerational nature of affairs, specifically the impact of the multigenerational transmission processes that contribute to infidelity. There are two ways that behavior patterns can be transmitted from one generation to the next: through repetition or reversal (Moultrup, 1990). In repetition, an individual connects with an unfaithful parent and repeats how they connect with others; in reversal, the individual interacts with others differently than their unfaithful parent.

Multigenerational transmission patterns in infidelity may also be influenced by liberal attitudes toward extradyadic relationships and sexuality issues (Hertlein, Ray, Wetchler, & Killmer, 2003). In the case of infidelity, persons who have engaged in infidelity are likely to be more sexually permissive (Treas & Giesen, 2000). As a result, their children may have been raised with the same values, may share the same values (also be more sexually permissive), and would therefore be more likely themselves to also engage in infidelity, resulting in a transmission of this pattern.

The therapist can use a genogram to assess the impact of emotional factors within each partner's family of origin. While the genogram can solicit important biological information about the makeup of the family, DeMaria, Weeks, and Hof (1994) suggested the implementation of an emotion-focused genogram to obtain information related to emotional management (and anger management patterns) within the family. A sexual genogram can add another dimension to the couple's intimate relationship (Hof & Berman, 1986). Many of our clients report that sex was never discussed at home, that sex education was learned from peers, and that sexuality is laden with guilt, shame, and mythology.

Multiple Dimensions of Infidelity

Specific aspects, elements, and features of infidelity will vary from case to case. The multiple presentations of infidelity must be assessed because they affect the meaning and definition of the infidelity for each partner (Weeks et al., 2003; Westfall, 1989). As stated, partners often disagree as to whether infidelity took place at all because of the presentation. For example, one person in the couple may justify that his or her relationship with the third party was primarily emotional rather than physical and would therefore not constitute infidelity. The dimensions of infidelity to be considered in the assessment phase are listed as follows:

- Duration of infidelity
- Frequency and types of communication
- Sexual contact between the affair partners
- Location of encounters
- Risk of discovery
- Degree of collusion by the betrayed partner
- Level of deception
- History of past infidelity

- Gender of the affair partner
- Type of infidelity
- Unilateral and bilateral infidelity (e.g., one primary partner becoming involved vs. both partners becoming involved)
- Relationship of the affair partner to either spouse/primary partner
- Perceived attractiveness of the affair partner
- Social context of infidelity (e.g., geographic community of the couple; socioeconomic group; ethnic, cultural, and religious affiliation)

The Therapist's Self

Throughout this chapter, therapists are advised to take stock of their own process in infidelity treatment. The topic of infidelity is one that centers to some degree on personal values and attitudes, for both clients and therapists. As such, therapists must consistently explore their neutrality in these cases and be mindful of whether they have adequate supervision (see, e.g., Hertlein, 2004; Hurlbert, 1992; Moultrup, 1990; Taibbi, 1983; Weeks et al., 2003). Additionally, infidelity work is emotionally draining; therefore, regulating the number of infidelity cases will ensure competent treatment and will prevent therapist fatigue.

Treatment

Treatment can commence after the crisis of disclosure has settled, the assessment is completed, and the therapist and clients have a good understanding of the numerous factors contributing to the occurrences of infidelity. While nothing excuses infidelity, the treatment needs to be systemic rather than focusing exclusively on the involved partner. This means that the problem is viewed within a broader framework of what it represents for and to the couple. To accomplish a systemic framework, the couple must be taught to think systemically. This can be a difficult task since each partner may be entrenched in his or her respective perceptions, justifications, and so forth. It gets even more complicated when infidelity stemmed from nonrelational factors. Nonetheless, a systemic approach focuses on how the infidelity impinges on the couple and how the individual factors that contributed to the infidelity affect the relationship. The betrayed partner is also helped to understand their part in accepting, coping, or unconsciously needing these factors.

There are three sections to the treatment component: intervening on the emotional level, intervening based on one's theory, and facilitating forgiveness. Each is next discussed in greater detail.

Emotional Interventions

Reactions to infidelity are intense and varied, yet they often fall within a range of predictable experiences for the unfaithful and the betrayed partners. The role of the therapist is to address emotional reactions as they erupt, to regulate the intensity of affect, and to normalize experiences when necessary. Couples appreciate information about processes that can be expected during recovery from infidelity. They are especially reassured that their emotional reactions are "normal" for a particular situation or phase of treatment. Also, they are more likely to comply with treatment when the rationale for interventions is explained. Thus, the therapist must be familiar with emotional experiences of the unfaithful partner, with how to keep this partner committed to treatment, and with how to address these feelings with sensitivity. Simultaneously, the powerful emotional responses of the betrayed partner must be anticipated and recognized.

One way to conceptualize infidelity is to approach treatment from a posttraumatic stress disorder (PTSD) perspective (see, e.g., Glass, 2002). Infidelity is often a devastating, destabilizing ordeal that threatens the foundations of the marriage or committed relationship (Weeks et al., 2003). As such, the betrayed partner can experience PTSD symptoms related to the trauma of the infidelity. The therapist helps to process emotions such as anxiety, lability, numbness, depression, aggression, jealousy, and loss of self-esteem (Glass, 2002; Lusterman, 2005). For example, the betrayed partner may ruminate obsessively about the discovery, about how and why the affair occurred, or about intimate scenarios between the spouse and the affair partner.

The emotional reactions of the unfaithful partner can also be unanticipated and bewildering. The therapist must expect that this person might not experience guilt or remorse but instead may feel sad that the affair has ended. Often, individual sessions are helpful for facilitating mourning related to the ending of the extradyadic relationship (Weeks et al., 2003). In other instances, the person who was unfaithful can feel relieved that the affair was disclosed or discovered. There may also be feelings of shame, guilt, and depression that become stimulated by observing pain in the betrayed partner.

Listen, Accept, and Moderate the Feelings

As the couple begins to discuss their feelings related to the infidelity and the current context of their relationship, they may have some difficulty navigating the strong emotional content in a way that is helpful and productive to their recovery process. In many cases, the couple will report that their conversations at home are circular, producing frustration without resolution; they might also become disappointed that each partner cannot understand the other's point of view. By the time they come to treatment, they may have developed a destructive pattern of communication that lacks empathy or other attempts to listen to each other's feelings. The therapist can be a model for listening to feelings. Listening does not necessarily involve agreement, but it is a first step toward mediating the communication and accompanying feelings about many aspects of the infidelity.

Identify Whether the Infidelity Provokes Other Feelings

In some cases, the infidelity itself may trigger other feelings such as anger, rage, rejection, betrayal, self-loathing, hatred, and abandonment (Spring, 1996; Weeks et al., 2003). The presence of such forceful emotions can further weaken the individual and can destabilize the couple's dynamics. Further, toxic emotional themes can persist in the relationship for a significant period of time after the infidelity is dealt with in treatment. It is imperative that the therapist speak with the couple about the potential for the development of these other feelings and address them immediately as they surface. Another component of treatment is to help the couple develop a long-term plan for management of these feelings.

Normalize Feelings

The feelings that emerge during treatment for infidelity can be unpredictable, unpleasant, and intolerable. At times, couples can be frustrated that they leave some sessions feeling that they have moved one step forward and two steps back. Normalizing the process of shifting emotions during the therapy process can increase the likelihood that the couple will remain in treatment during the low and high tides. The therapist should also normalize the duration of intense, residual, and obsessive feelings that will likely be experienced.

It is common that the person involved in infidelity may believe that once it is discovered, the betrayed partner should rapidly get beyond his or her pain and suffering. This dynamic can be destructive because the betrayed partner needs to discuss what happened and his or her feelings must be validated. The therapist should normalize the feeling of each partner while explaining that talking about painful issues is a key to recovery. In some instances, individual sessions are helpful for processing protracted anger, shame, grief, and other feelings that may need more attention.

Maintain Neutrality and Balance
Although most therapists working with couples believe they are capable of maintaining a neutral stance, infidelity work can be especially challenging. The partners can rapidly become polarized in positions of perpetrator and victim, each attempting to pull the therapist onto his or her side. The therapist should anticipate that the potential for collusion and triangulation is always present in infidelity work. Using a systemic framework is the antidote to collusion and triangulation; the therapist can structure sessions, can direct questions, and can control treatment in such a way as to maintain neutrality.

Encourage a Refrain on Making a Decision about the Outcome of the Relationship
During infidelity treatment, ambivalence about the outcome of the relationship is common. In addition to ambivalence, the emotions surrounding the infidelity, such as anger and rage, jealousy, and fear are very strong (Weeks et al., 2003). The couple may also report that their relationship feels turbulent, chaotic, and precarious. Therapists need to normalize these feelings for the couple as well as to advise them that decisions about the outcome of the relationship should not be made until the relationship becomes more stable.

Reduce Polarization
Each member of the couple may believe that he or she is the most injured party and that his or her feelings and actions are justified. The partner who was unfaithful may feel that he or she was "pushed" to engage in infidelity, placing blame on the shoulders of the uninvolved partner. Also, the wounded party might feel that treatment should revolve around "fixing" the faults of the unfaithful partner. In these cases, the therapist should ask each partner to listen to and acknowledge feelings of the other. This process can be tricky and prolonged, yet it is an essential step toward recovery. Active listening should be reinforced between sessions by assigning the couple specific time-limited tasks related to feelings in general (Weeks et al., 2003).

As a moderator, the therapist promotes safety by monitoring and controlling the direction of the conversation. For example, if the betrayed partner continues to seek factual information about the affair, the therapist can redirect the conversation to identify what need he or she is trying to satisfy and to help that partner connect with and identify the emotions he or she is feeling. The therapist then helps this partner to articulate these needs. The unfaithful partner is helped to listen without being defensive and to acknowledge the pain, hurt, and damage resulting from the infidelity (Weeks et al., 2003).

Reframing is another method to reduce the polarization within a couple. The purpose of a reframe is to help the couple view the problem differently or take away a different meaning from the infidelity (Weeks et al., 2003). If the infidelity resulted from relationship conflict, then the reframe can help the couple view the problem systemically or as a symptom of difficulties within the marriage. Nonetheless, the therapist must emphasize that infidelity and the deception that surrounds it is never acceptable in a committed relationship. For more detail on reframing with couples struggling with infidelity, see Weeks et al.

Working from a Theoretical Perspective

When the therapist is able to manage the emotions in the room and generate more safety and stability for the couple, he or she should intervene from a theoretical perspective. This involves the use of a set of beliefs or principles that will guide the therapist in selecting interventions. The problem with most of the infidelity literature, however, is the absence of a coherent theoretical model. A notable exception is the work of Johnson (2005), who used an emotionally focused therapeutic approach to guide the therapist in making decisions about managing infidelity, forgiveness, recreating trust, and rebuilding the damaged relationship.

Why Did This Couple Have This Problem?

The first step in operating from a theoretical perspective in infidelity cases is for the therapist to continue to assess the possible reasons for the infidelity. Then, a hypothesis is generated based on the information gathered about the individual partners, their relationship, and other loyalty ties. The therapist gradually develops a theory that guides treatment and assists in further comprehension of the problem. For example, did the infidelity serve as a means to remain loyal to one's family? Is this a case where the involved partner is sexually compulsive? Are there commitment fears on the part of one or both partners, thus resulting in the infidelity being used as a way to avoid commitment with the primary partner?

Another approach used in the treatment of infidelity is the deficit theoretical model. The underlying assumption of this model is that the couple is having problems because there is something "missing" from the relationship. The missing aspects of the relationship are fulfilled through engaging in infidelity (Hertlein, 2004). When using the deficit model, the therapist's map for treatment involves assessing for the aspects of the relationship which are missing. Next, the therapist is guided theoretically to help the partners to develop ways to meet each other's needs.

Evaluate Therapeutic Stance on Key Issues

Therapists must become familiar with theoretical issues of infidelity treatment, take a position within the issues, and be decisive. Problems arise rapidly, and the therapist must be armed with strategies, particularly when the issues are ethically taxing. Nelson (2000) conducted research examining how expert therapists conceptualize treatment in Internet infidelity cases. He discovered that a therapist's stance on certain key issues (e.g., holding a secret, individual versus conjoint sessions, amount of revealed information, monitoring activities of the unfaithful partner) affects the treatment. Many of the key issues also apply to the management of other forms of infidelity. In these cases, there is not one "right or wrong" answer. Once clear, therapists will understand specifically how their treatment will be dictated especially when divisive issues are involved. Weeks et al. (2003) discussed the different ethical approaches to use when the therapist learns that a violation of the relationship has occurred.

Intervene Consistent with Case Conceptualization

Once the therapist identifies a schema for why this couple has this problem and has clarity about a theoretical position, intervention can begin. Intervention must be consistent with both the case conceptualization and how the partners fall on the continua of divisive issues previously mentioned. For example, Chrissy, 32, and Robert, 35, came to treatment because Chrissy had been discovered having an affair with Robert's brother. According to her account, this was the fourth instance of infidelity in her marriage to Robert. During the assessment phase, Chrissy reported that her parents had also been unfaithful to one another. If the therapist believes that Chrissy is having affairs because she is consistently missing something that she needs in her relationship with Robert, therapy might revolve around having her express her needs and seeking ways for the relationship to be structured to meet those needs. In contrast, if the therapist believes that Chrissy's infidelity is her way of remaining loyal to her family of origin, the treatment will focus on intergenerational issues.

Forgiveness

Forgiveness is a critical process in infidelity treatment because it is necessary for repairing the damaged relationship and promoting healing. In many cases, people believe that they understand what it means to forgive, but this definition can vary across situations, people, and points in the life cycle. Often, betrayed partners need assistance in discussing whether to forgive the many parts of the infidelity and how to do so (Legaree, Turner, & Lollis, 2007). Forgiveness is a process that takes time and happens in small increments. Often, the guilty party will seek forgiveness quickly to bypass the painful elements of healing and to move away from the infidelity. Understandably, accelerating or circumventing the forgiveness process will further victimize the betrayed partner (Weeks et al., 2003).

Forgiveness is different from accepting or accommodating. Acceptance is typically equated with exonerating the unfaithful partner from guilt, excusing the actions, and removing the responsibility for the actions. Acceptance, though often requested by the unfaithful partner, is not effective in infidelity treatment because there is no obligation for behavior change or a commitment to work toward the relationship (Weeks et al., 2003). Forgiveness involves a series of processes that are initiated by genuine expressions of remorse and apology. The eventual outcome allows the betrayed partner to work toward releasing anger and resentment and eventually experiencing compassion toward the unfaithful partner.

Weeks et al. (2003) proposed that the therapist should facilitate empathy, humility, commitment, and hope when conducting sessions around forgiveness. The unfaithful partner is helped to compose and disseminate a sincere apology, specific to the numerous parts of the betrayal, and to demonstrate commitment to behavioral change. The purpose of the apology is a genuine attempt to repair the relationship and must be communicated with sincerity (ibid.). Within the course of the apology, the unfaithful partner needs to convey genuine regret, sorrow, and remorse. Apologies should be judiciously timed to be heard; if the timing is right, an empathic response is triggered in the wounded partner (ibid.). When forgiveness is achieved, the betrayed partner will begin to stop seeking revenge or demanding justice, will reduce their feelings of anger and resentment, and will move toward restoration of trust in the primary relationship (Case, 2005).

As stated earlier, therapists must evaluate their personal position on the topic, become aware of the clients beliefs and values, and intervene with a clear course of action. Legaree et al. (2007) reviewed strategies for conceptualizing forgiveness to help the therapist develop a plan that fits his or her own value system and that of the couple. Additionally, Gordon and Baucom (1999) presented a model of forgiveness for infidelity based partially on relational ethics, focusing on cognitive, emotional, and behavioral tasks. Weeks and colleagues (2003) offered therapeutic strategies for dealing with the ethical challenges of infidelity work.

Consolidation

After the emotions have become quiet and the forgiveness work is in progress, the couple can reflect on the future of their relationship. It is a time when therapy can proceed in only one of two directions. In some cases where too much damage has occurred, the couple might decide to terminate their relationship. In other instances, a period of rebuilding commences. The consolidation phase of infidelity treatment has many classifications: "recommit or quit" (Spring, 1996), "moving on" (Gordon & Baucom, 1999; Gordon et al., 2005), or "restructuring/rebuilding the relationship" (Lusterman, 1998; Spring, 1996; Weeks et al., 2003). It is the point of treatment when the couple takes inventory, makes sense of what has occurred, and determines the direction of their lives.

A unique element of this integrative approach (which includes the intersystems approach) is the utilization of Sternberg's (1986) triangular theory of love in the consolidation phase (Weeks et al., 2003). Love is composed of three interactive elements: commitment, intimacy, and passion. Commitment, the cognitive element of love, describes whether couples stay together. Intimacy, the second component, addresses emotional and physical closeness between the partners. Passion refers to the affections, feelings of longing, and sexual attraction within a relationship (Sternberg, 1986).

In establishing whether the couple wants to advance together or individually, the therapist and partners need to consider several critical questions:

1. Do both partners want commitment, intimacy, and passion?
2. Do both partners want the same levels of commitment, intimacy, and passion?
3. What levels of individuation and togetherness does each partner want in his or her relationship?

4. What prevents each partner's ability to express himself or herself freely along these components?
5. Is there a realistic understanding of what love involves for each partner?
6. Is there a realistic understanding of what each partner can offer?

These six questions will help the couple to identify how they would like to move forward, either individually or together. It will also provide an opportunity for the therapist and couple to work to develop a new foundation on which to proceed.

Research and Future Directions

Research in the field of infidelity is rich with ideas, opinions, and recommended treatments. Yet much of this information can be confusing to the therapist in need of direction with such difficult cases. Inconsistent findings, definitional issues, and many contradictions typify the available data on infidelity. Moreover, most researchers fail to consider the intersystemic aspects of infidelity, forgiveness, and reconciliation. Future research should take into account the factors that create vulnerability in an individual or couple and the intergenerational issues that may contribute to infidelity.

To date, much of the professional literature about infidelity has not helped to make sense of the complexity of this phenomenon. Many published studies lack empirical validation about specific therapeutic interventions for infidelity. Also, there is little consensus on theoretical approaches to guide the therapist in treating infidelity. Finally, there is confusion in the literature regarding the conceptualization of the forgiveness process and how therapists select a therapeutic model for the work of forgiveness (Legaree et al., 2007). Considering the importance of infidelity treatment and the existing inconsistencies within this body of literature, we support continued qualitative and quantitative research in this field.

References

Allen, E. S. & Baucom, D. H. (2004). Adult attachment and patterns of extradyadic involvement. *Family Process, 43*, 467–488.
Amato, P. R. & Rogers, S. J. (1997). A longitudinal study of marital problems and subsequent divorce. *Journal of Marriage and the Family, 59*, 612–624.

Atkins, D. C., Baucom, D. H., & Jacobson, N. S. (2001). Understanding infidelity: Correlates in a national random sample. *Journal of Family Psychology, 15*(7), 735–749.

Atkins, D. C., Yi, J., Baucom, D. H., & Christensen, A. (2005). Infidelity in couples seeking marital therapy. *Journal of Family Psychology, 19*(3), 470–473.

Atwater, L. (1979). Getting involved: Women's transition to first extramarital sex. *Alternative Lifestyles, 2*(1), 33–68.

Barton, C. & Alexander, J. F. (1981). Functional Family therapy. In A. Gurman & D. K. Kniskern (Eds.), *Handbook of family therapy.* New York: Brunner/Mazel.

Blow, A. & Hartnett, K. (2005). Infidelity in long-term committed relationships I: A methodological review. *Journal of Marital and Family Therapy, 31*(2), 183–216.

Blumstein, P. & Schwartz, P. (1983). *American couples: Money, work, sex.* New York: Morrow.

Bogaert, A. F. & Sadava, S. (2002). Adult attachment and sexual behavior. *Personal Relationships, 9*, 191–204.

Brown, E. (1991). *Patterns of infidelity and their treatment.* New York: Brunner/Mazel.

Brown, E. M. (1999). *Affairs: A guide to working through the repercussions of infidelity.* San Francisco: Jossey-Bass.

Buunk, B. (1980). Extramarital sex in the Netherlands: Motivation in social and marital context. *Alternative Lifestyles, 3*, 11–39.

Case, B. (2005). Healing the wounds of infidelity through the healing power of apology and forgiveness. *Journal of Couple and Relationship Therapy, 4*(2–3), 41–54.

Charny, I. (1992). Catering and not catering affairs: The proper and improper pursuit of extramarital relationships. In I. W. Charny (Ed.), *Existential/dialectical marital therapy* (pp. 220–244). New York: Brunner/Mazel.

Choi, K. H., Catania, J. A., & Dolcini, M. M. (1994). Extramarital sex and HIV risk behavior among US adults: Results from the National AIDS Behavioral Survey. *American Journal of Public Health, 84*, 2003–2007.

Christopher, C. F. & Sprecher, S. (2000). Sexuality in marriage, dating, and other relationships: A decade review. *Journal of Marriage and the Family, 62*, 999–1017.

Collins, N. L. & Feeney, B. C. (2000). A safe haven: Support-seeking and caregiving processes in intimate relationships. *Journal of Personality and Social Psychology, 78*(6), 1053–1073.

DeMaria, R., Weeks, G., & Hof, L. (1994). Focused genograms: Intergenerational assessment of individuals, couples, and families. Philadelphia: Brunner/Mazel.

Drigotas, S. M., Safstrom, C. A., & Gentilia, T. (1999). An investment model prediction of dating infidelity. *Journal of Personality and Social Psychology, 77*(3), 509–524.

DuPree, W. J, White, M. B., Olsen, C. S., & Lafleur, C. T. (2007). Infidelity treatment patterns: A practice-based evidence approach. *American Journal of Family Therapy, 35*(4), 327–341.

Forste, R. & Tanfer, K. (1996). Sexual exclusivity among dating, cohabitating, and married women. *Journal of Marriage and Family, 58,* 33–47.

Friedman, E. H. (1991). Bowen theory and therapy. In A. S. Gurman and D. P. Kniskern (Eds.), *Handbook of family therapy* (Vol. 2, pp. 134–170). New York: Brunner/Mazel.

Glass, S. P. (2002). Couple therapy after the trauma of infidelity. In A. Gurman & N. Jacobson (Eds.), *Clinical handbook of couple therapy* (3rd ed., pp. 488–507). New York: Guilford Press.

Glass, S. & Staehel, J. C. (2002). *Not "just friends": Protect your relationship from infidelity and heal the trauma of betrayal.* New York: Free Press.

Glass, S. P. & Wright, T. L. (1985). Sex differences in type of extramarital involvement and marital dissatisfaction. *Sex Roles, 12,* 1101–1120.

Glass, S. & Wright, T. (1992). Justifications for extramarital relationships: The association between attitudes, behaviors, and gender. *Journal of Sex Research, 29*(3), 361–387.

Gordon, K. C. & Baucom, D. H. (1999). A multitheoretical intervention for promoting recovery from extramarital affairs. *Clinical Psychology: Science and Practice, 6*(4), 382–399.

Gordon, K. C., Baucom, D. H., & Snyder, D. K. (2005). Treating couples recovering from infidelity: An integrative approach. *JCLP/In Session, 61*(11), 1393–1405.

Gottman, J. M. & Notarius, C. I. (2000). Decade review: Observing marital interaction. *Journal of Marriage and the Family, 62,* 927–947.

Hansen, G. L. (1987). Extradyadic relations during courtship. *Journal of Sex Research, 23,* 382–390.

Hertlein, K. M. (2004). *Internet infidelity: An examination of family therapist treatment decisions and gender biases.* Unpublished doctoral dissertation, Virginia Polytechnic Institute and State University, Blacksburg.

Hertlein, K. M., Ray, R., Wetchler, J., & Killmer, J. M. (2003). The role of differentiation in extradyadic relationships. *Journal of Couple and Relationship Therapy, 2*(4), 33–50.

Hertlein, K. M. & Weeks, G. R. (2007). Two roads diverging in a wood: The current state of infidelity research and treatment. *Journal of Couple and Relationship Therapy, 6*(1–2), 95–107.

Hof, L. & Berman, E. (1986). The sexual genogram. *Journal of Marital and Family Therapy, 12,* 39–47.

Humphrey F. G. (1985). *Extramarital affairs and their treatment by AAMFT therapist.* Paper presented at the meeting of the American Association of Marriage and Family Therapy, New York.

Hurlbert, D. (1992). Factors influencing a woman's decision to end an extramarital sexual relationship. *Journal of Sex and Marital Therapy, 18*(2), 104–113.

Johnson, S. M. (2005). Broken bonds: An emotionally focused approach to infidelity. *Journal of Couple and Relationship Therapy, 4*(2–3), 17–29.

Legaree, T., Turner, J., & Lollis, S. (2007). Forgiveness and therapy: A critical review of conceptualizations, practices, and values found in the literature. *Journal of Marital and Family Therapy, 33*(2), 192–213.

Lieberman, B. (1988). Extrapremarital intercourse: Attitudes toward a neglected sexual behavior. *Journal of Sex Research, 24,* 291–299.

Liu, C. (2000). A theory of marital sexual life. *Journal of Marriage and the Family, 62,* 363–374.

Lusterman, D. (1998). *Infidelity: A survival guide.* New York: MJF Books.

Lusterman, D. (2005). Helping children and adults cope with parental infidelity. *Journal of Clinical Psychology, 61*(11), 1439–1451.

Mikulincer, M. & Shaver, P. R. (2005). Attachment theory and emotions in close relationships: Exploring the attachment-related dynamics of emotional reactions to relational events. *Personal Relationships, 12,* 149–168.

Moultrup, D. J. (1990). *Husbands, wives, and lovers: The emotional system of the extramarital affair.* New York: Guilford Press.

Nelson, T. S. (2000). *Internet Infidelity: A modified Delphi study.* Unpublished doctoral dissertation, Purdue University, West Lafayette, IN.

Penn, C., Hernandez, S., & Bermudez, M. (1997). Using a cross-cultural perspective to understand infidelity in couples therapy. *American Journal of Family Therapy, 25*(2), 169–185.

Pittman, F. (1989). *Private lies: Infidelity and the betrayal of intimacy.* New York: W. W. Norton & Co.

Prins, K. S., Buunk B. P., & Van Yperen, N. W. (1993). Equity, normative disapproval, and extramarital relationships. *Journal of Social and Personal Relationships, 10,* 39–53.

Rholes, W. S., Simpson, J. A., Campbell, L., & Grich, J. (2001). Adult attachment and the transition to parenthood. *Journal of Personality and Social Psychology, 81,* 421–435.

Shaw, J. (1997). Treatment rationale for internet infidelity. *Journal of Sex Education and Therapy, 22*(1), 29–34.

Spanier, G. B. & Margolis, R. L. (1983). Marital separation and extramarital sexual behavior. *Journal of Sex Research, 19,* 23–48.

Spring, J. A. (1996). *After the affair: Healing the pain and rebuilding the trust when a partner has been unfaithful.* New York: HarperCollins.

Sternberg, R. (1986). A triangular theory of love. *Psychological Review, 93*(2), 119–135.

Taibbi, R. (1983). Handling extramarital affairs in clinical treatment. *Social Casework: The Journal of Contemporary Social Work, 64*(4), 200–204.

Thompson, A. (1983). Extramarital sex: A review of the research literature. *Journal of Sex Research, 19*(1), 1–22.

Thompson, A. P. (1984). Emotional and sexual components of extramarital relations. *Journal of Marriage and the Family, 46,* 35–42.

Treas, J. & Giesen, D. (2000). Sexual infidelity among married and cohabitating Americans. *Journal of Marriage and the Family, 62,* 48–60.

Walster, E., Traupmann, J., & Walster, G. W. (1978). Equity and extramarital sexu-
    ality. *Archives of Sexual Behavior, 7*(2), 127–141.
Weeks, G. R., Gambescia, N., & Jenkins, R. E. (2003). *Treating infidelity: Therapeutic
    dilemmas and effective strategies.* New York: W. W. Norton & Co.
Westfall, A. (1989). Extramarital sex: The treatment of the couple. In G. Weeks
    (Ed.), *Treating couples: The intersystem model of the Marriage Council of
    Philadelphia* (pp. 163–190). Philadelphia: Brunnel/Mazel.
Wiederman, M. W. (1997). Extramarital sex: Prevalence and correlates in a national
    survey. *Journal of Sex Research, 34,* 167–174.
Wiggins, J. D. & Lederer, D. A. (1984). Differential antecedents of infidelity in mar-
    riage. *American Mental Health Counselors Association Journal, 6,* 152–161.

14

Sexual Pharmacology
Love Potions, Pills, and Poisons

Johan Verhulst
Jonathan K. Reynolds

Contents

Introduction

Sexual behavior is essential for the survival of the human species, not just because it leads to reproduction but also because it facilitates social bonding and attachment. Consequently, one would expect that millions of years of evolution produced a very reliable human reproductive system with built-in redundancies, resulting in a robust sex drive, unfailing physiological mechanisms, and simple, consistent patterns of reproductive behavior and responsiveness. In reality, however, humans exhibit an enormous variety of sexual behaviors and preferences (Kinsey, Pomeroy, & Martin, 1948; Kinsey, Pomeroy, Martin, & Gebhardt, 1953), while population studies reveal a surprisingly high prevalence of sexual problems and dysfunctions (Lauman, Paik, & Rosen, 1999). Clearly, human sexuality appears to be characterized by diversity and fragility rather than by evolutionary conformity and sturdiness.

A reason for this discrepancy may be that the cultural world in which we live is at odds with our evolved dispositions. Modern humans lead a very different life from our ancestors. Consider the fact that, at least in the industrialized world, people now have access to an abundance of (fast) food. With an insistent propensity to eat, such access easily leads to obesity, diabetes, and other chronic diseases that affect sexuality (Nesse & Williams, 1996; Rosen, Wing, Schneider, & Gendrano, 2005). Life expectancy has more than doubled, and many people expect to maintain sexual activity at an advanced age regardless of the physiological effects of aging (Bradford & Meston, 2007). And maybe most importantly, our bodies are constantly being exposed to human-made chemicals: industrial toxins and pollutants, recreational drugs, and a whole range of powerful pharmaceuticals that often cause sexual problems. One can reasonably assume that chemical exposure contributes to a significant portion of the sexual dysfunctions in the population. This chapter reviews the impact of drugs on sexual functioning. First, we focus on chemicals that can *cause* sexual problems and then concentrate on those that are used to *treat* dysfunctions.

In the past, sexual dysfunctions were thought of as "problems of living" that might require sex therapy, which consisted predominantly of psychoeducation and counseling. Currently, they are increasingly seen as medical disorders, thus requiring medications. In fact, pharmacological treatment of sexual dysfunctions has become "big business," and sexual pharmacology is now an academic specialty area of research and knowledge (Ashton, 2007; Crenshaw & Goldberg, 1996; Segraves & Balon, 2003). In this chapter, we ask the question of whether sexuality has been overly "medicalized," and we advocate a systemic perspective.

The range of sexual problems usually includes the following:

1. *Sexual dysfunctions,* that is, problems of desire, arousal, orgasm, and painful sex
2. *Gender dysphorias,* such as transsexualism and transvestism
3. *Compulsive sexual behaviors,* such as paraphilias and nonparaphilic sexual addictions

This chapter focuses on the pharmacology of sexual dysfunctions. Indeed, with the exception of possible hormone treatments, there are no specific, well-tested medications for gender dysphorias and paraphilias. As for sexual addictions, the only commonly used drugs are selective serotonin reuptake inhibitors (SSRIs) like Prozac (Eli Lilly and Company, Indianapolis, Indiana). Indeed, these can be useful in high doses, often by reducing the truly compulsive component of the sexual behavior (Stein, Black, Shapira, & Spitzer, 2001).

Chemicals That Affect Sexual Function

Many *environmental toxins* such as mercury, lead, and organic solvents have been implicated in reproductive problems, including decreased libido and impaired fertility. In recent years particular attention has been paid to a group of ubiquitous environmental contaminants that have the potential, even at a low dose, to alter the normal functioning of the endocrine system in wildlife and humans by disrupting the production of androgens and estrogens or by directly affecting the receptors (Andersson, Grigor, Meyts, Leffers, & Skakkebaek, 2001; Brosens & Parker, 2003; Snyder, Westerhoff, Yoon, & Sedlak, 2003). The chemicals belonging to this group are called *environmental endocrine disruptors.* They include the well-known *dioxins* and are found in many products, from dairy foods to pesticides and plastics. Concerns have been raised about their possible role in breast and ovarian cancers, in birth defects, in early onset of puberty, in declining sperm counts in men, and in many other syndromes, including sexual dysfunctions (Naz, 1999). In animals they can even interfere with mating behavior across subsequent generations (Crews et al., 2007). Though the detrimental effects of these endocrine disruptors have been clearly demonstrated in wildlife, the evidence that relatively low-level exposure causes reproductive problems in humans remains somewhat tentative (Van den Berg et al., 2006). Clinicians may want to stay alert to further developments in this area.

On the other hand, when it comes to medications and recreational drugs there is not much doubt about their capacity to disrupt sexual functioning. Consider the number of people who take one or more prescribed medications on a daily basis (Raoli & Schapper, 2006), and then add the number of people who regularly abuse alcohol, nicotine, marijuana, sedatives, stimulants, or opiates. The total represents a sizeable section of the population who are exposed to chemicals, many of which are capable of impairing sexuality. A modern sex therapist should therefore always obtain a complete list of all the drugs the patient is taking, including prescribed medications, herbal medicines, "neutriceuticals," and alcohol and other recreational drugs.

Drugs of Abuse

People who regularly abuse drugs of any kind are at markedly increased risk of developing sexual problems. Several authors have reviewed the evidence for this association (Johnson, Phelps, & Cottler, 2004; Peugh & Belenko, 2001; Ravaglia, Marchioni, Costa, Maurelli, & Moglia, 2004; Segraves & Balon, 2003).* These studies confirm that alcohol intoxication increases subjective arousal while inhibiting physiological arousal. Chronic alcohol abuse may cause erectile dysfunction (ED). Cigarette smoking has been convincingly related to ED. Chronic marijuana use tends to depress sexual desire. Sedatives such as benzodiazepines inhibit sexual functioning. Stimulants like amphetamines or cocaine can at first enhance desire and arousal, but chronic use often leads to low libido and impotence. Opiates such as heroin, codeine, methadone, and oxycodone can all cause diminished libido, arousal problems (with erectile failure in men), and lack of ejaculation and orgasm. It should also be noted that most drugs, particularly alcohol, facilitate sexual risk taking and violence (Bancroft, 2000).

Consequently, a patient's sex history needs to always be complemented with a substance use history and vice versa. Understanding the link between sexual functioning and drug use can motivate the patient to pursue abstinence (Miller & Rollnick, 2002), and drug abstinence is, indeed, the most effective first-line treatment for desire, arousal, and orgasm problems in chemically dependent patients. Table 14.1 summarizes the incidence of sexual dysfunction for the most commonly used recreational drugs.

---

* Most studies were conducted on male subjects and there is a lack of data on females. We have generalized the data to the whole population, which is a logical extension rather than being data based.

TABLE 14.1   Sexual Side Effects of Recreational Drugs

Drug Name	Sexual Adverse Effects (Peugh, 2001)
Alcohol	Decreased libido, erectile dysfunction; ejaculation difficulties, orgasm difficulties, decreased lubrication, painful intercourse
Nicotine	Erectile dysfunction
Cocaine	Decreased or increased libido, erectile dysfunction, ejaculation difficulties
Amphetamines	Increased libido, orgasm difficulties, erectile dysfunction, ejaculation difficulties
Phencyclidine (PCP)	Decreased libido
Opiates	Increased or decreased libido, erectile dysfunction, ejaculation difficulties, orgasm difficulties
Marijuana	Increased libido, but conflicting information
Methylenedioxymethamphetamine (MDMA, or Ecstasy)	Erectile dysfunction, orgasm difficulties
Volatile nitrates	Erectile dysfunction, prolonged orgasm

Prescription Drugs

Drugs of abuse are not the only culprits. Many prescribed medications disturb sexual response. The following may give an idea of the extent of the problem: A search through a reputed clinical pharmacology database (Gold Standard Inc. [n.d.], 2007) produced 736 medications that were specifically listed as decreasing libido, 651 that cause erectile dysfunction, 211 with reported anejaculation, and an additional 57 with orgasm dysfunction.

Psychiatric medications are particularly notorious in this respect: Almost all of them—with a few notable exceptions—affect sexual function (Ashton, 2007; Gitlin, 1994; Stimmel & Guttierez, 2006). Indeed, diminished desire, arousal, and orgasm problems are known side effects of the most commonly used antidepressants, sedatives, antipsychotics, and mood stabilizers. The issue is compounded by the fact that psychiatric medications are among the most prescribed and the most widely used pharmaceuticals. Table 14.2 summarizes the incidence of sexual dysfunction for psychiatric medications.

Consider the newer antidepressants. Primary care physicians and psychiatrists routinely prescribe these medications to treat not only depressive and anxiety syndromes but also other conditions such as fibromyalgia,

TABLE 14.2 Sexual Side Effects of Psychiatric Medications

Drug Name	Sexual Adverse Effects
Antipsychotics (Typical)	
Chlorpromazine (Thorazine; GlaxoSmithKline, Philadelphia, Pennsylvania)	Decreased libido, erectile dysfunction, ejaculation difficulties, priapism (Heel, Broqden, Speight, & Avery, 1979)
Fluphenazine (Prolixin; Bristol-Myers Squibb, New York)	Sexual dysfunction, (Kelly, 2005)
Thioridazine (Mellaril; Novartis Pharmaceuticals, East Hanover, New Jersey)	Erectile dysfunction, ejaculation difficulties, orgasm difficulties, priapism (Blair & Simpson, 1966; Kotin, Wilbert, Verburg, & Soldinger, 1976)
Haloperidol (Haldol; Ortho-McNeil Pharmaceutical, Raritan, New Jersey)	Erectile dysfunction, painful ejaculation (Mitchell & Popkin, 1982)
Pimozide (Orap; Gate Pharmaceuticals, North Wales, Pennsylvania)	Decreased libido, erectile and ejaculation difficulties (Ananth, 1982)
Antipsychotics (Atypical)	
Clozapine (Clozaril; Novartis Pharmaceuticals, East Hanover, New Jersey)	Priapism, diminished sexual desire, sexual dysfunction (Cutler, 2003; Ziegler & Behar, 1992)
Ziprasidone (Geodon; Pfizer, New York)	Anorgasmia (Carey, 2006)
Risperidone (Risperdal; Janssen Pharmaceutica, Titusville, New Jersey)	Orgasmic dysfunction, priapism, vaginal dryness (Carey, 2006, p. 12)
Olanzapine (Zyprexa; Eli Lilly and Company, Indianapolis, Indiana)	Decreased libido, priapism (Cutler, 2003)
Quetiapine (Seroquel; AstraZeneca Pharmaceuticals, Westborough, Massachusetts)	Decreased libido, priapism (Cutler, 2003)
Antidepressants (SSRIs)	
Citalopram (Celexa; Forest Pharmaceuticals, New York)	Decreased libido, orgasm difficulties, ejaculation difficulties, erectile dysfunction, vaginal dryness, priapism (Carey, 2006; Dent, Brown, & Murney, 2002; Montejo, 2001)
Escitalopram (Lexapro; Forest Pharmaceuticals, New York)	Decreased libido, delayed orgasm (Carey, 2006)
Paroxetine HCL (Paxil; GlaxoSmithKline, Philadelphia, Pennsylvania)	Decreased libido, orgasm difficulties, ejaculation difficulties, erectile dysfunction, vaginal dryness (Carey, 2006)
Fluoxetine (Prozac; Eli Lilly and Company, Indianapolis, Indiana)	Decreased libido, orgasm difficulties, ejaculation difficulties, erectile dysfunction, vaginal dryness (Carey, 2006)

Drug Name	Sexual Adverse Effects
Sertraline (Zoloft; Pfizer, New York)	Decreased libido, orgasm difficulties, ejaculation difficulties, erectile dysfunction, vaginal dryness (Carey, 2006)
Fluvoxamine maleate (Luvox; Solvay Pharmaceuticals, Marietta, Georgia)	Decreased libido, orgasm difficulties, ejaculation difficulties, erectile dysfunction, vaginal dryness (Carey, 2006)

Antidepressants (MAOIs)

Isocarboxazid (Marplan; Oxford Pharmaceutical Services, Inc., Totowa, New Jersey)	Erectile dysfunction, ejaculation difficulties, lack of orgasm (Moss, 1983)
Phenelzine (Nardil; Pfizer, New York)	Erectile dysfunction, ejaculation difficulties, orgasm difficulties, priapism (Harrison et al., 1986; MMitchell & Popkin, 1983)
Tranylcypromine (Parnate; GlaxoSmithKline, Philadelphia, Pennsylvania)	Erectile dysfunction, ejaculation difficulties (Mitchell & Popkin, 1983)
Selegiline transdermal (Emsam; Bristol-Myers Squibb, New York)	Decreased libido, erectile dysfunction, ejaculation difficulties, orgasm difficulties (Somerset Pharmaceuticals, 2006)

Antidepressants (Tricyclics)

Amitriptyline (Elavil; AstraZeneca Pharmaceuticals, Westborough, Massachusetts)	Decreased libido, erectile dysfunction, ejaculation difficulties (Hekimian, Friedhoff, & Deever, 1978; Mitchell, 1983; Niniger, 1978; Petrie, 1980)
Clomipramine (Anafranil; Novartis Pharmaceuticals, East Hanover, New Jersey)	Decreased libido, impotence, ejaculation difficulties, orgasm precipitated by yawning (Hekimian, 1978; Mitchell & Popkin, 1983; Monteiro, Noshirvani, Marks, & Lelliot, 1987; Petrie, 1980)
Desipramine (Norpramin; Sanofi-Aventis, Bridgewater, New Jersey)	Decreased libido, erectile dysfunction, orgasm difficulties (Mitchell & Popkin, 1983; Petrie, 1980)
Doxepin (Sinequan; Pfizer, New York)	Decreased libido, ejaculation difficulties (Mitchell & Popkin, 1983)
Imipramine (Tofranil; Novartis Pharmaceuticals, East Hanover, New Jersey)	Decreased libido, erectile dysfunction, ejaculation difficulties, orgasm difficulties (Harrison et al., 1986; Hekimian et al., 1978; Mitchell & Popkin, 1983; Monteiro et al., 1987; Petrie, 1980)

(continued)

TABLE 14.2   Sexual Side Effects of Psychiatric Medications (continued)

Drug Name	Sexual Adverse Effects
Nortriptyline (Pamelor; Novartis Pharmaceuticals, East Hanover, New Jersey)	Decreased libido, erectile dysfunction (Mitchell & Popkin, 1983)

Antidepressants (Others)

Bupropion (Wellbutrin; GlaxoSmithKline, Philadelphia, Pennsylvania)	Possibly improved sexual function; sometimes decreased libido (Carey, 2006)
Duloxetine (Cymbalta; Eli Lilly and Company, Indianapolis, Indiana)	Decreased libido, orgasm difficulties (Carey, 2006)
Trazodone (Desyrel; Apothecon, Inc., Princeton, New Jersey)	Increased libido, ejaculation difficulties, orgasm difficulties, priapism (Pecknold & Langer, 1996)
Venlafaxine (Effexor; Wyeth, Madison, New Jersey)	Decreased libido, orgasm difficulties, ejaculation difficulties, erectile dysfunction, vaginal dryness (Carey, 2006, p. 3)
Mirtazapine (Remeron; Organon, West Orange, New Jersey)	Decreased libido, orgasm difficulties, ejaculation difficulties, erectile dysfunction, vaginal dryness (Montejo et al., 2001)

Anxiolytics (Benzodiazepines)

Alprazolam (Xanax; Pfizer, New York)	Decreased libido, erectile dysfunction, ejaculation difficulties, orgasm difficulties (Uhde, Tancer, & Shea, 1988)
Diazepam (Valium; Roche Pharmaceuticals, Nutley, New Jersey)	Decreased libido, ejaculation difficulties, orgasm difficulties, erection difficulties (Balon, Ramesh, & Pohl, 1989)
Lorazepam (Ativan; Biovail Pharmaceuticals, Inc., Bridgewater, New Jersey)	Decreased libido (Khandelwal, 1988)

Anxiolytics (Other)

Buspirone (BuSpar; Bristol-Myers Squibb, New York)	Priapism (Coates, 1990)

Mood Stabilizers

Barbiturates	Decreased libido, erectile dysfunction (Mattson et al., 1985)
Carbamazepine (Tegretol; Novartis Pharmaceuticals, East Hanover, New Jersey)	Erectile dysfunction (Mattson et al., 1985)
Phenytoin (Dilantin; Pfizer, New York)	Decreased libido, erectile dysfunction, priapism (Mattson et al., 1985)

Drug Name	Sexual Adverse Effects
Divalproex sodium (Depakote; Abbott Laboratories, Abbott Park, Illinois)	Decreased libido, orgasm difficulties (Schneck, Thomas, & Gundersen, 2002)
Lamotrigine (Lamictal; GlaxoSmithKline, Philadelphia, Pennsylvania)	Possibly improved sexual function (Husain, Carwile, Miller, & Radtke, 2000)
Topiramate (Topamax; McNeil-PPC, Inc., New Brunswick, New Jersey)	Erectile dysfunction, orgasm difficulties (Hogan, Wallin, & Baer, 1980; Sun, Lay, Broner, Silberstein, Tepper, & Newman, 2006)
Gabapentin (Neurontin; Pfizer, New York)	Ejaculation difficulties, orgasm difficulties (Labbate & Rubey, 1999)

premenstrual syndrome, and chronic pain. About half of the patients that receive these medications will experience sexual dysfunction (Clayton et al., 2002; Williams et al., 2006). We also know that a large number of patients on antidepressants fail to take them as prescribed: At six months after the initial prescription that number approaches 60% (Stein, Cantrell, Sokol, Eaddy, & Shah, 2006). One can reasonably assume that the onset of sexual dysfunction is a major factor in the decision to stop treatment.

Many of the *nonpsychiatric medications* commonly used in the treatment of chronic medical conditions also affect sexual function. Examples include antihypertensive medications, diuretics, hormones, antiepileptics, and chemotherapeutics. Table 14.3 features some commonly used nonpsychiatric medications and their sexual side effects.

When all the drugs that have been implicated in causing sexual problems are considered, an interesting fact stands out: Few of these substances inevitably cause sexual dysfunction in *all* the patients that take them. Some people seem more sensitive to sexual side effects than others, something that is usually explained by pointing to each individual's unique genetic and physiological characteristics. However, sexual function is determined by many other factors as well. In the case of a chronic disease that is being treated with medications, for instance, it should be remembered that the chronic disease itself may affect sexual function. An example would be hypertension, which can weaken the arousal response by damaging small blood vessels. Furthermore, the hypertension patient has to come to terms with having a chronic, and possibly progressive, disease. He or she has to cope with the treatment, which usually includes the instruction to lose weight and to change his or her lifestyle. Such psychological challenges and worries can interfere with sexual desire and arousal. Then there is

TABLE 14.3   Sexual Side Effects of Some Commonly Used Medications

Drug Name	Sexual Adverse Effect
Opiates	
Methadone (Dolophine; Roxane Laboratories, Inc., Columbus, Ohio)	Decreased libido, erection difficulties, orgasm difficulties, ejaculation difficulties (Brown, Balousek, Mundt, & Fleming, 2005)
Morphine (MS Contin; Purdue Pharma, Stamford, Connecticut)	Decreased libido, impotence (Ruan, 2007)
Blood-Pressure-Lowering Agents (Beta-Adrenergic Receptor Blockers)	
Propranolol (Inderal; Wyeth, Madison, New Jersey)	Decreased libido, impotence, painful ejaculation (Bathen, 1978)
Atenolol (Tenormin; AstraZeneca Pharmaceuticals, Westborough, Massachusetts)	Impotence (Heel, Broqden, Speight, & Avery, 1979)
Metoprolol (Lopressor; Novartis Pharmaceuticals, East Hanover, New Jersey)	Impotence (Novartis Pharmaceuticals Corporation, 2006)
Labetalol (Trandate; Prometheus, Inc., Newport, Rhode Island; Normodyne, Ivax Pharmaceuticals, Miami, Florida)	Decreased libido, impotence, ejaculation difficulty, priapism (Flamenbaum et al., 1985)
Timolol (Blocadren; Merck & Co., Inc., Whitehouse Station, New Jersey)	Decreased libido, impotence (McMahon, Shaffer, Hoskins, & Hetherington, 1979)
Blood-Pressure-Lowering Agents (Calcium Channel Antagonists)	
Nifedipine (Adalat; Bayer Pharmaceuticals Corporation, Pittsburgh, Pennsylvania)	Priapism (Rayner, May, & Walls, 1988)
Verapamil (Calan; Pfizer, New York)	Impotence (King, Pitchon, Stern, Schweitzer, & Schneider, 1983)
Diltiazem (Cardizem LA; Biovail Pharmaceuticals, Inc., Bridgewater, New Jersey; Tiazac; Forest Pharmaceuticals, New York)	Sexual dysfunction (Carey, 2006)
Amlodipine (Norvasc; Pfizer, New York)	Sexual dysfunction (Carey, 2006)
Blood-Pressure-Lowering Agents (Sympatholytics)	
Clonidine (Catapres; Boehringer Ingelheim, Ridgefield, Connecticut)	Decreased libido, impotence, ejaculation difficulties (Khan, Carml, & Perry, 1970; Papadopoulos, 1980; Stevenson & Umstead, 1984)
Methyldopa (Aldomet; Merck & Co., Inc., Whitehouse Station, New Jersey)	Decreased libido, impotence, ejaculation difficulties, gynecomastia (Aldrige, 1982; Bulpitt & Dollery, 1973; Hogan, Wallin, & Baer, 1980; Newman & Salerno, 1974; Stevenson & Umstead, 1984)

Drug Name	Sexual Adverse Effect
Blood-Pressure-Lowering Agents (Diuretics)	
Hydrochlorothiazide (Hydrodiuril; Merck & Co., Inc., Whitehouse Station, New Jersey)	Decreased libido, impotence, decreased vaginal lubrication (Yendt, Guay, & Carcia, 1970)
Spironolactone (Aldactone; Pfizer, New York)	Decreased libido, impotence; gynecomastia, decreased vaginal lubrication (Aldrige, 1982; Greenblatt & Koch-Weser, 1973; Stevenson & Umstead, 1984)
Blood-Pressure-Lowering Agents (Angiotensin Receptor Antagonist)	
Irbesartan (Avapro; Bristol-Myers Squibb, New York)	Decreased libido, impotence (Carey, 2006)
Other Drugs	
Digoxin (Lanoxin; GlaxoSmithKline, Philadelphia, Pennsylvania)	Decreased libido, impotence (Neri, Zukerman, Aygen, Lidor, & Kaufman, 1987)
Metoclopramide (Reglan; Baxter, Deerfield, Illinois)	Impotence, decreased libido (Bathen, 1978; Berlin, 1986)

the spouse's perception of both the illness and the sick patient, which can affect his or her responsiveness. We also know that the quality of the partner relationship itself plays a major role in sexual health (Byers, 2005). As for psychiatric illnesses, consider, for instance, the most widely used antidepressants—selective serotonin reuptake inhibitors (SSRIs). They are notorious for causing sexual dysfunction, but it is also necessary to keep in mind that depression itself impairs sexual functioning (Balon, 2006). Furthermore, coming to terms with depression and dealing with its causes and its meaning is stressful, and, even more importantly, depression almost always "infects" sufferers' intimate relationships and induces response patterns in their partner that may interfere with sexual function.

All the physiological, psychological, and relational factors interact and modify the direct pharmacological impact of the medications. As a result, the same drug may produce severe sexual problems in some patients while seemingly having little effect on others.

Medications That Facilitate Sexual Function

Sexual desire arises spontaneously; it largely escapes direct volitional control (Levine, 2003). In other words, just *wanting* to desire someone does not change whether that person turns you on. And trying to force someone else to feel desire usually has the opposite effect. Similarly, arousal and orgasm are spontaneous *responses* and are quite impervious to intentions and wishes, effort, and willpower. The zealous pursuit of an erection or an orgasm actually distracts from the sexual experience itself and can lead to dysfunction (Masters & Johnson, 1970). In other words, the more a person attempts to control desire and sexual response, the more he or she risks falling short of expectations. It should come as no surprise then that sexual behavior often engenders a sense of powerlessness and a fear of failure. Consequently, the interest in products that promise sexual control is high.

Since ancient times there has been a search for aphrodisiacs (i.e., "love potions") that instill desire, improve erections, enable "endurance," or facilitate multiple orgasms. Fabled aphrodisiacs include "Spanish fly" (a beetle extract that causes genital irritation), bull testicles, mandrake and ginseng roots, and certain foods such as oysters. The "herbal Viagra," peddled in a stream of email spam, is a well-known traditional aphrodisiac derived from the bark of a West African tree (*Corynanthe yohimbe*). It contains yohimbine, which has been used with limited success to facilitate erection (Sonda, Mazo, & Chancellor, 1990).

Sometimes what is promised is the fountain of youth (i.e., control over the processes of aging and decline). Dihydroepiandrosterone (DHEA)—an adrenal steroid, which is a precursor of estrogen and testosterone—for instance, is available over the counter as a supplement and is sold as the ultimate antiaging drug: a chemical that increases libido and sexual energy and that restores general health and youthful vitality. However, research has concluded that there is little evidence for its effectiveness, while concerns persist about potential long-term harm (Sreekumaran et al., 2006).

The human desire to control sexual functioning did not escape the attention of the medical-pharmaceutical industry. However, the products that were initially developed did not reach a broad market (Jiann, Yu, & Su, 2004). Penile implants, for instance, are appreciated by patients with total and irreversible erectile failure but are not an acceptable treatment for occasional ED. Vacuum devices that help to draw blood to the penis involve rather "mechanical" behavior during sex, thus interfering with the more romantic aspects of sexuality. Directly injecting prostaglandin E (Caverject; Pfizer, New York) into the penis, though quite effective and basically painless, is a treatment approach that draws more squeamish than excited reactions from men. Inserting the same chemical in the form of transurethral suppositories (Muse; Vivus, Mountain View, California) into the urethra with the help of a small device only marginally increases its acceptability.

Observing the sexual side effects of physical castration on unfortunate victims, humans have always suspected that the testes must contain a sex-promoting substance. Experiments of transplanting testicular tissue were already begun in the 18th century. When in 1935 the critical agent was isolated and given the name *testosterone*, hopes were high for an easy-to-administer product that would stimulate libido and strengthen erections (Freeman, Bloom, & McGuire, 2001; Sengoopta, 2006). When it was discovered that women produce testosterone, too—albeit in smaller amounts—there was an assumption that the hormone might also increase female libido. However, the initial enthusiasm abated as the side effects became evident: from oily skin and acne to a likely increased risk of prostate and breast cancer (Kaufman & Vermeulen, 2005; Sengoopta, 2006). As for efficacy, testosterone injections work well in men who are suffering from clinical hypogonadism due to an insufficient physiological production of testosterone. However, using the hormone to "supplement" the normally declining levels of testosterone in older men is more controversial: Studies show that low doses are ineffective, whereas high doses may carry serious long-term risks (Kaufman & Vermeulen, 2005). The effect of testosterone on libido in women is even more controversial (NAMS Board of Trustees, 2005) but is nevertheless still being explored. A recent study suggests that testosterone, administered through transdermal patches, may improve desire and satisfaction in menopausal women with hypoactive sexual desire (Shifren et al., 2006). However, the U.S. Food and Drug Administration (FDA) found the data insufficiently convincing and did not approve the indication. In summary, the attempts to control sexual functioning with therapeutic devices and hormones have been somewhat disappointing: Though effective for specific indications, they are not unambiguously helpful for the more common varieties of sexual problems.

Viagra and the Phosphodiesterase Type 5 (PDE5) Inhibitors

Everything changed with the development of sildenafil, or Viagra (Pfizer, New York), a product that was announced to be effective for ED. Its release in the United States in March 1998 was anticipated with the same excitement as the initial tour of the Beatles a few decades earlier. Indeed, for the first time in history, bona fide pharmaceutical research had developed a simple pill that could be taken "as needed" and that proved to be effective for the treatment of erectile failure, a common sexual problem. The drug could be used regardless of whether the etiology was thought to be psychological or physiological. Furthermore, Viagra's known mechanism of action through inhibition of an enzyme called PDE5 suggested a new and advanced scientific understanding of the physiology of the sexual response (Meston & Frohlich, 2000; Stahl, 2001).

Getting men to admit to erectile problems and to ask their physician for a Viagra prescription still required sophisticated marketing efforts. Politicians and athletes modeled a new way of thinking about having difficulty achieving or maintaining an erection: Men no longer needed to be ashamed of being "impotent." Instead, they now had a medical condition, ED—a condition common even among respected politicians and "macho" race-car drivers. In advertisements, celebrities testified to Viagra's effectiveness while at the same time selling the purely medical conceptualization of ED. Side effects proved to be quite manageable (e.g., headache, nasal congestion, flushing); however, the drug's incompatibility with nitrates raised concerns, and the risk for serious reactions such as vision loss and vascular incidents was shown to be quite rare but nevertheless real.

Given Viagra's broad worldwide appeal, other pharmaceutical companies set out to develop their own PDE5 inhibitor variants. Vardenafil, or Levitra (Bayer Pharmaceuticals Corporation, Pittsburgh, Pennsylvania), claimed to be better tolerated with fewer side effects, and tadalafil, or Cialis (Eli Lilly and Company, Indianapolis, Indiana) promised to be effective for at least 36 hours, thus giving the client enough time to "choose the moment." In other words, we now have several products to treat males with ED. But what about female arousal disorders? Unfortunately for the pharmaceutical company, a lack of evidence for Viagra's effectiveness in women thwarted the plan to market it in the form of a pink pill for women to complement the blue pill for men.* Furthermore, when Viagra was released for men, the drug company, fearful of stirring up a moral debate, was quick to point out that this drug targets the genitals and not the brain or mind. In other words, it facilitates the genital response to sexual desire, but the subject still has to be receptive to sexual stimuli and get into the mood for sex. It seems that this initial hesitation about affecting "the mind" has been overcome. Indeed, there are currently drugs based on testosterone or apomorphine in clinical trials that are designed to treat "low sexual desire." Given the reported prevalence of female low desire, which

---

* A recent report shows that women can be helped with PDE5 inhibitors for arousal problems and delayed orgasm, when caused by antidepressants (Nurnberg et al., 2008).

is around 30% (Lauman et al., 1999), women are the primary target population for these drugs. How the marketing effort will deal with the potential for abuse is unclear. Will it become possible for males to effectively pressure their partner to take a medication when she "has a headache?"

A downside of sexual pharmacology is that it creates the potential for drug-facilitated sexual coercion. Certain drugs are already used for flagrantly coercive sex. For instance, date rape is facilitated when the perpetrator surreptitiously slips methylenedioxymethamphetamine (MDMA, or Ecstasy), Rohypnol (Roche Pharmaceuticals, Nutley, New Jersey), or methamphetamine in his partner's alcoholic beverage (Theron, 2000). The newer sexual pharmacological products may enable a more subtle and covert coercion. For instance, a spouse, feeling totally dominated by the partner, may unconsciously use a sexual dysfunction as a way to resist him or her. Sex may be the only area in which one can say "no" by hiding behind the excuse of having an uncontrollable problem. But if a medication for that problem is available one might feel compelled to take it. And if the drug is effective in spite of the psychological resistance, the relational homeostasis is disrupted, with unpredictable consequences.

The Medicalization of Sex

In the 1970s and early 1980s, sexual dysfunctions were assumed to be primarily caused by psychological traumas and experiences that perturbed the natural cycle of desire, arousal, and release (Masters & Johnson, 1970). At the same time it was realized that the symptoms were often linked to a medical condition. Consequently, a biopsychosocial approach to evaluation and treatment was required.

Thus clinicians were instructed to carefully investigate all the determinants of the problem and, if the dysfunction seemed due to a medical condition, to refer the patient to the appropriate medical specialist. Therefore, if the condition is *primary* or *lifelong* (i.e., having existed since puberty) the possibility of an endocrine disorder with hypogonadism or of a genetic abnormality such as Klinefelter syndrome has to be ruled out. If it is *secondary* or *acquired* (i.e., having developed after a period of sexual adequacy), clinicians would further explore the history of the problem. A man with erectile difficulties could have Peyronie's disease, especially if he reports a past trauma to the penis. But the erectile problem would likely be psychogenic if it developed, say, after an incident of severe sexual humiliation. If the patient's symptoms are present during all sexual activity (*global*), the clinician should be more suspicious of the possibility of a medical etiology than if the patient's symptoms are *situational*. Thus if symptoms only appear during sex with a specific partner and not in other circumstances, it can be safely assumed that the etiology is psychological.

Traditionally, only dysfunctions due to a medical disease call for medical treatment. Thus, some men with irreversible neurological or vascular damage that prevents an erectile response benefit from penile implants, and patients with hypogonadism can receive hormone replacement. But many of the medical conditions that are linked to sexual dysfunction have no direct treatment options. An example would be disabling spinal cord injuries. In those cases sex therapists can still be helpful with psychoeducation, behavioral exercises, and relational problem solving so that sexual satisfaction can be achieved where sexual performance is limited. When biological issues such as alcohol or nicotine abuse or obesity and lack of physical exercise play a role, the therapist needs to also address these biological "lifestyle" factors in the therapy. Sex therapists have to attend to the medical-biological factors, if present, and then focus on the more common and general determinants of sexual dysfunction: problematic childhood upbringing, traumatic psychological experiences, relational and sociocultural dynamics.

The previously described traditional, biopsychosocial approach to the treatment of sexual dysfunctions persisted into the 1990s, even as the effect of chemicals in general and medications in particular became increasingly recognized (Ashton, 2007). Physicians became more familiar with the sexual side effects of psychiatric medication and realized that these same side effects can sometimes be exploited to produce a beneficial effect. For instance, because SSRI antidepressants tend to delay orgasm, one can use them to treat premature ejaculation. Or, one can attempt to use the sex-positive, dopaminergic effect of another antidepressant, Wellbutrin (bupropion, GlaxoSmithKline, Philadelphia, Pennsylvania), to counteract the sex-negative effects of other medications (Balon, 2006).

The advent of Viagra really heralded a shift from the biopsychosocial framework toward a narrower biomedical model (Loe, 2004). Sexual dysfunctions are seen increasingly as medical disorders that require mostly "corrective" pharmaceuticals and less and less as more general "problems of living" that require a counseling relationship with the patient in which all the etiological variables are explored and much of the therapy focuses on improving sexual communication. There appears to be a tendency in current medical practice to write the pertinent prescription first and to worry about the multiple causes of the dysfunction and about sexual communication later.

There are a number of reasons why the availability of Viagra would trigger such a profound shift in thinking. Male ED is not uncommon and is a source of great anxiety and concern among men, and Viagra can indeed be helpful in many clearly "organic" as well as clearly "psychogenic" cases, thus suggesting that the exploration of all probable etiological factors is but a waste of time. The notion that primary health-care providers can offer a simple prescription to, hopefully, "make the problem go away" has strong appeal in the era of managed care. Additionally, the medical perspective seems inspired by recent advances in our understanding of how the brain really works, what chemicals are involved in its various functions, and how messages are exchanged with other parts of the body, including the genitals. It is easy to imagine a future in which chemists will be able to design specifically targeted pharmaceuticals that work at the neurogenital level, regardless of other causal factors and regardless of the subjective history and meaning of the disturbance.

The shift toward a narrow medical conceptualization of sexual dysfunctions, inspired by the promise of biomedical science, is part of the broader societal trend to medicalize normal problems of living. The term *medicalization* refers to the tendency to define inherent challenges of the human condition and common problems of everyday life as subject to medical diagnosis and treatment (Conrad, 2005; Stein, Seedat, Iversen, & Wessely, 2007; Tiefer, 1996). A man no longer "has a problem achieving erections": He now has a medical condition, ED. Similarly, a person is no longer obese: A person has "metabolic syndrome." Being distressed after a trauma is *posttraumatic stress disorder,* requiring medical treatment rather than the honing of a person's coping skills; premenstrual tension is late luteal phase dysphoric disorder, and so on. Who is responsible for the trend to "pathologize" all problems of living? Clearly, both patients and health-care providers are influenced by the economic reality that only conditions listed in the *Diagnostic and Statistical Manual of Mental Disorders,* 4th ed., text revision (*DSM-IV-TR;* APA, 2000) are reimbursed by insurance companies. Yet most authors point to the pharmaceutical industry with the following hypothesis: To sell drugs the media is flooded with direct-to-consumer advertising in which everyday symptoms are labeled as illness (Hollon, 2005; Rubin, 2006; Wienke, 2006). A recent study of prescription drug advertisement on television concluded that the ads "provide limited information about the causes of a disease or who may be at risk; they show characters that have lost control over their social, emotional, or physical lives without the medication; and they minimize the value of health promotion through lifestyle changes" (Frosch, Krueger, Hornik, Cronholm, & Barg, 2007, p. 6).

Medical Disorder or Problem of Living?

The key question, of course, is whether medicalization is ultimately harmful, "neutral," or perhaps beneficial for people with problems. In the case of ED the answer, at first view, seems to be that the medical approach is beneficial. Randomized, placebo-controlled studies have shown PDE5 inhibitors to be highly effective (Berner, Kriston, & Harms, 2006). In addition to improved erectile function, men who use these drugs experience more sexual pleasure and increased sexual self-confidence. And not only the men benefit: Improvement in the male correlates positively with improvement in the female partner, and both feel better about their relationship (Dean et al., 2006; Goldstein et al., 2005; Heiman et al., 2007; Muller, Ruof, Grof-Morgenstern, Porst, & Benkert, 2001). The advertising campaigns have taken this sexual problem "out of the closet," have reduced its stigma, and have turned it into a condition men can easily admit to and seek help for.

However, some research findings suggest that the reality is more complex. Of all the men with ED only about 15% try PDE5 inhibitors (Nicolosi et al., 2006; O'Donnell, Araujo, Hatzichristou, & McKinlay, 2006), and 50% of the men who try PDE5 medications discontinue the treatment (Seftel, Mohammed, & Althof, 2004). These data raise additional questions that remain unanswered:

- What percentage of men who meet the criteria for ED nevertheless consider the condition not to be a problem, or at least not enough of a problem to warrant seeking help?
- What percentage of these men find medical help still too intimidating or shameful?
- What percentage experience the medical approach as somehow "missing the mark" and believe that they need "something different"?
- In what percentage of men is the inability to achieve an erection caused by a lack of desire, which remains untreated?
- Of the people who accepted medical treatment and then discontinued it, what percentage was disillusioned because the drug did not meet their expectations?

- In what percentage did erections become possible but related psychosocial issues possibly remained unresolved?

Clearly, the new sexual pharmacology affects not just a defined biological system but also broader psychological, interpersonal, and social systems. We return to these issues later in the chapter.

These questions also tie in to the core objection of the critics of medicalization. Regardless of the effectiveness of the medical treatment, what tends to be harmful is the formulation of the problem itself—that is, the fact that people think of it as a disease. In our culture, when we are suffering from a medical disorder we hand the problem over to a medical professional. We submit to diagnosis and treatment. And, expecting help from medical care, there is less need for us to learn to cope, to overcome, or to endure—and all this in spite of calls for patient responsibility, doctor–patient partnership, and informed consent. Consequently, seeing common problems of daily living (and their concomitant negative moods and anxieties) as medical disorders to be left to medical professionals is likely to decrease our sense of agency and autonomy.

It would therefore be naive to dismiss the concerns about medicalization as merely reflecting a turf battle between physicians and other providers or as a failure to appreciate the real contributions of the pharmaceutical industry and the effectiveness of the drugs. It is highly unlikely that the dispute is about finding some kind of objective, "real" boundary between medical disorders and nonmedical problems of living. The core issue is that the way a recognized expert labels a person's complaint has actual consequences: Labels induce patterns of thinking and behaving that can be beneficial or harmful for the patient. Failure to assess these consequences leads to poor practice. For instance, it is inappropriate to simply send a man who developed erectile problems in the context of a hostile relationship home with the diagnosis of ED and a Viagra prescription. The consequences of such a medical response are never 100% predictable, but they are most likely to range from unhelpful to confusing and harmful. It would be equally inappropriate to suggest to a man who progressively develops ED in the context of a satisfactory sexual and intimate relationship that he needs counseling for his normal problem of living. Initiating treatments without having conducted a broad and comprehensive assessment could be called unethical.

In summary, complaints, in our culture, refer either mainly to a medical disorder, which requires medications, or to a nonmedical problem of living, which requires counseling and practical advice (Verhulst et al., 2005).

The question of whether a professional "expert" should define a complaint as one or the other or as a combination of both is at the heart of the evaluation process. Ultimately, that question is a pragmatic one: Which approach, or combination of approaches, is at this point in time in the patient's best interest? Of course, there are corollary issues: Does the patient agree with the caregiver's formulation? Can he or she be persuaded to adopt the same point of view? If caregiver and help seeker espouse contradictory approaches, treatment is likely to fail.

Systemic Sexual Pharmacology

PDE5 inhibitors are unique in that they were specifically designed for the treatment of a sexual dysfunction. They are likely to be followed by many new products as the field of sexual pharmacology develops. During the almost 10 years that PDE5 inhibitors have been on the market, a number of problems have been noted—for example, they only reach a small fraction of people with ED, and there is a low adherence to treatment among those who take them. We have argued that these problems are related to the medicalization of sex. These pharmaceuticals are distributed in the context of a medical model, which tends to define sexual dysfunctions as biological disorders of the neurogenital system. However, our current experience with PDE5 inhibitors strongly suggests that sexual pharmacology can be much more effective if employed in the context of a broader, systemic model that fosters a comprehensive assessment and understanding of all relevant, interdependent systems (Perelman, 2005; Weeks & Gambescia, 2000).

Of course, no one would deny that clinicians working in this area need to have a good understanding of the *physiological* effects of medications. But one also needs to recognize how the *individual* psychology of the patient as well as of the partner modulates the use and the pharmacological impact of drugs. Even more relevant are the interactional dynamics of the *relationship*. Finally, one needs to take into account the influence of broader supraordinate systems such as the *sociocultural* and the *economic-political* environment in which we live. We will briefly review each one of these nonphysiological systems.

We have suggested that the need to control one's sexuality is a major individual motivational factor in the decision to take, and to persist in taking, a PDE5 inhibitor. The patient may feel torn between this wish for control and the fear of needing, and becoming dependent on, an "unnatural product." Or the patient may discover that the ability to perform sexually has less value in his life than he thought. Research shows that the majority of men attribute significantly greater importance to having a harmonious family and a good relationship with their wife or partner than to having a satisfying sex life (Sand, Fisher, Rosen, Heiman, & Eardley, 2008). A patient or partner may be reluctant to resume drug-facilitated sex after a long period of abstinence, especially if he experiences himself or the partner now as old or undesirable. Clearly, sex therapists need to explore the meaning of the symptom and the meaning of taking medications before initiating treatment.

Partner and relationship factors play an essential role. Research shows that relational factors affect not only whether a PDE5 inhibitor is used but also its efficacy (Heiman et al., 2007). If the decision to take PDE5 inhibitors is unilaterally made without meaningful input of the partner, or if the man uses the pill as a means to pressure his spouse for sex, one can expect the latter to make a countervailing effort to restore the power balance. The spouse's resistance to medication-facilitated sex can be open and assertive or, if she has become overly submissive and compliant, indirect and passive-aggressive. Conversely, if a man has become resentful of his spouse, he may use his dysfunction as an acceptable excuse for sexually rejecting her. Resuming sex with the help of PDE5 inhibitors may also be less acceptable if the relationship has become adjusted to sexless intimacy, or if past sexual intercourse was a standardized routine without much joy. Again, prescribing medications without involving the partner and evaluating the acceptability of the medication for the relationship will markedly reduce the efficacy of the treatment.

As for the sociocultural system, we have discussed the trend toward medicalization of sexual problems, and we affirmed the importance of negotiating a pragmatic formulation of the problem with both the patient and the partner instead of always indiscriminately following a medical disease model. We also noted the role of the economic and political system as it influences the availability of, and access to, various treatment options. Such is the case when insurance companies reimburse only for certain diagnoses or clearly favor pills over psychotherapy.

Primary Care and the Systemic Perspective

It seems clear that the initial assessment of sexual dysfunctions requires a biopsychosocial, systemic approach (Weeks & Gambescia, 2000). In principle, the task of performing such a comprehensive assessment could be assigned to any health-care provider with a basic knowledge of human sexuality. In practice, however, people who experience sexual dysfunction are most likely to first consult their primary care physician (Perelman, 2005). And indeed, the medical literature instructs primary care physicians to perform a comprehensive evaluation of sexual problems, to weigh the various biopsychosocial factors, and to design a multidimensional treatment plan, which may involve medications, counseling, advice, skills training, communication training, psychoeducation, and referrals to other specialists, including sex therapists (Perelman, 2005; Seftel et al., 2004).

However, in reality the contemporary health-care system, with its focus on productivity, limits the time a physician can spend with a patient, making such a comprehensive assessment during a primary care visit virtually impossible. Add to this the fact that physicians often lack specific training in the psychosocial aspects of sexuality and in how to approach these therapeutically; as a result, sexual problems are most likely to be quickly responded to with a prescription and therefore overly medicalized.

Dealing with complex psychosocial questions is a familiar challenge for primary care physicians. In the past, doctors gave wise advice for problems of living. However, fatherly advice from one's physician has gone out of fashion, not only because of our current aversion to paternalism and medicine's increasing focus on technology but also because the modern psychotherapeutic techniques and modalities have made old-fashioned advice much less acceptable. But physicians are still given the task of recognizing problems of living, knowing how to deal with these problems, and avoiding harmful medicalization. One solution is for the medical doctor to join forces with a mental health professional, dividing the tasks between them. An alternative solution is the one originally proposed by Michael Balint in the 1950s. He established a format of small-group discussions that were especially designed to develop the psychological skills of family practitioners, working under intense time pressure (Balint, 1964). Maybe the time is ripe for primary care physicians to form Balint-inspired sexuality interest groups?

In conclusion, clinical experience with sexual pharmacology highlights the need to integrate these new and powerful therapeutic tools in a systemic approach to evaluation and management, an approach that is in short supply at the entry point for sexual care (i.e., with the primary care physician) and that is undermined by a general trend toward medicalization. How the field of sex therapy meets these challenges will determine its future.

References

Aldrige, S. A. (1982). Drug-induced sexual dysfunction. *Clinical Pharmacy, 1*, 141.

Ananth, J. (1982). Impotence associated with pimozide. *American Journal of Psychiatry, 139*(10), 1374.

American Psychiatric Association (APA) (2000). *Diagnostic and statistical manual of mental disorders* (4th ed., text revision). Washington, DC: Author.

Andersson, A. M., Grigor, K. M., Meyts, E. R., Leffers, H., & Skakkebaek, N. E. (2001). *Hormones and endocrine disruptors in food and water.* Copenhagen: Munksgaard.

Ashton, A. K. (2007). The new sexual pharmacology: A guide for the clinician. In S. R. Leiblum (Ed.), *Principles and practice of sex therapy* (4th ed., pp. 509–541). New York: Guilford Press.

Balint, M. (1964). *The doctor, his patient and the illness* (2nd ed.). London: Pitman Medical.

Balon, R. (2006). SSRI-associated sexual dysfunction. *American Journal of Psychiatry, 163*(9), 1504–1509.

Balon, R., Ramesh, C., & Pohl, R. (1989). Sexual dysfunction associated with diazepam but not with clonazepam. *Canadian Journal of Psychiatry, 34*(9), 947–948.

Bancroft, J. (2000). Individual differences in sexual risk taking. In J. Bankroft (Ed.), *The role of theory in sex research* (pp. 177–212). Bloomington: Indiana University Press.

Bathen, J. (1978). Propranolol erective dysfunction relieved. *Annals of Internal Medicine, 88*(5), 716–717.

Berlin, R. G. (1986). Metoclopramide-induced reversible impotence. *Western Journal of Medicine, 144*(3), 359–361.

Berner, M. M., Kriston, L., & Harms, A. (2006). Efficacy of PDE-5-inhibitors for erectile dysfunction. A comparative meta-analysis of fixed-dose regimen randomized controlled trials administering International Index of Erectile Function in broad-spectrum populations. *International Journal of Impotence Research, 18*(3), 229–235.

Blair, J. H. & Simpson, G. M. (1966). Effect of antipsychotic drugs on reproductive functions. *Diseases of the Nervous System, 27*(10), 645–647.

Bradford, A. & Meston, C. M. (2007). Senior sexual health: The effects of aging on sexuality. In L. VandeCreek, F. L. Peterson, & J. W. Bley (Eds.), *Innovations in clinical practice: Focus on sexual health* (pp. 35–45). Sarasota, FL: Professional Resources Press.

Brosens, J. & Parker, M. G. (2003). Oestrogen receptor hijacked. *Nature, 423*, 487–488.

Brown, R., Balousek, S., Mundt, M., & Fleming, M. (2005). Methadone maintenance and male sexual dysfunction. *Journal of Addictive Diseases, 24*(2), 91–106.

Bulpitt, C. J. & Dollery, C. T. (1973). Side effects of hypotensive agents evaluated by a self-administered questionnaire. *British Medical Journal, 3*(5878), 485–490.

Byers, E. S. (2005). Relationship satisfaction and sexual satisfaction: A longitudinal study of individuals in long-term relationships. *Journal of Sex Research, 42*(5), 113–118.

Carey, J. C. (2006). Pharmacological effects on sexual function. *Obstetrics Gynecology Clinics of North America, 33*(4), 599–620.

Clayton, A. H., Pradko, J. F., Croft, H. A., Montano, C. B., Leadbetter, R. A., Bolden-Watson, C., et al. (2002). Prevalence of sexual dysfunction among newer antidepressants. *Journal of Clinical Psychiatry, 63*(4), 357–366.

Coates, N. E. (1990). Priapism associated with Buspar. *Southern Medical Journal, 83*(8), 983.

Conrad, P. (2005). The shifting engines of medicalization. *Journal of Health and Social Behavior, 46*, 3–14.

Crenshaw, T. L. & Goldberg, J. P. (1996). *Sexual pharmacology: Drugs that affect sexual function.* New York: Norton.

Crews, D., Gore, A. C., Hsu, T. S., Dangleben, N. L., Spinetta, M., Schallert, T., et al. (2007). Transgenerational epigenetic imprints on mate preference. *Proceedings of the National Academy of Sciences, 104*(14), 5942–5946.

Cutler, A. J. (2003). Sexual dysfunction and antipsychotic treatment. *Psychoneuroendocrinology, 28*(Suppl. 1), 69–82.

Dean, J., Hackett, G. I., Gentile, V., Pirozzi-Fanna, F., Rosen, R., Zhao, Y., et al. (2006). Psychosocial outcomes and drug attributes affecting treatment choice in men receiving sildenafil citrate and tadalafil for the treatment of erectile dysfunction: Results of a multicenter, randomized, open-label, crossover study. *Journal of Sexual Medicine, 3*, 650–661.

Dent, L. A., Brown, W. C., & Murney, J. D. (2002). Citalopram-induced priapism. *Pharmacotherapy, 22*(4), 538–541.

Flamenbaum, W., Weber, M. A., McMahon, F. G., Materson, B. J., Carr, A. A., & Poland, M. (1985). Monotherapy with labetalol compared with propranolol. Differential effects by race. *Journal of Clinical Hypertension, 1*(1), 56–69.

Freeman, E. R., Bloom, D. A., & McGuire, E. J. (2001). A brief history of testosterone. *Journal of Urology, 165*(2), 371–373.

Frosch, D. L., Krueger, P. M., Hornik, R. C., Cronholm, P. F., & Barg, F. K. (2007). Creating demand for prescription drugs: A content analysis of television direct-to-consumer advertising. *Annals of Family Medicine, 5*, 6–13.

Gitlin, M. J. (1994). Psychotropic medications and their effects on sexual function: Diagnosis, biology, and treatment approaches. *Journal of Clinical Psychiatry, 55*, 406–473.

Gold Standard, Inc. (n.d.) Clinical Pharmacology. Retrieved February 1, 2007 from: http://clinicalpharmacology.com

Goldstein, I., Fisher, W. A., Sand, M., Rosen, R., Mollen, M., Brock, G., et al. (2005). Women's sexual function improves when partners are administered vardenafil for erectile dysfunction: A prospective, randomized, double-blind, placebo-controlled trial. *Journal of Sexual Medicine, 2,* 819–832.

Grant, A. C. & Hyunjue, O. H., (2002). Gabapentin-induced anorgasmia in women. *American Journal of Psychiatry, 159*(7), 1247.

Greenblatt, D. J. & Koch-Weser, J. (1973). Gynecomastia and impotence: Complications of spironolactone therapy. *Journal of the American Medical Association, 223*(1), 82.

Greenburg, H. R. (1971). Inhibition of ejaculation by chlorpromazine. *Journal of Nervous and Mental Disease, 152*(5), 364–366.

Halvorsen, J. G. (2003). The clinical evaluation of common sexual concerns. *CNS Spectrum, 8*(3), 217–224.

Harrison, W. M., Rabkin, J. G., Ehrhardt, A. A., Stewart, J. W., McGrath, P. J., Ross, D., et al. (1986). Effects of antidepressant medication on sexual function: A controlled study. *Journal of Clinical Psychopharmacology, 6*(3), 144–149.

Heel, R. C., Broqden, R. N., Speight, T. M., & Avery, G. S. (1979). Atenolol: A review of its pharmacological properties and therapeutic efficacy in angina pectoris and hypertension. *Drugs, 17*(6), 425–460.

Heiman, J. R., Talley, D. R., Bailen, J. L., Oskin, T. A., Rosenberg, S. J., Pace, C. R. et al. (2007). Sexual function and satisfaction in heterosexual couples when men are administered sildenafil citrate (Viagra) for erectile dysfunction: A multicentre, randomized, double-blind, placebo-controlled trial. *BJOG: An International Journal of Obstetrics and Gynecology, 114*(4), 437–447.

Hekimian, L. J., Friedhoff, A. J., & Deever, E. (1978). A comparison of the onset of action and therapeutic efficacy of amoxipine and amitriptyline. *Journal of Clinical Psychiatry, 39*(7), 633–637.

Hogan, M. J., Wallin, J. D., & Baer, R. M. (1980). Antihypertensive therapy and male sexual dysfunction. *Psychosomatics, 21*(3), 234, 236–237.

Hollon, M. F. (2005). Direct to consumer advertising: A haphazard approach to health promotion. *Journal of the American Medical Association, 293,* 2030–2033.

Holtkamp, M., Weissinger, F., & Meierkord, H. (2005). Erectile dysfunction with topiramate. *Epilepsia, 46*(1), 166–167.

Husain, A. M., Carwile, S. T., Miller, P. P., & Radtke, R. A. (2000). Improved sexual function in three men taking lamotrigine for epilepsy. *Southern Medical Journal, 93*(3), 335–336.

Jiann, B. P., Yu, C. C., & Su, C. C. (2004). Impact of introduction of sildenafil on other treatment modalities for erectile dysfunction: A study of nationwide and local hospital sales. *International Journal of Impotence Research, 16*(6), 527–530.

Johnson, S. D., Phelps, D. L., & Cottler, L. B. (2004). The association of sexual dysfunction and substance use among a community epidemiological sample. *Archives of Sexual Behavior, 33*(1), 55–63.

Kaufman, J. M. & Vermeulen, A. (2005). The decline of androgen levels in elderly men and its clinical and therapeutic implications. *Endocrine Reviews, 26,* 833–876.

Kelly, D. L. & Conley, R. R. (2006). A randomized double-blind 12-week study of quetiapine, risperidone or fluphenazine on sexual functioning in people with schizophrenia. *Psychoneuroendocrinology, 31*(3), 340–346.

Khan, A., Carml, G., & Perry, H. M. (1970). Clonidine (Catapres): A new antihypertensive agent. *Current Therapeutic Research: Clinical and Experimental, 12*(1), 10–18.

Khandelwal, S. K. (1988). Complete loss of libido with short-term use of lorazepam. *American Journal of Psychiatry, 145*(10), 1313–1314.

King, B. D., Pitchon, R., Stern, E. H., Schweitzer, P., & Schneider, R. R. (1983). Impotence during therapy with verapamil. *Archives of Internal Medicine, 143*(6), 1248–1249.

Kinsey, A. C., Pomeroy, W. B., & Martin, C. E. (1948). *Sexual behavior in the human male.* Philadelphia, PA: W. B. Saunders.

Kinsey, A. C., Pomeroy, W. B., Martin, C. E., & Gebhardt, P. H. (1953). *Sexual behavior in the human female.* Philadelphia, PA: W.B. Saunders.

Kotin, J., Wilbert, D. E., Verburg, D., & Soldinger, S. M. (1976). Thioridazine and sexual dysfunction. *American Journal of Psychiatry, 133*(1), 82–85.

Labbate, L. A. & Rubey, R. N. (1999). Gabapentin-induced ejaculatory failure and anorgasmia. *American Journal of Psychiatry, 156*(6), 972.

Lauman, E. O., Paik, A., & Rosen, R. C. (1999). Sexual dysfunction in the United States: Prevalence and predictors. *Journal of the American Medical Association, 281,* 537–544.

Levine, S. B. (2003). The nature of sexual desire: A clinician's perspective. *Archives of Sexual Behavior, 32,* 279–285.

Loe, M. (2004). *The rise of Viagra: How the little blue pill changed sex in America.* New York: New York University Press.

Masters, W. J. & Johnson, V. E. (1970). *Human sexual inadequacy.* Boston, MA: Little Brown and Co.

Mattson, R. H., Cramer, J. A., Collins, J. F., Smith, D. B., Delgado-Escueta, A. V., Browne, T. R., et al. (1985). Comparison of carbamazepine, phenobarbital, phenytoin, and primidone in partial and secondarily generalized tonic-clonic seizures. *New England Journal of Medicine, 18,* 313(3), 145–151.

McMahon, C. D., Shaffer, R. N., Hoskins, H. D., & Hetherington, J. (1979). Adverse effects experienced by patients taking timolol. *American Journal of Opthamology, 88*(4), 736–739.

Meston, C. M. & Frohlich, P. F. (2000). The neurobiology of sexual function. *Archives of General Psychiatry, 57,* 1012–1030.

Miller, T. A. (2000). Diagnostic evaluation of erectile dysfunction. *American Family Physician, 61*(1), 95–104.

Miller, W. R. & Rollnick, S. (2002). *Motivational interviewing: Preparing people for change* (2nd ed.). New York: Guilford.

Mitchell, J. E. & Popkin, M. K. (1982). Antipsychotic drug therapy and sexual dysfunction in men. *American Journal of Psychiatry, 139*(5), 633–637.

Mitchell, J. E. & Popkin, M. K. (1983). Antidepressant drug therapy and sexual dysfunction in men: A review. *Journal of Clinical Psychopharmacology, 3*(2), 76–79.

Monteiro, W. O., Noshirvani, H. F., Marks, I. M., & Lelliot, P. T. (1987). Anorgasmia from clomipramine in obsessive-compulsive disorder. *The British Journal of Psychiatry: The Journal of Mental Science, 151,* 107–112.

Montejo, A. L., Llorca, G., Isquierdo J. A., & Villademoros, F. R. (2001). Incidence of sexual dysfunction associated with antidepressant agents: A prospective multicenter study of 1022 outpatients. Spanish Working Group for the Study of Psychotropic-Related Sexual Dysfunction. *Journal of Clinical Psychiatry, 62*(Suppl. 3), 10–21.

Moss, H. B. (1983). More cases of anorgasmia after MAOI treatment. *American Journal of Psychiatry, 140*(2), 226.

Muller, M. F., Ruof, J., Grof-Morgenstern, J., Porst, H., & Benkert, G. (2001). Quality of partnership in patients with erectile dysfunction after sildenafil treatment. *Pharmacopsychiatry, 34,* 91–95.

Naz, R. K. (Ed.). (1999). *Endocrine disruptors: Effects on male and female reproductive system.* Boca Raton, FL: CRC Press.

Neri, A., Zukerman, Z., Aygen, M., Lidor, Y., & Kaufman, H. (1987). The effect of long-term administration of digoxin on plasma androgens and sexual dysfunction. *Journal of Sex & Marital Therapy, 13*(1), 58–63.

Nesse, R. E., & Williams, G. C. (1996). *Why we get sick: The new science of Darwinian medicine.* New York: Vintage Books.

Newman, R. J. & Salerno, H. R. (1974). Sexual dysfunction due to methyldopa. *British Medical Journal, 12*(4, 5936), 106.

Nicolosi, A., Laumann, E. O., Glasser, D. B., Brock, G. B., King, R., & Gingell, C. (2006). Sexual activity, sexual disorders and associated help-seeking behavior among mature adults in five Anglophone countries from the Global Survey of Sexual Attitudes and Behaviors (GSSAB). *Journal of Sex & Marital Therapy, 32,* 331–342.

Niniger, J. E. (1978). Inhibition of ejaculation by amitriptyline. *American Journal of Psychiatry, 135*(6), 750–751.

North American Menopause Society (NAMS) Board of Trustees. (2005). The role of testosterone therapy in postmenopausal women: Position statement of the North American Menopause Society. *Menopause, 12,* 496-511.

Novartis Pharmaceuticals Corporation (2006, May). Lopressor (Metoprolol) Prescribing information, Suffern, NY.

Nurnberg, H. G., Hensley, P. L., Heiman, J. R., Croft, H. A., Debattista, C., & Paine, S. (2008). Sildenafil treatment of women with antidepressant associated sexual dysfunction: A randomized controlled trial. *Journal of the American Medical Association, 300*(4), 395–404.

O'Donnell, A. B., Araujo, A. B., Hatzichristou, D., & McKinlay, J. B. (2006). Phosphodiesterase-5 (PDE-5) inhibitor use in middle-aged and older men with erectile dysfunction: results from the Massachusetts Male Aging Study. *Journal of Urology, 175*(suppl.), 325.

Papadopoulos, C. (1980). Cardiovascular drugs and sexuality: A cardiologist's review. *Archives of Internal Medicine, 140*(10), 1341–1345.

Pecknold, J. C. & Langer, S. F. (1996). Priapism: trazodone versus nefazodone. *Journal of Clinical Psychiatry, 57*(11), 547–548.

Perelman, M. A. (2005). Psychosocial evaluation and combination treatment of men with erectile dysfunction. *Urologic Clinics of North America, 32*, 431–445.

Petrie, W. M. (1980). Sexual effects of antidepressants and psychomotor stimulant drugs. *Modern Problems of Pharmacopsychiatry, 15*, 77–90.

Peugh, J. & Belenko, S. (2001). Alcohol, drugs and sexual function: A review. *Journal of Psychoactive Drugs, 33*(3), 223–232.

Raoli, S. & Schapper, S. M. (2006). Medication therapy in ambulatory medical care: United States, 2003-04. *National Center for Health Statistics: Vital Health Statistics, 13*(63).

Ravaglia, S., Marchioni, E., Costa, A., Maurelli, M., & Moglia, A. (2004). Erectile dysfunction as a sentinel symptom of cardiovascular autonomic neuropathy in heavy drinkers. *Journal of the Peripheral Nervous System, 9*(4), 209–214.

Rayner, H. C., May, S., & Walls, J. (1988). Drug points: Penile erection due to Nifedipine. *British Medical Journal, 296*(6615), 136.

Rosen, R. C., Wing, R., Schneider, S., & Gendrano, N. (2005). Epidemiology of erectile dysfunction: The role of medical comorbidities and lifestyle factors. *Urological Clinics of North America, 32*, 403–417.

Rosen, R. C. (2007). Erectile dysfunction: Integration of medical and psychological approaches. In S. R. Leiblum (Ed.), *Principles and practice of sex therapy* (4th ed., pp. 277–310). New York: Guilford Press.

Ruan, X. (2007). Drug-related side effects of long-term intrathecal morphine therapy. *Pain Physician, 10*(2), 357–366.

Rubin, L. C. (2006). Advertising madness. In L. C. Rubin (Ed.), *Psychotropic drugs and popular culture* (pp. 85–110). Jefferson, NC: McFarland.

Sand, M. S., Fisher, W., Rosen, R. C., Heiman, J. R. & Eardley, I. (2008). Erectile dysfunction and constructs of masculinity and quality of life in the multinational Men's Attitudes to Life Events and Sexuality (MALES) study. *Journal of Sexual Medicine, 5*(3), 583–594.

Schneck, C. D., Thomas, M. R., & Gundersen, D. (2002). Sexual side effects associated with valproate. *Journal of Clinical Psychopharmacology, 22*(5), 532–534.

Seftel, A. D., Mohammed, M. A., & Althof, S. E. (2004). Erectile dysfunction: Etiology, evaluation, and treatment options. *Medical Clinics of North America, 88*, 387–416.

Segraves, R. T. & Balon, R. (2003). *Sexual pharmacology: Fast facts*. New York: W. W. Norton.

Sengoopta, C. (2006). *The most secret quintessence of life: Sex, glands, and hormones, 1850–1950*. Chicago: University of Chicago Press.

Shifren, J. L., Davis, S. R., Moreau, M., Waldbaum, A., Bouchard, C., DeRogatis, L., et al. (2006). Testosterone patch for the treatment of hypoactive sexual desire disorder in naturally menopausal women: Results from the INTIMATE NM1 Study. *Menopause, 13*(5), 770–779.

Snyder, S. A., Westerhoff, P., Yoon, Y., & Sedlak, D. L. (2003). Pharmaceuticals, personal care products, and endocrine disruptors in water: Implications for the water industry. *Environmental Engineering Science, 20*(5), 449–469.

Somerset Pharmaceuticals (2006, April). Emsam (selegiline transdermal system) continuous delivery for once-daily application. Prescribing information, Tampa, FL.

Sonda, L. P., Mazo, R., & Chancellor, M. B. (1990). The role of yohimbine for the treatment of erectile impotence. *Journal of Sex & Marital Therapy, 16*(1), 15–21.

Sreekumaran Nair, K., Rizza, R. A., O'Brien, P., Dhatariya, P., Short, K. R., Nehra, A., et al. (2006). DHEA in elderly women and DHEA or testosterone in elderly men. *New England Journal of Medicine, 355*(16), 1647–1659.

Stahl, S. M. (2001). The psychopharmacology of sex, part 1: Neurotransmitters and the 3 phases of the human sexual response. *Journal of Clinical Psychiatry, 62,* 80–81.

Stein, D. J., Black, D. W., Shapira, N. A., & Spitzer, R. L. (2001). Hypersexual disorder and preoccupation with Internet pornography. *American Journal of Psychiatry, 158*(10), 1590–1594.

Stein, D. J., Seedat, S., Iversen, A., & Wessely, S. (2007). Post-traumatic stress disorder: Medicine and politics. *Lancet, 369,* 139–144.

Stein, M. B., Cantrell, C. R., Sokol, M. C., Eaddy, M. T., & Shah, M. B. (2006). Antidepressant adherence and medical resource use among managed care patients with anxiety disorders. *Psychiatric Services, 57*(5), 673–680.

Stevenson, J. G. & Umstead, G. S. (1984). Sexual dysfunction due to antihypertensive agents. *Drug Intelligence & Clinical Pharmacy, 18*(2), 113–121.

Stimmel, G. L. & Guttierez, M. A. (2006). Sexual dysfunction and psychotropic medications. *CNS Spectrum, 11*(8 Suppl. 9), 24–30.

Sun, C., Lay, C., Broner, S., Silberstein, S., Tepper, S., & Newman, L. (2006). Reversible anorgasmia with topiramate therapy for headache: A report of 7 patients. *Headache, 46*(9), 1450–1453.

Theron, L. (2000). Ecstasy (MDMA), mepthamphetamine and date rape (drug-facilitated sexual assault): A consideration of the issues. *Journal of Psychoactive Drugs, 38*(1), 1–12.

Tiefer, L. (1996). The medicalization of sexuality: Conceptual, normative, and professional issues. *Annual Review of Sex Research, 7,* 252–282.

Uhde, T. W., Tancer, M. E., & Shea, C. A. (1988). Sexual dysfunction related to alprazolam treatment of social phobia. *American Journal of Psychiatry, 145*(4), 531–532.

Van den Berg, M., Birnbaum, L. S., Denison, M., De Vito, M., Farland, W., Feeley, M., et al. (2006). The 2005 World Health Organization reevaluation of human and mammalian toxic equivalency factors for dioxins and dioxin-like compounds. *Toxicology Science, 93*, 223–241.

Verhulst, J., Gardner, R., Sutton, B., Beahrs, J., Kerbeshian, J., Looney, J., et al. (Group for the Advancement of Psychiatry Research Committee). (2005). The social brain in clinical practice. *Psychiatric Annals, 35*(10), 803–811.

Weeks, G. R. & Gambescia, N. (2000). *Erectile dysfunction: Integrating couple therapy, sex therapy and medical treatment.* New York: Norton.

Wienke, C. (2006). Sex the natural way: The marketing of Cialis and Levitra. In D. Rosenfeld, & C.A. Faircloth (Eds.), *Medicalized masculinities* (pp. 45–64). Philadelphia, PA: Temple University Press.

Williams, V. S. L., Baldwin, D. S., Hogue, S. L., Fehnel, S. E., Hollis, K. A., & Edin, H. M. (2006). Estimating the prevalence and impact of antidepressant-induced sexual dysfunction in 2 European countries: A cross-sectional patient survey. *Journal of Clinical Psychiatry, 67*(2), 204–210.

Yendt, E. R., Guay, G. F., & Carcia, D. A. (1970). The use of thiazides in the prevention of renal calculi. *Canadian Medical Association Journal, 102*(6), 614–620.

Ziegler, J. & Behar, D. (1992). Clozapine-induced priapism. *American Journal of Psychiatry, 149*(2), 272–273.

15

A Systemic Approach to Sensate Focus

Gerald R. Weeks
Nancy Gambescia

Contents

Introduction

Sensate focus was introduced by Masters and Johnson (1970) and refined by Kaplan (1974). At the time, it was an innovative psychological approach to the treatment of sexual problems. We now appreciate that sexual functioning, to a large extent, is more complex and precarious than previously understood, yet this primarily behavioral method continues to be a fundamental element of most sex therapy treatments. Sexual problems are affected by the interaction of numerous biopsychosocial systems; consequently, prevailing treatments now merge physiological (medical) and psychological approaches (Lieblum, 2007). Thus, current therapies, while incorporating sensate focus techniques, are more comprehensive than originally stipulated by Masters and Johnson and Kaplan.

To face the challenges of sex therapy today, we have developed a systemic approach that is easily integrated into a biopsychosocial treatment model. We believe that sexual problems originate within the couple, become rooted within their dynamics, and are maintained by the couple's beliefs and behaviors. Accordingly, sensate focus treatment must concentrate on the couple rather than one partner (Weeks, 2005). The couple struggles with the sexual problem and works together to remedy it. The process of sex therapy, in our view, permits the couple to grasp and practice systemic techniques. We believe couples want to understand the treatment process and will be more likely to cooperate if the underlying principles are explained and make sense to them. Gradually, the partners comprehend their role in creating barriers to intimacy rather than focusing on a symptomatic partner. Over time, they learn to recognize their own sensual preferences and dislikes and to communicate in a mutual fashion about them. Ultimately, partners collaborate to build a mutually satisfying and flexible sexual relationship.

We have elected to review our application of sensate focus in one chapter rather than to repeat the general principles throughout the text. Even so, various contributors may elaborate or discuss this procedure as it relates to the particular sexual issue they are describing. The exercises presented in this chapter can be used in treating almost every type of sexual dysfunction. For more detailed or specific applications of sensate focus, the reader is directed to examine our publications that focus on erectile dysfunction (ED, Weeks & Gambescia, 2000), on hypoactive sexual desire disorder (HSDD, Weeks, 1987, 1995; Weeks & Gambescia, 2007), and on a review of assignments used to treat specific sexual dysfunctions (Gambescia & Weeks, 2006). Also, we recommend a concise and practical text by Wincze and Carey (2001).

The Role of Cognitive-Behavioral Homework

Many of our clients report that they feel powerless with respect to owning and controlling their sexual feelings. Often, they believe the misguided notion that sexual gratification is something that "happens" to them. During the process of relationship/sex therapy, such misconceptions are corrected, and the couple learns to take responsibility for their own sensual and sexual relationship. In time, they understand that pleasurable sexual intimacy is carefully created, fostered, and nurtured.

The systemic treatment of sexual dysfunctions is accomplished through a combination of techniques we described in prior texts (given in the previous section) as well as through psychoeducation, bibliotherapy, guided imagery, and cognitive restructuring (Lieblum, 2007; Wincze & Carey, 2001). Many of these procedures occur in the therapist's office—providing accurate information about sexual anatomy and physiology, correcting irrational thinking, and dispelling sexual myths. Partners learn to recognize and stop negative thoughts, to substitute positive cognitions, and to integrate various relaxation techniques that can be used in sexual situations (Lazarus, 1965; Wolpe, 1958).

The most practical use of psychotherapy, however, is to extend the learning experience beyond the therapy hour and the boundaries of the office (Gambescia & Weeks, 2006). Through sensate focus assignments, partners can practice skills they have learned in the office and can experience sensual and sexual touch within a familiar, relaxed, comfortable environment. The therapist prescribes detailed cognitive and sensual behavioral homework that incorporates sensual and eventually sexual touch. Each assignment involves small incremental steps that help to build confidence, competence, and an increased sense of efficacy in overcoming the sexual problem.

Promoting Compliance

The idea of homework may have onerous connotations to one or both partners. As they discuss their reactions to the concept, various alternative terms may emerge until there is agreement about the nature of the tasks and what they are called. Ultimately, the couple must understand that homework is not something that the therapist imposes on disinclined partners. Instead, it is a systemic process in which broad parameters are selected by the therapist, and the couple is helped to design each step with the therapist's oversight. Compliance is encouraged through this collaborative process and by providing a rationale for assignments. Clients want to know how a particular activity will help them (Weeks & Gambescia, 2000, 2002). This collaborative approach encourages couples to take ownership of their therapy and responsibility for factors that promote improvement.

Pessimism and Skepticism

Sexual dysfunctions produce stress, worry, and unhappiness for the individual and the partner (Althof, Rowland, McNulty, & Rothman, 2005; Chevret, Jaudinot, Sullivan, Marrel, & Solesse De Gendre, 2004). Couples often attempt to remedy the dilemma on their own using information they have found on the Internet or from books. By the time they present for treatment, the partners are often frustrated and pessimistic that any treatment can help them, particularly psychotherapy. They have doubts that "just talking" about the problem will produce results. It is important for the therapist to anticipate skepticism and normalize their fears. For instance, it is helpful to reframe that their feelings of hopelessness are natural given the amount of energy they have put into correcting the situation. The couple's efforts should be reinforced before proceeding to explain how sex therapy can help them to understand the genesis of the sexual problems and the ways of treating it.

Commitment

It is essential for the therapist to continually assess the level of commitment of each partner in two general areas: (1) to their relationship; and (2) to the process of therapy. One or both partners may be ambivalent, tenuous, or unequally committed. The couple will need to make their relationship a priority and to agree to work together constructively in the office and at home. As expected, commitment is a necessary condition for successful completion of the homework exercises. Devoted partners encourage each other when progress is slow, when issues become painful, and when the tendency is to give up. Ultimately, commitment is an important factor in overcoming skepticism and pessimism. This process is also helpful in preventing relapse (McCarthy, 1997, 1999).

Conversely, partners who are locked in conflict and cannot cooperate with each other will need some marital work before attempting sex therapy (Althof, 2003). This detail must be explained to the partners, particularly those who are impatient and want to proceed directly with sex therapy. The therapist must help the couple understand the systemic premise that sexual difficulties are embedded within their relationship dynamics (Weeks & Gambescia, 2000, 2002). When the couple is ready, they will work to resolve the relationship issues that would interfere with successful treatment of sexual problems. Once they are able to work together and support each other, treating the sexual problems will be more successful.

The Systemic Perspective

When Masters and Johnson (1970) and Kaplan (1974) pioneered the idea of sensate focus, they were not thinking systemically. Their therapeutic concentration was on the symptomatic partner rather than on the couple. In effect, the so-called nondysfunctional partner served as a surrogate cotherapist at home in helping the sexually dysfunctional partner. We believe that sexual problems are best understood and treated by viewing the reciprocal role of each partner within a greater context of their relationship; emotional and physical intimacy is a mutual process (Weeks, 1987, 1995). Our experience has been that sexual difficulties negatively impact intimacy patterns. By the time couples seek treatment, both partners have a sexual problem in the broadest sense, and the treatment must focus on the ailing relationship. One individual may manifest the symptoms, but the other is likely to have developed a sexual problem as well. Moreover, the chronic nature of sexual problems can produce emotional and sexual disconnection due to frustration, anger, and disappointment. A typical scenario is the partner who develops inhibited sexual desire in response to a man with recurrent ED or the couple who avoids sex altogether.

Often, in the initial phases of treatment, partners are frustrated and want to blame the other or to view them as the cause for the problem. They have little understanding that the fundamental difficulty resides within the relationship. Through the guidance of the systemically oriented therapist, partners gradually accept that the development, maintenance, and treatment of sexual dysfunctions must involve both partners. For instance, they learn that blaming is an ineffective method of conflict resolution because it misses the point, systemically speaking. Eventually, they realize the broader systemic understanding that the behavior of each mutually affects the other; problems are shared, and solutions require a joint approach rather than a one-sided focus.

Sensate Focus Exercises

Sensate focus offers a structured, gradual, and flexible approach to the treatment of sexual difficulties. Yet, when not essential to solving sexual problems, this method is useful in facilitating many aspects of the couple's emotional, intimate, and sexual relationship. The exercises are designed for the partners to focus on the sensual aspects of intimacy rather than on sexual performance (Kleinplatz, 1996). Each partner is required to concentrate on his or her own varied wants, needs, and sensual experiences. Furthermore, couples are guided to practice a series of detailed incremental exercises aimed at increasing the interpersonal awareness of each other's needs. During the process, the couple is encouraged to communicate wishes, desires, likes, and dislikes about sensual and sexual interactions. Using sensate focus exercises, the couple creates constructive mutual experiences and enjoys positive anticipation for future sensual activity.

Understanding Sensate Focus

Sensate focus exercises were originally designed with the express purpose of helping couples enjoy pleasurable sensory experiences and overcome the destructive impact of sexual anxiety. In the preliminary version of sensate focus, however, there was little elaboration about technique and other elements we believe are essential for the therapist to comprehend (Masters & Johnson, 1970). For instance, a major and often unacknowledged element is the powerful benefit in articulating what is desired or perhaps disliked in sexual intimacy. Through guidance and coaching, partners learn to communicate, often for the first time, without embarrassment (Maurice, 1999).

Another factor that the therapist must appreciate is the strong relationship between anxiety and sexual performance. Sex therapy couples obsess and worry about sexual problems. The performance anxiety that is experienced can be related to attaining a particular behavior or a particular feeling state. Further, the anticipation of a problem (anticipatory anxiety) and the self-monitoring that occurs during sexual activity interferes with pleasure and perpetuates the problem. This contagious process adds to the anxiety experienced by both partners in intimate situations. They agonize about functioning (performance anxiety), yet it is not performance anxiety alone that produces the sexual difficulty but the dysfunctional thinking associated with it (Wincze & Carey, 2001; e.g., Am I going to lose my erection? Why can't I feel desire?). Performance anxiety has a detrimental effect on most sexual functioning, including the ability to feel desire (Weeks & Gambescia, 2002). The goal of treatment, therefore, is to eliminate or to significantly reduce sexual anxiety.

The theoretical foundation of the original concept of sensate focus is systematic desensitization, a treatment designed to reduce anxiety (Wolpe, 1958, 1992). Sensate focus is a specific application of systematic desensitization in which partners are helped to overcome anxiety and negative associations to sexual intimacy (Lazarus, 1965). The couple is gradually and judiciously exposed to situations that once made them anxious; however, they learn to use relaxation techniques in such circumstances. Over time and repeated trials, partners are no longer anxious about sensual or sexual touching.

To promote desensitization, the exercises must allow the couple to experience sensual (and eventually sexual) behaviors in an anxiety-free context. Therefore, the blueprint of the exercises must carefully fit the situation. Additionally, the process must be gradual and measured. That is, each exercise must be designed so that it is a small step in the direction of a specific goal. The graduated increments must be so small that each exercise is experienced as a success, not a failure. Since the emphasis is on experiencing good sensations rather than on sexual performance, success is much more likely. Progressively, the partners learn to relax in intimate situations, and functioning and pleasure return to sexual intimacy.

Sensate focus exercises, in our opinion, are designed to interrupt the cycle of avoidance that is so destructive to relational satisfaction. This feature is often undervalued or avoided in many discussions of sensate focus. Avoidance of sex will spill over to affectional and sensual contact because physical touch is viewed as a prelude to sexual interaction. Before long, the partners evade touching, cuddling, and other forms of physical affection. Merely doing sensate focus exercises is a success because it breaks the cycle of avoidance around physical interaction.

Nine Functions of Sensate Focus

Properly implemented, the sensate focus exercises accomplish multiple purposes and objectives. These objectives must be communicated to the couple to help them become aware of what they are doing and why. The partners will appreciate knowing the principles behind each exercise as well as the richness of an assignment that appears so simplistic on the surface. As a result, the partners can anticipate that if they carry out a particular assignment, they will achieve certain experiences and goals.

The therapist and clients must keep in mind that each exercise represents a step within a continuum from simple to complex and from affectional to sensual to sexual. Each successive codesigned exercise is based on the couple's ability to start in a particular place and to move forward at a successful and comfortable pace. The nine functions of sensate focus are as follows.

1. Help Each Partner Become More Aware of His or Her Own Sensations

Couples in sex therapy become so focused on solving a particular sexual dilemma that they worry whenever they want to be intimate. Instead of experiencing pleasurable feelings, they think about negative experiences in the past. Eventually, the partners suppress and lose touch with their own sensuality and the pleasurable aspects of physical intimacy. This negative process is interrupted through the first objective of sensate focus. The individual partners are directed to focus on their own pleasurable sensual experiences. The therapist asks them straightforwardly to think about what they feel in the moment and not worry about anything else. This simple directive gives each partner the opportunity to freely explore his or her own sensual feelings without worrying about the sexual problem or what the other person might want. We have found that couples have more difficulty with this instruction than expected. They might complain that they do not want to be selfish or that the homework is overly simplistic. In actuality, they often need several tries to successfully complete portions of the assignment that involve concentrating on their own pleasure.

2. Focus on One's Own Needs for Pleasure and Worry Less about the Problem or the Partner

The second purpose of sensate focus emerges from the first. Our clients become so distracted by intrusive antisexual thoughts that they fail to enjoy sensual and sexual pleasure. These cognitions are usually about the sexual problem or the partner. The goal of much of their sexual activity is about pleasing the partner, not the self. This second function of sensate focus helps the partners to censor thoughts that distract them from their own enjoyment. We often incorporate cognitive techniques such as thought-stopping and thought substitution to promote pleasurable sensations (Beck, 1976, 1995). The couple must be helped to understand that worry and anxiety actually create distance between them and preclude mutually enjoyable sensual and sexual experiences.

3. Communicate Sensual and Sexual Needs, Wishes, and Desires

Most couples we have treated engage in very little communication about sensual or sexual matters. Typically, they are too inhibited to ask for what they actually want. Additionally, they have not developed a feeling of being physically proficient with each other. Physical interactions in the past have contributed to feelings of incompetence, awkwardness, or embarrassment with respect to articulating their emotions. To improve the overall quality and satisfaction of the couple's sexual life, they need to learn how to communicate with each other. Furthermore, verbalizing sensual needs, wishes, and desires is a prerequisite to moving to the sexual portions of the assignments. Two basic instructions are given to the couple. They are told to *notice* and *verbalize* what they like and need to keep the feelings pleasurable. Couples will require a significant amount of encouragement, praise, and patience in getting started with this stage. Through successful completion of this third objective, the partners develop an awareness of their own needs and learn that they can become masterful in providing and receiving the pleasure they seek.

Sensate focus exercises provide an ideal setting for this communication to be practiced. Exercises begin in small incremental steps; therefore, it is easier for the couple to discuss what they like during a sensual back rub than during genital stimulation. The couple should be asked how they feel about communicating with each other in this way. It is also essential to have them consider the reasons for failing to communicate needs and preferences in the past. The therapist should also have the partners discuss the kinds of overt and covert messages they received in their families of origin and the impact of such learning on present sexual beliefs. Each time an exercise is prescribed, the therapist must ask about the couple's communication. It would be a major mistake to assume the couple suddenly gains this skill after the first exercise. Competent communication is shaped and reinforced over many trials (Bandura, 1969). Sometimes the couple will experience a successful week and will subsequently forget the lessons of the prior week. Tracking this aspect of treatment requires great consistency on the part of the therapist.

4. Increase Awareness of the Partner's Sensual and Sexual Needs

Many of our clients are unable to talk to each other about sensual and sexual preferences, or they believe that such discussions are unnecessary. We have often heard the mythological notion that the partner should know what is desired without being told. A particularly dangerous variation is the linking of love with telepathic abilities; if the partner really loved the other, he or she would know what to do. This belief can only lead to anxiety, anger, disappointment, and irritation. Additionally, both partners feel chronically frustrated and helpless because each believes that the other partner does not care about him or her. In reality, important information about preferences was never communicated. This is a classic example of mind reading in the sexual realm.

Reciprocity is a key element of this fourth function of sensate focus. Each partner is encouraged to notice or ask about what is pleasurable to the other. Sensitivity to the partner is promoted, thereby enhancing the mutuality of the experience for both. The couple becomes more aware and appreciative of the positive sensual and sexual aspects of being together rather than focusing on problems. The partners must ask for what they want and explore what the other person would like. This interactional process heightens mutual sexual and sensual sensitivity in the partners.

5. Expand the Repertoire of Intimate, Sensual Behaviors

Our experience in working with hundreds of couples has shown that sexual behavior tends to become highly patterned over time. Inevitably, couples settle into a limited repertoire with little variety and experimentation. The fifth goal of sensate focus is for the couple to be experimental and creative and to try new sensual behaviors. This objective occurs "naturally" as the partners enhance their sensory awareness and develop a better understanding of their affectional, sensual, and sexual needs. The therapist might say, "Try as many things as you can think of to give yourself and your partner pleasure. Be creative. Think about what you would like. Tell your partner, and listen carefully to what your partner tells you." The impact of the exercise is to help the couple explore an extensive menu of physical pleasure. They can now spontaneously select from a wide variety of experiences that they know will be pleasurable and have permission to try opening up to new activities. The therapist must follow up in the next session by encouraging the couple to discuss the new behaviors they have attempted.

6. Learn to Appreciate Foreplay as a Goal Start
   Rather than a Means to an End

Sex therapy couples often truncate foreplay because so much of their concentration has been on solving a sexual problem. Additionally, men and women tend to approach foreplay, or non-goal-oriented sex, very differently. Generally, men fail to appreciate the role of foreplay as an end in itself rather than a prelude to intercourse. Women tend to want more touching, holding, affection, and sensuality in their lives. Unfortunately, it is all too common that men trade affection for sex and that women trade sex for some affection. During the sensate focus process, couples are prohibited from having intercourse and are instructed to work on developing their sensuality. In this way, they begin to discover the value of non-goal-oriented sex. This sixth function of sensate focus is designed to break a formulaic approach to sex, thereby freeing the couple to explore and negotiate the type of sensual pleasure they wish to share. The couple begins to appreciate foreplay, or nonsexual pleasure, as a goal in itself. It is not connected to a pressure-filled notion that any foreplay must and should lead to intercourse.

7. Create Positive Relational Experiences

Unlike past encounters that have been negative in terms of effect or outcome, sensate focus exercises are experienced positively particularly if they are well designed, well timed, and well sequenced. The therapist wants to help the couple generate as many positive physical and communicative interactions as possible. Gottman (1994) empirically showed that the happiest or most satisfied couples are those who experience quantitatively the most positive interactions. The positive relational outcome constitutes the seventh goal of the sensate focus exercises. Affirming interactions create positive anticipation, promote a good feeling about the relationship, and help the couple to believe that they are moving in the right direction, in general.

8. Build Sexual Desire

Typically, sex therapy clients present for treatment after their sensual and sexual relationship has deteriorated significantly. Often they report diminished sexual desire and a global avoidance of physical interactions. The therapist must inquire about the level of desire at the beginning and throughout the duration of treatment. Through sensate focus, performance anxiety is gradually removed from sensual touch. The couple can enter a sensual experience anticipating a positive outcome because each encounter is enjoyable in itself and is not linked to a performance goal. This eighth objective involves enjoying the positive rewards of sensate focus, specifically, increases in sexual desire and willingness to be together physically. When the couple discusses the exercise in each therapy session, each partner evaluates the other for levels of interest and enthusiasm. Frequently, the partners will interpret enthusiasm about the exercises as a measure of sexual desire.

9. Enhance the Level of Love, Caring, Commitment, Intimacy, Cooperation, and Sexual Interest in the Relationship

The last objective of sensate focus results from the couple's commitment to their relationship and to the process of therapy. They entered treatment despite significant pessimism and participated actively in the homework exercises. Throughout the duration, they prioritized their relationship.

Although they may have entered therapy thinking that just one person had a problem, they learned to appreciate how the problem has impacted their relationship and how their relationship may have contributed to the problem (Weeks & Gambescia, 2000, 2002). The therapeutic process opened up to the couple far more exploration than they had anticipated. Working together as a couple, with each partner taking responsibility for his or her part, is a powerful message for them regarding the strength of their relationship. Couples will begin to discern this positive message as the therapy proceeds.

On the other hand, if one partner is reluctant to or refuses to engage in the exercises, it could indicate a lack of interest in the other. This fact is especially true when one partner gets ahead of the other or when one is stuck or resistant. The therapist must help the couple to see explicitly that disinterest in the process might reflect a lack of commitment to the relationship. If treatment is going well, the therapist must praise the couple for working hard but especially for their commitment to each other. Couples enjoy hearing good news, and they like to be praised for their commitment and hard work.

The therapist should help the couple to understand the most salient functions of sensate focus for their situation and at different times as they progress. Through discussions about the utility of such homework, the couple learns that their role is active rather than passive in creating positive intimate experiences. The next section describes the sensate focus exercises and their application.

Readiness for Sensate Focus Assignments

When using sensate focus, it is helpful to remember that it is a tool for the couple. As we all know, couples will only use tools if they are ready. Part of being prepared involves having motivation and a positive attitude about wanting to do the exercise. To determine a couple's readiness, the therapist describes what is involved in the sensate focus, noting each partner's reactions. Additionally, the therapist will want to inquire directly to determine if the couple is prepared to proceed to the systemically oriented sensate focus exercises:

- Do the two of you believe that you are ready for assignments that involve physical touch?
- Physical touch can be sensual and/or sexual. What does it mean for the two of you to be *sensual* with each other?

- What does it mean for the two of you to be *sexual* with each other?
- How are the two concepts *sensual* and *sexual* alike or different?
- In what ways do the two of you think you are sensual/sexual beings?
- What does it mean to experience sexual pleasure?
- What do the two of you like most/least about being sexual?
- What does it mean to actually communicate your sensual/sexual feelings and wants?
- Can the two of you think of any negative consequences of experiencing sensual/sexual pleasure?
- Can the two of you think of any ways that you might avoid these exercises?

If the attitude is generally positive, the therapist can proceed with the exercise. However, if one or both partners expresses hesitation, ambivalence, or negative attitudes about the exercises it is necessary to process those feelings first.

Structure and Application of Sensate Focus

A word of caution is necessary regarding the structure and application of sensate focus exercises. Some authors present a variety of predetermined formats involving sizeable progressions or steps (Kaplan, 1974; Masters & Johnson, 1970). Typically, the format describes two large stages: sensual and sexual. We find that any design that proposes large progressions and/ or predetermined exercises is ineffective at best and often detrimental. Therapists can misinterpret the staging process and can prescribe steps that are too large or that do not fit the specific situation. This is a major reason for noncompliance or premature termination of treatment.

For sensate focus to be successful, the exercises must be constructed in several graduated increments and designed according to the specific needs of the couple as they progress through treatment. Every assignment is created assiduously and is modified as necessary. All pressure and anxiety must be removed from the sensual or sexual situation to ensure a positive outcome. Desensitization to sexual anxiety is gradual and systematic; thus, treatment requires a series of many steps that are based on the successful completion of the last. The therapist needs to continually assess the type of physical interaction and communication that produce successful completion of each step.

The specific assignments are practiced at home at least three times per week. Repetition provides plentiful opportunities to gradually change behavior and to break old habits that contributed to sexual difficulties. Therapy sessions, therefore, should occur on a weekly basis to monitor and modify the assignments, and the therapist must be available for clarification between sessions if necessary (Wincze & Carey, 2001). It is important for partners to understand that sensate focus permits occasions and opportunities for them to rebuild their sensual and sexual relationship. Also, couples often need prompting to relax and enjoy the unhurried pace rather than to accelerate the process.

Couples complete only the required behavioral increment each time; thus, the burden of responsibility and resulting performance pressures are eliminated (Wincze & Carey, 2001). The therapist must be mindful that couples will sometimes go beyond the limits of the assignment. In such instances, the therapist must reinforce the principles behind the pacing and structure of the exercises and the dangers of moving too quickly.

Proscribing Intercourse

At the outset, the couple is instructed to avoid intercourse and any activity that is sexual. The rationale for this proscription must be explained to the couple. In effect, avoiding all sexual activity helps to create a nondemand atmosphere, removes performance pressure, and promotes relaxation. The couple should be reminded that repeated pleasurable encounters will eventually lead to an improved physical relationship. Most couples report a sense of relief when they discuss their feelings about not having sexual activity initially. They have grown weary of attempting performance-oriented sex only to have a problem.

Creating a Sensual Environment

A critical element of sensate focus is the practice of taking responsibility for creating a private, relaxing, physical environment that will foster sensual intimacy. We usually recommend a location that is outside of the bedroom because of the negative associations to this physical setting. Additionally, the situation must be free from interruptions. Time together in a relaxed manner is the priority. Our clients often plan, for example, pleasant music, massage oil, scented candles, controlled lighting, and comfortable temperatures. The use of recreational drugs is prohibited. Although we do not recommend alcohol, a small amount can promote relaxation, if desired.

The couple selects convenient times that are sufficient and unhurried yet not too long. Each partner will function as a giver and a receiver with each assignment. We have found that it is prudent to establish ahead of time the order of who goes first before the couple tries the exercises for the first time. Subsequently, they can alternate to preserve a balance.

Sensual Pleasuring

The first broad category phase of sensate focus commences with a series of graduated exercises involving sensual touch. The couple must be prepared and must comprehend that sensual pleasuring does not involve sexual interaction of any type. As mentioned earlier, the goal is to promote self-awareness, to help the partners reconnect with sensual feelings, and to have a series of positive interaction with each other.

We often begin by asking the couple to describe the kinds of touching that they find to be mutually enjoyable, such as cuddling or holding hands. The therapist should determine the style of contact that has been positive historically and should avoid areas that have been problematic in the past. The couple and therapist discuss pragmatic aspects such as whether clothing is to be worn, the specific activities that will be performed, and the location. Some couples virtually have not touched each other for months. Clearly, the sensual experience will need to be broken down into small comfortable units, commensurate with their tolerance for physical contact. The therapist stresses that both partners must be comfortable with the starting point and progression of each exercise and suggests various kinds of touch involving the hands, feet, scalp, and the face.

It is important to be very clear in giving the instructions for each assignment. The following statement is typical of how we might set up this exercise, regardless of the amount of contact: "Your first task will be to do a touching exercise. It is not a sexual exercise; instead the focus is on having a sensual experience." It is necessary to have the couple discuss their ideas and feelings about what constitutes sensual touch: "You will need to set aside about 20 minutes for the main part of this experience. During that 20 minutes, take turns touching each other in a sensual manner. The touch can resemble a gentle massage (of the specific body parts that were determined in session). Each of you will have about 10 minutes. Rather than touching each other at the same time, please take turns. By taking turns you will be able to focus either on what you are feeling or what the other person would like to receive from you. The goal of this exercise is not to get sexually stimulated; however, if you happen to feel aroused, just take note of it." The therapist should help the couple to discuss how they would feel if either or both became aroused. They need permission to anticipate the possibility but not to act on their arousal during the exercise.

During the initial steps or progressions of sensual pleasuring, the giver chooses the type of touch while the receiver takes in as much pleasurable sensation as possible and concentrates on what is feeling good. Then, the receiver becomes an active participant directing the giver by communicating what is enjoyable to maintain pleasurable sensations. Communicating will give the partners practice in learning how to ask first for sensual and later for sexual activities. After a few successful trials, the couple is instructed to be creative and experimental, to ask for different kinds of touch to experience various sensations. The receiver is not to worry about the giver but to focus on the self when on the receiving end. This sounds like an easy exercise to do, but we have found that couples need a lot of practice before everything begins to flow, especially the communication.

The therapist encourages positive anticipation: "It would be better if you did not just make this a cold and clinical exercise. Try to get in the mood by thinking positive thoughts, remembering past pleasant experiences together, and saying things to each other during the day to create a positive mood." Thought-stopping and thought substitution are encouraged: "Take note of any negative thoughts or feelings that occur during this exercise, but do not dwell on them. Instead, think about pleasurable aspects of sensual touching. We will discuss any negative reactions in session. If you find yourself thinking about problems you have experienced in the past, stop these thoughts immediately and focus on your own pleasure. You will succeed to the extent that you are able to give each other and yourself pleasurable sensual feelings." Typically, the couple begins each therapy session by reporting about the completed homework exercises. Each encounter should be thoroughly debriefed to move on to designing the next assignment. In general, we are interested in what the couple enjoyed best and least, if the exercises went smoothly, and if there were any problems for either partner. In contemplating the next assignment, the therapist considers the hierarchy and the importance of small steps to ensure success. With each successive assignment, the therapist discusses where he or she would like to start and makes sure each partner is comfortable with the plan. Use behaviorally objective language so the couple knows exactly what is expected. The following questions are typical of what we ask in the follow-up:

- How did the exercise go? (Start with an open-ended question to see what they thought was most significant.)
- How many times were you able to do it?
- Who initiated the exercises? How did you decide?
- Was the experience enjoyable or pleasurable? In what ways?
- What did you like most about it?
- What was it like to create a sensual environment?
- Were your ideas about a comfortable setting alike or different?
- Was there anything you did not like?
- What was it like when you were the receiver?
- What was it like being on the giving end?
- Did you let your partner know what felt good? How?
- Did you let your partner know what you wanted? In what way? If not, what prevented you?
- How did it feel to communicate your wants?
- Did you feel your partner gave you enough feedback about what he or she felt and what he or she wanted?
- Did you feel turned on during the exercise?
- Were you able to stay focused on just the sensual experiences and not think about the problem you have been experiencing?
- Did you notice that you were avoiding the exercise?
- Was it easy or difficult to find time?
- Were you able to stop the self-monitoring we talked about?
- Were you able to stop any negative thoughts that occurred to you?

The therapist may design other questions depending on the material presented or queries targeted toward the specific problem at hand. For example, a man with ED might be asked what it was like not to have to worry about getting an erection. His partner also could be given an opportunity to express her related feelings.

The sensual pleasuring exercises are broken down into small behavioral units depending on the couple's weekly report. The process could take one, two, or several weeks depending on where they started and the progress made in achieving certain goals. Sometimes the couple will need to remain on the same exercise for two or three weeks or take a step back. Setbacks are to be expected, and the couple must be helped to view these instances as opportunities for growth. It is important not to rush this process, especially when the couple is pressing ahead for more than they are able to achieve.

Sensual Pleasuring with Erotic Stimulation

When the couple is able to comfortably give each other a full-body non-genital massage, they can advance to the next series of assignments. The second general category of sensate focus exercises incorporates breast and genital stimulation, although the prohibition against intercourse is still in effect. The intent is to help the couple enjoy sexual stimulation as a goal in itself within an anxiety-free environment. Each exercise begins with non-sexual touching and gradually progresses to include prearranged touch that is sexually stimulating. The therapist must take the same precautions in formatting graduated assignments that are built on successful completion of the last. Remind the partners to focus on the pleasurable sensations and to interrupt any negative cognition that may emerge.

Over time and successful trials, the couple is encouraged to allow the sexual sensations build to whatever level is desirable. The longing and arousal that accompany genital and breast stimulation may lead to noncoital orgasm but is not necessary. In fact, this goal is never stated; prescribing a particular goal state (e.g., orgasm or erection) can increase performance anxiety. Though orgasm is permitted, if desired, men should be cautioned to orgasm only if they have an erection.

Moving through these steps may take several trials and weeks. Couples will require encouragement during the process and reminders about the reasons for gradual steps. Progress is closely monitored with a review at the beginning of each session. At the end of each session, another homework assignment is given that will promote further success, feelings of competence, and connection between partners. After several trials of sensual pleasuring with erotic stimulation, most men with ED are beginning to experience the return of their erections, and other dysfunctions are gradually dissipating.

Transitioning to Intercourse

When the couple has successfully completed several successful trials of sensate focus with erotic stimulation, they can progress to sexual intercourse, if desired. As with other stages of sensate focus, intercourse can be dissected into many steps such as degree of penetration, penetration without thrusting, or penetration without orgasm.

Nondemand intercourse, by definition, does not require any particular type of performance; thus, if intercourse is desired without orgasm, it should be acceptable. If a partner does not want to have intercourse, he or she should be free of the demand, and the value of the intimate encounter should not be diminished. Prior sensate focus exercises have taught the couple to experience sex in a variety of ways. Intercourse is just one way of having sex; it is not the ultimate goal of sex (Gambescia & Weeks, 2006).

Many couples have been conditioned to believe that coitus alone is the crucial objective of sexual expression. This sort of dysfunctional thinking can make transitioning to intercourse difficult. The therapist must anticipate that unrealistic notions about performance and sexual desire might continue even if they have been discussed previously. These ideas must be processed as they emerge. Also, the couple must comprehend that sexual desire can fluctuate, is not necessarily synchronous, and need not be present at the beginning of sexual activity (Perel, 2006; Weeks & Gambescia, 2002). Desire can emerge as the individuals relax and begin to experience pleasure from intimate touch.

If the couple decides to have intercourse, instruct them to focus on the sensations, positive thoughts, fantasies, and other techniques that have helped to make the experience pleasurable. Repeat that the partners should not worry about what they feel. Rather, they can enjoy the fact that they are doing something that brings them closer and builds positive experiences (Gambescia & Weeks, 2006).

Conclusion

Sensate focus is recognized as a practical treatment for many sexual difficulties (Maurice, 1999); however, information regarding appropriate implementation of the exercises is often omitted from the description of the exercises. Frequently, therapists make the erroneous assumption that the technique is simple and therefore that they should know how to use it. In clinical supervision, we often hear reports that therapeutic disasters resulted from incorrect usage of sensate focus. We believe that proper application of sensate focus can make the difference between therapeutic success and failure. This simple yet powerful method can increase the sense of cohesion, love, caring, commitment, cooperation, and intimacy between partners provided it is implemented properly in a collaborative way with the couple.

We have devoted this chapter to the discussion of many aspects of sensate focus such as structuring the exercises, timing, pacing, function, selection of activities, and structure. Moreover, we have also emphasized the use of sensate focus in a systemic or balanced way. Each partner has a contribution to the development and maintenance of the sexual problem and will need to work collaboratively to resolve it. We are guided by systemic principles that recognize the need for both partners to actively participate in treatment.

Sensate focus facilitates the communication of sensual and sexual preferences and dislikes, a difficult endeavor for most sex therapy clients. This method also reduces sexual anxiety and helps couples attain a greater degree of emotional and physical closeness. We have found that both partners benefit equally from the experience. Thus, we are constantly thinking about mutual benefit. Sensate focus keeps both partners interested, motivated, and happier with the progress of therapy because they are always gaining something for themselves while seeing improvement in the sexual relationship.

References

Althof, S. (2003). Therapeutic weaving: The integration of treatment techniques. In S. B. Levine, C. B. Risen, & S. E. Althof (Eds.), *Handbook of clinical sexuality for mental health professionals* (pp. 359–376). New York: Brunner-Routledge.

Althof, S., Rowland, D., McNulty, P., & Rothman, M. (2005). Evaluation of the impact of premature ejaculation on a man's self esteem, confidence, and overall relationship. *Program and abstracts of the Sexual Medicine Society of North America: Abstract 4*, New York.

Bandura, A. (1969). *Principles of behavior modification*. New York: Holt, Rinehart & Winston.

Beck, A. T. (1976). *Cognitive therapy and the emotional disorders*. New York: International Universities Press.

Beck, J. (1995). *Cognitive therapy: Basics and beyond*. New York: Guilford.

Chevret, M., Jaudinot, E., Sullivan, K., Marrel, A., & Solesse De Gendre, A. (2004). Impact of erectile dysfunction on sexual life of female partners: Assessment with the index of sexual life questionnaire. *Journal of Sex and Marital Therapy, 30*(3), 157–172.

Gambescia, N. & Weeks, G. (2006). Sexual dysfunction. In N. Kazantzis & L. L'Abate (Eds.), *Handbook of homework assignments in psychotherapy: Research, practice, and prevention* (pp. 351–368). Norwell, MA: Kluwer Academic Publishers.

Gottman, J. (1994). *What predicts divorce: The relationship between marital processes and marital outcomes*. Hillsdale, NJ: Lawrence Erlbaum.

Kaplan, H. (1974). *The new sex therapy*. New York: Brunner/Mazel.

Kleinplatz, P. (1996). The erotic encounter. *Journal of Humanistic Psychology,* *36*(3), 108–123.

Lazarus, S. S. (1965). The treatment of a sexually inadequate man. In L. P. Ullmann & L. Drasner (Eds.), *Case studies in behavior modification* (pp. 243–260). New York: Holt, Rinehart & Winston.

Lieblum, S. R. (2007). Sex therapy today: Current issues and future perspectives. In S. R. Lieblum (Ed.), *Principles and practice of sex therapy* (4th ed., pp. 3–25). New York: Guilford Press.

Masters, W. H. & Johnson, V. (1970). *Human sexual inadequacy.* Boston: Little, Brown.

Maurice, W. (1999). *Sexual medicine in primary care.* St Louis: Mosby.

McCarthy, B. (1997). Strategies and techniques for revitalizing a nonsexual marriage. *Journal of Sex & Marital Therapy, 23,* 231–240.

McCarthy, B. W. (1999). Relapse prevention strategies and techniques for inhibited sexual desire. *Journal of Sex & Marital Therapy, 25,* 297–303.

Perel, E. (2006). *Mating in captivity: Reconciling the erotic and the domestic.* New York: HarperCollins.

Weeks, G. R. (1987). Systemic treatment of inhibited sexual desire. In G. Weeks & L. Hof (Eds.), *Integrating sex and marital therapy: A clinical guide* (pp. 183–201). New York: Brunner/Mazel.

Weeks, G. R. (1995). Inhibited sexual desire. In G. Weeks & L. Hof (Eds.), *Integrative solutions: Treating common problems in couples therapy* (pp. 215–252). New York: Brunner/Mazel.

Weeks, G. R. (2005). The emergence of a new paradigm in sex therapy: Integration. *Sexual and Relationship Therapy, 20,* 89–104.

Weeks, G. R. & Gambescia, N. (2000). *Erectile dysfunction: Integrating couple therapy, sex therapy, and medical treatment.* New York: W. W. Norton.

Weeks, G. R. & Gambescia, N. (2002). *Hypoactive sexual desire: Integrating sex and couple therapy.* New York: W. W. Norton.

Wincze, J. P. & Carey, M. P. (2001). *Sexual dysfunction: A guide for assessment and treatment* (2nd ed.) New York: Guilford Press.

Wolpe, J. (1958). *Psychotherapy by reciprocal inhibition.* Stanford, CA: Stanford University Press.

Wolpe, J. (1992). *The practice of behavior therapy* (4th ed.). Boston: Allyn & Bacon.

16

Solution-Focused Brief Therapy for the Treatment of Sexual Disorders

Terry S. Trepper
Sophia Treyger
Jennifer Yalowitz
Jeffrey J. Ford

Contents

Introduction

The history of approaches to the treatment of sexual dysfunction has, for the most part, paralleled the theoretical models in popular use at the time (cf. Wiederman, 1998). For the first half of the 20th century, sexual dysfunctions were treated with the prevailing psychoanalysis (Levine & Ross, 1977). As behavioral interventions started to appear in the mid-20th century, they began to be applied to sexual dysfunctions (e.g., Lazarus, 1963; Lazarus & Rachman, 1957; Wolpe, 1958), culminating with the major defining work by Masters and Johnson (1970). Since then, a number of other contemporary psychotherapy models and practices have been applied, including cognitive-behavioral therapies (e.g., McCabe, 2001); systemic therapies (e.g., Schnarch, 2001); medical treatments including prosthetics and medication (Leiblum & Rosen, 2001); and models integrating cognitive, behavioral, systemic, and medical (Weeks & Gambescia, 2000, 2002). Most recently, postmodern therapies, which are a paradigm shift from the problem-focused, label-dependent, and pathology-based therapies, have begun to be applied to helping clients with sexual concerns (Green & Flemons, 2007). Solution-focused therapy falls within this group.

Solution-focused brief therapy (SFBT) (De Shazer, 1985, 1988, 1991, 1994; De Shazer et al., 2007) is a strengths-based, resiliency-oriented approach to psychotherapy. SFBT reverses the traditional psychotherapy interview process by asking clients to describe a detailed resolution of the problem that brought them into therapy, thereby shifting the focus of treatment from problems to solutions. This small but iconoclastic shift has resulted in an approach that has become increasingly popular all around the world and is used as not only a therapy approach but also in education (Franklin, Biever, Moore, Clemons, & Scamardo, 2001; LaFountain & Garner, 1996; Littrell, Malia, & Underwood, 1995; Springer, Lynch, & Rubin, 2000), business systems (Berg & Cauffman, 2002), social services (Berg, 1994; Pichot & Dolan, 2003), and myriad other areas that benefit from solution building. Within the psychotherapy field, SFBT has been used to treat most problems and populations, including family therapy (e.g., Campbell, 1999; McCollum & Trepper, 2001), couples therapy (e.g., Hoyt & Berg, 1998; Murray & Murray, 2004), and treatment of sexual abuse (Dolan, 1991).

With SFBT being as popular as it is among clinicians worldwide, and with a solid and growing research base supporting its use for so many varied problems and clinical populations (see, e.g., Lambert et al., 1998), it is surprising then that only one paper on SFBT for the treatment of sexual dysfunctions and disorders appears in the literature (Ford, 2006).

The purpose of this chapter is to describe the use of SFBT as an approach to the treatment of sexual dysfunctions and disorders.* Because it is a resilience-based positive psychology approach that corresponds well to the human sexuality experience, SFBT is an ideal approach to use as the general framework for sex therapy.

Although many sexual concerns can be ameliorated with SFBT as the primary approach, other specific interventions, either behavioral or medical, can be integrated with SFBT. Working within the paradigm of solution-focused brief therapy, individual and couples dynamic, family of origin, and other important elements affecting a relationship are addressed in sex therapy via conversations directed by the couple.

---

* It is common convention for *sexual dysfunctions* to refer to the physiological response-based problems that occur along the sexual arousal cycle, such as erectile dysfunction or vaginismus, and for *sexual disorders* to refer to the myriad of other sexual problems, such as paraphilias, gender-identity disorder, and problems related to the "coming out" process. We believe SFBT is an appropriate approach for the treatment of both of these classes of sexual problems.

The Solution-Focused Brief Therapy Approach

Solution-focused brief therapy is a paradigm shift from the long-established focus in psychotherapy on problem formation and problem resolution. SFBT therapists focus instead on client strengths and resiliencies by examining clients' previous solutions and exceptions to the problem and then, through a series of interventions, encourage the client to do more of those behaviors. SFBT is future oriented and goal directed. And though SFBT is often identified with its innovative techniques, the real story of SFBT lies in the belief that clients know what is best for them and to effectively plan how to get there.

What follows is a brief description of the SFBT tenets and general and specific interventions, as applied to sexual problems (for a complete description of the theory and practice of SFBT in general, see de Shazer et al., 2007). Descriptions of how other systems (e.g., individual, dyadic, family of origin) affect couples are illuminated within this framework.

SFBT Tenets

If It Isn't Broken, Don't Fix It
This is the major tenet of SFBT. As de Shazer et al. (2007) put it, "Theories, models, and philosophies of intervention are irrelevant if the client has already solved the problem" (p. 1). Sex therapists have long recognized that many clients are doing quite well and really only require short-term support or "permission" to continue doing or feeling what they are doing (Annon, 1976). It is very common in solution-focused sex therapy for clients to rate themselves quite high on their scale (see next section) during the first session. To begin a complete sex therapy program would be inappropriate in these situations. Instead, offering compliments for the presession positive changes, support for their relationship, and encouragement for them to continue to do so well is preferable and is most likely to lead to a brief therapy experience. To begin a session, a solution-focused approach would include inquiring into what the couple would like to maintain in their sexual and general relationship. At times, the couple will collectively identify behaviors, cognitions, and beliefs that both partners agree on that enhance their sexual relationship. Many times this includes descriptions of macrosystemic variables such as family-of-origin or dyadic issues.

If Something Is Working, Do More of It

If the clients are already in the process of solving the problem, they need to be encouraged to do more of it. The SFBT therapist listens very carefully for examples of solutions to their sexual concerns that are already occurring and encourages the clients to continue doing what is working. Doing what works cuts across many dimensions, and asking couples to describe details of successful sexual encounters as well as in their general relationship not only provides the therapist with information to use for encouragement but also allows the couple to build confidence in their own abilities to solve their problems. Sexuality consists of different realms, and the therapist in inquiring about what has been working could focus on the following dimensions: part of a conversation would involve inquiring into each partner's satisfaction with sexual technique since physically applying enough physical stimulation to bring a partner to his/her sexual threshold makes it possible to achieve orgasm; psychologically, each partner would define intimacy and how it has been affecting sex; how in-laws affect sex in a positive direction could be described. For example, if a woman notices that she is able to experience an orgasm when she and her partner make love in private situations (e.g., when their young child is visiting her grandmother), the couple might be encouraged to arrange for more "grandmother retreats" for the child or to organize their home in such a way as to allow for maximum privacy.

If It's Not Working, Do Something Different

To complete the first three obvious tenets, this suggests that no matter how good it seems to be, if a "solution" is not working, it is not a solution. For example, when couples try to "solve" their sexual problems by avoiding having sex, this is usually not a useful solution. In traditional behavioral sex therapy, if clients fail to do their homework, they are usually assigned the task again. In SFBT sex therapy, however, if a couple does not complete a homework suggestion or experiment, the task is dropped and something different is offered. This not only moves the couple away from what is not working but also does so without creating self-doubt or self-deprecation on the part of the couple for "failing" a task. The therapist may also ask what the couple would like to change, seeking a description of their preferred future. At this time, the couple may mention behaviors that extend to other factors affecting their sex life, such as family-of-origin issues or making decisions together with shared meaning. Insofar as the couple is given the opportunity to identify these multisystemic issues, the therapist frames his or her questions based on the couple's preferred solutions. Whatever the couple identifies as needing change, the therapist encourages the couple to try solutions and to experience for themselves whether it will make a difference.

Small Steps Can Lead to Big Changes

SFBT is a minimalist approach where solutions are constructed through a series of small, manageable steps, assuming that once small changes are made, these will gradually lead to much bigger systemic change without major disruption. Many changes begin internally for individuals, whether it is a change in a way of thinking or a gesture toward a partner. A gesture, for example, can break a cycle affecting the couple's dynamic and creates a feedback loop. In essence, these gestures provide feedback, which can create a different dynamic. SFBT therapists listen carefully to minute yet milestone details, which may be easily overlooked in therapy, and ask for more details illuminating the change in dynamics. The descriptions often shed light on a larger story, leaving the couple to continue to create change within their relationship and around their relationship (with, e.g., family, work relationships). Often, things like the process of coming to therapy or making private time or having a "cuddle night" can lead to a sexual encounter, which will break the "avoidance cycle," which will then lead to one or both initiating sex more, and so forth. For example, the wife of a couple with whom our team worked was experiencing moderate but inconsistent vaginismus prior to therapy. As a result of first-session scaling, she noted that a small change would be for her and her husband to hold hands when they took their evening walk. She noted at the next session that when they made love that week, she felt more "relaxed" and did not have a vaginismus episode. The small change of hand-holding in some way allowed for more relaxed feelings that contributed most likely to a better sexual encounter.

The Solution Is Not Necessarily Directly Related to the Problem

SFBT spends little or almost no time focusing on the origins or nature of the problem. Whereas almost all other psychotherapy models and approaches have problem-leading-to-solution sequences, SFBT reverses this. Instead, the SFBT therapist and clients work backward to accomplish the goal by carefully and thoroughly examining the client's experiences to find times when at least a portion of the desired solution exists or could potentially exist in the future. Solutions traverse many dimensions that have little to do with the problem, which is mainly the sexual issue. The couple may speak about adjusting their schedules to provide time for intimacy or about more reliance on friends or neighbors, which helps them seek information to enhance pleasure as possible solutions.

Couples often assume incorrectly that the solution to their sex problem has to do with sex directly. For example, a partner may buy sexy underwear for his mate, but this may lead to her feeling pressure and to be more sex avoidant. At the same time, some seemingly unconnected *solutions* to low sexual desire and sex avoidance that we have seen emanating from clients include a partner helping with the dishes, arranging for a babysitter every Friday night, taking evening walks, starting an exercise program together, or taking dancing lessons. As can be seen, none of these idiosyncratic solutions would seem at face value to have anything to do with the "problem" directly. These solutions utilize the strengths of the couple as a unit because the couple is identifying and executing the solutions together.

The Language for Solution Development Is Different from What Is Needed to Describe a Problem

The language of problems is different from the language of solutions. *Problem talk* tends to be negative and past focused and often suggests permanence of a problem. *Solution talk* is usually more positive, hopeful, and future focused and suggests that problems are transient (McGee, Vento, & Bavelas, 2005; Tomori & Bavelas, 2007). For example, the diagnosis of hypoactive sexual desire disorder (HSDD) does little to help the therapist or the client to discover solutions a couple may have stumbled onto but have "forgotten." And understanding the dysfunctional relationship patterns or attachment issues of one or both partners may be interesting but will not ultimately be what leads to solutions to the problem.

No Problems Happen All the Time; Exceptions Can Always Be Utilized

This tenet follows naturally from the tenet of problem transience and suggests that people almost always display exceptions to their problems, even small ones. Most clients with any of the sexual dysfunctions or disorders do not have the problem all of the time. (There are exceptions to this, such as in the case of physiogenic erectile dysfunction.) For example, a client with premature ejaculation was able to recall a number of times when he was able to control his orgasm by slowing his thrusting or changing his positions. He agreed to an "experiment" where he did these self-discovered techniques the next times he and his partner made love.

The Future Is Both Created and Negotiable
This tenet suggests that people are not locked into their diagnoses but instead are the architects of their own destiny. To this end, the future is a hopeful place, one filled with sexual pleasure and contentment. A very important and useful tool in identifying solutions is through couples speaking of their preferred or ideal future sexually. The preferred future inevitably includes how each partner individually influences the other partner and how the couple comes together as a unit to achieve success. The couple and relationship is the point from which solutions are identified and the couple's unique dynamic itself fuels solutions.

Ongoing Interventions

A Positive, Collegial, Solution-Oriented Stance
Sex therapists typically present a fun, sex-positive, playful stance. This fits well with the SFBT general tenor of being positive, respectful, and hopeful. In addition, the SFBT sex therapist offers a collegial rather than an expert stance. Also, the SFBT sex therapist assumes that clients are motivated, successful, resilient, and full of previous positive sexual experiences that need to be learned about, nurtured, and encouraged. They believe that the client has the capacity to understand the multiple dynamics that might play into the maintenance of sexual problems. SFBT considers what other models view as "resistance" as either natural protection, a realistic desire to be cautious and go slow, or a therapist error in suggesting interventions that do not fit the clients' situation. The SFBT therapist "leads from one step behind" (Cantwell & Holmes, 1994).

Looking for Previous Solutions and Exceptions
Most clients have had what they would consider great sex at some time in their relationship or have had recent times when their specific problem did not happen or was less serious. SFBT therapists are trained to listen attentively for any small evidence or memory of a previous solution and to set up the therapeutic environment to nurture those memories. From the first session on, the SFBT therapist asks about, listens for, and encourages detailed discussion about previous solutions and exceptions to the problem. Clients come to learn to pay attention between sessions to such small changes and solutions across all areas of their experience (e.g., physiological changes, relational changes) so that they can report on those the next session.

Questions versus Directives or Interpretations

Questions are obviously an important element of communication and are an important part of all models of sex therapy. In SFBT, however, questions are the primary communication tool; as such, they are a major intervention in and of themselves. Most models of sex therapy offer directives or interpretation. The SFBT sex therapist generally uses questions to elicit previous solutions and exceptions and to encourage detailed discussion about past successes, previously great sex times, and even recent experiences that were a little better than before. Such questions can help the client to focus on changes made across several areas of their lives (e.g., individual biology, psychology, dyadic issues).

- "What were some small, positive changes you noticed since the two of you decided to come in for therapy?"
- "What were some times recently when your sex life was just the way you would like it to be?"
- "Did you know that she really liked it when you touched her that way?"
- "Would you be willing to try an experiment this week?"

Present- and Future-Focused Questions Versus Past-Oriented Focus

One of the cornerstones of SFBT is its focus on the present and future rather than the past. Questions that focus on clients' present successes and plans for future maintenance are more useful and lead to better outcomes than questions that focus on the past. Focusing on how they want their future sex life to be allows clients to maintain hope, which will in turn drive continued positive change. The therapist can ask the client to identify positive changes across many dimensions of the individual's or couple's life, including physiological and interpersonal.

Compliments

Supporting what clients are already doing successfully and acknowledging the difficulty of their problems encourages change while communicating that the therapist has been listening, understands, and cares (Berg & Dolan, 2001). SFBT sex therapists spend a good deal of time in complimenting clients about their hopes, their specific goals, and their successes. Compliments serve not only to make partners feel good about themselves but also to help their partner see their strengths and good intentions. This indirectly serves to break negative-feeling cycles, suspiciousness, and, ultimately, avoidance. The therapist can use compliments across many areas of the couple's lives. For example, the therapist can compliment the clients for better self-care strategies, which may address physiological limitations complicating the sexual picture. Sex therapists often compliment each partner individually, highlighting each partner's strengths within the relationship (as the therapist ties the compliment to the relationship dynamic) and the couple as a unit. Compliments may focus on how the couple works as a team to set up boundaries, therefore increasing intimacy and cohesiveness, or how the couple tackles financial issues, which reduces the stress on an individual partner.

Gentle Nudging to Do More of What Is Working

Once a positive framework has been created and some exceptions and previous solutions have been revealed, the SFBT therapist intervenes with gentle questioning, encouragement, and soft "nudging" to do more of what is working via some of the specific interventions that follow.

Specific Interventions

Presession Change

The purpose of this intervention is to allow the SFBT sex therapist to punctuate, explore, and get details about the positive changes that may have occurred before therapy began. This is the first topic of conversation to be about changes and solutions and exceptions rather than about problems. The therapist might say, "We have found that many couples, once they decide to come in for therapy, begin to see changes. I am wondering what changes you have noticed, even small ones, since you called for your appointment."

There are two possible answers to this question. First, the clients may say that there were no changes and that things were still bad. In this case, the therapist asks, "How can I be helpful to you today" or "What might need to happen to make this a really useful session?" or even "How have you managed to keep things from getting worse?" This would lead to a discussion that would elucidate some resiliencies, strengths, and hope. Each individual brings his or her own experiences to therapy, and an example of hope is in the mere fact that despite ambivalent or negative feelings about therapy each partner is in therapy to support one another. An example of strength is the willingness to divulge personal information in a genuine and honest way to a stranger. It is a powerful statement to the therapist and to each partner of the couple's commitment to change. It is also a powerful statement to others affecting the couple's dynamic that the couple is constructing boundaries around their relationship and privately with solidarity, thus enhancing their relationship.

Second, the clients may say that some changes have happened or that things have improved. In this case, the therapist explores those changes at length, uses them as the basis for therapy goals, and encourages more of those changes.

Solution-Oriented Goals

It is possible the presession change questions will lead to clear and specific goals, in which case the therapist can ask, "So if all of your times were like it was last Friday when you made love and it was 'great,' would that be how you would like it? Is that your goal?" Even if no changes were noted before the first session, the therapist can obtain goals the same way, by asking about how their sexual relationship once was, perhaps months or even years ago, or about a recent exception. Of course, the clients could also be asked, "How can I help you make this a great session *today*?" or "What would make this a great relationship?" or some version of this.

Goals in SFBT are usually offered in the more of the positive rather than less of the negative format. If the couple have trouble offering any more than less of the negative (e.g., "I want him to stop pressuring me to have sex") ask, "What would he (or the two of you) be doing *instead*?"

Miracle Question

One of the most common and important interventions in SFBT, the *Miracle Question* (de Shazer et al., 2007, pp. 37–60) can be helpful for clients who are having difficulty setting goals or who can articulate a desired feeling but not the concomitant behaviors (e.g., "I just want to *feel* more"). The Miracle Question can lead to a clear, specific, and scalable goal. It can also lead to clients feeling more hopeful about their future. The basic question can be asked like this:

> Suppose tonight you were to go to sleep, and during this sleep, a wonderful, deep, restful, peaceful sleep, a miracle were to happen. And this miracle is that your problem is solved, over. Now, you wake up in the morning, and you don't know this has happened, and because you were asleep you didn't know this miracle had happened. Without you saying a word, what would be the first small thing your partner would notice that was different? What would be the first small thing *you* would notice was different?

Another reason SFBT therapists ask the Miracle Question is that the very description of the miracle often leads to the emotional reaction of experiencing the miracle. For example, clients' body language usually relaxes (if previously tense) or their facial expressions lighten up or, with sexual miracles, they show signs of sexual interest. In all sexual response models, desire precedes physical sexual change. For couples who have had a long hiatus in sexual activity and intimacy, a pique in sexual interest may be all that it takes to initiate intimacy or a sexual encounter.

Scaling

Scaling is both an SFBT approach to assessment and a format for using solution-oriented language. Some SFBT therapists use scaling as the primary intervention in sessions. Part of the beauty of scaling is its deceptive simplicity, which allows all manner of clients to benefit and all types of problems to be addressed. It may be used at any time in the process but is best asked first during the first session, using some version of the following:

> On a scale of 0–10, let's say a 10 were as good as you could ever hope your sex life could be and 0 as awful as it could be. I would like to know from each of you three things: Where do you think it is *now* (pause to get answer from each); where was it at its worst (pause to get answers); and where would you be happy for it to be at the end of counseling?

Having this scale gives the therapist a great deal to work with. The therapist might say, "So you are at a 3 now, and it was a 2 at its worst. What has changed to move it up the scale a whole point?" This leads to a discussion of small changes the couple has already noticed in their sex life and/or relationship. Also, the therapist can ask, "What would it take for you to move up from a 3 to a 4?" This leads to small, observable, behavioral changes that can be "assigned" for the next week. These assignments are preferable to the therapist-initiated ones most common in behavioral sex therapy, since they emanate from the client. It also makes change feel incremental and manageable. The advantage with scaling is that the couple may use multiple scales addressing different dimensions in their lives. There are times when each individual has described a unique miracle and the couple together has described their miracle. In scaling, each partner is asked how each might move up the scale with the help of the partner or outside resources such as medication or renewed relationships with important others.

"Instead" Questions

This intervention is useful when clients offer a goal or a description of their problem that is a reduction of a negative behavior (e.g., "I want her to stop avoiding sex so much"). The therapist, using a small but significant shift in the language, asks, "What would you want for the two of you to be doing *instead*?" This may lead to an answer like, "Maybe talking more, maybe being romantic more," which could lead to the question from the therapist, "What would 'being romantic more' look like?" Now the talk has morphed into "solution talk" and a more positive view. Systemically, the instead question inevitably leads to less defensiveness between partners, because it is about the hope for the future, offered in a constructive way, rather than about a complaint about the past.

Listening for and Punctuating Solutions and Exceptions
This is a basic, ongoing intervention that fundamentally differentiates SFBT from traditional problem-focused approaches. The SFBT therapist listens continuously for small bits of information from the couple suggesting a previous solution that may have been successful but that was forgotten or for naturally occurring exceptions that have gone unnoticed. These changes might have occurred throughout several areas of the clients' experience, such as within the couple's relationship or within each person's individual psychology. These are then punctuated by the following:

1. Repeating the clients' words.
2. Being surprised, very interested—the classic "Wow!" response.
3. Having the couple give details about the previous solution or exception.

For example, a couple, in the course of describing all of the times the male partner has failed to get an erection, casually mention that when the female partner one time playfully teased him orally, he not only got an erection but also had sex with a certain vigor that he had not shown in a long time. As this was said in passing, while explaining why things were "so bad," it might have been easy for the therapist to miss this exception. Instead, the therapist responded with interest and fascination, having the clients describe it in detail and shifting the focus from that of failure to that of success.

"How" Questions
This is another basic and ongoing intervention that differentiates SFBT from traditional problem-focused therapies. The SFBT therapist tries to ask questions that ask *how* rather than *why*. The many reasons for this small but important linguistic shift are beyond the scope of this chapter (for a complete discussion of the philosophic-linguistic origins of SFBT,

see de Shazer et al., 2007, pp. 133–141). Suffice it to say that the question of *how* organizes the discussion around actions and descriptions of successes, which solidify and punctuate those successes and make them more likely to occur again. Examples of *how* questions in sex therapy might include the following:

- "How were you able to keep from coming longer last night?"
- "How were you two able to spend so much more time in making love?"
- "How did you decide to buy that sexy outfit for yourself?"

Compliments in the Clients' Own Language

Compliments, while of course common in all psychotherapies, are a particularly important intervention in and of themselves in SFBT, since they serve to maintain the stance that the clients are the experts on themselves, to support the positive and cooperative frame of the sessions, and to punctuate the small changes across many areas that clients have been making as they move up the scale. Compliments should focus on what the clients have done to maintain change and are best offered using the exact words the clients used to describe changes made, hopes, and goals. If possible, compliments should be used to remind partners of positive sexual changes, behaviors, and feelings that are occurring.

Experiments and Homework Assignments

In most models of sex and other psychotherapies, intersession assignments are given by the therapist. In SFBT, therapists often end the session by suggesting "experiments" the clients can do if they so choose. These are almost always based on something the client is already doing (an exception), thinking, or feeling that is in the direction of their goal. Sometimes, the therapist may ask the clients to come up with their own experiments. And since, unlike other approaches such as cognitive-behavioral therapy, homework is not required for change to take place, if clients do not complete an assignment it is not viewed as resistance and is not even really addressed. It is merely assumed by the therapist to be the "wrong experiment." To this end, *resistance* is not considered a relevant or useful concept.

Using SFBT with Specific Sex Therapy Interventions

We have found that SFBT is quite effective for a number of the most common sexual dysfunctions and often resolves these without other interventions. However, there are times when specific behavioral, skill-building, or medication interventions could be helpful or are necessary for the clients to reach their goals. How do SFBT sex therapists integrate SFBT with traditional sex therapy or medical interventions?

Following the first SFBT tenet, if the SFBT approach is working (i.e., the clients can articulate their goals and are moving toward their goals), no specific sex therapy interventions would usually be needed. Following the second tenet—and common sense—if the approach alone is not moving the couple toward their goals or if they are moving toward their relational goals but not their sexual goals, then it may be useful to include specific sex therapy or medication. Some of the ways that clients may be invited to think about including skill building or medication may include the following:

- "Has anyone ever talked to you about Viagra or other medications for erection problems? (This type of question also addresses the factors within the intersystems approach in that it allows for the therapist to address biological concerns with the couple, which, for some couples, may be contributing to the maintenance of the sexual problem.)
- "Some people have found doing more structured exercises to slow down their lovemaking to be helpful."
- "I have seen many couples who have found trying a few exercises, along with massage and touching, to help them with premature ejaculation. Do you think learning more about this may be helpful?"

In each of these examples, the couple is invited to think about including skill building or medication rather than the therapist assigning it. While this may seem like a small distinction, it is not insignificant and usually leads to greater compliance and cooperation in therapy (Adams & Jurich, 1991). It is important that when the assignments are given, they are offered parenthetically as a part of SFBT. We usually use the following general protocol when offering skill assignment:

- Start the session with scaling.
- Ask what is better or different, being sure to focus on individual, relational, and societal factors.
- Ask if they still are interested in trying a specific new skill.
- If yes, describe it; if not, continue with SFBT interventions.
- Describe the skill or exercise. It is often helpful to begin it with, "Couples seem to really enjoy this exercise" and then to describe it and then say, "What do you two think about it? Is it something you may want to try?"

If they say no, or hesitate, compliment them on wishing to go slowly and ask them to think about it during the week.

- If they say that they would like to do it, ask how they hope the specific assignments and sex therapy focus they are going to work on today will help them achieve their goals.
- Make the exercise an "experiment."
- When through, ask how what they have worked on will help them, for example, achieve their goals or move up the scale.
- Take a break, give compliments, and make assignments.

Case Example

Amy and Robert, a couple in their early 30s, were referred for sex therapy by her obstetrician/gynecologist for low sexual desire. Amy, a stay-at-home mother, and her husband, Robert, a laborer, had been high school sweethearts and got married in their early 20s. They now have three children, ages 6, 9, and 12. For many years since the birth of their last child, Amy has had little to no interest in sex and has become increasingly concerned that lack of desire was eroding what was once a "happy marriage." She explained that she would like the marriage to continue since other than the sexual difficulties, she and Robert have a strong partnership and friendship, albeit strained from current problems.

Amy explained that she experiences a lack of desire. She is often tired at the end of the day and is not interested in sex with Robert. In fact, she has become so distant that she rebukes any sign of affection in fear that it will turn into further demands for sex. From Robert's perspective, he feels that she has completely "shut him out." He, in turn continually questions why she is so disinterested.

Since the birth of their first child approximately 12 years ago, Amy stated that she has felt a diminished sex drive. Initially, neither partner was overly concerned and attributed the difference to an adjustment to motherhood that included intense involvement with their child and a depletion of energy. As Amy's low desire continued, Robert increased his determination to "solve the problem." Five years ago Amy was diagnosed with atrial fibrillation and began taking digoxin. Robert became convinced that the medication was causing or contributing to a lack of desire, and her physician did not rule out that possibility. Amy said she felt defeated by her "condition" and explained that she really didn't know why she wasn't interested in sex, although she did acknowledge that her medication seemed to slow her down.

Session 1

Amy and Robert were asked how the therapist might be helpful to them. Amy stated that she would like their sex life to be more like it was in the early days of their marriage. When asked what that would look like, she said they would "get back our sex life." She and Robert agreed that there are no set numbers to the amount of sex they would have, just "what works" for them. Robert's goals were to not be afraid that he will always be refused sex and to have Amy initiate sex "sometimes." Amy spoke about what she enjoys sexually. She loved to "snuggle" and be affectionate without the pressure that it will "always lead to sex." She admitted to missing this closeness and comfort but didn't like to "feel pushed." The therapist then asked about exceptions: "Was there a time when things were different?"

Robert recalled a time in the last few years when he "got so tired of pushing" that he "gave up" and made a conscious decision to wait for Amy to be the initiator. For a while nothing happened. Then one night she snuggled up to him and "spooned" him. The next night she initiated intercourse. The therapist asked, "If your sex life were like this all of the time, would that be what you would like?" Both agreed it would.

The therapist then asked each the Miracle Question. Both described, in detail, days that included intimacy. When asked to describe what that would look like, Amy said, "We'd be talking more. You know, just about 'stuff.' And he'd be listening, and I'd be listening." She also said they would make love and that she would feel close and safe enough to initiate sex. The therapist then asked her to describe in detail, for example, how she would initiate, what Robert would say and do, and what she would do. Robert's Miracle was filled with many "well, she wouldn't say" or "she wouldn't do" statements. The therapist each time asked, "What would Amy say *instead*?" and "What would Amy do *instead*?" Robert soon was able to describe a Miracle very similar to Amy's, filled with both physical and nonphysical intimacy.

The therapist asked each to scale himself or herself based on three questions. First, "On a scale from 1 to 10, if 10 were your 'Miracle' all of the time, and a 0 were the opposite, where are you *right now*?" Amy scaled this a 6 and Robert a 5. Second, "Where were you each before you decided to come in to therapy?" Amy scaled this a 3, as did Robert. The therapist expressed amazement. "How did you two move up from 3s to a 5 and a 6?" This led to a short discussion about their commitment to each other, their love, and their optimism that things will get better. Third, "And finally, where would you two be content to be at the end of counseling?" Both rated that an 8.

The therapist ended the session by complimenting Amy and Robert on their commitment to each other, their articulateness, and their hard work. They were then asked to think about what they would need to do to maintain their relatively high scaled numbers (5 and 6) or may even move up ever so slightly (e.g., to a 5.25 and 6.25) and to pay attention this week to what each did (themselves and their partner) to maintain or move the numbers up.

Session 2

Amy and Robert began the session by talking about their success. They spent every night during the previous week snuggling on the couch while watching television. As this was a change, the therapist expressed astonishment and delight at the change and asked them to describe this snuggling in great detail. After that, they scaled their intimacy level for the past week: Amy rated herself at a 7 and Robert a 6. Again, the therapist responded with enthusiasm, and asked, "How did you two go up a whole point each?" This led to discussion about how meaningful it was that each was trying, that they enjoyed the closeness, and ultimately that both loved to touch. In addition, Amy said she really appreciated Robert's "backing off" from asking for sex and instead appreciated that he seemed to "understand" her more.

Robert expressed concern that they had been through this cycle before and was concerned that by backing off and letting Amy take the lead that once the initial interest wanes, she would revert back to low or no desire. The therapist acknowledged his concern and asked what they both thought would help them maintain their "numbers." Amy said that they need to continue doing what they're currently doing so that she can continue not to feel pressured and can become more comfortable in the initiator role. The therapist asked the clients to make their own "assignment" between now and the next session, and they both thought they should continue to do what they were doing. The therapist ended the session by complimenting Amy for noticing that Robert had listened to her and Robert for being such a caring and attentive lover, one who "really listens" to his partner and tries to please her in a way that she wants.

Session 3

Amy and Robert again had what they described as a "successful week" and maintained their high numbers when scaled 7 and 6, respectively. When asked how they continued to remain so high, Amy said she thought that once the "pressure is off," she feels safer, more comfortable, and in control. Robert, when asked how he has been able to pay such good attention to Amy's needs, explained that he knows it will make the situation better for Amy and that it takes the pressure off. The therapist asked Amy how it was for her having Robert make this "shift," and she explained that it "makes me go to him more." She now felt that she could put her arm around him in bed without feeling like it would lead to sexual pressure.

The couple, when asked what a slightly higher number on the scale would be for each of them, both noted that a little more "romantic time alone" would move the numbers up. They then discussed how difficult that is with children. The therapist asked about a recent time when this had occurred, and they recalled a "date" they had taken a few months earlier. The therapist asked if they could, as an experiment, have another such "date" before the next session. They both agreed and finished the session by discussing how this could happen.

Session 4

The therapist began the session by asking them, "What was different since I last saw you?" They shared that they had indeed gone on their date. The therapist again displayed amazement that they were able to actually do it and asked for a detailed description. It turns out Amy was the one who initiated the date and planned for it. She had arranged for his parents to watch their children so they had their house to themselves. Amy spent much of the day thinking about Robert and becoming excited about the date. She also, unknown to him, secretly planned the evening's date to end with lovemaking. She even lit candles and had rose petals on the bed as a surprise for Robert when they came home from dinner. They did indeed have sex for the first time in many months. They were both very pleased with the evening, and Robert seemed particularly pleased that she had planned it and had taken the initiative.

After a long, detailed discussion of their date, the therapist asked them to scale themselves. They both scaled their Miracle at an 8. The therapist, after expressing surprise and delight with the very high scales, asked, "How have you gotten to an 8?" Amy said that coming to therapy, talking about their situation, "feeling that Robert really hears what I needed," and seeing Robert try so hard all allowed her to think about him more and in a "more sexual way." The therapist, after complimenting them for being so romantic and fun, asked what would help them to maintain the 8, to which they both responded that they would like to do this again. The therapist asked when they would like to come back, and they thought three weeks would give them enough time to have another date.

Session 5

Amy and Robert said that they were both talking more and that while spending more time together were holding hands more, cuddling, and kissing. They also had gone on two "dates," which both ended in lovemaking, and had even had sex another time spontaneously before going to bed. The therapist asked them to scale their Miracles, and both scaled it a 9. The therapist noted that they had gone beyond their goal of an 8 and asked how they did this. They said that when everything is pushed out of the picture (e.g., kids, feeling tired, not feeling well) they both greatly enjoy one another sexually. Robert also said that it seemed that for the first time in their marriage, Amy had begun to be more comfortable talking about her likes rather than just her dislikes sexually. She said that she had also been more willing to let Robert touch her more intimately and to engage in foreplay. The therapist complimented them for their willingness to open up to one another and experience so much pleasure. To the therapist's surprise, when asked what they thought they should do to maintain the 9, Robert expressed an interest in working on a project with Amy that was nonsexual: He wanted to repaint their daughter's room and wanted it to be a "team effort." Amy was also surprised but was quite willing to oblige.

The therapist asked what would be most helpful to them at this point. They suggested that they call the therapist if they felt themselves "slipping," and the therapist agreed. In follow-up phone conversations, Amy and Robert reported that they had sustained their high level of satisfaction with their intimacy, both sexual and nonsexual.

Summary and Conclusions

It should be noted that, from an SFBT point of view, this case example demonstrated a successful outcome because the couple achieved the goals they had described. Since the SFBT approach does not deal with "issues" beyond the clients' frame of reference, the couple's goals are considered both valid and clinically sufficient. In this situation, the couple not only offered a cogent goal, which was based on their combined Miracles, but also had exceptions to their problem, which could be incorporated into the therapy. In the course of the application of this approach, the couple had changed their dysfunctional avoidant behavioral pattern without ever having to have it described to them, which might have accidentally (and ironically) solidified this pattern further by causing them to focus on the meaning of the *avoidance*. This is part of the elegance of the SFBT approach: It actually leads to the result that many problem-focused models end up with (or hope to end with) but does so more briefly and with less risk.

Solution-focused brief therapy can be a useful approach for the treatment of sexual dysfunctions and is quite compatible with the interactional approaches described in this book. SFBT's positive, collegial, supportive, and resiliency-based structure offers an ideal framework from which to work with the presenting problems treated by sex therapists. The use of medication (e.g., sildenafil citrate for erectile dysfunction) or other specific behavioral skills (e.g., the squeeze technique to reduce immediate orgasm for premature ejaculation) can be offered concomitantly within an SFBT framework if the client-initiated, exception-based interventions do not result in the clients achieving their goals. Given the increased evidence for its effectiveness with many other clinical problems and populations, it is hoped that clinical research on SFBT will be expanded to empirically examine the effectiveness of SFBT for the treatment of sexual problems.

References

Adams, J. & Jurich, J. (1991). Effects of Solution Focused Therapy's "Formula First Session Task" on compliance and outcome in family therapy. *Journal of Marital & Family Therapy, 17*, 277–290.

Annon, J. (1976). The PLISSIT model: A proposed conceptual scheme for behavioral treatment of sexual problems. *Journal of Sex Education and Therapy, 2*, 1–15.

Berg, I. K. (1994). *Family based services: A solution-focused approach.* New York: Norton.

Berg, I. K. & Cauffman, L. (2002, January–February). Solution focused corporate coaching. *Lernende Organisation,* 1–5.

Berg, I. K. & Dolan, Y. (2001). *Tales of solutions: A collection of hope-inspiring stories.* New York: Norton.

Berg, I. K. & Miller, S. D. (1992). *Working with the problem drinker: A solution-focused approach.* New York: Norton.

Campbell, J. (1999). Crafting the "tap on the shoulder": A compliment template for solution-focused therapy. *American Journal of Family Therapy, 27,* 35–47.

Cantwell, P. & Holmes, S. (1994). Social construction: A paradigm shift for systemic therapy and training. *Australia and New Zealand Journal for Family Therapy, 15*(1), 17–26.

Cockburn, J. T., Thomas, F. N., & Cockburn, O. J. (1997). Solution-focused therapy and psychosocial adjustment to orthopedic rehabilitation in a work hardening program. *Journal of Occupational Rehabilitation, 7,* 97–106.

De Shazer, S. (1985). *Keys to solution in brief therapy.* New York: Norton.

De Shazer, S. (1988). *Clues: Investigating solutions in brief therapy.* New York: Norton.

De Shazer, S. (1991). *Putting difference to work.* New York: Norton.

De Shazer, S. (1994). *Words were originally magic.* New York: Norton.

De Shazer, S., Berg, I. K., Lipchik, E., Nunnally, E., Molnar, A., Gingerich, W., et al. (1986). Brief therapy: Focused solution development. *Family Process, 25,* 207–221.

De Shazer, S., Dolan, Y., Korman, H., Trepper, T. S., McCollum, E. E., & Berg, I. K. (2007). *More than miracles: The state of the art in solution focused brief therapy.* New York: Haworth Press.

De Shazer, S. & Isebaert L. (2003). The Bruges Model: a solution-focused approach to problem drinking. *Journal of Family Psychotherapy, 14,* 43–52.

Dolan, Y. (1991). *Resolving sexual abuse: Solution-focused therapy and Ericksonian hypnosis for survivors.* New York: Norton Professional Books.

Dolan, Y. (1998). *One small step: Moving beyond trauma and therapy to a life of joy.* Papier-Machier Press.

Eakes, G., Walsh, S., Markowski, M., Cain, H., & Swanson, M. (1997). Family-centered brief solution-focused therapy with chronic schizophrenia: A pilot study. *Journal of Family Therapy, 19,* 145–158.

Ford, J. J. (2006). Solution focused sex therapy of erectile dysfunction. *Journal of Couple and Relationship Therapy, 5,* 65–79.

Franklin, C., Biever, J., Moore, K., Clemons, D., & Scamardo, M. (2001). The effectiveness of solution-focused therapy with children in a school setting. *Research on Social Work Practice, 11,* 411–434.

Gingerich, W. J. & Eisengart, S. (2000). Solution-focused brief therapy: A review of the outcome research. *Family Process, 39,* 477–498.

Green, S. & Flemons, D. (2007). *Quickies: The handbook of brief sex therapy: Revised and expanded.* New York: Norton.

Hoyt, M. F. & Berg, I. K. (1998). Solution-focused couple therapy: Helping clients construct self-fulfilling realities. In F. M. Dattilio (Ed.), *Case studies in couple and family therapy: Systemic and cognitive perspectives* (pp. 203–232). New York: Guilford Press.

LaFountain R. M. & Garner N. E. (1996). Solution-focused counseling groups: the results are in. *Journal for Specialists in Group Work, 21,* 128–143.

Lambert, M. J., Okiishi, J. C., Finch, A. E., & Johnson, L. D. (1998). Outcome assessment: From conceptualization to implementation. *Professional Psychology: Research and Practice, 29,* 63–70.

Lazarus, A. (1963). The treatment of chronic frigidity by systematic desensitization. *Journal of Nervous and Mental Diseases, 136,* 272–278.

Lazarus, A. A. & Rachman, S. (1957). The use of systematic desensitization in psychotherapy. *South Africa Medical Journal, 31,* 934–937.

Leiblum, S. R. & Rosen, R. C. (2000). Introduction: sex therapy in the age of Viagra. In S. R. Leiblum & R. C. Rosen (Eds.), *Principles and practice of sex therapy,* (3rd ed., pp. 1–13). New York: Guilford Press.

Levine, E. M. & Ross, N. (1977). Sexual dysfunctions and psychoanalysis. *American Journal of Psychiatry, 134,* 646–651.

Lindforss, L. & Magnusson, D. (1997). Solution-focused therapy in prison. *Contemporary Family Therapy, 19,* 89–103.

Littrell, J. M., Malia, J. A., & Vanderwood, M. (1995). Single-session brief counseling in a high school. *Journal of Counseling and Development, 73,* 451–458.

Leiblum, S. R. & Rosen, R. C. (2001). Introduction: Sex therapy in the age of Viagra. In S. R. Leiblum & R. C. Rosen (Eds.), *Principles and practices of sex therapy* (3rd ed., pp. 1–16). New York: Guilford.

Masters, W. H. & Johnson, V. E. (1970). *Human sexual inadequacy.* New York: Little, Brown.

McCabe, M. P. (2001). Evaluation of a cognitive behavior therapy program for people with sexual dysfunction. *Journal of Sex & Marital Therapy, 27,* 259–271.

McCollum, E. E. & Trepper, T. S. (2001). *Creating family solutions for substance abuse.* New York: Haworth Press.

McGee, D., Vento, A., & Bavelas, J. B. (2005). An interactional model of questions as therapeutic interventions. *Journal of Marital and Family Therapy, 31,* 371–384.

Murray, C. E. & Murray, T. L. (2004). Solution-focused premarital counseling: Helping couples build a vision for their marriage. *Journal of Marital and Family Therapy, 30,* 349–358.

Newsome, W. S. (2004). Solution-focused brief therapy groupwork with at-risk junior high school students: Enhancing the bottom line. *Research on Social Work Practice, 14,* 336–343.

O'Hanlon, W. (2000). *Do one thing different: Ten simple ways to change your life.* New York: Harper Books.

Pichot, T. & Dolan, Y. (2003). *Solution-focused brief therapy: its effective use in agency settings.* New York: Haworth Press.

Rosen, R. C. & Leiblum, S. R. (1995). Treatment of sexual disorders in the 1990s: An integrated approach. *Journal of Consulting and Clinical Psychology, 63,* 877–890.

Schnarch, D. (2001). Desire problems: A systemic perspective. In S. R. Leiblum & R. C. Rosen (Eds.), *Principles and practices of sex therapy* (3rd ed., pp. 17–56). New York: Guilford.

Springer, D. W., Lynch, C., & Rubin A. (2000). Effects of a solution-focused mutual aid group for Hispanic children of incarcerated parents. *Child and Adolescent Social Work, 17,* 431–442.

Tomori, C. & Bavelas, J. B. (2007). Using microanalysis of communication to compare solution-focused and client-centered therapies. *Journal of Family Psychotherapy, 18*(3), 25–43.

Van Lankveld, J. J. D. M. (1998). Bibliotherapy in the treatment of sexual dysfunctions: A meta-analysis. *Journal of Consulting and Clinical Psychology, 66,* 702–708.

Weeks, G. R. & Gambescia, N. (2000). *Erectile dysfunction: Integrating couple therapy, sex therapy, and medical treatment.* New York: Norton.

Weeks, G. R. & Gambescia, N. (2002). *Hypoactive sexual desire: Integrating sex and couple therapy.* New York: Norton.

Wiederman, N. W. (1998). The state of theory in sex therapy—The use of theory in research and scholarship on sexuality. *Journal of Sex Research, 34,* 167–174.

Wolpe, J. (1958). *Psychotherapy by reciprocal inhibition.* Stanford, CA: Stanford University Press.

Zimmerman, T. S., Jacobsen, R. B., MacIntyre, M., & Watson, C. (1996). Solution-focused parenting groups: An empirical study. *Journal of Systemic Therapies, 15,* 12–25.

17

Sex Therapy
A Panoramic View

Gerald R. Weeks
Nancy Gambescia
Katherine M. Hertlein

Contents

A Look Behind: Where We've Been

Masters and Johnson (1966; 1970), pioneers in the field of sex therapy, emphasized the notion that there is no such thing as an uninvolved partner in treating sexual dysfunctions. Following the lead of the early marital therapists, sex therapists recognized that the couple, rather than the individual client, was the focal point of treatment. This concept continues to be indispensable to modern-day sex therapy. In the early phases of sex therapy, however, the treatment process failed to recognize the systemic aspects of the couple's relationship, the interplay between relationship and sexual dynamics, and the reciprocal nature of sexual dysfunctions. In fact, one partner was often viewed as the identified patient while the other partner functioned as a cotherapist who facilitated the completion of treatment assignments at home (Masters & Johnson, 1970).

Lack of a Systemic Focus

Having the couple in the office together did not necessarily promote a systemic understanding of the many factors that contributed to and maintained the couple's sexual problems. The intimate, relational, familial, environmental, and social issues operating within the couple's intimate relationship were rarely recognized or addressed (Gurman & Fraenkel, 2002). Emily Mudd, distinguished sex counselor, educator, and researcher and founder of Philadelphia's Marriage Council, noted the absence of a systemic focus in the work of Masters and Johnson (Weeks, personal communication, 1992). Mudd recognized that Masters and Johnson did not clearly view the couple as the recipient of treatment, despite her work to educate them. She reported that they had difficulty understanding how the role of the partner helps to create or sustain sexual difficulties or to truly understand systemic thinking.

Behavioral Concentration

The therapeutic approach of Masters and Johnson (1970) and other leading sex therapists (Heiman & LoPiccolo, 1988; Kaplan, 1974; Rimm & Masters, 1974) can unquestionably be described as behavioral. Their treatment centered on the correction of problems such as faulty learning, lack of education, misinformation, negative sexual attitudes, and paucity of sexual experience. Psychodynamic or relational techniques were employed only if the behavioral treatments failed to produce a favorable outcome (Kaplan, 1974). Incremental homework assignments were recommended to reduce sexual anxiety, to increase sexual performance, and to enhance sexual pleasure (as discussed in Gambescia & Weeks, 2006). Treatment protocols emphasized education, permission, communication training, and the use of cognitive and behavioral techniques (LoPiccolo, 1978). Various highly regarded sex therapy texts used the same behaviorally oriented principles and techniques, including homework assignments (Leiblum & Rosen, 2000b; Wincze & Carey, 1991). In general, there was little appreciation of the numerous systemic factors that could precipitate and maintain sexual problems (Weeks, 2005).

Bifurcation of Marital and Sex Therapy

The conjoint format, used in both marital and sex therapy, did little to ensure that the two fields were integrated. Marital therapy concentrated on the relational issues, and sex therapy addressed sexual problems. This identity problem obstructed the development and continues to limit the capacity of the field of sex therapy. Masters and Johnson (1966; 1970) were aware that couples and sex therapy were dissimilar, and others reinforced the divide. For example, in the text *Treating Sexual Disorders* (Charlton & Yalom, 1997), various topics related to the biopsychoassessment and treatment of sexual dysfunctions were included. In one chapter, "Couple Therapy of Sexual Disorders," Borrelli-Kerner and Bernell (1997) highlighted the lack of intersection between the two fields, noting that sex therapy is "short term, ten- to twenty-session, goal-directed treatment specifically designed to ameliorate sexual symptoms. For the most part, other dynamics are considered only when they affect the sexual arena.... In our experience, the difference between sex and couple therapies is one of timing and focus rather than of philosophy" (p. 166). To a large extent, the gulf between the fields of marital and sex therapy continues to exist. Gurman and Fraenkel (2002), in a review of couple therapy, noted, "... The worlds of the 'marital' or 'couple' therapist and 'sex therapist' seem rarely to intersect" (p. 239).

A Look Around: Where We Are

A Shift in Perspective: The Need for Integration in Therapy

Contrary to the earlier perspectives about the nature of sexual problems and their associated treatments, we view sex therapy as a unique subset of couple therapy. In most instances, sex therapy involves working with the couple, and, regardless of the presentation, the couple, rather than one partner, is the recipient of treatment. We have found, time after time, that partners in treatment will reveal co-occurring sexual problems in addition to the relational and emotional difficulties they are experiencing. Because of the implications a problematic sexual relationship might have for couples, their relationship cannot be ignored when dealing with sexual problems (Crowe, 1995; Weeks, 2004). In effect, relationship dynamics become embedded in the couple's sexual system and vice versa.

Weeks and Hof (1987) argued that sex therapy and couples therapy must be viewed from an integrative perspective. Their book *Integrating Sex and Marital Therapy* was the first text to conceptualize sexual problems from a systems perspective arguing that in sex therapy the couple must be treated as a couple rather that focusing on a symptomatic partner. This view of sex therapy was later expanded in texts on the treatment of erectile dysfunction (ED) and hypoactive sexual desire disorder (HSDD; Weeks & Gambescia, 2000, 2002). One of the most significant contributions in Weeks and Gambescia (2000 and in Weeks, Gambescia, and Jenkins (2003) is the instruction that sex therapists attend to the three components that constitute Sternberg's (1999) triangle of love: commitment, intimacy, and passion. For instance, a fear of intimacy or lack of commitment can significantly impact the sexual relationship (Weeks & Gambescia, 2000; 2002; Woody, 1992). Gehring's (2003) research supports this contention, as he found that a couple's sexuality is better expressed under circumstances when the partners embrace intimacy in their relationship. Thus, it is necessary for sex therapists and couples therapists to have the ability to work with all three aspects of the love triangle because each is important to the maintenance of a nourishing relationship (Weeks, 2005).

Perhaps the most noteworthy paradigm shift in the field of sex and marital therapy is the intersystems approach described by Weeks (1989; 1994; 2004). This approach attends to the biological, psychological, and sociocultural factors operating in the lives of individuals experiencing sexual problems. Rather than believing the sexual dysfunction is one partner's

problem, this integrative approach uses a systemic lens that views the dysfunction within the context of the couples relationship. The result is a more
comprehensive and less restrictive treatment modality. Other theorists
are beginning to argue for the integration of medical and psychological
treatment in sex therapy (see Leiblum, 2007) and systemically oriented sex
therapy (Woody, 1992). These trends suggest that the field of sex therapy is
recognizing that sexual problems can be very much affected by the context
held by the individual, the couple, and the larger systems.

Acknowledgment of the Interplay between Biology and Sexuality

Therapists are becoming increasingly aware of the undeniable interaction
between certain medications and sexual functioning, yet until the mid
1990s the primary source of information related to this relationship was
the *Physician's Desk Reference* (1996). In 1996, Crenshaw and Goldberg
published a revolutionary text focusing specifically on the biochemistry of
sex and the effects that various medications have on sexual functioning.
The introductory chapters of *Sexual Pharmacology* review the research
on what is known about the biochemical process in sexual functioning.
The remainder of the volume examines studies performed by others in the
field and original research conducted by the authors. The detrimental sexual side effects of some of the major classes of medications are included,
such as antidepressants, antianxiety medications, and antihypertensive
medications. Whenever possible the authors present alternative pharmacotherapy that would have fewer or no sexual side effects. An implicit goal
of the volume is to suggest the development of medications with fewer
sexual side effects and antidotes for those medications with sexual side
effects (ibid.). Today, several additional texts focus on medications and
their effect on sex (e.g., Ashton, 2007; Segraves and Balon, 2003).

Medicalization of Sex Therapy

In 1998, Pfizer Pharmaceuticals (New York) released the drug sildenafil
(Viagra), which produced a major change in the treatment of ED and gen-
erated the development of two similar drugs, vardenafil (Levitra; Bayer
Pharmaceuticals Corporation, Pittsburgh, Pennsylvania) and tadalafil
(Cialis; Eli Lilly and Company, Indianapolis, Indiana). These oral agents,
called phosphodiesterase type 5 (PDE5) inhibitors, help to promote and

restore erectile functioning to many men. Globally, an estimated 25 to 30 million men consume these relatively safe and effective oral medications (Rosen, 2007). Because of this medicalization of sex treatment, an evolution in the field of sex therapy occurred. Many men experiencing sexual dysfunction today often seek medications over psychotherapy to resolve sexual problems (Weeks & Gambescia, 2000).

PDE5 inhibitors can be successful in restoring erectile functioning, yet they should not be considered a miraculous course to a satisfying sex life. Bypassing the psychological treatment route often involves circumventing the partner's issues, needs, and contributions to the problem. Although successful in many cases, our clinical experience shows that PDE5 inhibitors cannot always "fix" sexual dysfunction if relationship problems are present. Further, the partner is often left out of decisions about treatment and can be surprised by the man's new interest in and capacity for erections. Many times, the woman is psychologically and physically unprepared for resuming sexual contact after a period of abstinence. Often, physicians do not have the time or training to discuss the man's psychological or relational issues, and the partner assessment is still seldom included in the clinical evaluation of disorders such as ED in medical settings (Leiblum, 2007).

The shift toward medicalization has significant implications, both positive and negative, for society and couples. Drug companies, for example, bear the burden of demonstrating that medications are effective, leading to renewed interest in the refinement of the etiology and definitions of the various dysfunctions as well as in the development of assessment instruments to measure the effects of the medical interventions. Women's sexual medical complaints are also being taken more seriously. Previously, physicians would often attribute pain symptoms in women to psychogenic causes rather than to organic problems (Binik, Bergeron, & Khalife, 2000), resulting in frequent misdiagnoses, to referrals to therapists who knew little of these disorders, and subsequently to an inability to receive the appropriate treatment. Currently, disorders including vulvodynia, dyspareunia, and vulvar vestibulitis are receiving much more attention (Basson, 2007; Binik, Bergeron, & Khalife, 2007; Heiman, 2007; Leiblum, 2007; Rosenbaum, 2007). In addition to pain disorders, pharmaceutical companies recognize the need for medications that will improve female functioning, especially lack of sexual desire. Numerous treatments to help restore sexual desire for women are being investigated.

Greater Openness Regarding Sexuality and Sexual Problems

The use of Viagra and other PDE5 inhibitors has led to a number of profound changes in treatment and public perceptions of ED (see, e.g., Sae-Chul & Sook, 2006). For instance, the shroud of secrecy related to ED and its treatment is removed through advertising of the oral agents, and an era of greater openness regarding sexual problems in general has begun. The public consciousness regarding sexuality, sexual function, and dysfunction is raised concurrent with an increased interest in medical and psychological treatments. Problems that were rarely discussed in the past, such as a couple's sexual intimacy, are increasingly becoming a part of the standard physical examination. This greater candor regarding sexuality may inspire people to seek out treatment who otherwise would not have disclosed their issues to a physician or psychotherapist. It also provides the opportunity for increased communication between the couple regarding their sexual lives and affords an opportunity for a couple to feel normalized when they experience sexual difficulties.

The Incorporation of Technology into Our Sexual Lives

Increasing advances in electronic, digital, and other technological products, such as the Internet, has had a significant effect on sexuality (Leiblum & Rosen, 2000b). The estimated number of people now using the Internet daily is at 1 billion worldwide, with the number still rapidly accelerating (Computer Almanac Industry, 2006). In addition, other forms of technology, including cell phones and wireless handheld computers, have altered the ways that we interact with one another. With 197 million Internet users in the United States alone, there are multiple effects on the definition of sexuality, sexual issues, and the manner in which it is acceptable to exhibit one's sexuality (Hertlein & Piercy, 2006).

Countless Internet sites provide information regarding sexual function, dysfunction, and sexually transmitted illnesses. Effectively, anyone with access to the Internet can search the Web and find almost any source of information or education. For many, the Internet constitutes an important avenue for healthy sexual pursuits. For example, the Kinsey Institute (2007) provides a list on their website of online sexuality-related resources, as does the Sexuality Information and Education Council of the United States (SIECUS) and a host of other sites. Finally, there are also counseling

sites that claim to provide a form of treatment for common sexual problems. While the ethics of online psychotherapy are hotly debated, there is
little doubt that the development of online cyber counseling and its variations are beginning to take form (Bloom & Walz, 2000).

The Internet also provides an unimaginable variety of sexually explicit
pictures, writings, and other material whose primary purpose is to produce
sexual arousal. Pornographic information is readily available, affordable,
and accessible to the consumer. Without leaving the home, individuals
can anonymously engage in sexually explicit viewing or locate those who
want to meet for sexual liaisons. The many venues of cybersex, such as
chat rooms and Web cameras (Webcams), have contributed to problematic
Internet usage with regard to sexuality (Cooper, 2002). For many, cybersex
has replaced or added to traditional forms of compulsive behavior such as
using print pornography or engaging in sex with prostitutes. Such behavior is damaging to sex addicts, their partners, and families. For example,
researchers such as Carnes (1991) and Schneider (2003) noted that many
sex addicts who use the Internet as a vehicle for their addiction have lost
or damaged their relationships because their partner views their behavior
as infidelity or a breach of the relationship contract. Additionally, Internet
sex has promoted the exploitation and victimization of children by sexual
predators, who, while anonymous, pose in a variety of ostensibly safe pre-
tenses. A more complete discussion of this topic can be found in Carnes
(1991), Kafka (2000), and the journal *Sexual Addiction and Compulsivity.*

Special Populations

Therapists are now challenged to recognize, to become comfortable with,
and to expand their knowledge base regarding special groups of individuals with sexual issues. New developments are occurring in sex therapy
in working with the aging and elderly populations, people with chronic
illnesses and disabilities, sexual minorities, and those with gender issues
(Barsky, Friedman, & Rosen, 2006; Carroll, 2007; Gill & Hough, 2007;
Haffey, Peterson, Bley, & Glaus, 2007; Nichols & Shernoff, 2007; Shaw,
2001; Stevenson & Elliot, 2007).

Ageism

As Americans are living longer and enjoying active lives, a rapidly growing
sexual minority is older clients. The idea that one's sex life ends at 50 is no
longer the norm. According to Davis (2007) 50-year-old men and women

are only at the midpoint of their sex lives. Therapists are encouraged to help clients over 50 realize that their sexuality can be replete with continued exploration, enjoyment, and gratification. Because people are living longer healthier lives, the therapist must address normative age-related changes in sexual function including delayed erection and prolonged refractory periods for men and the progressive drying of the vagina (atrophy) for women. In some of these cases penile–vaginal intercourse is not possible or desired, yet the couple can be helped to explore other avenues for expressing and enjoying sexuality.

One key to helping clients think more positively is for therapists to reevaluate their own beliefs about sex. Gill and Hough (2007) proposed that instead of conveying to these clients that they will never again achieve the sexual satisfaction that they once enjoyed or expected to enjoy, therapists should focus more on the positive aspects of what their clients can and are able to achieve in their present situation. Moreover, the sex therapist must utilize a more comprehensive biopsychosocial approach with all clients, especially the aging population. Many treatments focus on medical solutions, and these remedies must be considered as an adjunct to the relational, cognitive, and behavioral aspects of treatment (Barksy, Friedman, & Rosen, 2006).

Chronic Illness and Disability

Sexual expression is an essential element of life for all persons, yet chronically ill and disabled individuals can struggle with various aspects of the sexual experience. Sex therapists today must acquire the knowledge and demonstrate the sensitivity necessary to modify current techniques and approaches when treating those in these special populations. There is a tremendous need to examine issues such as the lack of privacy, body image concerns, sex education, sexual function and reproduction, and ways to deal with stereotypes and prejudices. It is important for therapists not to label those with disabilities as sexually dysfunctional based on their own preconceptions of what is and what is not functional (Giulio, 2003). In a book targeted toward the general population, Joannides (2004) addressed this issue by including a chapter outlining ideas to enhance one's sex life when one partner is affected by disability. Similar steps need to be taken by the academic community to ensure the continuation of effective delivery of treatment. The treatment of chronic illness and disability is an area where medical family therapy, multidisciplinary treatment, and sex therapy all interface.

Sexual Minorities

While there is a trend toward greater acceptance of sexual minority groups, clients who present with lesbian, gay, bisexual, and transgender (LGBT) identities continue to be pathologized by many therapists. Additionally, LGBT clients are particularly vulnerable to the adverse effects of social oppression, discrimination, and prejudice. They often suffer from internalized shame, guilt, and homophobia, all of which interfere with sexual intimacy (Haffey et al., 2007). Although research has shown that sexual minorities have many of the same types of sexual problems experienced by heterosexual individuals (Meana, Rakipi, Weeks, & Lykins, 2006), lesbian, gay, and bisexual (LGB) couples typically request treatment for difficulties specific to their preferred sexual practices (Bradford, 2004; Connolly, 2004; Nichols & Shernoff, 2007; Tunnell & Greenan, 2004). Because LGB lifestyles and sexual practices are frequently misunderstood, therapists unintentionally impose a limiting heterosexual template on assessment and treatment of sexual dysfunctions (Haffey et al., 2007) and tend to pathologize their variances.

Transgender individuals must be differentiated from LGB sexual minorities because their major issue is with core gender identity (as a male or a female) rather than that of sexual orientation (the genders to which one's feelings, thoughts, fantasies, and attraction are focused) (Coolhart & Torres Bernal, 2007). Transgender clients and their loved ones must be helped to cope with the integration of their changing identities and roles. Often, transgender clients seek medical treatments to modify their gender presentation, and the therapist musk interface with other health-care providers to achieve a gender transition. Finally, new information is becoming available about transgender persons (Carroll, 2000; Lev, 2004), including guidelines of care established by the Harry Benjamin International Gender Dysphoria Association.

Therapists working with sexual minority clients must educate themselves on how to best approach treatment for LGBT persons with sensitivity. The American Psychological Association proposed major guidelines that require therapists to understand their own and society's attitudes toward sexual minorities (as cited in Haffey et al., 2007). Moreover, therapists must understand and be respectful of LGBT relationships, families, challenges, and circumstances. When needed, therapist must seek consultation or make the appropriate referrals.

The Paraphilias

There is a great deal of information in the *Diagnostic and Statistical Manual of Mental Disorders*, 4th ed., text revision (*DSM-IV-TR*; APA, 2004) concerning the diagnosis of paraphilia-related disorders, yet there is little research and empirical evidence about these behaviors and treatment outcomes (Kafka, 2007). Such disorders typically involve sexual urges, fantasies, or behaviors with nonhuman objects, children, nonconsenting adults or engaging in the humiliation or suffering of oneself or another person. Many therapists prefer not to pathologize sexual behavior that involves willing adults, even if the behavior might be considered socially inappropriate or deviant. In general, these cases require multiple types of interventions including visiting more than one mental health professional, focusing on psychoeducation, cognitive and behavioral therapies, support groups, marital therapy, or pharmacotherapy (ibid.). Therapists are urged to seek available information about treatment, to encourage clients to communicate with their providers and partners, to have positive attitudes, and to focus on the things that are possible (Gill & Hough, 2007). Ultimately there appears to be a great need for more research and literature relating to the paraphilias to establish a wider knowledge base as to how they are best effectively treated.

Theoretical Gaps in Sex Therapy

The field of sex therapy has improved considerably since its inception, yet large gaps in our current treatment approaches remain. Kleinplatz (2001) attested to the absence of a theoretical foundation for sex therapy and the preponderance of stereotypical assumptions, gender biases, and a biological orientation. Fraser and Solovey (2004) concurred that historically, the field of sex therapy has often circumvented cultural, contextual, and interpersonal issues while overfocusing on performance oriented sex. A review of the literature using keywords like *sex therapy* and *theory*, *sex research* and *theory*, *sex* and *theory*, and *sexual theory* reveals no new references since a special issue of the *Journal of Sex Research* published in 1998. In that issue, Wiederman (1998) observed that the field of sex therapy has been dominated by techniques that are not theoretically grounded. In the early days of sex therapy, it was often sufficient to provide the clients with some education and simple techniques. As the public became more edu-cated, the "easy" cases disappeared, leaving therapists with many puzzling and difficult cases to treat (ibid.). For example, Masters and Johnson (1970) claimed that retarded ejaculation was an easy problem to treat and had a high success rate. In our experience, this problem ranks as one of the most complex and difficult.

Weiss (1998) also contended that sex therapy has been largely atheo-retical, providing a detailed list of 39 distinctive theoretical structures in psychology and the application of some of these techniques to sex therapy. Unfortunately, none of these theories has been consistently adopted, has explanatory power, or has been scrutinized empirically in this field. The most recent model to appear in this field has been sexual script theory, which asserts that the subjective understanding of an individual's sexuality determines preferences in sexual behavior (ibid.). Unfortunately, Gagnon (1990), the proponent of the theory, has been unable to show how these scripts are internalized and reinforced. It seems that sex researchers have not shown a great deal of interest in how systems theory could be applied to sex therapy and that such application has been rare. Clearly, not much has changed in the field of sex therapy. For instance, Jurich and Myers-Bowman (1998) were only able to locate seven research articles based on systems theory in sex therapy from 1974 to 1995.

Looking Ahead: Future Directions

The Effect of Increased Medicalization

The current research on the treatment of sexual dysfunctions conducted by pharmaceutical companies has both positive and negative implications for the future of sex therapy. First, pharmaceutical companies will con-tinue to provide the impetus for research in sexual physiology and neu-rological processes because producing drugs that facilitate erections or assist with orgasm involves a detailed understanding of the physiologi-cal mechanisms. Conversely, however, as medicalization continues, drug companies may spend more research dollars on developing new medica-tions rather than on exploring alternative treatment methods. This trend clearly has influenced the public's proclivity for rapid, effortless, medical solutions for sexual problems. It is likely that funding agencies may also shift in the direction of medical solutions, leading to decreased funding

for psychologically oriented sex research and sex therapy. Such a movement may be perpetuated by stagnation of new developments in the field
of sex therapy (Leiblum & Rosen, 2000b).

Other disadvantages of the medicalization of treatment for sexual dysfunctions have been demonstrated through the use of PDE5 inhibitors
for the treatment of ED. Often, unrealistic expectations are operative in
the man's preference for medication and the disinclination to recognize
and address the psychological etiologies. This set of circumstances can
have detrimental effects on his partner, the relationship, and the man's
self-esteem (Weeks & Gambescia, 2000, 2002). A "quick fix" is not always
guaranteed because sexual functioning involves more than physiological
tumescence. Noncompliance to successful medical treatment underscores
the fact that augmenting erections does not correct insidious and pervasive
individual, relational, contextual issues such as anxiety, depression, and
lack of desire for the partner. Additionally, as stated earlier, the partner is
often left out of the man's decision to use medications and is often sexually symptomatic as well. Frequently, over time the man has compensated
for the lack of desire in his partner with a decreased sexual frequency or
erectile difficulties. The use of medications may increase desire or enhance
a man's ability to perform but is not likely to increase the partner's desire
or interest in sex. Sudden performance changes in the man will offset a
functional (albeit less-than-optimal) sexual homeostasis and can inflame
the underlying relational dissatisfaction.

The interplay of psychological and organic factors sustaining ED,
HSDD, and other sexual difficulties suggests that a comprehensive treatment approach is more favorable than a strictly medical approach (Weeks
& Gambescia, 2000, 2002). Despite burgeoning medical advances in the
field, sexual functioning remains a biopsychosocial issue, and the need for
greater integration in the field of sex therapy is more relevant than ever.
The role of the therapist, therefore, must expand and adapt to the challenges of sex therapy today.

Infusing Theory into Practice

The field of sex therapy is continually emerging and in search of a strong
theoretical base. Therapists can easily become wedded to one theory or no
theory or view themselves as technically eclectic rather than theoretically
integrative. We propose that any theories that eventually gain dominance

will need to be integrative in nature to attend to all of the aspects of sexuality and factors that affect a couple's sexual life. For instance, Aanstoos (2001) proposed a novel idea that sexuality is a way of being that cannot be measured or directly observed but rather sensed, felt, or experienced. Thinking of sexuality and sexual arousal as phenomena rather than acts will help individuals better understand their own sexual connections by allowing them to focus on experience rather than outcome. This approach emphasizes thinking of the chemistry created during a sexual encounter as an atmosphere bursting with unique sensations rather than as a mere act (ibid.). Proponents of this idea feel that sexuality should include elements of imagination and freedom from rationality.

Armstrong (2006) proposed that revitalizing a humanistic method to sexuality and sex therapy would benefit the field of sex therapy. In this approach, it is necessary to understand and treat the individuals in their interpersonal and experiential contexts. Tiefer (2006) concurred that there is a need for those involved in the field of sex therapy to have a stronger philosophical foundation when approaching individuals' struggles with sexually related issues. She asserted that revamping the humanistic approach to sexuality will prevent the field of sex therapy from having a focus that is too narrow or commercialized. In summary, the fields of sex research, human sexuality, and sex therapy are in need of much more theoretical grounding, debate, and research.

Developing and Utilizing Integrative Approaches

Despite advances in the field of sex therapy over the past few decades, many practitioners continue to resort to individually oriented cognitive-behavioral treatments. Recent publications reflect an increasing emphasis on medical issues and basic science and fewer systemically conceived interventions (Lieblum, 2007). Further, sex and marital therapy continue to be regarded as separate entities, and this divide is widened by increasing medical advances. We believe the primary future direction for sex therapy is in the development of integrative and multidisciplinary treatment.

This text argues for the application of a comprehensive, integrative approach to the assessment and treatment of sexual dysfunctions that will bridge the gap between marital and sex therapies and will provide a systemic rather than individualistic methodology. The intersystems approach developed by Weeks (1989, 1994, 2004, 2005) provides such an innovation, as it incorporates four major foci:

1. The medical, social, and, psychological issues related to the individual partners
2. Interactional (couple) dynamics
3. Family-of-origin considerations
4. The larger societal/cultural issues impinging on the couple.

Over the past 20 years, the intersystems approach has added significantly to the existing clinical literature on general psychotherapy (Weeks & Cross, 2004), couples and sex therapy (Weeks & Hof, 1987, 1995; Weeks & Treat, 2001), specific sexual dysfunctions (Weeks & Gambescia, 2000, 2002), and infidelity (Weeks et al., 2003). We welcome new discoveries that are being made in neuroscience, biology, physiology, or the medical aspects of sexuality as these can be integrated into the intersystems perspective. Thus, we believe there is considerable room for psychotherapeutic advancement in the field of sex therapy, especially for systems-oriented therapists.

We expect that the field of sex therapy will continue to produce clinical and research data that concentrate on behaviorally oriented treatment, new medical developments (Lieblum, 2007), and systems-oriented psychology (Weeks, 1987). Nevertheless, we fear that the field will continue to become more divided because the training of the members of each camp will not be able to transcend their professional experience. The behaviorists will continue to be behaviorists, and systems thinkers will continue to be systems thinkers with little overlap or interest in the others approach. We believe that systems theory best explains the interlocking nature of sexual dysfunction, as is demonstrated in cases of erectile dysfunction and lack of sexual desire (Weeks & Gambescia, 2000; 2002) and that sex and relationship therapy should be integrated. Clinicians who share the common goal of treating intimate relationships should be amenable to assimilating new information, regardless of the orientation.

Education/Training Implications

Coupled with the momentum of the traditional behavioral approach, the intersystems approach is beginning to gain widespread acceptance. Despite this, the reason many therapists have not used the intersystems approach is because they view it as too complex. In effect, this approach is rather user-friendly, although the therapist must attend to many issues related to the individual, relationship and family of origin and to factors related to larger system in which the couple and individual is embedded. A therapist practicing from an integrative perspective needs to be well trained in the modalities of individual, couples, and family therapy. This training represents a significant investment and dedication to systemic thinking—an appreciation of the interaction of all of the components of a situation. Many graduate programs for training sex, marital, and family therapists have recognized the value in utilizing such an integrative approach.

The medical field needs to be educated that the etiology of a sexual problem can frequently be an interaction between biological and psychological factors. Such information will encourage appropriate referrals to be made on behalf of individuals and couples experiencing sexual problems and will likely reduce the dependence on medical solutions for complicated problems. Practitioners who recognize the psychogenic and relational risk factors for sexual problems often admit that they do not have the time or training to address these issues, yet they do not consult with a psychotherapist unless they have forged a relationship. Coordinated treatment between medical and psychological practitioners is a step toward reducing feelings of failure, anxiety, and hopelessness in individuals and partners experiencing problems with sexual intimacy.

Research

The trends in research in academics and psychotherapy have shifted toward demonstrating that psychotherapy is effective. Unfortunately, the outcome research in sex therapy is relatively limited in depth (Schover & Leiblum, 1994). This is somewhat surprising, given the reliance on behavioral methods frequently utilized in sex therapy. It is imperative that the field of sex therapy continue to grow by testing the effectiveness of the models or the critical components of treatment. In a review of sex research published by the Society for the Scientific Study of Sexuality, Heiman and Meston (1997) cite the problems in sex dysfunction research as including the lack of control groups, limited funding, and manuals for treating sex problems.

Heiman and Meston (1997) also reviewed the existing effectiveness studies and noted that the areas for future research include sexual desire disorders, dyspareunia in both women and men, and delayed orgasm in men.

Rather than comparing which model is better than another, some researchers have explored a "common factors" approach, which identifies the factors common in each of the models that contribute to effective treatment. Sex therapy has, thankfully, not been excluded from this analysis. Donahey and Miller (2000) cited the role of extratherapeutic factors as being a significant component in therapy, stating, "By being mindful of the significant role that client strengths, capabilities, resources, social supports, and the fortuitous events that weave in and out of client's lives play in everyday practice, sex therapists can enhance their contribution to treatment outcome" (p. 222). Further, they highlighted the importance of the relationship between the client and therapist, explored the role of hope and expectancy and its impact on the sex therapy process, and provided strategies to help a therapist determine appropriate model or technique selection. Research topics along this line might include testing the degree to which the extratherapeutic factors shift outcome based on the nature of a couple's presenting problem, the role of the therapist–client relationship in sex therapy with same-sex couples, or how a couple's sense of failure in sexual functioning mitigates their feelings of hope and expectancy, thus altering the therapeutic outcome. Incorporating the common factors approach and research into sex therapy will continue to make research in this field stay in step with the developments in psychology, counseling, and systemic therapy.

One Final Look

The field of sex therapy is still relatively new when compared with other scientific fields such as biology or physics. Thus, we have the time and opportunity to build formal theories, to develop new treatment protocols, and to test them using a variety of methods. This book represents the first major comprehensive effort to change the paradigm for the field of sex therapy and its application to a wide spectrum of sexual problems. Our intervention strategies stress integration, systemic thinking, and coordinating of treatment modalities. The field needs to be revitalized through much more theory building, research, professional cross-fertilization, and changing the way students are trained in graduate programs toward the integration of the fields of sex and marital therapy. Rather than think of sex therapy as a young field, we can think of it as a field entering a new era that will lead to many new developments.

References

Aanstoos, C. (2001). Phenomenology of sexuality. In P. Kleinplatz (Ed.), *New directions in sex therapy: Innovations and alternatives* (pp. 69–90). Philadelphia: Brunner/Routledge.

American Psychiatric Association (APA) (1980). *Diagnostic and statistical manual of mental disorders* (3rd ed.). Washington, DC. Author.

American Psychiatric Association (APA) (1987). *Diagnostic and statistical manual of mental disorders* (3rd ed., rev.). Washington, DC. Author.

American Psychiatric Association (APA) (1994). *Diagnostic and statistical manual of mental disorders* (4th ed.). Washington DC: Author.

Anonymous (2001). Special: Harry Benjamin international gender dysphoria association's the standard of care for gender identity disorders—Sixth version. *International Journal of Transgenderism, 5,* 1.

Armstrong, L. (2006). Barriers to intimate sexuality; Concerns and meaning-based therapy approaches. *Humanist Psychologist, 34*(3), 281–298.

Ashton, A. (2007). The new sexual pharmacology: A guide for the clinician. In S. Leiblum (Ed.), *Principles and practice of sex therapy* (4th ed., pp. 509–542). New York: Guilford.

Barsky, J., Friedman, M., & Rosen, R. (2006). Sexual dysfunction and chronic illness: The role of flexibility in coping. *Journal of Sex & Marital therapy, 32,* 235–253.

Basson, R. (2007). Sexual desire/arousal disorders in women. In S. Leiblum (Ed.), *Principles and practice of sex therapy* (4th ed., pp. 25–53). New York: Guilford.

Borrelli-Kerner, S. & Bernell, B. (1997). Couple therapy of sexual disorders. In R. S. Charlton & I. D. Yalom (Eds.), *Treating sexual disorders* (pp. 165–200). San Francisco: Jossey-Bass.

Binik, Y., Bergeron, S., & Kahlife, S. (2000). Dyspareunia. In S. Leiblum & R. Rosen (Eds.), *Principles and practice of sex therapy* (3rd ed., pp. 154–180). New York: Guilford.

Binik, Y., Bergerson, S., & Khalife, S. (2007). Dyspareunia and vaginismus: So-called sexual pain. In S. Leiblum (Ed.), *Principles and practice of sex therapy* (4th ed., pp. 124–156). New York: Guilford.

Bloom, J. & Walz, G. (2000). Cybercounseling and cyberlearning. Greensboro, NC: ACA/CAPS, Inc.

Borrelli-Kerner, S. & Bernell, B. (1997). Couple therapy of sexual disorders. In R. S. Charlton (Ed.), *Treating sexual disorders* (pp. 165–199). San Francisco: Jossey-Bass.

Bradford, M. (2004). Bisexual issues in same-sex couple therapy. *Journal of Couple & Relationship Therapy, 3,* 43–51.

Carnes, P. (1991). *Don't call it love.* New York: Bantam.

Carroll, R. (2000). Assessment and treatment of gender dysphoria. In S. Leiblum and R. Rosen (Eds.), *Principles and practice of sex therapy* (3rd ed., pp. 368–398). New York: Guilford.

Carroll, R. (2007). Gender dysphoria and transgender experiences. In S. Leiblum (Ed.), *Principles and practice of sex therapy* (4th ed., pp. 477–508). New York: Guilford.

Charlton, R. S. & Yalom, I. D. (Eds.). (1997). *Treating sexual disorders.* San Francisco: John Wiley & Sons, Inc.

Computer Almanac Industry (2006). Worldwide Internet users top 1 billion in 2005. Retrieved December 19, 2006, from: http://www.c-i-a.com/pr0106.htm.

Connolly, C. (2004). Clinical issues with same-sex couples: A review of the literature. *Journal of Couple & Relationship Therapy, 3,* 3–12.

Coolhart, D. & Torres Bernal, A. (2007, May–June). Transgender in family therapy. *Family Therapy Magazine,* 36–42.

Cooper, A. (Ed.) (2002). Sex and the internet: A guidebook for clinicians. New York: Brunner-Routledge.

Crenshaw, T. & Goldberg, G. (1996). *Sexual pharmacology.* New York: W.W. Norton.

Crowe, M. (1995). Couple therapy and sexual dysfunction. *International Review of Psychiatry, 7,* 195–204.

Davis, L. (2007). Golden sexuality: Sex therapy for seniors. In L. Vandecreek, F. Peterson Jr., & J. Bley (Eds.), *Innovations in clinical practice: Focus on sexual health* (pp. 261–273). Sarasota, FL: Professional Resource Press.

Donahey, K. M. & Miller, S. D. (2000). Applying a common factors perspective to sex therapy. *Journal of Sex Education and Therapy, 25,* 221–230.

Fraser, J. & Solovey, A. (2004). A catalytic approach to brief sex therapy. In S. Green & D. Flemons (Eds.), *Quickies: The handbook of brief sex therapy* (pp. 189–212) New York: W.W. Norton.

Gagnon, J. (1990). The explicit and implicit use of the scripting perspective in sex research. *Annual Review of Sex Research, 1,* 1–43.

Gehring, D. (2003). Couple therapy for low sexual desire: A systemic approach. *Journal of Sex & Marital Therapy, 29,* 25–38.

Gill, K. & Hough, S. (2007). Sexual health of people with chronic illness and disability. In L. VandeCreek, F. Peterson Jr., & J. Bley (Eds.), *Innovations in Clinical Practice: Focus on sexual health* (pp. 223–243). Sarasota, FL: Professional Resource Press.

Giulio, G. (2003). Sexuality and people living with physical or developmental disabilities: A review of key issues. *Canadian Journal of Human Sexuality, 12,* 53–68.

Gurman, A. S. & Fraenkel, P. (2002). The history of couple therapy: A millennial review. *Family Process, 41*(2), 199–260.

Haffey, B., Peterson, F. Jr., Bley, J., & Glaus, K. (2007). Addressing sexual health concerns of sexual minority clients. In L. VandeCreek, F. Peterson Jr., & J. Bley (Eds.), *Innovations in clinical practice: Focus on sexual health* (pp. 209–221). Sarasota, FL: Professional Resource Press.

Heiman, J. (2007). Orgasmic disorders in women. In S. Leiblum (Ed.), *Principles and practice of sex therapy* (4th ed.) (pp. 84–123). New York: Guilford.

Heiman, J. & LoPiccolo, J. (1988). *Becoming orgasmic.* New York: Prentice Hall.

Heiman, J. & Meston, M. (1997). Empirically validated treatment for sexual dysfunction. In R. Rosen, C. Davis, & J. Ruppel Jr. (Eds.), *Annual review of sex research: An integrative and interdisciplinary review* (Vol. 8, pp.148–194). Mount Vernon, IA: Society for the Scientific Study of Sexuality.

Hertlein, K. M. & Piercy, F. P. (2006). Internet infidelity: A critical review of the literature. *Family Journal, 14*(3), 366–371.

Joannides, P. (2004). *The guide to getting it on* (4th ed.). Waldport, OR: Goofy Foot Press.

Jurich, J. & Myers-Bowman, K. (1998). Systems theory and its application to research on human sexuality. *Journal of Sex Research, 35,* 72–87.

Kafka, M. (2000). The paraphilia-related disorders: Nonparaphilic hypersexuality and sexual compulsivity/addiction. In S. Leiblum & R. Rosen (Eds.), *Principles and practice of sex therapy* (3rd ed., pp. 471–503). New York: Guilford.

Kafka, M. (2007). Paraphilia-related disorders: The evaluation and treatment of nonparaphilic hypersexuality. In S. Leiblum (Ed.), *Principle and practice of sex therapy* (4th ed., pp. 442–476). New York: Guilford.

Kaplan, H. (1974). *The new sex therapy: Active treatment of sexual dysfunctions.* New York: Times Books.

Kinsey Institute (2007). *Sexuality information links.* Retrieved April 19, 2007 from: http://www.indiana.edu/~kinsey/resources/sexlinks.html

Kleinplatz, P. (Ed.) (2001). *New directions in sex therapy: Innovations and alternatives.* Philadelphia: Taylor & Francis.

Leiblum, S. (2007). Persistent genital arousal disorder: Perplexing, distressing, and underrecognized. In S. Leiblum (Ed.), *Principles and practice of sex therapy* (4th ed., pp. 54–83). New York: Guilford.

Leiblum, S. & Rosen, R. (2000a). Introduction: Sex therapy in the age of Viagra. In S. Leiblum & R. Rosen (Eds.), *Principles and practice of sex therapy* (3rd ed., pp. 1–16). New York: Guilford.

Leiblum, S. & Rosen, R. (2000b). *Principles and practice of sex therapy* (3rd ed.). New York: Guilford.

Lev, A. I. (2004). *Transgender emergence: Therapeutic guidelines for working with gender-variant people and their families.* Binghamton, NY: Hayworth Clinical Practice Press.

LoPiccolo, J. (1978). Direct treatment of sexual dysfunction. In J. LoPiccolo & L. LoPiccolo (Eds.), *Handbook of sex therapy* (pp.1–17). New York: Plenum.

Masters, W. H. & Johnson, V. (1966). *Human sexual response.* Boston: Little, Brown.

Masters, W. H. & Johnson, V. (1970) *Human sexual inadequacy.* Boston: Little, Brown.

Meana, M., Rakipi, R., Weeks, J., & Lykins, A. (2006). Sexual functioning in a non-clinical sample of partnered lesbians. *Journal of Couple & Relationship Therapy, 5*(2), 1–22.

Physician's Desk Reference (50th ed.) (1996). NJ: Thompson PDR.

Rimm, D. & Masters, J. (1974). *Behavior therapy: Techniques and empirical findings.* Oxford: Academic Press.

Rosen, R. (2007). Erectile dysfunction: Integration of medical and psychological approaches. In S. Leiblum (Ed.), *Principles and practice of sex therapy* (4th ed., pp. 277–310). New York: Guilford.

Rosenbaum, T. (2007). Physical therapy management and treatment of sexual pain disorders. In S. Leiblum (Ed.), *Principles and practice of sex therapy* (4th ed., pp. 157–180). New York: Guilford.

Sae-Chul, K. & Sook, P. (2006). Five years after the launch of Viagra in Korea: Changes in perceptions of erectile dysfunction treatment by physicians, patients, and the patients' spouses. *Journal of Sexual Medicine, 3*(1), 132–137.

Schneider, J. (2003). The impact of compulsive cybersex behaviours on the family. *Journal of Sexual and Relationship Therapy, 18*(3), 329–354.

Schover, L. & Leiblum, S. (1994). Commentary: The stagnation of sex therapy. *Journal of Psychology & Human Sexuality, 6,* 5–30.

Segraves, R. & Balon, R. (2003). *Sexual pharmacology: Fast facts.* New York: W. W. Norton.

Shaw, J. (2001). Approaching sexual potential in relationship: A reward of age and maturity. In P. Kleinplatz (Ed.), *New directions in sex therapy: Innovations and alternatives* (pp. 185–209). Philadelphia: Brunner-Routledge.

Sternberg, R. (1999). *Love is a story: A new theory of relationships.* Oxford: Oxford University Press.

Stevenson, R. & Elliot, S. (2007). Sexuality and illness. In S. Leiblum (Ed.), *Principles and practice of sex therapy* (4th ed., pp. 313–349). New York: Guilford.

Tiefer, L. (2006). Sex therapy as a humanistic enterprise. *Sexual and Relationship Therapy, 21,* 359–375.

Weeks, G. (Ed.). (1989). *Treating couples: The intersystem model of the Marriage Council of Philadelphia.* New York: Brunner/Mazel.

Weeks, G. (1994). The intersystem model: An integrative approach to treatment. In G. Weeks & L. Hof (Eds.), *The marital-relationship therapy casebook* (pp. 3–34). New York: Brunner/Mazel.

Weeks, G. (2004). Integration in sex therapy. *Sexual and Relationship Therapy, 19,* S11–S12.

Weeks, G. (2005). The emergence of a new paradigm in sex therapy: Integration. *Sexual and Relationship Therapy, 20,* 89–103.

Weeks, G. & Cross, C. (2004). The intersystem model of psychotherapy: An integrative systems treatment approach. *Guidance and Counseling, 19,* 57–64.

Weeks, G. & Gambescia, N. (2000). *Erectile dysfunction: Integrating couple therapy, sex therapy, and medical treatment.* New York: W.W. Norton.

Weeks, G. & Gambescia, N. (2002). *Hypoactive sexual desire: Integrating sex and couple therapy.* New York: W.W. Norton.

Weeks, G., Gambescia, N., & Jenkins, R. (2003). *Treating infidelity.* New York: W. W. Norton.

Weeks, G. & Hof, L. (1987). *Integrating sex and marital therapy.* New York: Brunner/Mazel.

Weeks, G. & Hof, L. (1995). *Integrative solutions: Treating common problems in couples therapy.* New York: Brunner/Mazel.

Weeks, G. & Treat, S. (2001). *Couples in treatment: Techniques and approaches for effective practice* (2nd ed.). New York: Brunner/Routledge.

Weiss, D. (1998). Conclusion: The state of sexual theory. *Journal of Sex Research, 35,* 100–114.

Wiederman, M. (1998). The state of theory in sex therapy. *Journal of Sex Research, 35,* 88–99.

Wincze, J. P. & Carey, M. P. (1991). *Sexual dysfunction.* New York: Guilford.

Woody, J. D. (1992). *Treating sexual distress.* Thousand Oaks, CA: Sage.

18

Epilogue
A Personal Note on Being a Sex Therapist

Prior to the publication of this text, we have never seen a book, chapter, or paper dealing with what it means to be a sex therapist. Hopefully, we have contributed to a greater understanding of our work through several discussions within the text that address this issue. The purpose of this volume has been to introduce the beginning therapist to the field of sex therapy and to introduce all therapists to a systems view of sex therapy. We want to encourage therapists to embrace sexual issues in treatment and to understand the complex interplay between the various systems contributing to any sexual problem. With the medicalization of psychotherapy and the increased focus on integrative approaches, this is a time for us as sex therapists to redefine our roles.

The field of sex therapy is met with numerous challenges. Because sex therapists are not licensed, it is critically important that the field have a strong credentialing process such as the one that can now lead to becoming a certified sex therapist. We know that the number of sex therapists, like most professionals, will diminish in number over the next few years as the baby boomers in this field retire. Though sex therapy practitioners are frequently credentialed as psychotherapists, psychiatrists, physicians, social workers, and other mental health professionals, many lay people do not understand the function of a sex therapist. Further, sex therapy is looked on with suspicion by the general public and is frequently put under much scrutiny. It is accorded low status among researchers who fail to understand the rigors of doing sex research and therapy. For these and many other reasons having to do with the sex negative culture internalized by the clinician, few therapists pursue becoming a sex therapist. Our wish is to see national sex therapy organizations recruiting more members, starting mentoring programs, maintaining strict credentialing, and providing certification. These processes would eliminate ambiguity, would regulate training and clinical experience, would legitimize the reputation of the sex therapist, and would grant the field the recognition it deserves. Only then will the public be assured that the practitioner has completed specific requirements that ensure a particular standard of care.

Along with these challenges, being a sex therapist means additional training beyond one's terminal degree and additional expense. So the question becomes, why do some therapists choose to enter and remain in this field? Part of the reason may be that sex is intrinsically interesting. Sexual behavior is expressed in an almost infinite variety of ways that reflect one's culture, family values, psychology, and biology.

Once past the newness of the field, clinicians can find that they have entered a world where few venture; sexual behavior is the most unique, personal, and hidden part of self. Whereas over the course of their career, from time to time all therapists hear the phrase, "I have never told anyone this...," sex therapists hear it every day. Our clients invite us into the most intimate part of their life, with some hesitation, and, depending on how we respond, they may invite us to understand that part of themselves completely. It is the ultimate privileged position for us to share in their vulnerability and truth about their sexuality. Our clients' sexuality is but one piece of the overall puzzle in their lives that often remains in the background. In sex therapy, it is the one area of their life where their pain, regret, grief, inhibitions, prohibitions, and many other feelings are now allowed expression directly.

Sex is one of the great joys of life that bonds couples together and can allow the individual to feel free to pursue sexual happiness, wholeness as a person, and freedom. In spite of the fact that what we do remains invisible to all but our clients, the effect is profound and the personal rewards transcend attempts at verbalization. We open ourselves to resonate with our clients' sexuality and in so doing reap the same rewards.

Index